T0214045

Lecture Notes in Computer Science   12691

More information about this subseries at http://www.springer.com/series/7407

Ting Hu · Nuno Lourenço ·
Eric Medvet (Eds.)

Genetic Programming

24th European Conference, EuroGP 2021
Held as Part of EvoStar 2021
Virtual Event, April 7–9, 2021
Proceedings

 Springer

Editors
Ting Hu (iD)
Queen's University
Kingston, ON, Canada

Nuno Lourenço (iD)
University of Coimbra
Coimbra, Portugal

Eric Medvet (iD)
University of Trieste
Trieste, Italy

ISSN 0302-9743 ISSN 1611-3349 (electronic)
Lecture Notes in Computer Science
ISBN 978-3-030-72811-3 ISBN 978-3-030-72812-0 (eBook)
https://doi.org/10.1007/978-3-030-72812-0

LNCS Sublibrary: SL1 – Theoretical Computer Science and General Issues

This Springer imprint is published by the registered company Springer Nature Switzerland AG
The registered company address is: Gewerbestrasse 11, 6330 Cham, Switzerland

Preface

The 24th European Conference on Genetic Programming (EuroGP) took place online, due to the COVID-19 pandemic restrictions, between 7–9 April, 2021.

Genetic Programming (GP) is an evolutionary computation branch that has been developed to automatically solve design problems, in particular computer program design, without requiring the user to know or specify the form or structure of the solution in advance. It uses the principles of Darwinian evolution to approach problems in the synthesis, improvement, and repair of computer programs. The universality of computer programs, and their importance in so many areas of our lives, means that the automation of these tasks is an exceptionally ambitious challenge with far-reaching implications. It has attracted a very large number of researchers and a vast number of theoretical and practical contributions are available by consulting the GP bibliography[1].

Since the first EuroGP event in Paris in 1998, EuroGP has been the only conference exclusively devoted to the evolutionary design of computer programs and other computational structures. In fact, EuroGP represents the single largest venue at which GP results are published. It plays an important role in the success of the field, by serving as a forum for expressing new ideas, meeting fellow researchers, and initiating collaborations. It attracts scholars from all over the world. In a friendly and welcoming atmosphere authors present the latest advances in the field, also presenting GP-based solutions to complex real-world problems.

EuroGP 2021 received 27 submissions from around the world. The papers underwent a rigorous double-blind peer review process, each being reviewed by multiple members of an international Program Committee.

Among the papers presented in this volume, 11 were accepted for full-length oral presentation (40% acceptance rate) and 6 for a short talk. Authors of both categories of papers also had the opportunity to present their work in poster sessions, to promote the exchange of ideas in a carefree manner.

The wide range of topics in this volume reflects the current state of research in the field. The collection of papers covers interesting topics including developing new operators for variants of GP algorithms, as well as exploring GP applications to the optimisation of machine learning methods and the evolution of complex combinational logic circuits.

Together with three other co-located evolutionary computation conferences (Evo-COP 2021, EvoMusArt 2021, and EvoApplications 2021), EuroGP 2021 was part of the Evo* 2021 event. This meeting could not have taken place without the help of many people. The EuroGP Organizing Committee is particularly grateful to the following:

---

[1] http://liinwww.ira.uka.de/bibliography/Ai/genetic.programming.html

- SPECIES, the Society for the Promotion of Evolutionary Computation in Europe and its Surroundings, aiming to promote evolutionary algorithmic thinking within Europe and wider, and more generally to promote inspiration of parallel algorithms derived from natural processes.
- The high-quality and diverse EuroGP Program Committee. Each year the members give freely of their time and expertise, in order to maintain high standards in EuroGP and provide constructive feedback to help the authors to improve their papers.
- Nuno Lourenço (University of Coimbra, Portugal) for his dedicated work with the submission and registration system.
- João Correia (University of Coimbra, Portugal) and Francisco Chicano (University of Málaga, Spain) for the Evo* publicity, social media service, and website.
- Sérgio Rebelo (University of Coimbra, Portugal) for his important graphic design work.
- Our invited speakers, Darrell Whitley and Susanna Manrubia, who gave inspiring and enlightening keynote talks.
- Finally, we express our continued appreciation to Anna I. Esparcia-Alcázar, from SPECIES, whose considerable efforts in managing and coordinating Evo* helped towards building a unique, vibrant, and friendly atmosphere.

April 2021

Ting Hu
Nuno Lourenço
Eric Medvet

Organization Committee

Program Co-chairs

Ting Hu	Queen's University, Canada
Nuno Lourenço	University of Coimbra, Portugal

Publication Chair

Eric Medvet	University of Trieste, Italy

Local Chairs

Francisco Fernández de Vega	University of Extremadura, Spain
Federico Divina	University Pablo de Olavide, Spain

Publicity Chair

João Correia	University of Coimbra, Portugal

Conference Administration

Anna Esparcia-Alcázar	Evo* Coordinator

Program Committee

Ignacio Arnaldo	Universidad Complutense de Madrid, Spain
R. Muhammad Atif Azad	Birmingham City University, UK
Wolfgang Banzhaf	Michigan State University, USA
Helio Barbosa	Federal University of Juiz de Fora, Brazil
Heder Bernardino	Federal University of Juiz de Fora, Brazil
Anthony Brabazon	University College Dublin, Ireland
Stefano Cagnoni	University of Parma, Italy
Mauro Castelli	Universidade Nova de Lisboa, Portugal
Ernesto Costa	University of Coimbra, Portugal
Marc Ebner	Universität Greifswald, Germany
Anna Esparcia-Alcázar	Universitat Politècnica de València, Spain
Francisco Fernández de Vega	Universidad de Extremadura, Spain
Gianluigi Folino	ICAR-CNR, Italy
James Foster	University of Idaho, USA
Christian Gagné	Université Laval, Canada

Contents

Short Talks

Long Talks

Quality Diversity Genetic Programming for Learning Decision Tree Ensembles

Stephen Boisvert[1]([✉]) and John W. Sheppard[2]([✉])

[1] Johns Hopkins University, Baltimore, USA
sboisve2@jhu.edu
[2] Montana State University, Bozeman, USA
john.sheppard@montana.edu

Abstract. Quality Diversity (QD) algorithms are a class of population-based evolutionary algorithms designed to generate sets of solutions that are both fit and diverse. In this paper, we describe a strategy for applying QD concepts to the generation of decision tree ensembles by optimizing collections of trees for both individually accurate and collectively diverse predictive behavior. We compare three variants of this QD strategy with two existing ensemble generation strategies over several classification data sets. We then briefly highlight the effect of the evolutionary algorithm at the core of the strategy. The examined algorithms generate ensembles with distinct predictive behaviors as measured by classification accuracy and intrinsic diversity. The plotted behaviors hint at highly data-dependent relationships between these metrics. QD-based strategies are suggested as a means to optimize classifier ensembles along this performance curve along with other suggestions for future work.

Keywords: Genetic programming · Decision tree ensemble · Quality diversity

1 Introduction

Decision tree induction is a supervised learning strategy in which labels for data points are predicted through a series of decisions modeled as nodes of a tree. That is, given a data point m consisting of a set of feature and value pairs, a tree τ attempts to predict $label(m)$, which is a value associated with m but unknown to the model. In order to perform the prediction $p(\tau, m)$, the model recursively applies tests to m, beginning at the root of the tree. Each test results in a decision that maps one or more input feature values to a choice of adjacent nodes. The corresponding branch is then traversed, and the process repeats until a leaf node is reached. The value of the ending leaf node then outputs $p(\tau, m)$.

At the cost of some simplicity, decision tree ensembles (or forests) can be formed in which the output labels of multiple decision trees are considered collectively in order to make a final prediction. That is, the ensemble prediction $p(T, m)$ combines $p(\tau, m), \forall \tau \in T$ to predict the value of $label(m)$. Using an

© Springer Nature Switzerland AG 2021
T. Hu et al. (Eds.): EuroGP 2021, LNCS 12691, pp. 3–18, 2021.
https://doi.org/10.1007/978-3-030-72812-0_1

ensemble necessarily implies some amount of dissimilarity of individual trees within the forest. Otherwise, the output of the complete ensemble would be equal to the output of any subset of that ensemble. Thus, there must be diversity within the ensemble population in order for the ensemble strategy to be effective.

Quality-Diversity (QD) algorithms are a class of population-based optimization algorithms that aim to output a collection of quantifiably high performing and diverse solutions [20]. While diversity is a common theme in evolutionary computation, the explicit diversity considered by QD algorithms is distinct from strategies that promote population diversity implicitly by increasing the use of stochastic methods. QD algorithms measure diversity by comparing the *behavioral characterizations* of individual solutions. Groups of similar individuals, called niches, are then identified, and a high performing representative for each behavioral niche is returned in the solution.

The concept of diversity and the application of decision tree formation are common subjects in the field of genetic programming [4,8]. In this paper, we examine the qualities of decision tree ensembles formed from the output of a QD optimization algorithm. Specifically, we formulate a QD algorithm such that individuals in the population are complete decision trees with fitness and diversity calculated from prediction behavior over the training data. We then compare the accuracy and diversity of the resulting QD ensembles to the corresponding metrics of ensembles formed by alternative means under the hypothesis that the QD-generated ensembles will outperform the other studied algorithms in terms of both accuracy and diversity.

The remainder of the paper is organized as follows. In the following section, we review concepts in the areas of decision trees, ensemble classifiers, and QD algorithms. In Sect. 3, we present the specific algorithms used in this paper in detail. In Sect. 4 we describe the experimental configurations, analyzing the results in Sect. 5. Finally, in Sect. 6 we summarize our conclusions and then suggest future work.

2   Background

2.1   Decision Tree Diversity

Decision tree ensembles require some amount of diversity in order to behave differently than a single tree. Breiman shows a particular relationship between the misprediction probability or *generalization error* (PE^*) of an ensemble, the strength (s) of the ensemble, and prediction correlation ($\bar{\rho}$) between individuals within that ensemble [6]. Specifically, while introducing the well-known "Random Forest" algorithm, it is shown that:

$$PE^* \leq \bar{\rho}(1 - s^2)/s^2,$$

where $-1 \leq s \leq 1$ is defined as the expectation of the *margin function*, which describes the confidence of the ensemble in predicting correct classification labels, and $\bar{\rho}$ is described as the mean value of the correlation in *raw margin function* between individual classifiers in the ensemble. The full proof will not be discussed here, though Breiman finally suggests a ratio of $\bar{\rho}/s^2$ such that "the smaller it is, the better." That this, both higher strength and lower correlation of individuals will reduce the theoretical bound on this error. In this way, concepts of both fitness and diversity are shown to be reasonable objectives for selecting members of a classifier ensemble.

Given this formulation, a natural way to describe the diversity of a population of decision trees is to describe the correlation of their outputs for a given input set. Several strategies have been proposed for this purpose, including the averaged Q statistic [15], a Kappa statistic [11], classification overlap [7], ensemble ambiguity [14], and the percentage correct diversity measure (PCDM) [2]. While the latest is perhaps unique in being proposed specifically for the purpose of thinning decision tree forests, all of these strategies attempt to measure forest diversity by comparing the outputs of individual trees.

The value used to determine whether the predictions of given trees are equal is a key distinguishing characteristic of the listed metrics. Some, such as the Kappa statistic, compare the direct outputs of the trees. That is, they compare $p_{raw}(\tau, m)$ values, each of which is a predicted output label for a data point m using a decision tree τ. Others first convert the tree predictions to binary values, indicating whether each prediction was correct or incorrect. That is, they compare $p_{correct}(\tau, m)$ where

$$p_{correct}(\tau, m) = \begin{cases} 1, & p_{raw}(\tau, m) = label(m) \\ 0, & p_{raw}(\tau, m) \neq label(m) \end{cases} \tag{1}$$

In this paper, we use p_{raw} for diversity calculations using a simple count of the data points in a sample that result in different outputs between two trees. That is, the diversity metric Δ_{raw} between two trees τ_1, τ_2 over the points m in a data sample M is calculated as the sum of:

$$\delta_{raw}(\tau_1, \tau_2, m) = \begin{cases} 0, & p_{raw}(\tau_1, m) = p_{raw}(\tau_2, m) \\ 1, & p_{raw}(\tau_1, m) \neq p_{raw}(\tau_2, m) \end{cases}$$

such that:

$$\Delta_{raw}(\tau_1, \tau_2, M) = \sum_{m \in M} \delta_{raw}(\tau_1, \tau_2, m) \tag{2}$$

The diversity of a decision tree ensemble T is then computed as the average pairwise Δ_{raw} between individuals in the ensemble. That is:

$$\bar{\Delta}_{raw}(T, M) = \frac{\sum_{(\tau_1, \tau_2) \in T \times T, (\tau_1 \neq \tau_2)} \Delta_{raw}(\tau_1, \tau_2, M)}{size(T) \times (size(T) - 1)} \tag{3}$$

This formulation provides a relatively simple way to interpret a reported diversity measure as a distance metric but does not attempt to account for differences in population size or other properties of M such as label representation. Therefore, it is important to not compare the reported $\bar{\Delta}$ measures between data sets or experimental configurations.

2.2   Decision Tree Induction

Common strategies for forming decision trees implement a greedy heuristic approach for determining the test to apply at each node. The tree is formed root-
to-leaf in a way that recursively maximizes a quantifiable *split criterion* over the
training data. This split criterion measures the predictive power of that node in
isolation. Examples of the split criterion include information gain, Gini impu-
rity, and prediction accuracy, though studies suggest that the difference between
these criteria often have minimal effect on the resulting trees [21].

The chosen decision is then applied to the training data, and the children
at the branches of the tree are trained using their respective data subsets. This
continues until some stopping condition is met, typically a level of accuracy
or a data sample size. Alternatively post-pruning can be applied to prevent
overfitting. Note that, for a given input M and a list of possible decisions, this
algorithm is deterministic and will produce identical trees. Thus, some additional
stochastic elements are needed when forming diverse decision tree ensembles.

One option for diversity injection is through the training data input to the
greedy tree formation algorithm. One popular and effective method, called *boot-
strap aggregating* or *bagging* [5], forms separate data sets for training different
trees by sampling data points at random (with replacement) from the original
training set [3]. That is, to form a training set M_{τ_1} used to train a tree τ_1,
random data points are selected from the original M until $|M_{\tau_1}| = |M|$.

A related strategy called boosting provides weights to the selection options
such that inaccurately classified points are more likely to be added to new training sets. A comparison suggests that bagging and boosting can each be more
effective than the other, depending on the amount of noise in the data set [11].

Alternatively, the structures of the trees can be built in a stochastic manner.
One option is to generate random trees without using information from the
training data. That is, a tree is generated where each test is selected as a random
feature and test value. Labels for leaf nodes are determined later by feeding in
the training data to the randomized decisions and examining the distributions at
the leaves [13]. This approach may result in unreachable nodes, however, which
can either be removed or saved for online learning.

Also, unreachable nodes can be prevented by partially using the training data
when forming decisions in the tree. One option is to select randomly from the
best n discovered decisions according to the split heuristic [11]. Another option
is to select a random set of attributes with a decision threshold chosen as the
half-way point between two randomly selected training points [17]. A particular
configuration of such trees are called a *Max-diverse Ensemble*.

2.3   Evolutionary Decision Tree Induction

Evolutionary computation has also been applied extensively to the stochastic
formation of decision trees [4]. In particular, genetic programming approaches
fit naturally to the tree structure of the decision tree classifiers. Also, more
traditional evolutionary algorithms have been applied to relatively rigid tree

structures. While discussing the full range and taxonomy of population-based implementations is outside the scope of this paper, we present the following information as relevant to the evolutionary component of our QD algorithm implementation.

When restricting the tree structure to binary trees of a maximum depth, each tree-encoding chromosome can be described with a fixed number of genes, where each gene represents a single node in the tree [1]. That is, the number of genes G to represent an individual is given by:

$$G = 2^{depth+1} - 1$$

where each gene can represent either a leaf-node or a sub-tree.

In our experiments, we share the gene encoding used by [22] with $node = \langle t, label, P, L, R, C, size \rangle$, where t is an identifying node number, P is a pointer to the parent node, L and R are pointers to the left and right children, $size$ indicates the height of the contained sub-tree, and C is a set of registers. If the node is an internal node, $C[0]$ represents the feature index used in the branching decision at that node while $C[1]$ represents the threshold of the decision. That is, the decision nodes use tests in the form of

$$feature_{C[0]} < C[1]$$

for real-valued features, or

$$feature_{C[0]} = C[1]$$

for discrete-valued features. If the node is a leaf node, C will contain an array of values representing the weighted labels of training data that reach the node. This information is then used to predict labels of testing data.

Using such a representation, the crossover operator can be implemented such that one random gene (and corresponding sub-tree) from two parents are swapped as used by the "standard GP" [22]. Note that in our implementation, we limit the selected genes to ensure they are of the same height so as to maintain the complete structure of the trees.

The mutation operator can be implemented by modifying the C[0] and C[1] registers for decision nodes according to some fixed rate. In this paper, the mutation operator chooses a random element for C[0]. For the test targets, mutation either adds a random value from the normal distribution to C[1] or selects uniformly from the set of discrete values. With these encodings and operators defined, we can use our tree representation in any standard population-based genetic framework.

2.4   QD Algorithms

Quality Diversity algorithms aim to produce populations containing locally-optimal representatives of regions in a *behavioral characterization* (BC) space.

The BC space is a problem-specific description of possible solutions that provides a mechanism for calculating the similarity between solutions. For example, in [10], a set of BCs represent the final position of the end of a robotic arm after applying a series of angular rotations to joints in the arm. Thus, it is expected that many possible solutions may result in similar or perhaps identical BCs.

A foundational example of a QD algorithm is the *Novelty Search with Local Competition* (NSLC) algorithm, which uses a "Pareto-based multi-objective" strategy to optimize explicitly for both novelty and quality during search [16]. This algorithm was applied to evolve a set of virtual creatures in a simulated robotic environment. The creatures were evolved to have diverse properties with local competition, ensuring that each returned representative showed relative success in achieving the goal of movement.

Another exemplary QD algorithm is *Multi-dimensional Archive of Phenotypic Elites* (MAP-Elites), which seeks to divide the behavior space into a grid, then "illuminate" the quality of the regions through high performing, representative individuals [19]. It is also noted that this strategy can be used as an optimizer by returning the overall highest performing individual while maintaining the benefits of diversity during the search process.

These algorithms share a common goal of producing populations containing locally-optimal representatives of behavioral niches. However, their structures have distinct characteristics. For example, MAP-Elites divides the behavioral feature space into a *grid* with a representative for each space, while NSLC allows for a more flexible *archive* where acceptance into the collection is determined by comparison to nearest neighbors. Work to unify these examples into a common framework has abstracted these differences into types of *container operators* [10].

Additionally, the selection of individuals to insert into future generations has been abstracted as a *selection operator* [10]. Examples of selection operators include *uniform random selection* and *score-proportionate selection*. A typical example of the latter is to establish a score for each individual proportional to its fitness or diversity, where a higher score increases the chance of being selected. A suggested type of score called the *curiosity score* provides higher values to individuals that produce new offspring that are added successfully to the container [10].

In this paper, we use the predictive behavior over the training set as the behavioral characterization of each tree. This metric is related to the label purity at leaf nodes. Distances to nearest neighbors in the behavioral space are then calculated as the defined Δ_{raw} metric from Eq. 2. Trees are added to an archive container with a minimum distance requirement between all individuals in the population. Newly generated trees can replace existing members of the container if they are sufficiently high-performing.

2.5   Ensemble Prediction

The final prediction of an ensemble is a combination of the predictions of the individual classifiers within that ensemble. The strategy chosen for this combination is critical to the effectiveness of the ensemble. Perhaps the simplest strategy is to apply a voting technique where the most frequent output among individuals is selected as the overall output [18]. These votes can also be weighted or ranked according to confidence of the prediction for one or more outputs [23]. More complex strategies, such as stacked generalization or meta-learning, apply a learning process to the combination [9].

For this paper, we use only the *sum rule* strategy for calculating ensemble output. In this strategy, each decision tree provides a confidence value for each possible output. For each decision, the confidence value is calculated as the percentage of the training label purity of the deciding leaf node. All confidence values are added over all trees in the ensemble, and the choice with the highest sum is chosen as the ensemble output [23]. However, we suspect that more intentionally complementary combination strategies could increase the effectiveness of any ensemble generation algorithm.

3 Implementation

3.1 Structure Restrictions

Our implemented algorithms all require the decisions within each internal tree node to be Boolean. That is, each test will either result in an evaluation of either *true* or *false*. If the test evaluates to *true*, the tree will return the prediction of its left subtree; otherwise, it will return the right subtree's prediction. In the case of real-valued features, each test will determine whether the value of a given feature in the input data point is below some threshold. For discrete-valued features, the test will determine whether the input feature value is equal to some test value.

3.2 Bagging

Our bagging implementation follows the description in Sect. 2.2 using a standard greedy algorithm. That is, to generate an ensemble $T_{bagging}$ of n binary decision trees $\{\tau_1, \tau_2, ..., \tau_n\}$, the algorithm first generates a set of n training sets $\{M_1, M_2, ..., M_n\}$, each of which contains elements selected randomly from the original training set M with replacement until $|M_i| = |M|$. Then:

$$\tau_i = GreedyHeuristic(M_i), \forall i \in \{1, 2, ..., n\}$$

The split criterion for each rule choice is calculated as the accuracy of predicting the labels of the elements in the M_{left} and M_{right} sub-groups as the majority label in each respective group. This essentially calculates the accuracy of treating each sub-group as a leaf, functioning as a measure of label purity. Recall from Sect. 2.2 that we would expect replacing accuracy with information gain or Gini impurity to have similar results. The greedy formulation terminates when the size of the input to $GreedyHeuristic$ is below a percentage of $|M_i|$.

3.3   Random Trees

The structures of the random trees examined in this paper are formed as complete, binary decision trees. To form each individual τ_{rnd} in an ensemble T_{rnd}, the algorithm picks a series of $2^{depth} - 1$ randomly generated training data features on which to base decisions for internal tree nodes. The threshold for each node is then determined root-to-leaf by calculating the mean value of the corresponding feature from two randomly chosen (with replacement) data points that traverse that node. For discrete-valued features, the corresponding feature value from a randomly chosen point is used for the equality condition. Up to 2^{depth} leaf nodes are labeled by feeding the training data M into the established trees and keeping a record of which $m \in M$ reach each node. Any decision nodes that are reachable by a number of points less than an established percentage of $|M|$ are converted into leaf nodes with their children nodes truncated. Note that such pruned trees will no longer be complete.

3.4   QD Trees

Our implementation of the QD algorithm for decision tree generation uses an *archive* container A where the pairwise distance between tree elements $\tau_i, \tau_j \in A$ is calculated as the diversity measure $\Delta_{raw}(\tau_i, \tau_j, M)$ from Sect. 2.1, Eq. 2. Given a minimum distance threshold Δ_{min}, this container will allow the addition of a new element τ_{new} based on its comparison to its nearest two neighbors τ_{first} and τ_{second} where:

$$\tau_{first} = \arg\min\{\Delta_{raw}(\tau_{new}, \tau_i, M), \forall \tau_i \in A\}$$

and:

$$\tau_{second} = \arg\min\{\Delta_{raw}(\tau_{new}, \tau_i, M), \forall \tau_i \in A \setminus \{\tau_{first}\}\}$$

Given this, τ_{new} will be added to A without affecting other members if its nearest neighbor is farther away than the minimum threshold. If both of the two nearest neighbors of τ_{new} are closer than the minimum threshold, τ_{new} will not be added to the container. However, if the nearest neighbor is closer than the threshold while the second nearest neighbor is farther, τ_{new} may replace its nearest neighbor if its fitness is higher, where fitness is measured as accuracy in predicting the labels of the training data set. Note this has a similar effect as our greedy tree formation such that trees with higher label purity in leaf nodes will have higher fitness. This is shown more precisely in Algorithm 1.

The container is initialized by generating a fixed number of τ_{rnd} trees and adding them to the container in order, as long as the diversity conditions are met as described above. Note that the first two decision trees are always added successfully to the container. Next Δ_{min} is tuned to ensure that the container capacity $|A|$ does not increase above a given size during initialization. This helps to ensure that the nearest neighbor calculations remain in an achievable range of computational complexity during the algorithm's execution.

Algorithm 1. Conditional Archive Addition

1: **procedure** ADDTREETOARCHIVE(τ_{new})
2:      $globals : Archive\ A,\ Data\ M,\ Constant\ \Delta_{min}$
3:      $\tau_{first} \leftarrow \tau_1$
4:      $\tau_{second} \leftarrow \tau_1$
5:      **for** τ_i in A **do**
6:           **if** $\Delta_{raw}(\tau_{new}, \tau_i, M) < \Delta_{raw}(\tau_{new}, \tau_{first}, M)$ **then**
7:                $\tau_{second} \leftarrow \tau_{first}$
8:                $\tau_{first} \leftarrow \tau_i$
9:           **else if** $\Delta_{raw}(\tau_{new}, \tau_i, M) < \Delta_{raw}(\tau_{new}, \tau_{second}, M)$ **then**
10:                $\tau_{second} \leftarrow \tau_i$
11:      **if** $\Delta_{raw}(\tau_{new}, \tau_{first}, M) < \Delta_{min}$ **then**
12:           $A \leftarrow A + \tau_{new}$
13:      **else if** $\Delta_{raw}(\tau_{new}, \tau_{second}, M) < \Delta_{min}$ **then**
14:           **if** $fitness(\tau_{new}) > fitness(\tau_{first})$ **then**
15:                $A \leftarrow A + \tau_{new}$
16:                $A \leftarrow A \setminus \tau_{first}$

The algorithm then executes for a specified number of generations. At each generation, two parent trees are selected from the container (with replacement), where the selection probability for each tree is proportional to its current *curiosity score*. Recall that the curiosity score indicates how successful the offspring of that tree have been in recent history. Crossover is then applied to the parent trees as described in Sect. 2.3. Specifically, randomly selected sub-trees from each parent tree at the same height are swapped. Note that the crossover operation results in two children. Each child undergoes mutation where each decision node may have its tested feature modified and its threshold reinitialized according to some probability. Failing this, a sample from the normal distribution is added to real-valued thresholds while discrete-valued thresholds are modified to an alternate value according to a second sampling from mutation probability.

The mutated children are then tested to determine if they should be added to the container. If the addition is successful, the curiosity scores of the parents are increased by 1. Otherwise, the curiosity scores of the parents are decreased by 0.5. For instance, the successful addition of one child and the failed addition of the other will result in a net curiosity score gain of 0.5 for each parent. After the set number of generations, the container is returned.

Finally, a decision tree ensemble T_{QD} of a fixed size n must be generated from the resulting container. Here, we test three different strategies. The *accuracy* strategy (QD Accuracy) chooses the n decision trees in the container with the highest fitness. The *diversity* strategy (QD Diverse) chooses n random trees from the container. The *hybrid* strategy (QD Hybrid) chooses $\frac{n}{2}$ trees with the highest fitness, then chooses the remaining trees randomly. Once chosen, each tree is pruned such that decisions reachable by a number of training samples less than a specified percentage of $|M|$ are replaced by leaf nodes. This is done to ensure sufficient data at the leaves to make a statistically reasonable prediction.

Table 1. Data set attributes

Data set	# Used points	# Used features	# Classes	Missing data?
Balance	626	4	3	No
Breast Cancer	699	9	2	Yes
Dermatology	366	34	6	Yes
Flags	194	28	8	No
Glass	214	9	6	No
Heart	270	12	3	No
Hayes-Roth	132	4	3	No
Ionosphere	351	34	2	No
Iris	150	4	3	No

4   Experiments

For our experiments, we execute the previously described algorithms and measure their classification performance over nine data sets selected from the UCI Machine Learning Repository [12]. Specifically, we compare the results of the QD Hybrid, QD Accuracy, and QD Diverse algorithms against those of the Bagging and Random algorithm baselines.

The data sets were selected for manageable data sizes, few missing attribute values and varying numbers of features (Table 1). For all used data sets, any missing attribute values are handled by removing the affected data points from consideration. Uniquely identifying attributes such as IDs and names are also removed from the data. Note that for this experiment, we predict the "religion" field of the Flags data set based on the other attributes.

All presented diversity and accuracy results are determined using 10-fold cross validation. That is, each point graphed in Fig. 1 is a result of this validation, and 10 such results are used in our statistical test. Note that the cross validation folds are stratified by class, ensuring proportionate representation of all classes within each division. Note that these diversity and accuracy metrics are the same metrics used in the construction of the ensembles with the QD variants. The use of alternative metrics for additional insights into the effectiveness of the classifiers is an opportunity for future work.

Each of the algorithms includes a pre-pruning hyperparameter that specifies the percentage of training points that much be reachable by every decision used in the tree. For these experiments, that setting is kept at a constant 1%. Additionally, each algorithm is configured to generate ensembles such that $|T| = 50$. The depth-limit of the randomly-generated and QD-generated trees is kept at 4.

Each QD algorithm variant is executed for 10,000 generations unless stated otherwise. Note that two children are created in each generation. For most experiments, Δ_{min} is chosen at initialization such that no more than 350 of 3,000 randomly initialized trees are added successfully to the container. If the container size goes above this threshold during initialization, the algorithm restarts with

Table 2. Median algorithm accuracy and diversity. **Bold** indicates $p < 0.05$

Data set	Bagging		Random		QD acc		QD div		QD hybrid	
	Acc	Div	Acc	Div	Acc	Div	Acc	Div	Acc	Div
Balance	0.842	16.68	**0.887**	**20.71**	0.871	17.38	**0.888**	20.17	**0.883**	18.63
Breast Cancer	0.958	3.08	**0.965**	**9.54**	**0.972**	4.80	0.963	9.63	**0.968**	7.40
Dermatology	**0.966**	2.26	0.775	19.80	0.949	16.21	0.863	**20.45**	0.942	18.92
Flags	0.478	10.31	0.419	11.12	**0.599**	11.40	0.481	**11.90**	0.587	**11.88**
Glass	0.621	7.92	0.658	10.80	**0.690**	9.11	0.621	**12.27**	**0.689**	10.17
Heart	0.652	7.82	**0.668**	8.95	**0.680**	8.37	**0.674**	9.34	**0.677**	9.05
Hayes-Roth	**0.781**	4.86	0.669	6.95	0.749	6.28	0.674	**7.07**	0.736	6.69
Ionosphere	**0.923**	2.80	0.832	9.50	0.891	8.38	0.849	**10.25**	0.886	9.33
Iris	**0.963**	0.44	0.953	3.43	0.953	1.05	0.947	**4.06**	0.953	2.72

a higher Δ_{min}. Note that reported diversity measures use the pairwise averaged $\bar{\Delta}$ value (Eq. 3), indicating the average number of data points in the testing set that have different predicted labels between two trees in the ensemble.

The mutation rate is set to 2%. Note that for discrete valued features, the sampling for the mutation may occur twice where a second sampling for modifying the threshold value will occur if the sampling for modifying the feature fails. For real valued features, the threshold is always modified by adding a sample from the normal distribution, $\mathcal{N}(0, 0.1)$.

5   Results

5.1   Algorithm Comparisons

Figure 1 plots the diversity and quality of the algorithms over the indicated data sets. Table 2 shows median accuracy and diversity metrics. Entries shown in bold are not significantly lower than the maximum value in the row according to the Wilcoxon Signed-Rank Test at the 95% confidence level.

5.2   Evolutionary Algorithm

Much of the niching behavior of the QD strategy can be attributed to the container, which enforces a level of diversity while allowing for quality improvements. Here, we investigate the change in algorithm behavior when the evolutionary components of the algorithm are replaced by the random tree generation strategy. Specifically, we examine the size of the container over time, the number of times an existing member of the container was replaced by a newly generated tree, and the average accuracy of the members of the container over the *training* data. As in other fitness metrics, the training data accuracy indicates a measure of the purity of the labels at the leaves of the decision trees. In this experiment, the number of generations is increased to 100,000, and Δ_{min} is increased by 25%. We show the results on the Glass data as a representative in Fig. 2.

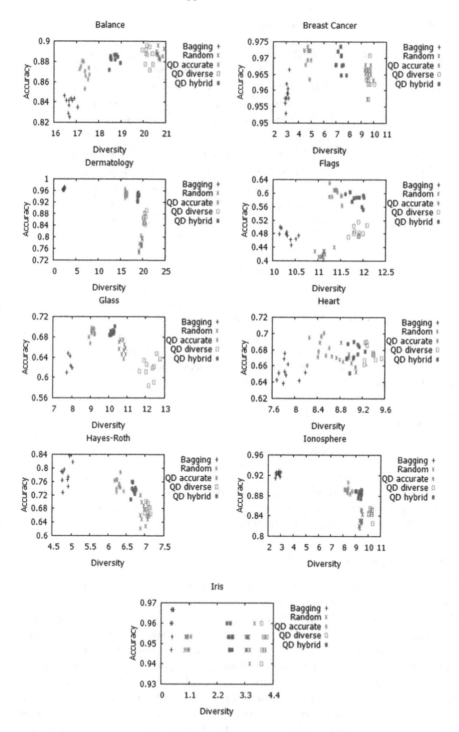

Fig. 1. Algorithm accuracy versus diversity for each of the nine data sets

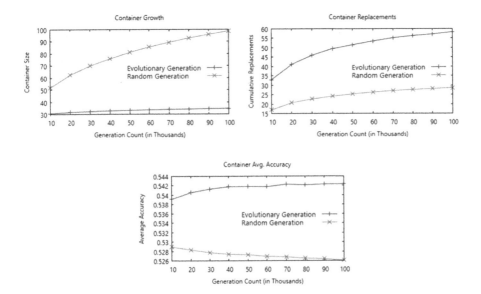

Fig. 2. Behavior of the QD algorithms vs. random generation on the Glass dataset

5.3 Binary Diversity

We examined the effect on performance of using the more common $p_{correct}$ (Eq. 1) to calculate $\Delta_{correct}$ rather than Δ_{raw} (Eq. 2) for the QD-hybrid algorithm, keeping all other settings constant. We found that the difference in accuracy was not statistically significant for the Glass, Ionosphere and Balance data sets tested. We consider these data sets to be representative of the accuracy/diversity relationship trends and label quantities of our data sets. Further experimentation with alternative diversity metrics, especially those less-directly tied to fitness, may prove interesting.

5.4 Ensemble Size

Finally, in Fig. 3, we briefly examine the change in behavior of ensemble classifiers of varying sizes. As an example, we replot the diversity and accuracy of class predictions on the Glass data set from ensembles consisting of 50, 25, 10 and 2 individual trees. All other parameters are held constant for this experiment.

6 Analysis

The effectiveness of the QD strategy is shown to be highly data-dependent, as is the correlation between ensemble diversity and accuracy. Data sets such as Breast Cancer, Flags, Glass, and Heart demonstrate a mid-range of diversity where accuracy tends to be higher. The Dermatology, Hayes-Roth, Ionosphere,

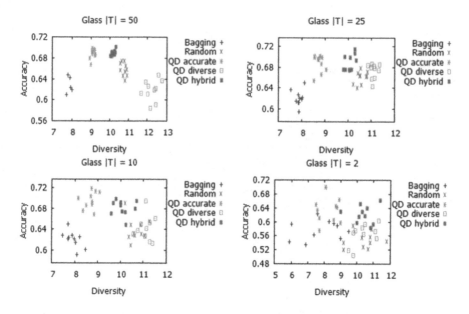

Fig. 3. Change in performance by ensemble size.

and Iris data sets show a trend for less diverse ensembles to be more accurate. The Balance data set shows the reverse trend where more diverse ensembles tend to have higher accuracy. The QD-Diversity algorithm shows particularly promising results in creating diverse ensembles, shown here to be significantly less diverse than the top performer in only one data set. The QD-Hybrid variant demonstrates the possibility of tuning the behavior of the ensemble by more carefully selecting the individuals from the container output.

There are several cases where the local optimization of the QD algorithm is apparent from the plots. For example, in the Dermatology graph in Fig. 1, we see the QD-Diverse ensemble outperform the Random ensemble, despite similar measures of diversity. Similar patterns are observed between QD-Hybrid and Random in the Ionosphere data set and between QD-Accurate and Random on the Flags data set. Indeed, Fig. 2 suggests that a primary effect of combining the QD container with the evolutionary algorithm versus random generation is to optimize existing members of the container locally, thus increasing accuracy.

Figure 3 demonstrates a trend for behavioral variance of the algorithms to decrease as ensemble size increases while maintaining distinct average behaviors. This suggests a substantial difference in the properties of the ensembles based on varying tree generation and selection methods.

7   Conclusion

We have presented a new application of QD algorithms in generating decision tree ensembles containing trees that are both fit and behaviorally diverse. Our experiments show that the benefit of diversity in such an ensemble is highly dependent on the data set. For data sets with very defined rules, aiming for more diverse ensembles may be counterproductive. However, for other data sets, the QD generation methods appear to offer effective strategies for tuning the performance of resulting ensembles. Furthermore, we have demonstrated that while the container plays an important role in the QD formulation by enforcing a degree of diversity, the evolutionary algorithm component also plays a key role by promoting local optimization to a greater degree than simple random tree generation. The QD strategies offer a promising method for exploring a locally optimized relationship between ensemble accuracy and diversity.

The parameters used in our experiments have been highly controlled in order to demonstrate the differences between the algorithms in generating ensemble members. Performance may be improved further by allowing for more complex and deeper tree structures. Further study of these algorithms at their respective peaks of performance may give more insight into the practical utility of QD-generated ensembles. More flexible genetic programming implementations may also promote quicker ensemble generation, allowing more opportunities to optimize container contents. Similarly, we have restricted the ensemble integration mechanism to highlight the difference between ensemble compositions. Using more advanced combination techniques could improve the performance of these ensembles by allowing for diverse "specializations." Long computation times led to using relatively simple data sets for our experiments. Though we demonstrate varying relationships between accuracy and diversity even among these data sets, using more complicated data may reveal additional insights. Finally, we have focused on using decision tree ensembles, but the concepts used in this paper may apply in a straightforward way to other types of classifiers. For example, it would be possible to replace the tree models with neural networks given appropriate crossover and mutation operators.

References

1. Bandar, Z., Al-Attar, H., McLean, D.: Genetic algorithm based multiple decision tree induction. In: Proceedings of the 6th International Conference on Neural Information Processing (ICONIP), vol. 2, pp. 429–434 (1999)
2. Banfield, R.E., Hall, L.O., Bowyer, K.W., Kegelmeyer, W.P.: A new ensemble diversity measure applied to thinning ensembles. In: Windeatt, T., Roli, F. (eds.) MCS 2003. LNCS, vol. 2709, pp. 306–316. Springer, Heidelberg (2003). https:// doi.org/10.1007/3-540-44938-8_31
3. Banfield, R.E., Hall, L.O., Bowyer, K.W., Kegelmeyer, W.P.: A comparison of decision tree ensemble creation techniques. IEEE Trans. Pattern Anal. Mach. Intell. **29**(1), 173–180 (2006)
4. Barros, R.C., Basgalupp, M.P., De Carvalho, A.C., Freitas, A.A.: A survey of evolutionary algorithms for decision-tree induction. IEEE Trans. Syst. Man Cybern. Part C (Appl. Rev.) **42**(3), 291–312 (2011)
5. Breiman, L.: Bagging predictors. Mach. Learn. **24**(2), 123–140 (1996). https://doi. org/10.1007/BF00058655

6. Breiman, L.: Random forests. Mach. Learn. **45**(1), 5–32 (2001). https://doi.org/10.1023/A:1010933404324

7. Brodley, C.E.: Recursive automatic bias selection for classifier construction. Mach. Learn. **20**(1–2), 63–94 (1995). https://doi.org/10.1023/A:1022686102325

8. Burke, E.K., Gustafson, S., Kendall, G.: Diversity in genetic programming: an analysis of measures and correlation with fitness. IEEE Trans. Evol. Comput. **8**(1), 47–62 (2004)

9. Chan, P.K., Stolfo, S.J.: On the accuracy of meta-learning for scalable data mining. J. Intell. Inf. Syst. **8**(1), 5–28 (1997). https://doi.org/10.1023/A:1008640732416

10. Cully, A., Demiris, Y.: Quality and diversity optimization: a unifying modular framework. IEEE Trans. Evol. Comput. **22**(2), 245–259 (2017)

11. Dietterich, T.G.: An experimental comparison of three methods for constructing ensembles of decision trees: bagging, boosting, and randomization. Mach. Learn. **40**(2), 139–157 (2000). https://doi.org/10.1023/A:1007607513941

12. Dua, D., Graff, C.: UCI machine learning repository (2017). http://archive.ics.uci.edu/ml

13. Fan, W., Wang, H., Yu, P.S., Ma, S.: Is random model better? On its accuracy and efficiency. In: Third International Conference on Data Mining, pp. 51–58. IEEE (2003)

14. Krogh, A., Vedelsby, J.: Neural network ensembles, cross validation, and active learning. In: Advances in Neural Information Processing Systems, pp. 231–238 (1995)

15. Kuncheva, L.I., Whitaker, C.J., Shipp, C.A., Duin, R.P.: Is independence good for combining classifiers? In: International Conference on Pattern Recognition, vol. 2, pp. 168–171. IEEE (2000)

16. Lehman, J., Stanley, K.O.: Evolving a diversity of virtual creatures through novelty search and local competition. In: Proceedings of the 13th Annual Conference on Genetic and Evolutionary Computation (GECCO), pp. 211–218. ACM (2011)

17. Liu, F.T., Ting, K.M., Fan, W.: Maximizing tree diversity by building complete-random decision trees. In: Ho, T.B., Cheung, D., Liu, H. (eds.) PAKDD 2005. LNCS (LNAI), vol. 3518, pp. 605–610. Springer, Heidelberg (2005). https://doi.org/10.1007/11430919_70

18. Merz, C.J.: Dynamical selection of learning algorithms. In: Fisher, D., Lenz, H.J. (eds.) Learning from Data. LNS, vol. 112, pp. 281–290. Springer, New York (1996). https://doi.org/10.1007/978-1-4612-2404-4_27

19. Mouret, J.B., Clune, J.: Illuminating search spaces by mapping elites. arXiv preprint arXiv:1504.04909 (2015)

20. Pugh, J.K., Soros, L.B., Stanley, K.O.: Quality diversity: a new frontier for evolutionary computation. Front. Robot. AI **3**, 40 (2016)

21. Raileanu, L.E., Stoffel, K.: Theoretical comparison between the Gini index and information gain criteria. Ann. Math. Artif. Intell. **41**(1), 77–93 (2004). https://doi.org/10.1023/B:AMAI.0000018580.96245.c6

22. Tanigawa, T., Zhao, Q.: A study on efficient generation of decision trees using genetic programming. In: Proceedings of the 2nd Annual Conference on Genetic and Evolutionary Computation (GECCO), pp. 1047–1052. ACM (2000)

23. Van Erp, M., Vuurpijl, L., Schomaker, L.: An overview and comparison of voting methods for pattern recognition. In: Proceedings of the Eighth International Workshop on Frontiers in Handwriting Recognition, pp. 195–200. IEEE (2002)

Progressive Insular Cooperative GP

Karina Brotto Rebuli[1,2]([⊠]) and Leonardo Vanneschi[1]([⊠])

[1] NOVA Information Management School (NOVA IMS),
Universidade Nova de Lisboa, Campus de Campolide, 1070-312 Lisbon, Portugal
{krebuli,lvanneschi}@novaims.unl.pt
[2] Dipartimento di Scienze Veterinarie, Università degli Studi di Torino,
Largo Paolo Braccini 2, 10095 Turin, Italy
karina.brottorebuli@unito.it

Abstract. This work presents a novel genetic programming system for multi-class classification, called progressively insular cooperative genetic programming (PIC GP). Based on the idea that effective multiclass classification can be obtained by appropriately joining classifiers that are highly specialized on the single classes, PIC GP evolves, at the same time, two populations. The first population contains individuals called specialists, and each specialist is optimized on one specific target class. The second population contains higher-level individuals, called teams, that join specialists to obtain the final algorithm prediction. By means of three simple parameters, PIC GP can tune the amount of cooperation between specialists of different classes. The first part of the paper is dedicated to a study of the influence of these parameters on the evolution dynamics. The obtained results indicate that PIC GP achieves the best performance when the evolution begins with a high level of cooperation between specialists of different classes, and then this type of cooperation is progressively decreased, until only specialists of the same class can cooperate between each other. The last part of the work is dedicated to an experimental comparison between PIC GP and a set of state-of-the-art classification algorithms. The presented results indicate that PIC GP outperforms the majority of its competitors on the studied test problems.

Keywords: Multiclass classification · Genetic programming ·
Cooperative evolution

1 Introduction

Genetic Programming (GP) [7] breads a population of computer programs (individuals) by mimicking the principles of Darwin's theory of evolution. At each step, stochastic operators of crossover and mutation are applied to generate new individuals, the most promising of which are probabilistically selected for the next generation. This selection step emulates Darwinian natural selection, introducing into GP the ecological relationship of competition. In classification tasks, GP individuals usually compete to generate a discriminating function

© Springer Nature Switzerland AG 2021
T. Hu et al. (Eds.): EuroGP 2021, LNCS 12691, pp. 19–35, 2021.
https://doi.org/10.1007/978-3-030-72812-0_2

that best separates the instances of each target class. In Multi-Class Classification (MCC) (i.e. for classification tasks with three or more target classes), a crucial question arises: how to discriminate the classes, all at once or in pairs? In practical terms, addressing this question means having either a single classifier to handle the entire classification task or to have as many classifiers as the number of classes to be modelled. GP has the potential to implement both these approaches. However, while very few successful studies have been presented so far concerning the first approach, if we consider the second one, the standard GP process should be changed from its basic design. In fact, GP should evolve solutions joining more than one program, since one different classifier is needed for each target class. This may be one of the reasons why GP is currently not considered a top algorithm for MCC, as clearly stated, for instance, in [3]. This work is intended to represent a first step towards the introduction of a robust and accurate GP system for MCC. We present the *Progressively Insular Cooperative* (PIC) GP. PIC GP is broadly characterized by two main populations, evolving at the same time. The first population evolves individuals that are specialized in the classification of one single target class. We call these individuals *specialists*. Specialists are grouped in *teams*, higher-level solutions that combine specialist outcomes to give the univocal algorithm prediction. Teams are evolved in the second population. The specialists population can conceptually be imagined as further partitioned into K subpopulations, where K is the number of target classes, each one containing the specialists of a particular class. In addition to the competition relationship, typical of natural selection, the two-level design of PIC GP presents an opportunity for the introduction of *cooperation* between individuals of different specialisations. Cooperation is a mutually beneficial interaction between species [1], that contrasts with intragroup competition, in which individuals work against each other. The cooperation is present in a team-based GP only if specialised individuals are allowed to interact over the evolution process. Simply joining them into a team, in itself, is not a cooperative, but a collaborative action, since the specialised individuals work together, but do not benefit from it. In PIC GP, the specialists can evolve with different levels of cooperation, that can be modified by tuning three simple parameters. Following the terminology used in [2], specialist subpopulations will be called *demes* when the level of cooperation between specialists is high, and *islands* when it is low or inexistent. The proposed method is called PIC GP because the algorithm begins with demes (high collaboration between specialists), that can be progressively transformed into islands (no cooperation at all). Given that PIC GP is introduced for the first time in this work, our first objective is to investigate the dynamics of PIC GP, by studying how parameters affect its evolution. In this phase, particular focus will be given to the study of selection, that directly influences the level of specialists cooperation. Secondly, we compare PIC GP with a set of state-of-the-art classification algorithms, in order to assess the competitiveness of PIC GP.

The manuscript is organized as follows: Sect. 2 presents a review of previous and related GP methods for MCC. Section 3 explains the functioning of PIC GP.

Section 4 describes our experimental study, first presenting the experimental settings and the employed test problems, and then discussing the obtained results. Finally, Sect. 5 concludes the paper and proposes ideas for future research.

2 GP for Multiclass Classification

In some previous work on MCC, GP was used as a wrapper method for data preprocessing, for posterior classification performed by other algorithms [3–6]. Other strategies use GP directly for dealing with the classification problem, without any posterior classifier procedure. When discriminating three or more classes, the very first decision is how to separate them. Three main possibilities have been investigated so far: all-vs-all, pairwise or one-vs-all.

All-vs-All. The all-vs-all strategy is the most simple extension of the binary classification approach. In this strategy, a single GP solution is generated and $K - 1$ thresholds are applied to its outcomes for a K classes problem. A single model must therefore be able to discriminate among all classes. For instance, Zhang and Smart [8] proposed a single classifier with $K - 1$ thresholds, dynamically evolved during the GP run. The same authors, in [9], used properties of Gaussian distributions of the classes to dynamically define the $K - 1$ thresholds of the GP multiclassifier solution. Usually, this approach is less likely to produce good models, since it has to handle all the problem complexity at once.

Pairwise. In the pairwise strategy, the problem of classifying K classes is decomposed into K classifiers, each one trained contrasting one target class with the others, in pairs. Thus, we can imagine that the training dataset represents $K * (K - 1)/2$ binary classification problems. The final algorithm result is given by a combination of the predictions of the K classifiers. Examples using GP with this strategy can be found in [10] and [11].

One-vs-All. In the one-vs-all category, to which PIC GP belongs, the problem of classifying K classes is decomposed into K binary classification problems, contrasting each class with all others at once, to generate K classifiers, one for each target class. The predictions of these K classifiers are then combined by means of an algorithm, able to output the final classification. In GP, these K classifiers can be evolved using one of the following approaches:

(1) *Independent runs approach.* The GP is simply run K times, one for each class, with the dataset split for the corresponding one-vs-all comparison. For example, Lin et al. [12] used the independent runs approach, proposing a multi-layer system with independent GP multi populations for MCC problems. In the last layer, the solutions obtained in the previous layers were combined in a single population, and a single GP solution was produced.

(2) *Same run, different subpopulations approach.* In this approach, the subpopulations can be totally isolated (in this case they are called islands), or they can exchange their individuals (demes). For example, Chen and Lu [13] used an island subpopulation approach, with the final prediction being decided by majority voting among the different models.

(3) *Same run, same population, independent individuals approach.* In this approach, the individuals evolve all in the same population, as in a standard GP
implementation, but at each generation they are evaluated and set to be
responsible for classifying one of the target classes. Smart and Zhang [14]
used this approach for evolving all classifiers in a single GP run, with solutions evaluated for every target class at each generation. For the GP prediction, the data instance was evaluated by all K solutions and was assigned
to the class to which it had the highest probability of belonging to.

(4) *Teams approach.* A team can be imagined as a tree, in which the root node
combines the results of its members. Each team member is a single threshold binary classifier, specialised in a corresponding class. Both the team
and its members evolve in the GP process. Thus, the two-level nature of
evolving K classifiers, that are combined into a single GP solution, becomes
explicit. Evolving only the specialists can produce strong individuals that
perform poorly for the combined prediction. Nevertheless, the specialists
should also evolve individually, to be able to improve the team's output.
For that to happen, it is necessary to define their individual evolution criteria, i.e. their individual fitnesses. Therefore, the team's approach creates
a new decision requirement, that is to define how the team fitness will be
distributed among the team's members. This is called the credit assignment
problem [17]. The team outcome will be the class whose specialist member
gives a positive result. Since more than one specialist can give a positive prediction, the team requires a disambiguation procedure to define which of the
positive classes will correspond to its final classification result. Haynes et al.
[15] published a pioneering work using the team's approach with Strongly
Typed GP. Their focus was in the role of crossover in making team populations evolve in coordination. The presented crossover operator essentially
controlled if individuals specialised in a target class could exchange genetic
material with individuals specialised in other target classes. In a later and
more complete publication, Haynes and Sen [16] explored more widely this
idea and concluded that the crossover that allowed the exchange of genetic
material among random different specialists was advantageous for the studied problem.

Some authors have also used hybrid methods, like we do in this work. For
instance, in [17], the authors applied the teams approach together with the
demes subpopulation approach for two binary classifications and a regression
problem with Linear GP. Lichodzijewski and Heywood [18] presented a mixed
independent individuals and team approach in a GP that evolves the training
subset, the individual binary classifiers and the team, each in a separate evolution
process. Soule and Komireddy [19] also presented a mixed independent individuals and teams approach, in which specialist individuals evolved in islands and
replaced team's members. Thomason and Soule [20] presented a variation of this
idea, in which teams are selected and replace individuals in islands. Generally
speaking, it is expected that the cooperation between specialists will favour the
search space exploration and that the competition will favour the search space

exploitation. In a traditional GP, the balance between exploration and exploitation is carried on mainly by crossover and mutation rates and the selection pressure. In a cooperative GP, the interaction among specialists can also help to control this balance. In a Linear GP study, Luke and Spector [21] found that restricting the interaction to individuals of the same specialisation improved the algorithm performance. Soule [22] studied a GP regression problem and concluded that heterogeneity among teams is necessary but not sufficient, while individuals' high specialisation, that is related with heterogeneity, is key for improving the algorithm performance. Nevertheless, it is still an open issue how to benefit from the balance between cooperation and the evolution of highly specialised individuals, to properly explore and exploit the search space, and this is the main motivation for our work.

In the present study, variations in the level of specialists cooperation over time were explored. Individuals can be distributed in class-based demes, work fully as islands or begin the algorithm in demes and progressively be detached into islands. Thus, by controlling the level of cooperation among specialists, exploration can be favoured in the beginning of the evolution and exploitation can be intensified as the algorithm evolves.

3   Progressive Insular Cooperative GP

The method presented in this work, Progressively Insular Cooperative (PIC) GP, is a one-vs-all mixed individuals and teams approach for cooperative MCC. Its general structure is exemplified in Fig. 1, for a 3-class classification problem, consisting in categorizing data observations into classes C_1, C_2 and C_3. The system is composed by two main populations, evolving at the same time: the population of specialists and the population of teams. The population of specialists is, in turn, partitioned into a number of subpopulations equal to the number of classes. Each one of these subpopulations i contains individuals specialised in the classification of class C_i. Each individual in the teams population joins one specialist from each one of the subpopulations. The subpopulations of specialists begin as demes (high level of cooperation between specialists), but further in the evolution they can become islands (no cooperation at all). The level of cooperation between specialists of different classes can be changed over the algorithm evolution. It is controlled by three parameters: the cooperation intensity rate (CIR), the CIR decrease rate and the generation in which the algorithm should turn the specialised subpopulations into islands, i.e. independent and isolated subpopulations, while previously they were allowed to interact (demes). Additionally, in PIC GP, the selection method is different from standard GP, in order to work with two parents at a time and foster cooperation. In PIC GP, specialists emerge independently from the teams evolution. Initially, teams are composed of the best individuals from the specialists population. As the teams are evolved, at each generation, the teams population is replaced half by teams offspring, half by new teams formed by evolved specialists. The following subsections describe in detail how each step of PIC GP works.

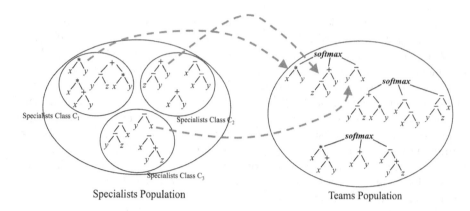

Fig. 1. A simplified graphical representation of the PIC GP system, for an ideal 3-classes classification problem. Two populations (the specialists population and the teams population) are evolved at the same time. The specialists population is, in turn, partitioned into a number of subpopulations equal to the number of classes. Each individual in the teams population contains one specialist coming from each one of these subpopulations.

3.1   Specialists Evolution Components

Specialists and Their Fitness. The solutions that we call *specialists* are trees, labelled with an attribute that represents a class. Let C be that class label. To classify instances, the tree has a logistic function ($S(x) = 1/(1 + e^{-x})$) at its root node and uses the threshold 0.5 for classes discrimination (in other words, instances with an output greater than 0.5 are classified as belonging to class C, while the other instances are identified as not belonging to class C), as it is usual, for instance, in Perceptron artificial neural networks. The chosen fitness function for the specialists is the *f-score* measure, because, contrarily to accuracy, it is a reliable measure of performance also in presence of unbalanced data. The definition of the class in which individuals are specialised can be done in two ways: it can be automatic, simply set by the class for which the individual has a higher fitness, or it can be assigned by the algorithm to balance the number of specialists in the population.

Specialists Initial Population. Like in traditional GP, the specialists population is initialised using the ramped half-and-half method [7]. Specialists are assigned to the class label for which they work better. To ensure that there will be specialists of all classes in the initial population, individuals in classes with exceeding specialists are relocated. For each class, only the N/K best individuals are kept, where N is the size of the entire specialists population and K is the number of class labels in the dataset. If there are more than N/K individuals specialised in a class, the remaining are randomly changed to other specialisation classes, in which the number of individuals is less than N/K.

Specialist Solutions Selection. If the algorithm is in islands phase, the selection is made with roulette wheel or tournament, as in a traditional GP. If the algorithm is in demes phase, the specialists selection algorithm works with two individuals at a time. To keep the balance of specialists in the population, the first parent is selected with roulette wheel or tournament selection from a specific deme. The second parent is selected with roulette wheel or tournament over the entire population, but the fitnesses are weighted by means of the *cooperation intensity rate* (CIR) parameter (see the paragraph below). This parameter controls the quantity of cooperation between individuals from different specialisations.

PIC GP Parameters: CIR, CIR Decrease Rate and Phase Change. The main parameter to control the intensity of the cooperation among specialists is the *cooperation intensity rate* (CIR). This parameter is used to lower the fitness of individuals from other specialisations, when specialists are competing in the second parent selection step. Let f_i be the usual fitness of specialist i; then the new fitness f_i' is equal to $(f_i * \eta)$ if k_i is different from k_1, and f_i' is equal to f_i otherwise, where $\eta \in [0,1]$ is the CIR, k_i is the ith individual's specialisation class and k_1 is the specialisation class of the first selected parent. The CIR can be decreased over the evolution by the *CIR decrease rate* parameter, according to: $\eta_g = \eta_{g-1} * \eta_{dec}$, where η_g is the CIR at generation g, η_{g-1} is the CIR at generation $g-1$ and η_{dec} is the CIR decrease rate. The decrease rate reduces constantly, at each generation, the rate of cooperation among specialists. However, if using tournament selection, this process cannot convert the algorithm into an island approach, since even with $\eta = 0$, it can happen that only individuals with fitness equal to zero are randomly chosen to take part in the tournament, and so even a zero-fitness individual can be selected (in other words, decreasing the fitness of an individual to zero does not guarantee that the individual will not be selected). Therefore, to transform the specialists subpopulations from demes to islands, a *phase change* parameter is needed. The value of this parameter corresponds to the generation in which the specialists subpopulations should be transformed from demes to islands.

With these three parameters (CIR, CIR decrease rate and phase change), the specialised subpopulations can begin the evolution with a defined level of cooperation, that is reduced over the generations, up to a moment in which they do not cooperate anymore.

Specialist Solutions Genetic Operators. For specialists crossover and mutation, in this work the PIC GP uses one point crossover with two offspring and one-point mutation [7]. However, the method is general and, in principle, any existing tree-based GP genetic operator can be used. When the algorithm is in demes phase, the offspring will be assigned to the class for which it works better. So, it does not depend on the parents specialisation class(es). When the algorithm is in islands phase, the specialisation class of the offspring is automatically the same as the specialisation class of the parents.

3.2   Teams Evolution Components

Teams Structure and Their Fitness. In the proposed system, a team is a tree with a prediction function at its root node, with arity equal to K, being K the number of target classes in the dataset, and with one specialist of each class (the team members) in each one of the root's subtrees. In the present work, the team root node has a softmax function, i.e.: $\sigma(\mathbf{z})_j = e^{z_j}/(\sum_{k=1}^{K} e^{z_k})$, with $j = 1, 2, ..., K$, where $\mathbf{z}$ is the K-dimensional vector of the specialists logistic outcomes and, for each $i = 1, 2, ..., K$, z_i is the ith component of vector $\mathbf{z}$. The specialists logistic outcomes are used as inputs for the softmax function and the team's prediction is the class with the higher softmax outcome. The teams fitness is the accuracy of the final algorithm classification.

Teams Initialisation. The teams population starts with one special team, created deterministically with the elite of each specialists subpopulations (i.e. the best individual in each specialists subpopulation). The other teams are created with specialists selected with a roulette wheel selection from the specialists' subpopulations.

Teams Genetic Operators. Crossover of teams exchanges entire specialists, randomly selected with uniform distribution, between parents. Mutation substitutes a random specialist by an individual with the same specialisation from the specialists population, selected with a roulette wheel selection.

4   Experimental Study

4.1   Test Problems and Experimental Settings

All experiments were run 30 times, each with a different data partition, where 80% of the observations were selected randomly with uniform distribution to form the training set, 10% to form the validation set and 10% the test set. The validation set was used for parameter tuning (the parameter setting chosen for the final experiments was the one that returned the best results on the validation set), while the (unseen) test set was used to report the final results. This is exactly the same data partitioning scheme as the one used in [26]. Three MCC datasets from the UCI Machine Learning Repository [23] were studied: the Iris (IRS), the Thyroid (THY) and the Yeast (YST).

The IRS was used to explore the PIC GP dynamics and how they are influenced by its parameters. IRS is a widely studied dataset, with 3 target classes (three flower species) and the simplicity of the data structure in this dataset is beneficial to the comprehension of the algorithm dynamics. The target class *setosa* is the easiest to classify, since it is linearly separable from the other two species, based on petal length and width. The *versicolor* is the hardest to classify, because it has all feature values in-between the other two classes. The THY and the YST datasets were used to compare PIC GP with other state-of-the-art classification algorithms.

In all runs, the trees were initialised with an initial maximum depth equal to 3. Specialists elitism and teams elitism (i.e. copy of the best individual in these populations, into the next generation, without modification) were always used. The primitive functions used to build the specialists were $+$, $-$, $\times$ and protected $\div$ (the denominator was replaced by the constant $10e^{-6}$ when it was zero). The terminal set was composed by ephemeral constants from $]0, 1[$, in addition to the dataset features. The other default parameter settings are presented in Table 1. They were decided in a preliminary experimental tuning phase, choosing the configuration that was able to return the best fitness on the validation set. The modified settings for each experiment on the IRS dataset are presented in the corresponding section.

Table 1. PIC GP base settings used in the experiments.

PIC GP settings	IRS	THY	YST
Trees maximum depth	6	10	10
Specialists population size	90	90	120
Parent 1 selection	Tournament size 3	Tournament size 3	Tournament size 3
Parent 2 selection	Tournament size 3	Tournament size 2	Roulette wheel
Crossover probability	0.8	0.8	0.8
Mutation probability	0.2	0.2	0.2
Maximum generations	250	250	300
Phase change	200	200	240
Initial CIR	1.00	1.00	1.00
CIR decrease	0.00	0.00	0.00

4.2   Experimental Results

Specialists Selection Methods. In the first set of experiments, we are interested in comparing between each other several different selection methods for the specialists populations. The methods used in these experiments were: tournament of size 3 for the first parent and roulette wheel for the second (T3_R); roulette wheel for the first parent and tournament of size 3 for the second (R_T3); tournament of size 3 for both parents (T3_T3); tournament of size 5 for the first parent and roulette wheel for the second (T5_R); roulette wheel for the first parent and tournament of size 5 for the second (R_T5); and tournament of size 5 for both parents (T5_T5). For all these selection methods, the best accuracy for the test partition was 1.000. The accuracy mean for the test partition was $0.978 \pm (0.036$ sd) for T5_T5, $0.967 \pm (0.042$ sd) for R_T5 and T3_T3, $0.953 \pm (0.056$ sd) for R_T3, $0.953 \pm (0.047$ sd) for T3_R and $0.951 \pm (0.068$ sd) for T5_R. The differences were not significant (p-value 0.267 for a one-way ANOVA test).

The selection methods for first and second parents have different effects in PIC GP. The selection of the first parent just controls the selection pressure inside the subpopulation of one single specialisation class. Besides the selection pressure, the selection of the second parent also controls the cooperation among specialists of different classes. This can be seen in Fig. 2, which shows the evolution of the amount of cooperation between specialists from different classes, for the tested selection methods. More in particular, this figure shows the average and standard deviation of the number of events in which individuals belonging to two different specialists subpopulations are selected for crossover.

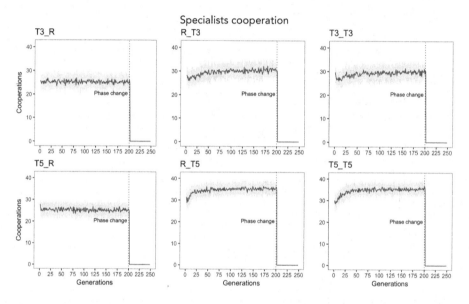

Fig. 2. Effect of the selection method of the second parent on the evolution of mean and standard deviation of the amount of the specialists cooperation (i.e. crossovers between specialists of different classes) against generations, for each specialists selection method.

Independently of the selection method used for the first parent, the amount of cooperation among specialists of different classes was the same for the same selection method used in the second parent (T3_R is very similar to T5_R; R_T3 to T3_T3; and R_T5 to T5_T5). Moreover, the bigger the tournament for the second parent, the more cooperation among different specialists happened in each generation. The first step of tournament selection is completely random, i.e. it is not related with the individuals' fitnesses. However, the number of individuals in each class subpopulation affects the selection pressure, favouring individuals of the more abundant subpopulation. In addition to the fact that the first parent is chosen to balance the number of individuals among the specialisation classes, favouring the more abundant class in the second parent selection increased the cooperation among classes. Since the *setosa* class is the easiest to discriminate, its specialists tend to have higher fitness and, hence, to be predominant in the population. This can be seen in Fig. 3, which shows the mean of the number of individuals in each class subpopulation for each generation of the T3_T3 and T5_T5 experiments. These plots show that in the demes phase of the algorithm, for both tournament sizes, the number of *versicolor* specialists tended to decrease, while the number of *setosa* specialists tended to increase. The number of *virginica* specialists tended to decrease for the tournament size 3 and to decrease in the beginning of the evolution process but to increase afterwards for the tournament size 5. So, in a situation under higher selection pressure, the difference in the fitnesses of *versicolor* and *virginica* specialists was more decisive for the selection method outcome.

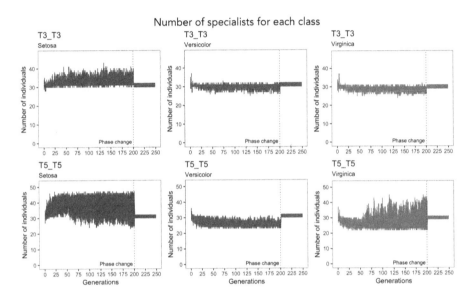

Fig. 3. Evolution of the number of specialised individuals in each class subpopulation against generations for each specialists selection method.

Cooperation Intensity Rate. The objective of this second part of our experimental study is to understand the influence of the CIR parameter on the dynamics of PIC GP. The following values of CIR were tested: 0.0, 0.2, 0.4, 0.6, 0.8 and 1.0. For all experiments, the CIR was kept constant for the entire PIC GP evolution. The best runs of all CIR experiments achieved accuracy of 1.000 for the test set for CIR 0.6 and CIR 0.8. The highest mean accuracy in the test set was obtained for CIR 0.6, 0.973 ± (0.041 sd). Nevertheless, the differences among the accuracies obtained in the CIR experiments were not statistically significant (p-value 0.843 for a one-way ANOVA test). As shown in Fig. 4, the amount of specialists cooperation presented different behavior for different CIR values.

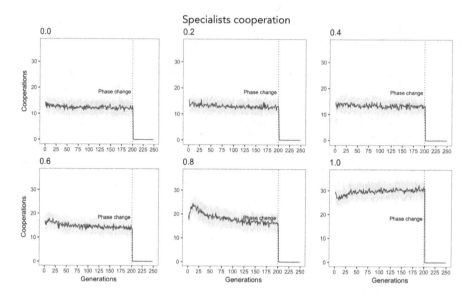

Fig. 4. Evolution of the mean and one standard deviation of the specialists interactions against generations for each CIR values experiment.

Table 2. Mean of differences between the mean fitnesses of the class subpopulations 50 generations before and 50 generations after the phase change.

Class	CIR	Before	After	Diff	CIR	Before	After	Diff	CIR	Before	After	Diff
setosa	0.0	0.845	0.913	0.086	0.4	0.843	0.902	0.059	0.8	0.873	0.893	0.020
versicolor		0.671	0.757	0.077		0.756	0.794	0.038		0.752	0.780	0.028
virginica		0.741	0.818	0.064		0.763	0.799	0.035		0.802	0.816	0.013
setosa	0.2	0.856	0.910	0.054	0.6	0.873	0.897	0.024	1.0	0.893	0.892	−0.001
versicolor		0.743	0.791	0.049		0.754	0.793	0.039		0.799	0.811	0.012
virginica		0.780	0.816	0.037		0.780	0.818	0.038		0.796	0.809	0.014

The specialists cooperation decreased slightly along the evolution in experiments with CIR from 0.0 to 0.4. For CIR equal to 0.6 and 0.8, they reached a maximum in the early generations, decreasing afterwards. For CIR equal to 1.0, in contrast, they steadily increased along the evolution. In general, the specialists cooperation increased with the increase of CIR. However, this correlation was not linear, because it also depends on the number of individuals in each class specialisation, since tournament was used as selection method. The bigger the difference in the number of individuals among the specialised subpopulations, the more the individuals of different specialisations cooperate when using the tournament selection for the second parent. For CIR values from 0.0 to 0.4, the number of individuals in each specialisation subpopulation was stable and balanced. For CIR equal to 0.6 and 0.8, the *setosa* specialists started to prevail at the expense of *versicolor* and *virginica* specialists. But this pattern tended to smooth with the algorithm evolution, more intensely for CIR equal to 0.6 and less for CIR equal to 0.8. For CIR equal to 1.0, the prevalence of *setosa* individuals lasted for the entire demes phase. The CIR value was also important for the mean fitness of class subpopulations during the evolution: with higher CIR values, i.e. with more cooperation between specialists of different classes, the mean fitness of the class subpopulations increased earlier for all classes. Furthermore, the mean fitness of the specialised subpopulations increased more with the phase change for smaller values of CIR, as Table 2 shows. Before the phase change, the subpopulations of specialists of the classes *setosa* and *versicolor* had higher mean fitness for CIR equal to 1.0 and the *virginica* class for CIR equal to 0.8. Comparing only the values before the phase change, the weakest class subpopulation (*versicolor*, which is the hardest to separate) presented the greatest difference (0.128) between the mean fitness with CIR equal to 0.0 and with CIR equal to 1.0. For the *virginica* class subpopulation, this difference was 0.055 and for the *setosa*, it was 0.048. After the phase change, *setosa* had the higher mean fitness with CIR equal to 0.0 (0.913), *versicolor* with CIR equal to 1.0 (0.811) and *virginica* with CIR equal to 0.0 and 0.6 (0.818). Table 2 also shows that the smaller the CIR value, the bigger the difference between the subpopulations mean fitness before and after the phase change. This is due to both smaller mean fitness values before the phase change and higher values after the phase change. Although with CIR equal to 0.0 the mean fitness of the specialised subpopulations increased more with the phase change, for the weakest classifier subpopulation (*versicolor*) the highest mean fitness was reached with CIR equal to 1.0, after phase change. This was not observed for the strongest classifier subpopulation (*setosa*), for which the highest mean fitness was reached with CIR equal to 0.0, after phase change. Thus, a higher CIR value favoured an improvement of the subpopulation of weaker classifiers.

Two interesting conclusions can be drawn from the results presented above. First, before the change of phase (i.e. in the demes phase) the cooperation among the specialists of different classes was helpful, especially for the weaker classifiers. Second, the islands phase is also important for subpopulations to evolve. Both demes and islands seem to be important for achieving the best algorithm performance.

Cooperation Intensity Decrease Rate. Now, we study the influence of the CIR decrease rate on the PIC GP dynamics. The following values of the CIR decrease rates were tested: $8.2e^{-4}$, $5.3e^{-4}$ and $2.6e^{-4}$, to decrease the CIR from 1.00 respectively to 0.85, 0.90 and 0.95 at the end of the demes phase. The constant decrease of the CIR worsened the algorithm final accuracy from 0.967 with no CIR decrease, to 0.920 with final CIR equal to 0.85 (p-value equal to 0.017 in a Tukey HSD test for this pair of means). For final CIR values equal to 0.90 and 0.95, the mean was also smaller than for the experiments without CIR decreasing (0.931 and 0.942, respectively), but the difference was not statistically significant.

These results indicate that for the IRS dataset, the maximum cooperation among specialists over the entire demes phase was beneficial.

Phase Change. We now present the experiments aimed at understanding the influence of the phase change on the dynamics of PIC GP. Four values of the phase change were tested: 0 (full islands evolution), 125, 200 and 250 (full demes). The accuracy mean was 0.980 ± (0.036 sd) for the phase change at generation 125, 0.967 ± (0.042 sd) for the phase change at generation 200, 0.962 ± (0.049 sd) for the phase change at generation 0 (full islands) and 0.960 ± (0.057 sd) for the phase change at generation 250 (full demes). These results indicate that combining the demes and islands phases can be convenient.

Comparison of PIC GP with Other Machine Learning Algorithms. The objective of this final part of our experimental study is to asses the competitiveness of PIC GP, by comparing its performance with a set of state-of-the art classification algorithms. In these experiments, the THY and the YST datasets were used.

Concerning the THY dataset, PIC GP achieved an accuracy of 0.992 on the test set. Thus, PIC GP outperformed some results found in the literature, without any fine tuning. For example, Tsakonas [24] tested four grammar-guided GP configurations on the THY dataset: with decision trees, with fuzzy rule-based training, with fuzzy petri-nets and with neural networks. The best obtained accuracies were respectively 0.976, 0.941, 0.940 and 0.940 for the test set. Ionita and Ionita [25] also compared methods of machine learning for this dataset. They found that the best runs for Naive Bayes (NB), Decision Trees, Multilayer Perceptron and Radial Basis Function Network achieved classification accuracies of 0.917, 0.969, 0.951 and 0.960, respectively. Finally, Zhang et al. [26] published a comparison among the following machine learning algorithms for MCC: Stochastic Gradient Boosting Decision Trees (GBDT), Random Forests (RF), Extreme Learning Machine (ELM), Support Vector Machine (SVM), C4.5, Sparse Representation based Classification (SCR), KNN, Logistic Regression (LR), AdaBoost (AB), NB and Deep Learning (DL). The best accuracies that they could obtain for each classifier for the THY dataset are presented in Table 3. As the table shows, PIC GP outperformed 9 of the 11 algorithms tested by the authors, and was slightly outperformed only by GDBT and RF.

Concerning the experiments on the YST dataset, PIC GP achieved an accuracy of 0.642 for the test set. The PIC GP performance for this dataset, obtained again without any fine tuning, is comparable with some results found in the literature, again confirming the robustness of the algorithm. Muñoz et al. [3], for instance, found a median accuracy of 0.562 for this dataset, using a MCC GP wrapper algorithm. The results for the 11 algorithms studied by Zhang et al. [26] are also presented in Table 3. PIC GP outperformed 10 over the 11 of those algorithms, and it was slightly outperformed only by ELM. The difference in accuracy to the best algorithm (ELM) was only 0.007, while to the worst (DL), it was 0.311.

Table 3. Best accuracy for PIC GP and the achieved accuracy for each classifier reported in [26] for the THY and the YST datasets. $^{(+)}$ indicates the algorithms that performed better than PIC GP, $^{(-)}$ those that performed worse to PIC GP.

Algorithm	THY dataset	YST dataset	Algorithm	THY dataset	YST dataset
PIC GP	0.992	0.642	SCR	$0.903^{(-)}$	$0.574^{(-)}$
GDBT	$1.000^{(+)}$	$0.622^{(-)}$	KNN	$0.903^{(-)}$	$0.574^{(-)}$
RF	$1.000^{(+)}$	$0.622^{(-)}$	LR	$0.931^{(-)}$	$0.621^{(-)}$
ELM	$0.903^{(-)}$	$0.649^{(+)}$	AB	$0.931^{(-)}$	$0.412^{(-)}$
SVM	$0.903^{(-)}$	$0.629^{(-)}$	NB	$0.903^{(-)}$	$0.595^{(-)}$
C4.5	$0.986^{(-)}$	$0.513^{(-)}$	DL	$0.903^{(-)}$	$0.331^{(-)}$

5   Conclusions and Future Work

A novel GP method for multiclass classification (MCC) was presented in this work, combining the advantages of evolving both individuals that are strongly specialized in the classification of the single target classes, and teams, that join those individuals to obtain the final prediction. Specialists and teams are evolved at the same time, in two independent populations, and the specialists population is further partitioned into a number of subpopulations, one for each different target class. The algorithm is named Progressively Insular Cooperative (PIC) GP, because its key feature is the possibility to control the level of cooperation between specialized individuals from a high level of cooperation (where the specialists subpopulations are demes), to a complete separation of the specialists subpopulations (islands). Even though the idea of using mixed teams and specialised subpopulations is not new, PIC GP contains, at least, the following elements of novelty: (1) the combination of the demes and islands phase in different stages of the evolution; (2) the parametrization to control the cooperation intensity; and (3) the functioning of the teams population, in which, at each generation, the teams evolution is combined with the input of new evolved specialists. The influence of the PIC GP parameters on the dynamics of the algorithm was studied on the Iris dataset, while PIC GP was compared to a set of state-of-the-art classification algorithms on the Thyroid and Yeast datasets (these three datasets are publicly available in the UCI Machine Learning Repository [23]). The presented results indicated that PIC GP outperformed the majority of its competitors, on both the Thyroid and Yeast datasets. Importantly, this work elucidated a major question that had no clear answer in the available literature: team-based GP can benefit both from the cooperation among specialists of different classes and from a more restricted process, where only an interaction among individuals specialized in the same class is allowed. The contribution of each approach to the algorithm's performance will depend on the performance of each group of specialised individuals. A demes approach helps weaker groups of specialist classifiers, because they may benefit from receiving crucial genetic material from stronger groups. An island approach, on the other hand, allows strong classifiers to evolve to their best potential. The presented results indicate that the combination of both approaches may be the best strategy, at least for the studied test problems. Starting with a demes approach is important to improve the weaker performers. Later, when all groups are strong, the algorithm can change to an islands approach, to allow all the specialised classifiers to reach their best performance.

Our current research is focused on a more exhaustive exploration of the PIC GP parameters. In particular, we are investigating other combinations of the settings, especially the CIR decrease rate and the phase change. In the near future, we are planning to begin a vast testing phase of PIC GP on numerous and more complex datasets.

Acknowledgments. This work was partially supported by FCT, Portugal, through funding of projects BINDER (PTDC/CCI-INF/29168/2017) and AICE (DSAIPA/DS/0113/2019).

References

1. Boucher, D.: Mutualism. Integr. Comp. Biol. **56**(2), 365–367 (2016)
2. Wilson, D.S.: Structured demes and the evolution of group-advantageous traits. Am. Nat. **111**(977), 157–185 (1977)
3. Muñoz, L., Silva, S., Trujillo, L.: M3GP – multiclass classification with GP. In: Machado, P., et al. (eds.) EuroGP 2015. LNCS, vol. 9025, pp. 78–91. Springer, Cham (2015). https://doi.org/10.1007/978-3-319-16501-1_7
4. Raymer, M.L., Punch, W.F., Goodman, E.D., Kuhn, L.A.: Genetic programming for improved data mining - application to the biochemistry of protein interactions. In: Genetic Programming 1996: Proceedings of the 1st Annual Conference, pp. 375–380. Morgan Kaufmann (1996)
5. Tan, X., Bhanu, B., Lin, Y.: Fingerprint classification based on learned features. IEEE Trans. Syst. Man Cybern. Part C (Appl. Rev.) **35**(3), 287–300 (2005)
6. Al-Madi, N., Ludwig, S.A.: Improving genetic programming classification for binary and multiclass datasets. In: IEEE Symposium on Computational Intelligence and Data Mining (CIDM), pp. 166–173 (2013)
7. Koza, J.R.: Genetic Programming: On the Programming of Computers by Means of Natural Selection. MIT Press, Cambridge (1992)
8. Zhang, M., Smart, W.: Multiclass object classification using genetic programming. In: Raidl, G.R., et al. (eds.) EvoWorkshops 2004. LNCS, vol. 3005, pp. 369–378. Springer, Heidelberg (2004). https://doi.org/10.1007/978-3-540-24653-4_38
9. Zhang, M., Smart, W.: Using Gaussian distribution to construct fitness functions in genetic programming for multiclass object classification. Pattern Recogn. Lett. **27**, 1266–1274 (2006)
10. Kishore, J.K., Patnaik, L.M., Mani, V., Agrawal, V.K.: Application of genetic programming for multicategory pattern classification. IEEE Trans. Evol. Comput. **4**(3), 242–258 (2000)
11. Silva, S., Tseng, Y.-T.: Classification of seafloor habitats using genetic programming. In: Giacobini, M., et al. (eds.) EvoWorkshops 2008. LNCS, vol. 4974, pp. 315–324. Springer, Heidelberg (2008). https://doi.org/10.1007/978-3-540-78761-7_32

12. Lin, J.Y., Ke, H.R., Chien, B.C., Yang, W.P.: Designing a classifier by a layered multi-population genetic programming approach. Pattern Recogn. **40**(8), 2211–2225 (2007)
13. Chen, Z., Lu, S.: A genetic programming approach for classification of textures based on wavelet analysis. In: 2007 IEEE International Symposium on Intelligent Signal Processing, pp. 1–6 (2007)
14. Smart, W., Zhang, M.: Using genetic programming for multiclass classification by simultaneously solving component binary classification problems. In: Keijzer, M., Tettamanzi, A., Collet, P., van Hemert, J., Tomassini, M. (eds.) EuroGP 2005. LNCS, vol. 3447, pp. 227–239. Springer, Heidelberg (2005). https://doi.org/10.1007/978-3-540-31989-4_20
15. Haynes, T., Sen, S., Schoenefeld, D., Wainwright, R.: Evolving a team. In: Working Notes for the AAAI Symposium on Genetic Programming (1995)
16. Haynes, T., Sen, S.: Crossover operators for evolving a team. In: Genetic Programming 1997: Proceedings of the Second Annual Conference (1997)
17. Brameier, M., Banzhaf, W.: Evolving teams of predictors with linear genetic programming. Genet. Program Evolvable Mach. **2**, 381–407 (2001). https://doi.org/10.1023/A:1012978805372
18. Lichodzijewski, P., Heywood, M.I.: Managing team-based problem solving with symbiotic bid-based genetic programming. In: Proceedings of the 10th Annual Conference on Genetic and Evolutionary Computation, GECCO 2008, p. 363 (2008)
19. Soule, T., Komireddy, P.: Orthogonal evolution of teams: a class of algorithms for evolving teams with inversely correlated errors. In: Riolo, R., Soule, T., Worzel, B. (eds.) Genetic Programming Theory and Practice IV. GEVO, pp. 79–95. Springer, Boston (2007). https://doi.org/10.1007/978-0-387-49650-4_6
20. Thomason, R., Soule, T.: Novel ways of improving cooperation and performance in ensemble classifiers. In: Proceedings of the 9th Annual Conference on Genetic and Evolutionary Computation, GECCO 2007, p. 1708 (2007)
21. Luke, S., Spector, L.: Evolving teamwork and coordination with genetic programming. In: 1996 Proceedings of the Conference on Genetic Programming (GP 1996) (1996)
22. Soule, T.: Heterogeneity and specialization in evolving teams. In: Proceedings of the Genetic and Evolutionary Computation Conference (GECCO 2000) (2000)
23. https://archive.ics.uci.edu/ml/
24. Tsakonas, A.: A comparison of classification accuracy of four genetic programming-evolved intelligent structures. Inf. Sci. **176**(6), 691–724 (2006)
25. Ionita, I., Ionita, L.: Prediction of thyroid disease using data mining techniques. Broad Res. Artif. Intell. Neurosci. **7**(3), 115–124 (2016)
26. Zhang, C., Liu, C., Zhang, X., Almpanidis, G.: An up-to-date comparison of state-of-the-art classification algorithms. Expert Syst. Appl. **82**, 128–150 (2017)

Regenerating Soft Robots Through Neural Cellular Automata

Kazuya Horibe[1,2,3(✉)], Kathryn Walker[1], and Sebastian Risi[1]

[1] IT University of Copenhagen, Copenhagen, Denmark
[2] Osaka University, Osaka, Japan
[3] Cross Labs, Cross Compass Ltd., Tokyo, Japan

Abstract. Morphological regeneration is an important feature that highlights the environmental adaptive capacity of biological systems. Lack of this regenerative capacity significantly limits the resilience of machines and the environments they can operate in. To aid in addressing this gap, we develop an approach for simulated soft robots to regrow parts of their morphology when being damaged. Although numerical simulations using soft robots have played an important role in their design, evolving soft robots with regenerative capabilities have so far received comparable little attention. Here we propose a model for soft robots that regenerate through a neural cellular automata. Importantly, this approach only relies on local cell information to regrow damaged components, opening interesting possibilities for physical regenerable soft robots in the future. Our approach allows simulated soft robots that are damaged to partially regenerate their original morphology through local cell interactions alone and regain some of their ability to locomote. These results take a step towards equipping artificial systems with regenerative capacities and could potentially allow for more robust operations in a variety of situations and environments. The code for the experiments in this paper is available at: http://github.com/KazuyaHoribe/RegeneratingSoftRobots.

Keywords: Regeneration · Soft robots · Neural cellular automata · Damage recovering

1 Introduction

Many organisms have regenerative capabilities, allowing them to repair and reconfigure their morphology in response to damage or changes in components [3]. For example, the primitive organisms Hydra and Planaria are particularly capable of regeneration and can thus achieve complete repair, no matter what location of the body part is cut off [29,49]. Furthermore, salamanders are capable of regenerating an amputated leg [48]. Many biological systems achieve regeneration by retaining information on the damaged parts [2].

© Springer Nature Switzerland AG 2021
T. Hu et al. (Eds.): EuroGP 2021, LNCS 12691, pp. 36–50, 2021.
https://doi.org/10.1007/978-3-030-72812-0_3

While biological systems are surprisingly robust, current robotic systems are fragile and often not able to recover from even minor damage. Furthermore, the majority of damage recovery approaches in robotics has focused on damage compensation through behavioral changes alone [6,8,20,26,41]; damage recovery through the regrowth of morphology has received comparable little attention.

In this present study, we develop a neural cellular automata approach for soft robot locomotion and morphological regeneration. Cellular automata (CA) were first proposed by Neumann and Ulam in the 1940s and consist of a regular grid of cells where each cell can be in any one of a finite set of states [35]. Each cell determines its next state based on local information (i.e. the states of its neighboring cells) according to pre-defined rules. In a neural cellular automata, instead of having hand-designed rules, a neural network learns the update rules [5,32,36]. In a recent impressive demonstration of a neural CA, Mordvintsev et al. trained a neural CA to grow complex two-dimensional images starting from a few initial cells [33]. In addition, the authors successfully trained the system to recover the pattern, when parts of it were removed (i.e. it was able to regrow the target pattern). The neural network in their work is a convolutional network, which lends itself to represent neural CAs [13]. Earlier work by Miller showed that automatically recovery of simpler damaged target patterns is also possible with genetic programming [32].

In this study, we extend the neural CA approach to simulated soft robots, which develop from a single cell, and are able to evolve the ability to locomote and regenerate. The results show that when the simulated soft robots are partially damaged, they are capable to move again by regrowing a morphology close to their original one. Our approach opens up interesting future research directions for more resilient soft robots that could ultimately be transferred to the real world.

2   Related Work

2.1   Evolved Virtual Creatures

The evolution of virtual creatures first began with Karl Sim's seminal work nearly three decades ago [44], with creatures composed of blocks interacting with their environment and other individuals in a virtual physical space, evolving their own body plans. Since then many researchers have explored the use of artificial evolution to train virtual creatures and even transferred some of these designs to the real world [9,10,14,18,30,40,42]. It should be noted, however, that in each of the above examples, the morphology of the evolved robot is fixed; it does not develop over its lifetime.

More recently, this research field has embraced approaches based on compositional pattern producing networks (CPPN) [4,7,45], which are a special kind of neural network. Furthermore, using CPPN-based approaches, researchers have been able to explore evo-devo virtual creatures, where development continues during interaction with the environment, further increasing the complexity of the final body plans [22,23]. However, the lifetime development of these creature tends to be limited to material properties, rather than growth of complete body parts.

Kriegman et al. also proposed a modular soft robot automated design and construction framework [24]. The framework's ability to transfer robot designs from simulation to reality could be a good match for our neural CA method in the future, which increases morphological complexity during development.

2.2 Cellular Automata

Instead of a CPPN-based approach, which relies on having access to a global coordinate system, we employ a neural cellular automata to grow virtual soft robots solely based on the local interaction of cells. As previously discussed, cellular automata (CA) were first studied by Neumann and Ulam [35] in the 1940s, taking inspiration from observations of living organisms. When correctly designed, CAs have been able to reproduce some of the patterns of growth, self-replication, and self-repair of natural organisms, only through local cell interactions.

Wolfram exhaustively examined the rules of one-dimensional CAs and classified them according to their behaviors [50]. Later, Langton discovered that behavior of CAs could be determined with a single parameter [27]. Similar dominant parameters and behaviors have been searched for in two-dimensional CAs using tools from information theory and dynamical systems theory [38].

More recently, optimization methods (e.g. evolutionary algorithms, gradient descent) have been employed to train neural networks that in turn dictate the behaviour (i.e. growth rules) of a CA. Such a CA is called a neural cellular automata [33,36,37]. Neural CAs are able to learn complex rules, which enable growth to difficult 2D target patterns [32,37], and can also regrow patterns when they are partially removed [33]. In this paper, we extend the work on neural CAs to soft robots, which can move and regrow once their morphologies are damaged.

2.3 Shape Changing Robots and Damage Recovery

Krigeman et al. evolved robots that were capable of adapting their resting volume of each voxel in response to environmental stress [25]. In recent years, not only the locomotion performance of organisms, but also their environmental adaptability through shape change has attracted attention. For a recent review of approaches that allow robots to transform in order to cope with different shapes and tasks, see Shah et al. [43].

In terms of damage recovery, traditionally approaches have focused on the robot's control system to combat loss of performance. Building on ideas from morphological computation and embodiment, more recently morphological change has been investigated as a mechanism for damage recovery. Such work includes that by Kriegman et al. [25], where silicone based physical voxel robots were able to recover from voxel removal. Furthermore, Xenobots, synthetic creatures designed from biological tissue [24], have shown to be capable of reattachment (i.e. healing after insult).

Our model uses only local information (i.e. each cell only communicates with its neighbors) and could be applied as a design method for regenerating soft robots composed of biological tissue using techniques which control gene expression and bioelectric signaling [1,47]. We believe that by using only local information, our method is particularly biologically plausible and therefore might work on real robots in the future, with the help of various biological tissues editing technologies. In particular, an exciting direction is to combine the approach with biological robots such as the Xenobots [24].

3 Growing Soft Robots with Neural Cellular Automata

The neural CA representation for our soft robot is shown in Fig. 1. For each cell, the same network maps the neighborhood cell's input to a new cell state. The cell states are discrete values from a finite set, which we map to a continuous value before passing it to the neural network. The dimension of the input layer corresponds to the number of cell neighbors (e.g. Neumann and Moor neighborhood). The neural network has one output for each possible cell state and is assigned the state that corresponds to the largest activated output.

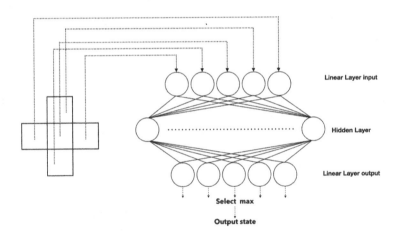

Fig. 1. Neural CA representation. The center cell and its neighboring cells are shown. Each cell state is an input to the neural network. The center cell transitions to the state with the highest network output.

We use a three-layer networks with tanh activation functions. We experiment with both **feed forward** (the hidden layer is a linear layer) and **recurrent networks** (the hidden layer is an LSTM unit [16]), which means that each cell has its own memory. The dimension of the hidden layer in this paper is set to 64 unless otherwise noted. The recurrent setup is inspired by recent experimental reports that organisms store information about the original morphology in a distributed manner in the bioelectrical signaling networks [28,31].

Following Mordvintsev et al. [33], the network has an additional alpha channel output (α) that determines the maturity of a cell. If α is greater than 0.1, the cell is tagged as "living". A cell with $0 < \alpha < 0.1$ is tagged as "growing". When the neural network is calculating the next state of a cell, the inputs from empty or growing cells are set to 0.0. This way, it is possible to gradually expand the area of mature cells from a few initial cells. Mature cells can also die and become empty; to guarantee that robots do not have any isolated and unconnected cells, isolated cells are removed before the robot is evaluated following the procedure below. First, we remove cells that are connected diagonally but not horizontally to eliminate physical simulation error in VoxCad. Second, we remove independent cells which do not have any neighboring cells. Both of these two steps are applied to each cell sequentially in the order of their indexes.

3.1 Soft Robot Simulator

All soft robot experiments are performed in the open-source physical simulator Voxelyze [15]. We consider a locomotion task for soft robots composed of a 7×7 and $9 \times 9 \times 9$ grid of voxels in 2D and 3D, respectively. We adopt the Dirichlet boundary condition, and the cell state of the outer frame is always empty. Thus, the actual maximum size of the soft robots is 5×5 (Fig. 2a) and $7 \times 7 \times 7$ (Fig. 3a). At any given time, a robot is completely specified by an array of resting volumes, one for each of its $7 \times 7 = 49$ and $9 \times 9 \times 9 = 729$ voxels. Each voxel is volumetrically actuated according to a global signal that varies sinusoidally in volume over time. The actuation is a linear expansion and contraction from their resting volume.

Following Cheney et al. [7], there are four types of voxels, denoted by their color: Red colored voxels can be thought of as muscle; they actively contract and expand sinusoidally at a constant frequency. Green colored voxels can also be though of as muscle, with their activation in counter-phase to red voxels. Dark blue colored voxels can be considered as bone; they are unable to expand and contract like the "muscle" voxels. Furthermore, they have a high stiffness value. The final type of voxel used in this experiment are colored light blue voxels. These are also passive but have a lower stiffness than dark blue bone voxels. The physical and environmental Voxelyze parameters also follow the settings in Cheney et al. [7].

Soft robots are evaluated for their ability to locomote for 0.25 s, or 10 actuation cycles in 2D (Fig. 2c) and for 0.5 s, or 20 actuation cycles in 3D (Fig. 3c, 3d). The evaluation times try to strike a balance between reducing computational costs while still giving sufficient time to observe interesting locomotion behaviours. Fitness is determined as the distance the robot's center of mass moves in 0.25 or 0.5 s. The distance is measured in units that correspond to the length of a voxel with volume one. Creatures with zero voxels after their growth are automatically assigned a fitness of 0.0.

3.2 Genetic Algorithm

To evolve a neural CA, we use a simple genetic algorithm [11,17] that can train deep neural networks [46]. The implemented GA variant performs truncation selection with the top T individuals becoming the parents of the next genera-tion. The following procedure is repeated at each generation: First, parents are selected uniformly at random. They are mutated by adding Gaussian noise to the weight vector of the neural network (its genotype): $\theta' = \theta + \sigma\epsilon$, where ϵ is drawn from $N(0, I)$ and σ is set to 0.03. Following a technique called elitism, top N^{th} individuals are passed on to the next generation without mutation.

4   Results

4.1   Evolving 2D Soft Robots

To confirm the promise of neural CAs for growing soft robots, we first apply them to simpler 2D robot variants. Here, robots have a maximum size of 7×7 voxels. Since the neural CA used a Moor neighborhood, the input dimension of the neural network was $9 \times 2 = 18$, which includes neighboring cell types and alpha values. The output layer has a size of 6, 5 for the different states of the cell (empty = 0, light blue = 1, dark blue = 2, red = 3, green = 4) plus one alpha channel. The first single soft & passive cell is placed at position $(3, 3)$ and 10 steps of development are performed. As result, 11 morphologies are obtained. (Fig. 2a). Afterwards, the final grown robot is tested in the physical simulator and allowed to attempt locomotion for 0.25 s (10 actuation cycles). The fitness of each robot is taken to be distance travelled by the robot from its starting point. These 2D experiments use a population size of 300, running for 500 generations. One evolutionary run on 8 CPUs took around 12 h.

Results are shown in Fig. 2, which were obtained from ten independent evo-lutionary runs, using both recurrent and feed forward networks. The training mean together with bootstrapped 95% confidence intervals is shown in Fig. 2b.

Evolution produced a variety of soft robots (Fig. 2c). A "Hook" type is distin-guished by its hook-like form and locomotion, which shakes the two sides of the hook and proceed to hook the remaining one side to the floor. The "S" shaped-robot is distinguished by its sharp and peristaltic motion with amplitude in the same direction as the direction of travel. The "Biped" has two legs and its loco-motion resembles that of a frog, with the two legs pushing the robot forward. The "L" type displays a sharp and winged movement. Finally, the "Zig-zag" shows a spring-like movement by stretching and retracting the zigzag structure. Enabling the cells to keep a memory of recent developmental states through a recurrent network improved performance, although only slightly (Fig. 2b). Inves-tigating what information the evolved LSTM-based network is keeping track of during development is an interesting future research direction.

4.2   Evolving 3D Soft Robots

In this section we now extend our methodology to grow 3D robots. For these 3D robots the maximum size of the morphologies is $9 \times 9 \times 9$. Since the neural CA uses a Moor neighborhood, the input dimension of the neural network is

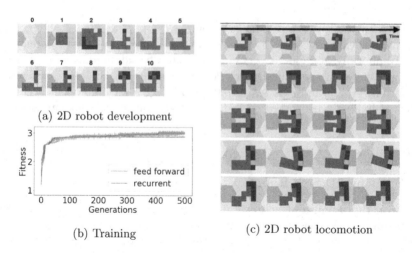

(a) 2D robot development

(b) Training

(c) 2D robot locomotion

Fig. 2. Evolution of 2D soft robots (a) Development of 2D soft robots through a neural cellular automata. (b) Training fitness for the recurrent/feed forward setup. (c) Time series of soft robot behaviors as they move from left to right. From top to bottom, we refer to them as Hook type, S-type, Biped, L-type, and Zigzag.

$3 \times 9 \times 2 = 54$. The hidden layer is set to 64. The output layer is set to $5 + 1 = 6$ dimensions with the number of states of the cell and the value of its own next step alpha value. The first single soft & passive cell is placed at position $(4, 4, 4)$ and 10 steps of growth are performed (Fig. 3a). The final soft robot grown after 10 steps is tested in the physical simulated and, as with the 2D robots, the distance of the robot's center of gravity from its starting point was used as part of the fitness function. Additionally we include a voxel cost in the fitness calculation: $Fitness = (Distance) - (VoxelsCost)$. We added a "voxel" cost because preliminary results indicated that without this additional metric all the soft robots simply acquired a box-like morphology. Including the voxel cost metric increased diversity in the population. Note that voxel cost is the number of voxels that are neither empty nor dead.

For our 3D experiments the evaluation time is increased to 0.5 s for 20 actuation cycles to adjust for the increased complexity of the robots. Each generation has a population size of 100 and the next generation is selected from the top 20%. The number of generations is set to 300. Note that both the generation number and population size are reduced from those values used in the 2D experiments as simulated the larger 3D robots has a higher computational cost. One evolutionary run on 1 CPU took around 80–90 h.

Results are based on 24 independent evolutionary runs for both the recurrent and feed forward treatment (Fig. 3b). Interestingly, the feed forward setup for the 3D robots has a higher fitness than the recurrent one, in contrast to the 2D soft robot results (Fig. 2b). We hypothesize that with the increased numbers of neighbors in 3D and more complex patterns, it might be harder to evolve an LSTM-based network that can use its memory component effectively.

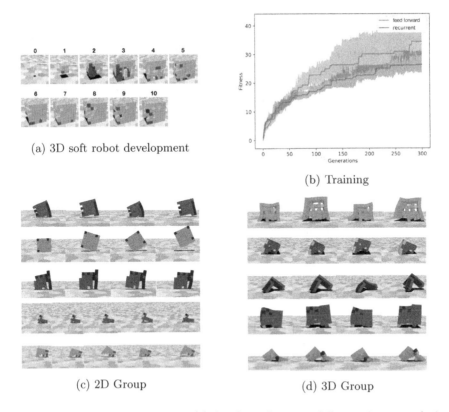

(a) 3D soft robot development

(b) Training

(c) 2D Group

(d) 3D Group

Fig. 3. Evolution of soft robots (a) A robots shown at different timesteps during its development. (b) Fitness over generations for the recurrent/feed forward setup. (c) Time series of common 2D soft robot behaviors as they move from left to right. From top to bottom, we refer to them as Jumper, Roller, Pull-Push, Slider, and Jitter. (d) Common grown 3D robots: Pull-Push, L-Walker, Jumper, Crawler, and Slider.

Because the dynamics of LSTM-based networks are inherently difficult to analyse, more experiments are needed to investigate this discrepancy further.

Similarly to CPPN-encoded soft robots [7], 3D robots grown by an evolved neural CA (Fig. 3) can be classified into two groups: the first group is the two-dimensional group of organisms (Fig. 3c), where planar morphology was acquired by evolution. Exemplary classes of locomotion in this group include the jumper, which is often composed of a single type of muscle voxel. Once a soft robot sinks down, it use this recoil to bounce up into the air and move forward. The morphology determines the angle of bounce and fall. The Roller is similar to a square; it moves in one direction by rotating and jumping around the corners of the square. The Push-Pull is a widely seen locomotion style. A soft robot pushes itself forward with its hind legs. During this push, it pulls itself forward, usually by hooking its front legs on the ground. The Slider has a front foot and a hind foot, and by opening and closing the two feet, it slides forward across the floor. The two legs are usually made of a single material. The Jitter moves by bouncing up and down from its hind legs to back. It has an elongated form and is often composed of a single type of muscle voxel. The second group is the three-dimensional group of organisms, as shown in Fig. 3d. The L-Walker resembles an L-shaped form; it moves by opening and closing the front and rear legs connected to its pivot point at the bend of the L. The Crawler has multiple short legs and its legs move forward in concert.

4.3 Regenerating Soft Robots

Here we investigate the ability of the soft robots to regenerate their body parts to recover from morphological damage. We chose three morphologies from the previous experiments, which are able to locomote well and as diverse as possible: the Biped (feed forward), Tripod (feed forward), and Multiped (recurrent). The morphologies of each of these three robots are shown in Fig. 4a and the locomotion patterns in Fig. 3d.

In these experiments, we damaged the morphologies such that one side of the robot was completely removed (Fig. 4a). In the left side of these damaged morphologies, the cell states were set to empty and the maturation alpha values were set to zero. For the recurrent network, the memory of LSTM units in each cell were also reset to zero.

We initially attempted regeneration using the original neural CAs of these three robots but regeneration failed and locomotion was not recovered. Therefore, we evolved another neural CA, which sole purpose it is to regrow a damaged morphology. In other words, one neural CA grows the initial morphology and the other CA is activated once the robot is damaged. Fitness for this second CA is determined by the voxel similarity between the original morphology and the recovered morphology (values in the range of $[0; 729]$). The maximum fitness of $9 \times 9 \times 9 = 729$ indicates that the regrown morphology is identical to the original morphology. We evolved these soft robots, which were allowed to grow for 10 steps, for $1,000$ generations with a population size of $1,000$. The next generation was selected from the top 20%.

For all three morphologies we trained both feed forward and recurrent neural CAs. The best performing network types for damage recovery were consistent with the original network type for locomotion in all morphologies (biped = feed forward, tripod = feedforward, multiped = recurrent). The results with the highest performing network type are summarised in Table 1 and damaged morphologies for each of the robots are shown in Fig. 4a. The results indicate that the Multiped was the hardest to reproduce, followed by the Biped and then the Tripod. The Tripod had a higher similarity than the other morphologies and the neural CA almost completely reproduced the original morphology with the exception of one cell. We hypothesise that regeneration for the Tripod is easier because it only requires the regrowth of one leg, a simple rod-like shape with only a few cells.

Table 1. Morphology similarity and locomotion recovery rate.

Morphology (Network)	Similarity	Locomotion		
		Original	Damaged	Regrown
Biped (feed forward)	98% (718/729)	40.4	27.2 (67%)	35.1 (86%)
Tripod (feed forward)	99% (728/729)	44.5	1.63 (3.6%)	20.3 (45%)
Multiped (recurrent)	91% (667/729)	42.7	5.36 (12%)	9.6 (22%)

For comparison, we then measured the locomotion of the original, damaged, and regrown morphology with an evaluation time of 0.5 s for 10 cycles in VoxCad. The ratio of regrowth and travel distance to the original morphology are shown in Table 1 and its locomotion in Fig. 5. The damaged Biped maintained 67% of its original locomotion ability; it replicated a similar locomotion pattern to the one observed in the L-Walker. As the Tripod lost one of its three legs, it was incapable of successful locomotion. Furthermore, the Multiped lost all locomotion – the robot simply collapsed at the starting position.

These results suggest that the location of the damage is important in determining how much the robot loses in terms of locomotion performance. For instance, in the case of the Biped, the left hand side and right hand side are symmetrical. This means that when the left hand side was removed, the right hand side was able to locomote in the same, almost unaffected way. Therefore, despite having the lowest similarity value between the initial and regrown morphologies, there is little loss in performance. In contrast the Tripod regained less than half the locomotion of the original morphology, despite regaining its original morphology almost completely. It would appear that the one voxel it is unable to regenerate is necessary to prevent the robot from spinning, allowing it to move forward. The damage recovery results show potential for soft robots capable of regrowth, but regrowth mechanisms that are not dependant of damage location are an important future research direction.

5 Discussion and Future Work

The ability to control pattern formation is critical for the both the embryonic development of complex structures as well as for the regeneration/repair of damaged or missing tissues and organs. Inspired by this adaptive capacity of biological systems, in this paper we presented an approach for morphological regeneration applied to soft robots.

We developed a new method for robot damage recovery based on neural cellular automata. While full regeneration is not always possible, the method shows promise in restoring the robot's locomotion ability after damage. The results indicate that the growth process can enhance the evolutionary potential of soft robots, and the regeneration of the soft robot's morphology and locomotion can provide some resilience to damage.

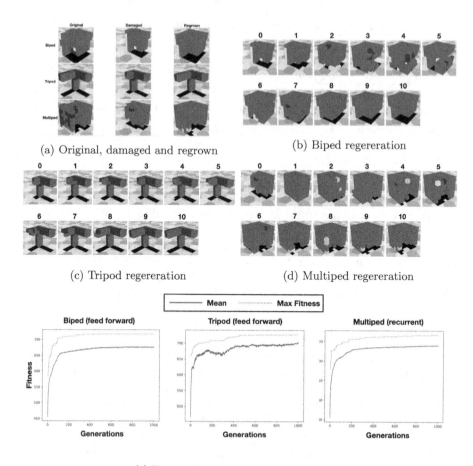

(a) Original, damaged and regrown

(b) Biped regereration

(c) Tripod regereration

(d) Multiped regereration

(e) Fitness function of each morphology

Fig. 4. Regenerating soft robots (a) Original, damaged, and regrown morphology. (b)–(d) Soft robot development after damage shown at different timesteps. (e) Training performance for recurrent/feed forward setup.

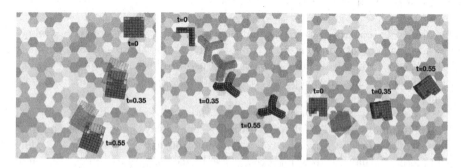

Fig. 5. Recovery of locomotion. The regrown morphologies are shown semi-translucent. From left to right: Biped, Tripod, and Multipod.

The fitness landscape of the developmental evolving soft robot is likely very complex, and the simple evolutionary algorithm employed in this paper is therefore getting stuck in some of these local optima. This limitation could explain why we needed two neural CA, one for growing the initial morphology and one for regeneration, and why it was sometimes difficult for evolution to find a network that could completely replicate the original morphology for damage recovery. We anticipate that the variety of quality diversity approaches that reward more exploration during evolutionary search [39], such as MAP-Elites [34], could allow for an even wider range of morphologies and escape some of these local optima.

Additionally, the locomotion and regeneration task in this paper is relatively simple. Exciting future work will explore more complex tasks (e.g. recovery form more types of damage) that could benefit from morphological growth/regeneration, such as object manipulation, adaptation to environmental changes, task-based transformation, and self-replication.

Recently, soft robots designed using computer simulations have recently been recreated in real robot using a variety of materials [19]. With the development of material science, a variety of soft robots that can change their shape have been born [12]. Currently, the technology of tissue culture has been developed, and hybrid robots with dynamic plasticity are being developed [21]. In the future, it may be possible to create a hybrid robot that can grow spontaneously and recover its function from damage by creating a soft robot designed using the proposed model with living tissue. Because the approach presented in this paper only relies on the local communication of cells, it could be a promising approach for the next generation of these hybrid robots.

Acknowledgements. This work was supported by the Tobitate! (Leap for Tomorrow) Young Ambassador Program, a Sapere Aude: DFF-Starting Grant (9063-00046B), and KH's Academist supporters (https://academist-cf.com/projects/119?lang=en) (Takaaki Aoki, Hirohito M. Kondo, Takeshi Oura, Yusuke Kajimoto, Ryuta Aoki).

References

1. Blackiston, D.J., Levin, M.: Ectopic eyes outside the head in Xenopus tadpoles provide sensory data for light-mediated learning. J. Exp. Biol. **216**(6), 1031–1040 (2013). https://doi.org/10.1242/jeb.074963
2. Blackiston, D.J., Shomrat, T., Levin, M.: The stability of memories during brain remodeling: a perspective. Communicative Integr. Biol. **8**(5), e1073424, September 2015. https://doi.org/10.1080/19420889.2015.1073424. https://www.tandfonline.com/doi/full/10.1080/19420889.2015.1073424
3. Carlson, B.M.: Principles of Regenerative Biology. Elsevier, Amsterdam (2011)
4. Cellucci, D., MacCurdy, R., Lipson, H., Risi, S.: One-dimensional printing of recyclable robots. IEEE Robot. Autom. Lett. **2**(4), 1964–1971 (2017). https://doi.org/10.1109/LRA.2017.2716418
5. Cenek, M., Mitchell, M.: Evolving cellular automata. Comput. Complexity: Theory Tech. Appl. **9781461418**, 1043–1052 (2013)
6. Chatzilygeroudis, K., Vassiliades, V., Mouret, J.B.: Reset-free trial-and-error learning for robot damage recovery. Robot. Auton. Syst. **100**, 236–250 (2018). https://doi.org/10.1016/j.robot.2017.11.010

7. Cheney, N., MacCurdy, R., Clune, J., Lipson, H.: Unshackling evolution: evolving soft robots with multiple materials and a powerful generative encoding. In: Proceeding of the Fifteenth Annual Conference on Genetic and Evolutionary Computation Conference - GECCO 2013, New York, New York, USA, p. 167. ACM Press (2013). https://doi.org/10.1145/2463372.2463404. http://dl.acm.org/citation.cfm?doid=2463372.2463404

8. Cully, A., Clune, J., Tarapore, D., Mouret, J.B.: Robots that can adapt like animals. Nature **521**(7553), 503–507 (2015). https://doi.org/10.1038/nature14422

9. Dellaert, F., Beer, R.D.: A developmental model for the evolution of complete autonomous agents. In: On Growth, Form and Computers, pp. 377–391. Elsevier (2003). https://doi.org/10.1016/B978-012428765-5/50053-0. https://linkinghub.elsevier.com/retrieve/pii/B9780124287655500530

10. Eggenberger-Hotz, P.: Evolving morphologies of simulated 3D organisms based on differential gene expression. In: Proceedings of the 4th European Conference on Artificial Life (ECAL97), pp. 205–213 (1997). http://citeseer.ist.psu.edu/viewdoc/summary?doi=10.1.1.52.5045

11. Eiben, A.E., Smith, J.E.: Introduction to Evolutionary Computing. Natural Computing Series. Springer, Heidelberg (2003). https://doi.org/10.1007/978-3-662-05094-1. http://link.springer.com/10.1007/978-3-662-05094-1

12. El-Atab, N., et al.: Soft actuators for soft robotic applications: a review. Adv. Intell. Syst. **2**(10), 2000128, October 2020. https://doi.org/10.1002/aisy.202000128. https://onlinelibrary.wiley.com/doi/10.1002/aisy.202000128

13. Gilpin, W.: Cellular automata as convolutional neural networks. Phys. Rev. E **100**(3), 032402, September 2019. https://doi.org/10.1103/PhysRevE.100.032402. https://link.aps.org/doi/10.1103/PhysRevE.100.032402

14. Hallundbæk Østergaard, E., Hautop Lund, H.: Co-evolving complex robot behavior. In: Tyrrell, A.A.M., Haddow, P.C., Torresen, J. (eds.) ICES 2003. LNCS, vol. 2606, pp. 308–319. Springer, Heidelberg (2003). https://doi.org/10.1007/3-540-36553-2_28

15. Hiller, J.D., Lipson, H.: Multi material topological optimization of structures and mechanisms. In: Proceedings of the 11th Annual Conference on Genetic and Evolutionary Computation - GECCO 2009, New York, New York, USA, p. 1521. ACM Press (2009). https://doi.org/10.1145/1569901.1570105. http://portal.acm.org/citation.cfm?doid=1569901.1570105

16. Hochreiter, S.: Long short-term memory. Neural Comput. **1780**, 1735–1780 (1997)

17. Holland, J.H.: Genetic algorithms. Sci. Am. **267**(1), 66–73 (1992)

18. Hornby, G.S., Lipson, H., Pollack, J.B.: Evolution of generative design systems for modular physical robots. In: Proceedings - IEEE International Conference on Robotics and Automation, vol. 4, pp. 4146–4151 (2001). https://doi.org/10.1109/ROBOT.2001.933266

19. Howison, T., Hauser, S., Hughes, J., Iida, F.: Reality-assisted evolution of soft robots through large-scale physical experimentation: a review. arXiv (2020). http://arxiv.org/abs/2009.13960

20. Kano, T., Sato, E., Ono, T., Aonuma, H., Matsuzaka, Y., Ishiguro, A.: A brittle star-like robot capable of immediately adapting to unexpected physical damage. Royal Soc. Open Sci. **4**(12), 171200 (2017). https://doi.org/10.1098/rsos.171200

21. Kriegman, S., Blackiston, D., Levin, M., Bongard, J.: A scalable pipeline for designing reconfigurable organisms. In: Proceedings of the National Academy of Sciences of the United States of America, vol. 117, no. 4, pp. 1853–1859 (2020). https://doi.org/10.1073/pnas.1910837117

22. Kriegman, S., Cheney, N., Bongard, J.: How morphological development can guide evolution. Sci. Rep. **8**(1), 1–10 (2018). https://doi.org/10.1038/s41598-018-31868-7. http://dx.doi.org/10.1038/s41598-018-31868-7

23. Kriegman, S., Cheney, N., Corucci, F., Bongard, J.C.: A minimal developmental model can increase evolvability in soft robots. In: Proceedings of the Genetic and Evolutionary Computation Conference, pp. 131–138. ACM, New York, NY, USA, July 2017. https://doi.org/10.1145/3071178.3071296. https://dl.acm.org/doi/10.1145/3071178.3071296

24. Kriegman, S., et al.: Scalable sim-to-real transfer of soft robot designs. In: 2020 3rd IEEE International Conference on Soft Robotics, RoboSoft 2020, pp. 359–366, November 2020. http://arxiv.org/abs/1911.10290

25. Kriegman, S., Walker, S., S. Shah, D., Levin, M., Kramer-Bottiglio, R., Bongard, J.: Automated shapeshifting for function recovery in damaged robots. In: Robotics: Science and Systems XV. Robotics: Science and Systems Foundation, June 2019. https://doi.org/10.15607/RSS.2019.XV.028. http://www.roboticsproceedings.org/rss15/p28.pdf

26. Kwiatkowski, R., Lipson, H.: Task-agnostic self-modeling machines. Sci. Robot. **4**(26), eaau9354, January 2019. https://doi.org/10.1126/scirobotics.aau9354. https://robotics.sciencemag.org/lookup/doi/10.1126/scirobotics.aau9354

27. Langton, C.G.: Computation at the edge of chaos: phase transitions and emergent computation. Phys. D: Nonlinear Phenomena **42**(1–3), 12–37 (1990). https://doi.org/10.1016/0167-2789(90)90064-V

28. Levin, M., Pezzulo, G., Finkelstein, J.M.: Endogenous bioelectric signaling networks: exploiting voltage gradients for control of growth and form. Ann. Rev. Biomed. Eng. **19**, 353–387 (2017). https://doi.org/10.1146/annurev-bioeng-071114-040647

29. Levin, M., Selberg, J., Rolandi, M.: Endogenous bioelectrics in development, cancer, and regeneration: drugs and bioelectronic devices as electroceuticals for regenerative medicine. iScience. **22**, 519–533 (2019). https://doi.org/10.1016/j.isci.2019.11.023

30. Lipson, H., Pollack, J.B.: Automatic design and manufacture of robotic lifeforms. Nature **406**(6799), 974–978, August 2000. https://doi.org/10.1038/35023115. http://www.nature.com/articles/35023115

31. McLaughlin, K.A., Levin, M.: Bioelectric signaling in regeneration: mechanisms of ionic controls of growth and form. Dev. Biol. **433**(2), 177–189 (2018). https://doi.org/10.1016/j.ydbio.2017.08.032

32. Miller, J.F.: Evolving a self-repairing, self-regulating, French flag organism. In: Deb, K. (ed.) GECCO 2004. LNCS, vol. 3102, pp. 129–139. Springer, Heidelberg (2004). https://doi.org/10.1007/978-3-540-24854-5_12

33. Mordvintsev, A., Randazzo, E., Niklasson, E., Levin, M.: Growing neural cellular automata. Distill **5**(2), e23 (2020). https://doi.org/10.23915/distill.00023. https://distill.pub/2020/growing-ca/

34. Mouret, J.B., Clune, J.: Illuminating search spaces by mapping elites. arXiv, pp. 1–15 (2015). http://arxiv.org/abs/1504.04909

35. von Neumann, J.: Theory of Self-Reproducing Automata. University of illinoi Press (1966). https://doi.org/10.2307/2005041. https://www.jstor.org/stable/2005041?origin=crossref

36. Wulff, N.H., Hertz, J.A.: Learning cellular automaton dynamics with neural networks. In: Proceedings of the 5th International Conference on Neural Information Processing Systems, pp. 631–638. Morgan Kaufmann Publishers Inc. (1992). https://doi.org/10.5555/2987061.2987139

37. Nichele, S., Ose, M.B., Risi, S., Tufte, G.: CA-NEAT: evolved compositional pattern producing networks for cellular automata morphogenesis and replication. IEEE Trans. Cogn. Dev. Syst. **10**(3), 687–700 (2018). https://doi.org/10.1109/TCDS.2017.2737082

38. Packard, N.H., Wolfram, S.: Two-dimensional cellular automata. J. Stat. Phys. **38**(5–6), 901–946 (1985)

39. Pugh, J.K., Soros, L.B., Stanley, K.O.: Quality diversity: a new frontier for evolutionary computation. Front. Robot. AI **3**, 1–17 (2016). https://doi.org/10.3389/frobt.2016.00040

40. Radhakrishna Prabhu, S.G., Seals, R.C., Kyberd, P.J., Wetherall, J.C.: A survey on evolutionary-aided design in robotics. Robotica **36**, 1804–1821 (2018). https://doi.org/10.1017/S0263574718000747

41. Ren, G., Chen, W., Dasgupta, S., Kolodziejski, C., Wörgötter, F., Manoonpong, P.: Multiple chaotic central pattern generators with learning for legged locomotion and malfunction compensation. Inf. Sci. **294**(May), 666–682 (2015). https://doi.org/10.1016/j.ins.2014.05.001. http://dx.doi.org/10.1016/j.ins.2014.05.001

42. Risi, S., Cellucci, D., Lipson, H.: Ribosomal robots. In: Proceedings of the 15th Annual Conference on Genetic and Evolutionary Computation, pp. 263–270 (2013). https://doi.org/10.1145/2463372.2463403

43. Shah, D., Yang, B., Kriegman, S., Levin, M., Bongard, J., Kramer-Bottiglio, R.: Shape changing robots: bioinspiration, simulation, and physical realization. Adv. Mater. **2002882**, 1–12 (2020). https://doi.org/10.1002/adma.202002882

44. Sims, K.: Evolving virtual creatures. In: Proceedings of the 21st Annual Conference on Computer Graphics and Interactive Techniques - SIGGRAPH 1994, vol. 4, pp. 15–22. ACM Press, New York, USA (1994). https://doi.org/10.1145/192161.192167. http://portal.acm.org/citation.cfm?doid=192161.192167

45. Stanley, K.O.: Compositional pattern producing networks: a novel abstraction of development. Genet. Program Evolvable Mach. **8**(2), 131–162 (2007). https://doi.org/10.1007/s10710-007-9028-8

46. Such, F.P., Madhavan, V., Conti, E., Lehman, J., Stanley, K.O., Clune, J.: Deep neuroevolution: genetic algorithms are a competitive alternative for training deep neural networks for reinforcement learning. arXiv, December 2017. http://arxiv.org/abs/1712.06567

47. Thompson, D.M., Koppes, A.N., Hardy, J.G., Schmidt, C.E.: Electrical stimuli in the central nervous system microenvironment. Ann. Rev. Biomed. Eng. **16**, 397–430 (2014). https://doi.org/10.1146/annurev-bioeng-121813-120655

48. Vieira, W.A., Wells, K.M., McCusker, C.D.: Advancements to the axolotl model for regeneration and aging. Gerontology **66**(3), 212–222 (2020). https://doi.org/10.1159/000504294

49. Vogg, M.C., Galliot, B., Tsiairis, C.D.: Model systems for regeneration: hydra. Development (Cambridge) **146**, 21 (2019). https://doi.org/10.1242/dev.177212

50. Wolfram, S.: Statistical mechanics of cellular automata. Rev. Mod. Phys. **55**(3), 601, March 1983. https://doi.org/10.1103/PhysRev.113.1178. https://link.aps.org/doi/10.1103/PhysRev.113.1178

Inclusive Genetic Programming

Francesco Marchetti[(✉)] and Edmondo Minisci

Intelligent Computational Engineering Laboratory, University of Strathclyde,
Glasgow, UK
{francesco.marchetti,edmondo.minisci}@strath.ac.uk

Abstract. The promotion and maintenance of the population diversity in a Genetic Programming (GP) algorithm was proved to be an important part of the evolutionary process. Such diversity maintenance improves the exploration capabilities of the GP algorithm, which as a consequence improves the quality of the found solutions by avoiding local optima. This paper aims to further investigate and prove the efficacy of a GP heuristic proposed in a previous work: the Inclusive Genetic Programming (IGP). Such heuristic can be classified as a niching technique, which performs the evolutionary operations like crossover, mutation and selection by considering the individuals belonging to different niches in order to maintain and exploit a certain degree of diversity in the population, instead of evolving the niches separately to find different local optima. A comparison between a standard formulation of GP and the IGP is carried out on nine different benchmarks coming from synthetic and real world data. The obtained results highlight how the greater diversity in the population, measured in terms of entropy, leads to better results on both training and test data, showing that an improvement on the generalization capabilities is also achieved.

Keywords: Genetic programming · Population diversity · Entropy · Benchmarks · Symbolic regression

1 Introduction

Genetic Programming [12] is known to be a powerful approach to perform Symbolic Regression (SR) , capable of autonomously finding a symbolic expression, which explicitly models a distribution of observed data, starting from no previous knowledge of such data. In the past years it was used for several kinds of applications, from pure symbolic regression [18], to optimization [11] and control system design [10,16,21]. Despite this abundance of applications, GP still suffers from several issues that affect different aspects of a GP algorithm and undermine its performances. In this work, one of such issues is tackled, namely the promotion and maintenance of diversity in a GP population.

© Springer Nature Switzerland AG 2021
T. Hu et al. (Eds.): EuroGP 2021, LNCS 12691, pp. 51–65, 2021.
https://doi.org/10.1007/978-3-030-72812-0_4

The importance of the population diversity in an evolutionary algorithm was treated by several publications in the past: in [5] diversity is addressed as a method to control exploration and exploitation during the evolutionary process, describing also different diversity measures; in [20] a survey of methodologies for promoting diversity in evolutionary optimization is presented; while in [4] different diversity measures are analyzed.

This work aims to contribute to the landscape of publications about diversity maintenance and promotion by performing a deeper analysis of a heuristic proposed in a previous work [15]: the Inclusive Genetic Programming. This heuristic is based on a different formulation of the evolutionary operations, such as crossover, mutation and selection, aimed to promote and maintain the diversity in a GP population. These evolutionary operations are based on the partition of the population into different niches according to the genotypic diversity of the individuals. Therefore, such heuristic pertains to the class of niching techniques [14]. Traditionally, the individuals are divided according to their genotypic (individual structure) or phenotypic (fitness value) characteristics [19], although recently also a niching approach based on the computational time necessary to execute the individuals was suggested by De Vega et al. [8]. Nonetheless, all these methods consist in dividing the population into different niches and evolve them separately to find different local optima. On the contrary, the approach proposed in this work aims to subdivide the population into niches and then take into account the individuals from different niches when performing the evolutionary operations so to have a flow of genes between the different niches. The concept of combining diverse individuals (e.g. individuals from different niches) rather than well performing ones was already explored in the past, for example by Aslam et al. [2], although their approach is based on the phenotypic diversity of the individuals and did not considered a subdivision of the population into niches. Instead they classified the individuals based on a measure called Binary String Fitness Characterisation, originally introduced by Day and Nandi [6], and also explored the concept of good and bad diversity.

In this work, the aim of the flow of genes between the different niches is to preserve also more complex structures, which would otherwise be lost due to bloat control operators, and to exploit them in order to avoid losing well performing genes which are contained in them. It could be argued that bloat control operators could be removed for this purpose, but nonetheless, they are useful to avoid having too big individuals which would become of difficult interpretation for the user. Indeed, bloat control and the GP population diversity are related, but it was not aim of this work to investigate this relation. Some examples of this relation are presented by De Jong et al. [7], where a multi-objective formulation of GP is used to avoid bloat and promote diversity; and by Alfaro-Cid et al. [1] where several bloat control operators and their influence on the population diversity were analyzed.

The reminder of this paper is organized as follows: in Sect. 2 the Inclusive Evolutionary Process is described; in Sect. 3 the benchmarks used in this work, the settings of the algorithms employed in the comparison and the produced results are presented. Finally in Sect. 4, conclusions and future work directions are discussed.

2   Inclusive Evolutionary Process

In this Section, the components of the evolutionary process that is at the foundation of the IGP are described. Such evolutionary process is based on a modified version of the evolutionary strategy $\mu + \lambda$ [3], as described by Algorithm 1. The differences from the standard version consist in: 1) the creation of the niches at the beginning of the evolutionary process and every time after a new offspring is generated; 2) the use of the Inclusive Reproduction; 3) the use of the Inclusive Tournament.

Algorithm 1. Pseudocode of the Inclusive $\mu + \lambda$

1: Evaluate fitness of the individuals in the population
2: Update Hall of Fame of best individuals
3: **while** Generation < Maximum Generation Number **do**
4:　　Create n niches according to the maximum and minimum length of the individuals in the population and allocate the individuals to their respective niche

5:　　Perform Inclusive Reproduction to produce λ offspring
6:　　Evaluate fitness of the individuals in the obtained offspring
7:　　Update Hall of Fame of best individuals
8:　　Create n niches according to the maximum and minimum length of the individuals considering both the parents and the offspring and allocate the individuals to their respective niche
9:　　Perform Inclusive Tournament Selection to select μ new parents
10: **end while**

2.1   Niches Creation

At the core of the Inclusive Evolutionary Process, there is the niching creation mechanism. The niches are created in an evenly distributed manner (linearly divided) between the maximum and minimum length (number of nodes) of the individuals in the population, then the individuals are assigned to the respective niche according to their length. The same number of niches is kept during the evolutionary process, but their size (the interval of individuals lengths that they cover) and the amount of individuals inside them change at every generation.

The variation of size of the niches allows for a shifting of the individuals between contiguous niches every time maximum and minimum lengths of the individuals in the population changes. Once the niches are created, both the reproduction and selection are performed considering individuals from different niches in order to maintain the population diversity. Figure 1 depicts the rationale behind the niches creation mechanism. In this example, a population composed by 10 individuals of length 1, 1, 2, 2, 3, 4, 4, 5, 7, 8 (without considering the root node) is considered and 10 niches are created. These niches span the lengths depicted in the figure and contain the individuals depicted inside them.

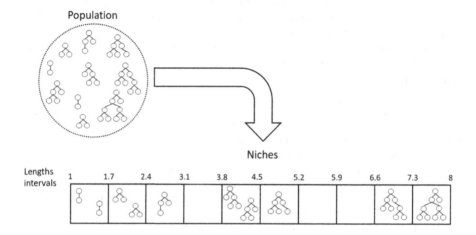

Fig. 1. Illustration of niches creation rationale.

2.2   Inclusive Reproduction and Inclusive Tournament

Algorithm 2 describes the mechanism behind the Inclusive Reproduction. Such mechanism consists in applying either crossover, mutation or 1:1 reproduction (the individual is passed unaltered to the offspring) using the individuals in the different niches. If the crossover is selected, a one point crossover is applied between two individuals which are selected from two different niches. About the two individuals chosen, one is the best of the considered niche, in order to pass the best performing genes to the future generation and the other is selected randomly in order to maintain a certain degree of diversity in the population. Moreover, a mechanism to avoid breeding between the same or very similar individuals is used (lines 16–20 in Algorithm 2). Here n_l is a preset constant defining the maximum number of loop iterations, needed to avoid possible infinite loops. If the mutation is selected, a mutation operator among those listed in Table 1 is applied to an individual randomly chosen from the chosen niche. Finally, if the 1:1 reproduction is selected, a randomly chosen individual from the chosen niche is passed to the offspring. The niches selected in all three previously described operations (crossover, mutation and 1:1 reproduction) are picked from a list of exploitable niches, which is continuously updated in order to avoid selecting always from the same niches.

Algorithm 2. Pseudocode of Inclusive Reproduction

1: **if** Crossover probability <0.8 **then**
2:     Mutation probability = Mutation probability -0.01
3:     Crossover probability = Crossover probability $+0.01$
4: **end if**
5: *Good Indexes* ← Indexes of filled niches
6: *List of exploitable niches* ← *Good Indexes*
7: **while** Size offspring $< \lambda$ **do**
8:     Choice ← Random number between $[0, 1]$
9:     **if** Choice $<$ Crossover Probability **then**
10:        **if** *List of exploitable niches* is empty **then**
11:            *List of exploitable niches* ← *Good Indexes*
12:        **end if**
13:        Select randomly two different niches from *List of exploitable niches*
14:        Remove chosen niches from *List of exploitable niches*
15:        Select the **best** individual from the first niche and select a **random** individual from the second niche
16:        n = 0
17:        **while** The selected individuals have the same fitness and n $< n_l$ **do**
18:            Repeat lines 10 to 15
19:            n = n + 1
20:        **end while**
21:        Apply crossover to the chosen individuals
22:        Add first child to offspring
23:        **if** Size of offspring $< \lambda$ **then**
24:            Add second child to offspring
25:        **end if**
26:     **else if** Choice $<$ Mutation probability + Crossover Probability **then**
27:        Repeat lines 10 to 15 but selecting only one category
28:        Select randomly one individual from the chosen category
29:        Perform mutation of the chosen individual
30:        Add mutated individual to the offspring
31:     **else**
32:        Repeat line 27, 28
33:        Add chosen individual to the offspring
34:     **end if**
35: **end while**

Algorithm 3. Pseudocode of Inclusive Tournament

1: **while** Number of selected individuals $< \mu$ **do**
2:    **for** i in number of niches **do**
3:       **if** Number of selected individuals from i-th niche $<$ total number of individuals in i-th niche **then**
4:          Select one individual in i-th niche with Double Tournament selection
5:       **end if**
6:    **end for**
7: **end while**

The Inclusive Tournament consists in performing a Double Tournament [13] on each niche as in Algorithm 3. For the Inclusive Tournament the niches are selected in a sequential manner and the double tournament on each niche is performed at most t times where t is the number of individuals inside the considered niche, to avoid having clones in the final population.

3 Algorithms Setup and Results

In this section the results obtained from a comparison between the IGP and the Standard Genetic Programming (SGP) are presented. The SGP is a standard formulation of GP.

3.1 Benchmarks

The benchmarks selected for the comparison were taken from [22]. These were selected since comprehend both synthetic and real world data, hence they cover a sufficient variety of problems. More on the benchmarks can be found in [22]. In this work the same number of samples and sampling technique to produce them as in [22] were used, except for the benchmarks *korns11*, where 5000 samples were used instead of 10000 to reduce the computational time, both on training and testing samples; and for the benchmark *S2* where the same number of training samples used for the x variable were also used for the y one.

3.2 SGP and IGP Settings

Both algorithms were implemented in Python 3 relying on the open source library DEAP [9]. The experiments were run on a Laptop with 16 GB of RAM and an Intel® Core™ i7-8750H CPU @ 2.20 GHz × 12 threads and multiprocessing was used. The code developed in this work is open source and can be found at https://github.com/strath-ace/smart-ml.

For both algorithms the bloat control mechanism implemented in the DEAP library was used with the limit height and size set as in Table 1. The mutation operators listed in Table 1 refers to the homonym functions in the DEAP library. Regarding the primitives listed in Table 1, *add3* and *mul3* are respectively a ternary addition and multiplication, while *plog* and *pexp* are respectively a protected natural logarithm and protected exponential, to avoid numerical errors. Regarding the crossover and mutation probability for the IGP, they changed dynamically during the evolutionary process as shown in lines 1–4 of Algorithm 2. This mechanism was introduced to incentivate the exploration at the beginning of the evolutionary process and the exploitation at the end of it. It was not adopted for the SGP since it was tested but did not introduce any improvement.

300 generations were chosen as stopping criteria to have a good compromise between the goodness of the results and a reasonable computation times.

3.3   Results

Both the SGP and IGP algorithms were run on nine different benchmarks consisting of synthetic and real world data as described in Sect. 3.1. On each benchmark the evolutionary process was repeated 100 times in order to obtain statistically significant results.

Table 1. Settings for the SGP and IGP algorithms. The percentages near the mutation mechanisms refers to the probability of that mutation mechanism to be chosen when the mutation is performed.

	SGP	IGP
Population size	300 individuals	
Maximum generations	300	
Stopping criteria	Reaching maximum number of generations	
Crossover probability	0.8	$0.2 \rightarrow 0.8$
Mutation probability	0.2	$0.8 \rightarrow 0.2$
Evolutionary strategy	$\mu + \lambda$	
μ	Population size	
λ	Population size $\times$ 1.2	
Number of ephemeral constants	1	
Limit height	15	
Limit size	30	
Selection mechanism	Double tournament	Inclusive tournament
Double tournament fitness size	2	
Double tournament parsimony size	1.2	
Tree creation mechanism	Ramped half and half	
Mutation mechanisms	Uniform (50%), Shrink (5%), Insertion (25%), Mutate Ephemeral (20%)	
Crossover mechanism	One point crossover	
Primitives set	$+$, $-$, $*$, *add3*, *mul3*, *tanh* *square*, *plog*, *pexp*, *sin*, *cos*	
Fitness measure	RMSE	

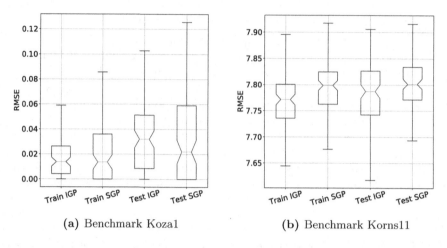

(a) Benchmark Koza1   (b) Benchmark Korns11

Fig. 2. RMSE of training and test data on synthetic benchmarks Koza1 and Korns11. The median and standard deviations values were evaluated over the results produced on 100 different runs.

Figure 7 depicts the evolution of the RMSE median values of the SGP and IGP algorithms during the evolutionary process on the nine benchmarks. The shaded areas represent the standard deviation interval. From these results it is clear how the IGP is always capable of finding better or equally performing individuals to those found with SGP and also it converges faster than SGP to a minimum. Moreover, the Figures from 2 to 6 show the RMSE median and standard deviation on the different benchmarks on both train and test data. As can be seen, IGP always outperforms the SGP in terms of generalization capabilities, achieving a lower (better) RMSE, except for the *koza1* benchmark were the IGP performs worse than the SGP. A possible explanation for this could be that the key feature of IGP, which is the greater diversity in the population, leads to bigger individuals than those obtained with SGP. Such bigger individuals could be overkill solutions for a simple test case like *koza1*, which could be solved more efficiently by smaller individuals.

To assess how and if the population diversity was maintained throughout the evolutionary process, the entropy of the population was considered as proposed in [17]. Figure 8 shows the entropy median and standard deviation values of the population of both the SGP and IGP during the evolutionary process for all the benchmarks. As for the fitness values, also the entropy median values were computed over the results obtained from 100 different runs.

The entropy was measured as in Eq. 1

$$entropy = -\sum(d * log(d)) \tag{1}$$

where d is the distribution of the individuals across the different niches without considering the empty ones. Assuming the example illustrated in Fig. 1, d would be the array $[0.2, 0.2, 0.1, 0.2, 0.1, 0.1, 0.1]$ and the corresponding entropy would

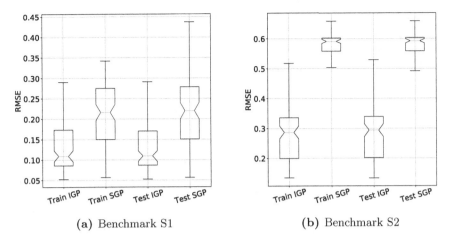

(a) Benchmark S1   (b) Benchmark S2

Fig. 3. RMSE of training and test data on synthetic benchmarks S1 and S2. The median and standard deviations values were evaluated over the results produced on 100 different runs.

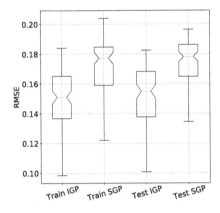

Fig. 4. RMSE of training and test data on synthetic benchmark UB. The median and standard deviations values were evaluated over the results produced on 100 different runs.

be 1.89. For sake of the comparison carried out in this work, also the population in the SGP algorithm was subdivided into niches to evaluate the entropy in the same way as was done in the IGP, although these were not used during the evolutionary process.

As can be seen in Fig. 8 the IGP is able to maintain an entropy value around 2.30 during the whole evolutionary process, while the SGP tends to decrease towards the end of the evolutionary process, meaning that the population tends to have more similar individuals, i.e. lose diversity, while the evolution proceeds.

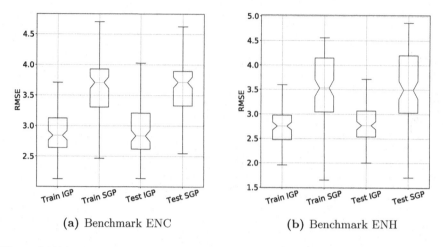

Fig. 5. RMSE of training and test data on real world benchmarks ENC and ENH. The median and standard deviations values were evaluated over the results produced on 100 different runs.

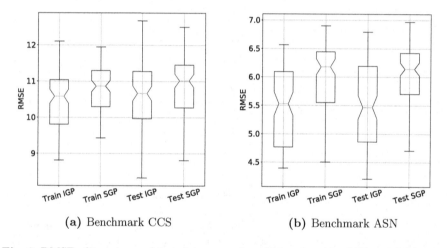

Fig. 6. RMSE of training and test data on real world benchmarks CCS and ASN. The median and standard deviations values were evaluated over the results produced on 100 different runs.

Now by looking at both Fig. 7 and 8, the results suggest that indeed the diversity maintenance plays an important role during the evolutionary process, resulting in a GP which can converge faster to the minimum, is more precise and has better generalization capabilities than a standard GP implementation.

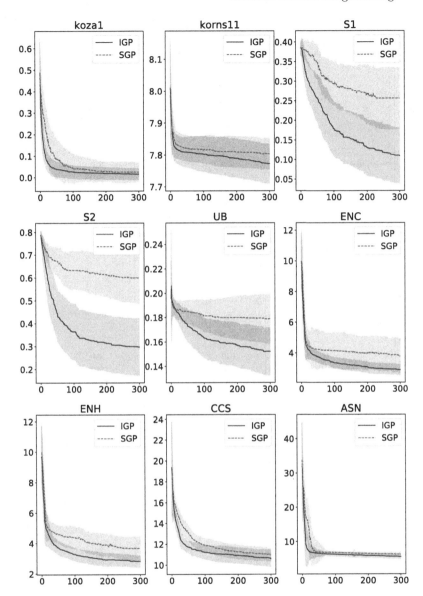

Fig. 7. Fitness function values of the SGP and IGP algorithms on the nine different benchmarks. On the ordinate is the RMSE while on the abscissa the number of generations. The solid and dashed lines represents the median values for the IGP and SGP respectively while the shaded regions are the standard deviation intervals

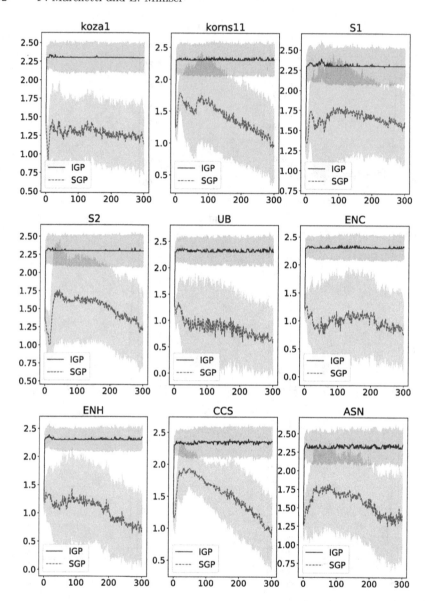

Fig. 8. Entropy values of the SGP and IGP algorithms on the nine different benchmarks. On the ordinate is the Entropy while on the abscissa the number of generations. The solid and dashed lines represents the median values for the IGP and SGP respectively while the shaded regions are the standard deviation intervals

4   Conclusions

In this paper an heuristic approach to promote and maintain the diversity in a genetic programming algorithm, the Inclusive Genetic Programming, is described and tested by comparing its performance with a standard genetic programming implementation. The comparison was performed and here presented on nine different benchmarks, composed by both synthetic and real world data and on each benchmark the evolutionary process was repeated 100 times both with IGP and SGP. Then, the obtained best behaving individuals were tested on a set of test data, different from the training data, to assess the generalization capabilities. The results show how the IGP almost always (8/9 benchmarks) outperforms the SGP by converging faster to a minimum, with a better final fitness function value and by possessing better generalization capabilities than the SGP. To assess the importance of the population diversity on this outcome, the population's entropy was analyzed and it was observed that indeed the IGP is capable of maintaining it approximately constant throughout the evolutionary process, while in the SGP it tends to diminish towards the end of the evolutionary process, meaning a decrease in the population diversity.

This work aims to be a positive contribution to the open problem of the exploration vs. exploitation in the GP community, by describing and analyzing a new effective heuristic which highlights the importance of the exploration achieved through the promotion and maintenance of population diversity. Future works could investigate the application of the proposed heuristic to other GP formulations like the MGGP in order to assess its applicability. Moreover, it would be interesting to combine it with other diversity maintenance strategies to further increase the obtained benefits.

References

1. Alfaro-Cid, E., Merelo, J.J., Fernández de Vega, F., Esparcia-Alcázar, A.I., Sharman, K.: Bloat control operators and diversity in genetic programming: a comparative study. Evol. Comput. **18**(2), 305–332 (2010). https://doi.org/10.1162/evco.2010.18.2.18206
2. Aslam, M.W., Zhu, Z., Nandi, A.K.: Diverse partner selection with brood recombination in genetic programming. Appl. Soft Comput. J. **67**, 558–566 (2018). https://doi.org/10.1016/j.asoc.2018.03.035
3. Beyer, H.G., Schwefel, H.P.: Evolution strategies - a comprehensive introduction. Natl. Comput. **1**(1), 3–52 (2002). https://doi.org/10.1023/A:1015059928466
4. Burke, E., Gustafson, S., Kendall, G., Krasnogor, N.: Advanced population diversity measures in genetic programming. In: Guervós, J.J.M., Adamidis, P., Beyer, H.G., Schwefel, H.P., Fernández-Villacañas, J.L. (eds.) Parallel Problem Solving from Nature – PPSN VII, pp. 341–350. Springer, Berlin Heidelberg, Berlin, Heidelberg (2002)
5. Crepinsek, M., Liu, S.H., Mernik, M.: Exploration and exploitation in evolutionary algorithms: a survey. ACM Comput. Surv. **45**(3), 1–33 (2013). https://doi.org/10.1145/2480741.2480752

6. Day, P., Nandi, A.K.: Binary string fitness characterization and comparative partner selection in genetic programming. IEEE Trans. Evol. Comput. **12**(6), 724–735
   (2008). https://doi.org/10.1109/TEVC.2008.917201
7. De Jong, E.D., Watson, R.A., Pollack, J.B.: Reducing bloat and promoting diversity using multi-objective methods. In: Proceedings of the Genetic and Evolutionary Computation Conference GECCO2001, vol. GECCO-2001, pp. 11–18 (2001)
8. Fernandez De Vega, F., et al.: Time and individual duration in genetic programming. IEEE Access **8**, 38692–38713 (2020). https://doi.org/10.1109/ACCESS.
   2020.2975753
9. Fortin, F.A., De Rainville, F.M., Gardner, M.A., Parizeau, M., Gagńe, C.: DEAP:
   evolutionary algorithms made easy. J. Mach. Learn. Res. **13**, 2171–2175 (2012)
10. Grosman, B., Lewin, D.R.: Lyapunov-based stability analysis automated by genetic
    programming. In: 2006 IEEE Conference on Computer Aided Control System
    Design, 2006 IEEE International Conference on Control Applications, 2006 IEEE
    International Symposium on Intelligent Control, pp. 766–771 (2009). https://doi.
    org/10.1109/CACSD-CCA-ISIC.2006.4776742
11. Khayyam, H., Jamali, A., Assimi, H., Jazar, R.N.: Genetic programming
    approaches in design and optimization of mechanical engineering applications. In:
    Jazar, R.N., Dai, L. (eds.) Nonlinear Approaches in Engineering Applications, pp.
    367–402. Springer, Cham (2020). https://doi.org/10.1007/978-3-030-18963-1_9
12. Koza, J.R.: Genetic programming as a means for programming computers by
    natural selection. Stat. Comput. **4**(2), 87–112 (1994). https://doi.org/10.1007/
    BF00175355. https://link.springer.com/content/pdf/10.1007%2FBF00175355.pdf
13. Luke, S., Panait, L.: Fighting bloat with nonparametric parsimony pressure. In:
    Guervós, J.J.M., Adamidis, P., Beyer, H.G., Schwefel, H.P., Fernández-Villacañas,
    J.L. (eds.) Parallel Problem Solving from Nature – PPSN VII, pp. 411–421.
    Springer, Berlin Heidelberg, Berlin, Heidelberg (2002)
14. Mahfoud, S.W.: Niching methods for genetic algorithms. Ph.D. thesis (1995)
15. Marchetti, F., Minisci, E.: A hybrid neural network-genetic programming intelli-
    gent control approach. In: Filipič, B., Minisci, E., Vasile, M. (eds.) BIOMA 2020.
    LNCS, vol. 12438, pp. 240–254. Springer, Cham (2020). https://doi.org/10.1007/
    978-3-030-63710-1_19
16. Oh, C.K., Barlow, G.J.: Autonomous controller design for unmanned aerial vehicles
    using multi-objective genetic programming. In: Proceedings of the 2004 Congress
    on Evolutionary Computation (IEEE Cat. No.04TH8753), vol. 2, pp. 1538–1545
    (2004). https://doi.org/10.1109/CEC.2004.1331079
17. Rosca, J.P.: Entropy-driven adaptive representation. In: Proceedings of the Work-
    shop on Genetic Programming: From Theory to Real-World Applications, pp. 23–
    32 (1995)
18. Schmidt, M., Lipson, H.: Symbolic regression of implicit equations. In: Riolo, R.,
    O'Reilly, U.M., McConaghy, T. (eds.) Genetic Programming Theory and Practice
    VII, pp. 73–85. Springer, US, Boston, MA (2010). https://doi.org/10.1007/978-1-
    4419-1626-6_5
19. Shir, O.M.: Niching in evolutionary algorithms. In: Rozenberg, G., Bäck, T., Kok,
    J.N. (eds.) Handbook of Natural Computing, pp. 1035–1069. Springer, Berlin Hei-
    delberg (2012). https://doi.org/10.1007/978-3-540-92910-9_32
20. Squillero, G., Tonda, A.: Divergence of character and premature convergence: a
    survey of methodologies for promoting diversity in evolutionary optimization. Inf.
    Sci. **329**, 782–799 (2016). https://doi.org/10.1016/j.ins.2015.09.056

21. Verdier, C.F., Mazo Jr., M.: Formal controller synthesis via genetic programming. IFAC-PapersOnLine **50**(1), 7205–7210 (2017). https://doi.org/10.1016/j.ifacol.2017.08.1362
22. Žegklitz, J., Pošík, P.: Benchmarking state-of-the-art symbolic regression algorithms. Genet. Programm. Evolvable Mach. (2020). https://doi.org/10.1007/s10710-020-09387-0

Towards Incorporating Human Knowledge in Fuzzy Pattern Tree Evolution

Aidan Murphy[1]([⊠]) [iD], Gráinne Murphy[1] [iD], Jorge Amaral[2] [iD],
Douglas Mota Dias[1,2] [iD], Enrique Naredo[1] [iD], and Conor Ryan[1] [iD]

[1] Lero, University of Limerick, Limerick, Ireland
`aidan.murphy@ul.ie`
[2] Rio de Janeiro State University, Rio de Janeiro, Brazil
`http://bds.ul.ie/`

Abstract. This paper shows empirically that Fuzzy Pattern Trees (FPT) evolved using Grammatical Evolution (GE), a system we call FGE, meet the criteria to be considered a robust Explainable Artificial Intelligence (XAI) system. Experimental results show FGE achieves competitive results against state of the art black box methods on a set of real world benchmark problems. Various selection methods were investigated to see which was best for finding smaller, more interpretable models and a human expert was recruited to test the interpretability of the models found and to give a **confidence** score for each model. Models which were deemed interpretable but not trustworthy by the expert were seen to be outperformed in classification accuracy by interpretable models which were judge trustworthy, validating that FGE can be a powerful XAI technique.

Keywords: Grammatical Evolution · Fuzzy logic · Explainable AI

1 Introduction

The number of machine learning (ML) applications has expanded massively since the turn of the millennium. ML algorithms these days have access to massive amounts of data and can run on massively parallel high-performance hardware. ML frameworks and systems now achieve near-perfect performance, which can outperform human agents. This has led to headline-grabbing AI success stories in chess and Go [34]. Global spending on artificial intelligence is estimated to hit $50 billion a year.

These results are not without their critics, though [20]. There often exists a trade-off between high accuracy and transparency. These models are referred

---

The authors are supported by Research Grants 13/RC/2094 and 16/IA/4605 from the Science Foundation Ireland and by Lero, the Irish Software Engineering Research Centre (www.lero.ie). The third and fourth authors are partially financed by the Coordenação de Aperfeiçoamento de Pessoal de Nível Superior - Brasil (CAPES) - Finance Code 001.

T. Hu et al. (Eds.): EuroGP 2021, LNCS 12691, pp. 66–81, 2021.
https://doi.org/10.1007/978-3-030-72812-0_5

to as 'black box' (BB) models. They do not allow their internal workings to be understood. They simply return input and output pairs. No knowledge of how a decision is made can be obtained from the system. A user, expert or otherwise, has no means to understand how a model arrived at a conclusion. This inability to interpret and check that the model has 'common sense' makes trusting the model difficult as well as making debugging and error checking an impossibility. These shortcomings have, too, been headline-grabbing and shown AI systems can exhibit racist and sexist behaviour [37].

To tackle these issues, a new area of research was spawned, XAI [1,2]. XAI aims to create interpretable models and methods that can somehow explain themselves without, or with minimal, impacting performance [4].

A recent addition to XAI has been Fuzzy Pattern Trees (FPTs) [14,36]. Based on fuzzy set theory, a FPT is a hierarchical tree structure. This is in contrast to most other fuzzy-based systems which use rules as representations. As a fuzzy model, it is easily interpretable due to its usage of linguistic labels. This interpretability, obviously, depends on the tree size not being excessively large. Grammatical Evolution has shown it can be a very effective approach for evolving accurate, and, crucially, small FPTs [22].

This paper sets out to validate the claim that these FPTs are intrinsically interpretable in their own right. It further wishes to show this interpretability can aid in the evolutionary process by finding faults in the best performing individuals found by the search. The system was tested on various real-live fairness benchmarks. The results show that FPTs may allow the identification of data or algorithmic bias that may be present in final models.

The remainder of this paper is organized as follows: Sect. 2 reviews the main background concepts GE, Fuzzy GE and XAI. Section 3 explains the proposals and describes the paper's contributions in more detail. Next, Sect. 4 presents the experimental set-up. It outlines all performance measures which were investigated. Section 5 presents the main results of the experiments described in 4. Finally, Sect. 6 summarises the research and discusses future work suitable for investigation.

2 Background

2.1 XAI

Papers and conference talks in the area of XAI and computer model interpretability has grown and is continuing to grow rapidly [1,13]. However, these conferences talks and papers have existed in a space where the term 'interpretability' has not been agreed upon or even well-defined [1,6,7,10]. There is not yet a consensus when exactly as to when a model has been 'explained' fully or indeed what an 'explanation' even is [6]. The terms *interpretable*, *understandable* and *intelligible* are often used interchangeably or without distinction [19]. In different contexts, interpretability may have differences; for example, a loan approving system may simply need to show that it is not discriminatory against any group, whereas a safety-critical system may need to describe every step in its internal logic [7].

Many of the explanations put forward in papers require some machine learning expertise [18]. They may look incomplete to somebody with no machine learning experience, while others may require some domain knowledge to interpret the results [21]. While a user of the model will undoubtedly have some domain knowledge, it is unclear if defining a model as interpretable implies that the user does have this knowledge.

Some work has been done to develop a rigid framework to define and evaluate interpretability [7]. They stress that human evaluation or abstraction is essential to any idea of judging interpretability.

Others argue that it is not enough for models to be interpretable and comprehensible but that they must also have logic and put forward some form of rationale to the user as to how a particular decision was arrived at [6].

Trust in a model or system is an often overlooked and important feature [27]. It may not be sufficient for a model to show high accuracy for a user to accept its outputs. A user may require sufficient evidence that the decisions are fair or ethical or legal. If the model is a BB or its logic is presented in a way that makes it difficult for a human to abstract knowledge from its results, they may refuse to use it, or may not be allowed to under the General Data Protection Regulation, GDPR [12].

If a domain expert is working in collaboration with a model, knowledge of its logic or internal workings may enable them to know when the model will predict something sub-optimally. More importantly, perhaps, it may also allow them to know in what areas the model will fail and its outputs can be discarded.

For a model to be useful, usable and fully 'explained' this paper proposes it should have the following properties: it must be transparent in its workings; have similar or better accuracy to any other model; be cogent in its statements (particularly for finding complex relationships); be able to incorporate domain knowledge; and deterministic.

2.2   Grammatical Evolution

Grammatical Evolution (GE) [30], often thought of as a variant of genetic programming (GP) [17], is a popular evolutionary computation technique. As with many evolutionary algorithms, GE's inspiration comes from nature and genetics. GE creates computer programs by mapping a binary string using a grammar. A key point to note is GE can produce programs in any arbitrary language, usually specified using a Backus-Naur Form (BNF) grammar [25,29] or Attribute Grammar (AG) [26]. The evolutionary operators of crossover and mutation do not occur on the actual computer program, but on the string which, combined with the grammar, creates the program. Therefore any representation the user wishes to use for the solution to aid interpretability is possible. The most popular way to represent the solutions is to use tree structures [31], which have been shown to be the most easily interpretable representations [15] and makes them quite transparent.

Therefore GE, or GP in general, may represent a better ML algorithm to leverage a humans ability to generalize/abstract with the strengths of computers.

GE finds solutions which best minimise (or maximise depending on the goal) an objective function. GE, however, allows much more knowledge and nuance to be built into its objective function than typical test set accuracy. Multi-objective [5] and many objective [16] optimisation are common in EAs. It would be easy to find explicitly what trade-off, if any, had to be made to accommodate this interpretability by creating a Pareto front, an attractive feature pointed out by [7]. The user has their pick of solutions. This allows the programs to have the highest possible fidelity while at the same time being interpretable to whomever is using them. GE can be trained to be highly accurate on particular cases if they are of important to the user. The objective function allows the user to personalize their goals more than traditional ML models by including ethics, fairness, legality, profit etc. as a component of the search.

Ideas like fairness are vague and hard to define. This allows the user to define these concepts in a way which is important to them. GE also allows for the human factors to be built into the solution [8]. If combined with an interactive GA [35], in which the person is directly responsible for giving a fitness score, solutions could take the form which maximises the utility of the person using them. That is to say, the search would look for a solution in the form which would be most suitable to the user interacting with it. This creates a personalized explanation, seen as a key facet in Machine Learning going forward [33].

This would normalise the concept of interpretability to the user and allow accuracy to be improved instead of trying to improve the vague idea of interpretability while keeping accuracy high. GE can have the user involved at every stage of the machine learning process. Before the search begins the user may set up the grammar and specify the objective. During run time they may impart domain knowledge in the form of subtrees or modules [23]. The user would be the main architect of the form of the solutions. All this would help build 'trust' in the model to the user, if it is needed.

2.3   Fuzzy GE

FPTs which use GE as their search technique were recently introduced [22]. This approach, FGE, showed competitive performance against black box methods and was shown to outperform another GP variant, Cartesian GP, on a set of benchmark classification problems [32].

In order to perform classification using FGE a set of FPTs are needed, one for each class that exists in the problem. These FPTs serve as the logical description of the class. This sets FGE apart from traditional classification approaches in GE which only require one expression to be evolved, regardless of the number of classes in the problem. To classify an individual a boundary or boundaries are decided upon. The output of the tree is then compared against this boundary and a decision is made about its classification. There are many downsides to this approach, much time, effort and expertise is required to optimise these boundaries [9].

FGE evolves one, large solution and treats the subtrees of this solution as it's FPTs, as seen in Fig. 1. The FPT which yields the largest output for an individual is declared the winner and that individual is designated as belonging to that class. This is illustrated in Fig. 2. The root node of the tree is responsible for this process. Representing each FPT as subtrees of one large solution combined with GE's inbuilt separation between search space and program space leads to another major advantage FGE experiences. No special or protected operators are needed for crossover or mutation. A simple grammar augmentation is all that is needed to tackle different problem specifications.

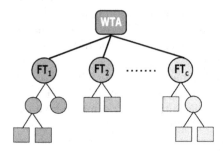

Fig. 1. Pictorial representation of a multi-classifier evolved by FGE, where FT_c is the fuzzy tree for each available class, and at the root the winner take all (WTA).

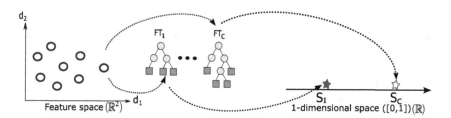

Fig. 2. Graphical depiction of the mapping process from the feature space to a 1-dimensional space [0,1] using a set of fuzzy trees FT_1 to FT_c.

3   Explainable GE

3.1   Reducing Size of Trees

A FPT serves as a class descriptor in each benchmark problem. It is therefore paramount for FPTs to be interpretable. This interpretability is only achieved if their size is kept as small as possible. It was seen previously that standard GE may be bloating individuals, leading to trees which are excessively large and contain worthless material. The addition of a simple parsimony pressure was seen to greatly reduce the size of individuals without having a noticeable effect on their fitness. It was not established if this simple procedure was the most effective at producing smaller, accurate FPTs. In this paper we investigate various methods for producing smaller trees were investigated and compared against standard GE and against each other, and consider both their size and accuracy. Each method is outlined below.

Intron Removal. In the context of GP, an intron is a section of an individual which does not have an effect on that individual's output. That is to say, it is a redundant piece of the individual. Despite their lack of involvement they can play an important part in evolution [24]. However, when trying to interpret an individual it is necessary to remove them as they may lead to confusion.

Strict/Easy Regularization. Two types of regularisation were used. The first was an easy regularization where a small penalty to fitness was applied based on the maximum depth of the solutions found. The second was a strict regularization. This procedure set the fitness to 0 if the max depth exceeded a certain threshold. Fitness was set as usual if it was below this threshold.

Double Tournament. The final procedure for bloat control implemented was double tournament. This strategy conducts 2 tournaments, one of which chooses the individual with the highest fitness while the other chooses the one with the smallest size. Both potential orders of series were investigated, that is, first fitness and secondly size, and vice versa.

3.2 FPT Representation

A FPT differs from other fuzzy based classifiers by adopting a hierarchical, tree structure. The leaf nodes of these trees are the fuzzified problem variables and the inner nodes are fuzzy logical and arithmetic operators. The information is propagated from the bottom to the top, similar to a regular GP classifier. The output of the tree is in the [0,1] interval. More formally, a FPT maps $f_i(\mathbf{x}) : \Re^n \to [0,1]$, where x are the input variables.

The following operators are used, where a and b are the inputs to the operator:

$$WTA = IF\{\}()..ELSE() \tag{1}$$
$$MAX = max(a, b) \tag{2}$$
$$MIN = min(a, b) \tag{3}$$
$$WA(k) = ka + (1 - k)b \tag{4}$$
$$OWA(k) = k \cdot max(a,b) + (1 - k)min(a,b) \tag{5}$$
$$CONCENTRATE = a^2 \tag{6}$$
$$DILATE = a^{\frac{1}{2}} \tag{7}$$
$$COMPLEMENT = 1 - a \tag{8}$$

where WTA, WA & OWA denote **Winner Takes All, Weighted Average** and **Ordered Weighted Average**, respectively, and k is a randomly created value in (0,1).

Figure 3 shows an example of an FPT which was trained on the **Heart** benchmark dataset. It represents the fuzzy concept – a fuzzy criterion for – the presence of heart disease. This tree was picked as it was considered as very interpretable by a domain expert, who was also very confident in the logic of this model.

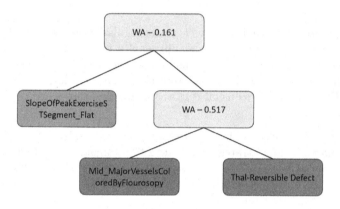

Fig. 3. Tree representing the interpretable class "Presence of Heart Disease", showing each variable with different color.

An interpretation of this tree could be:

The presence of heart disease is strongly determined by three criteria. The first criteria is that a reversible defect was found while conducting a Thallium Stress Test. The second is that the number of major vessels coloured by fluoroscopy was moderate. The third criteria is the slope of the peak exercise ST segment was flat. Criteria I and II are the major contributors to the decision roughly contributing equally, with criterion III has a small but not insignificant effect.

3.3   Human in the Loop

The goal of many ML processes is to replace a human agent by a model which makes as good as, or better, decisions than a human would. The main obstacle is a machines inability to reason or abstract. The goal of so-called strong AI is to develop systems that possess this 'common sense' [11]. However, until such time as that is available it is reasonable to add this common sense into a model through human interaction. Therefore, a solution to the short comings of modern ML models and interpreting them lies in creating models which are transparent, unambiguous and which place humans prominently in their design, a human in the loop ML algorithm.

In order to create a fully Explainable GE system, meeting all the criteria highlighted above, it is essential a human is incorporated in the evolutionary cycle as much as possible. However, it is first necessary to empirically validate that FPTs are, in fact, interpretable. The depth at which FPTs cease to become interpretable also requires investigation. This required an extra operation to be performed. This involved giving each model to a domain expert who ranked each model's interpretability.

4 Experimental Setup

The hypothesis that FGE meets all, or most, of the criteria of an interpretable model was tested. That is to say, FGE provides a transparent model which can be understood and attains accuracy comparable to other, black box ML approaches. Five selection methods were tested on six benchmark problems. These benchmark datasets were chosen as they have been identified as problems which often produce models containing bias or discrimination. Insight into the logic of any model trained on this data would, therefore, be very useful.

The grammar used can be seen in Fig. 4. The FPTs for each class are contained within the WTA node, the $<exp>$ non-terminals. To extend the grammar for multi-class classification, the simple addition of more $<exp>$ symbols in the expression are needed. For example, three classes would need the addition of one more $<exp>$ symbol and so on. Constants were created using digit concatenation [3].

$$< start >::=WTA(< exp >, < exp >)$$
$$< exp >::=max(< exp > , < exp >) \mid$$
$$min(< exp > , < exp >) \mid$$
$$WA(< const > , < exp > , < exp >) \mid$$
$$OWA(< const > , < exp > , < exp >) \mid$$
$$concentrate(< exp >) \mid$$
$$dilation(< exp >) \mid$$
$$complement(< exp >) \mid$$
$$x_1 \mid x_2 \mid x_3 \mid...$$
$$< const >::=0. < digit >< digit >< digit >$$
$$< digit >::=0 \mid 1 \mid 2 \mid....$$

Fig. 4. Grammar used to evolve a Fuzzy Pattern Tree. Extra $<exp>$, as needed, can be added in the WTA node to make it a multi-class grammar.

4.1   GE Parameters

The experiments were run with a population size of 500 and for 50 generations. For each run, Sensible Initialisation was used to create the initial population and effective crossover was also employed [28]. At the beginning of each run, the data was split randomly 75% for training and the remaining 25% for test. This was repeated so each run had a different, randomized training and test data. The exception was Census Income, which came with the data already partitioned and was used as such. There was a total of 30 runs per experiment.

Two selection methods were employed. Tournament selection and double tournament selection. Double tournament selection involved performing two, nested tournaments. For experiments FGE$_{DT1}$, the first tournament winner was decided by fitness with the second tournament winner being the individual with the smaller size. FGE$_{DT2}$ was the inverse of this, the first tournament considered size while the second was determined by an individual's fitness (Table 1).

Table 1. List of parameters used for FGE

Parameter	Value
Runs	30
Total generations	50
Population	500
Elitism	Best individual
Selection	Tournament, Double tournament
Crossover	0.9 (Effective)
Mutation	0.01
Initialisation	Sensible

4.2   Fitness Function

The fitness function used for each experiment, except FGE$_{L1}$ & FGE$_{L2}$, was 1 - RMSE. That is to say, FGE, FGE$_{DT1}$ and FGE$_{DT2}$ use the fitness function shown in Eq. 9.

$$F = 1 - RMSE \tag{9}$$

The fitness function for FGE$_{L1}$, is calculated to penalise solutions with a large size. It is computed as follows;

$$F_{L1} = 1 - RMSE - MaxDepth \times 0.001 \tag{10}$$

Finally, the fitness function for FGE$_{L2}$, is calculated to allow solutions attain a max depth of 2. It is computed as follows;

$$F_{L2} = \begin{cases} 1 - RMSE, & \text{if } MaxDepth < 3 \\ 0, & \text{otherwise} \end{cases} \tag{11}$$

The max depth of a solution is the largest path which exists in any FPT of an individual.

4.3 Fairness Benchmarks

The experiments are run on six binary classification benchmark datasets, all of which can be found online in the UCI repository. A summary of all the datasets can be seen in Table 2. These datasets are often used as benchmarks in AI fairness experiments, an area XAI could prove fruitful in.

Table 2. Benchmark datasets for the classification problems, taken from the UCI repository.

Datasets	Short	Class	Vars	Instances
Bank marketing	Bank	2	20	41,188
Census income	Census	2	14	45,222
German credit	Credit	2	20	1,000
ProRepublica recidivism	Recid	2	52	7,214
ProRepublica violent recidivism	V/Recid	2	52	4,743
Heart disease	Heart	2	13	303

4.4 Expert Validation

An expert was sought out to empirically validate the interpretability of the FPTs. A domain expert, a doctor working in a local hospital, was sought out to examine the results from the Heart experiments. The best individual from each run was saved and parsed into a tree. This gave 150 graphs of the trees, 30 for each of the 5 selection methods. These trees were then presented to the domain expert over Zoom. The evaluation consisted of two steps. The expert was first asked to evaluate the trees in terms of interpretability. Afterwards, the expert was asked to score the logic of the model. That is to say, do the variables and operators in the make sense medically. Both of these were scored from 1, lowest, to 5, highest.

5 Results

The experimental results are summarized in Table 3 showing the best performance from 30 runs of FGE and the various selection methods as well as other ML approaches.

The first five columns show the results for FGE, FGE with fitness function in Eq. 10 applied, FGE with fitness function in Eq. 11 applied, FGE with double tournament selection, first considering size then fitness, and finally FGE with double tournament selection, first fitness then size. The sixth column shows the results for Support Vector Machine (SVM) and seventh Random Forest (RF). Finally, column eight shows the result of a Logistic Regression (LR).

Table 3. Classification performance comparison of each selection method used with FGE, showing the classification accuracy on the test data for the best solution found averaged across the 30 runs.

Dataset	FGE	FGE_{L1}	FGE_{L2}	FGE_{DT1}	FGE_{DT2}	SVM	RF	LR
Bank	0.89	0.89	0.89	0.89	0.89	0.91	0.91	0.84
Census	0.79	0.78	0.81	0.80	0.78	0.85	0.85	0.79
Credit	0.71	0.70	0.71	0.70	0.70	0.73	0.76	0.71
Recid	0.71	0.72	0.69	0.72	0.70	0.74	0.74	0.56
V/Recid	0.83	0.83	0.83	0.83	0.83	0.84	0.84	0.54
Heart	0.79	0.77	0.77	0.77	0.75	0.82	0.82	0.81

No one selection method for FGE was seen to outperform any other selection method with respect to accuracy. Among all FGE experiments, FGE_{DT1} found the best solutions on 4/6 benchmark problems. However, it also achieved the worst performance on the Recid problem. No selection method was seen to statistically significantly outperform any other.

A Friedman test was carried out on the data to compare the performance of all the classifiers. This test showed evidence that the RF classifier was statistically significantly better than all others, achieving or matching the best performance on each problem. As a BB model, though, it does not allow any further knowledge to be extracted. FGE was able to achieve very competitive results against the BB approaches. FGE was outperformed by 5% on the Credit dataset, achieving 71% in both FGE and FGE_{L2} compared to the best performing technique RF which found 76%. FGE accomplished 81% accuracy on the Census problem, 4% worse than both SVM and RF which obtained 85% accuracy. For the Bank, Recid and V/Recid problems, FGE evolved solutions which were within 2% of those found by either SVM or RF.

On all but one problem FGE was seen to outperform the interpretable ML algorithm considered, LR. FGE significantly exceed the performance of LR on the Bank, Recid and V/Recid problems. FGE found better solutions on the Census dataset by 2%, 81% vs 79%, while both achieved parity on the Credit dataset, attaining 71% accuracy. The Heart problem was the sole exception to this, it was seen to favour LR by 2%.

At the end of each run, the best of run individual underwent an intron removal process, outlined above, to remove any bloat which may exist in the program. The mean size of the FPTs in the final individual found in each of the 30 runs are shown in Table 4. The best results (smallest trees) are highlighted in bold.

Table 4. Size comparison between each approach. Best results are in bold.

Dataset	FGE	FGE_{L1}	FGE_{L2}	FGE_{DT1}	FGE_{DT2}
Bank	7.90	2.82	**1.83**	8.33	4.70
Census	10.13	6.70	**1.96**	9.80	8.03
Credit	10.63	7.53	**2.00**	12.90	10.67
Recid	10.90	5.33	**2.00**	10.13	10.33
V/Recid	8.17	3.97	**2.00**	9.40	8.57
Heart	10.63	5.85	**2.00**	9.40	8.57

Unsurprisingly, as the most rigid selection technique, FGE_{L2} finds by far the smallest individuals. FGE_{L1} and FGE_{DT2} are next best at finding small individuals. They are, however, more than double the size of the solutions found by FGE_{L2} on average.

The results of the human expert's analysis can be seen in Table 5. FGE_{L2} was the best performing method for finding interpretable solutions, with all 30 runs finding trees attaining scores of 4 or 5. The next best performing method was FGE_{L1}, with 8/30 being scored 4 or 5, followed by FGE_{DT1}, having 6 interpretable solutions. The worst performing methods were FGE_{DT2} and FGE, both only finding 4 interpretable solutions in their 30 runs. A plot showing the decrease in interpretability as depth increases is seen in Fig. 5. The plot suggests that any reasonable indication of interpretability disappears after trees have exceeded depth 5 or 6.

Table 5. Count of Interpretability scores for the best individual in each run for each selection type. There are 30 individuals for each selection type.

	Interpretability score				
Selection type	1	2	3	4	5
FGE	19	2	5	4	0
FGE_{L1}	14	3	5	5	3
FGE_{L2}	0	0	0	2	28
FGE_{DT1}	20	1	3	4	2
FGE_{DT2}	19	1	6	3	1

To validate that the FPTs were indeed transparent and clear in their statements, the logic of the models deemed interpretable (those scoring 4 or 5) was examined by the domain expert. This gave 52 of the original 150 models. Any models flagged as having 'incorrect' logic, that is to say the confidence score was 1 or 2, were separated from the population. Similarly, models with marginal trust, those with a confidence score of 3, were separated.

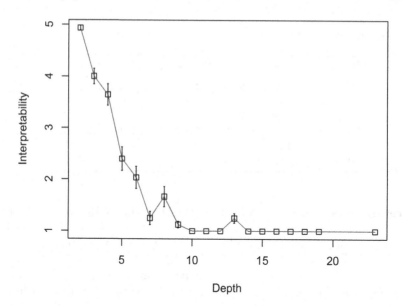

Fig. 5. Decrease in human interpretability as the maximum depth of the model increases

This left 24 models, described in Table 6, which were deemed interpretable and inspired confidence. The mean accuracy of those models is 77.1%, shown in Table 7. When marginal models were included, those with confidence score of 3, the number of models jumps to 39, as shown in Table 6, and the mean accuracy marginally increased to 77.3%, as seen in Table 7. Models which have been deemed to have 'correct' logic perform ~2% better than those adjudged to have 'incorrect' logic. This is despite both groups containing almost identical fitness on the training data. By investigating the models and judging their logic, an expert is able to improve the overall performance of the population by identifying models which are likely to be over-trained. This process is also an effective way for an expert to build trust in the models which are being evolved.

Table 6. Selection methods of FGE models with interpretability score ≥ 4.

Confidence score	FGE	FGE$_{L1}$	FGE$_{L2}$	FGE$_{DT1}$	FGE$_{DT2}$
≤ 2 (Incorrect logic)	2	2	5	2	2
≥ 4 (Correct logic)	0	3	19	1	1
≥ 3 (Correct & Marginal logic)	2	6	25	4	2

Table 7. Accuracy of FGE models with interpretability score ≥ 4.

Confidence score	Number	Accuracy
≤ 2 (Incorrect logic)	13	75.2%
≥ 4 (Correct logic)	24	77.1%
≥ 3 (Correct logic & Marginal logic)	39	77.3%

6 Conclusion

This paper empirically evaluates the suitability of FGE as an XAI approach by analysing the Fuzzy Pattern Trees it produced.

The experimental results show that FGE has a competitive performance on real world classification tasks. These models were then presented in comprehensible terms to a human domain expert, a medical doctor. This expert was able to validate the interpretablity of the models and to extract the knowledge obtained in the learning process of the model. This was validated by comparing the performance of models which the domain expert labeled their logic as 'incorrect' vs those the domain expert labeled as 'correct'. Models with 'incorrect' logic were seen to perform worse than those deemed as 'correct'.

The next major step in this work is the inclusion of the human expert in more stages of the evolutionary process. Pre-processing by picking membership function values, encapsulating information into modules and incorporating domain knowledge in the grammar, setting maximum depth size of the individuals, being involved in the selection process are some of the many possibilities going forward. This would enable GE to tailor its search to the expertise and capabilities of the user.

References

1. Adadi, A., Berrada, M.: Peeking inside the black-box: a survey on explainable artificial intelligence (XAI). IEEE Access **6**, 52138–52160 (2018)
2. Arrieta, A.B., et al.: Explainable artificial intelligence (XAI): concepts, taxonomies, opportunities and challenges toward responsible AI. Inf. Fusion **58**, 82–115 (2020)
3. Azad, R.M.A., Ryan, C.: The best things don't always come in small packages: constant creation in grammatical evolution. In: Nicolau, M., et al. (eds.) EuroGP 2014. LNCS, vol. 8599, pp. 186–197. Springer, Heidelberg (2014). https://doi.org/10.1007/978-3-662-44303-3_16
4. Carvalho, D.V., Pereira, E.M., Cardoso, J.S.: Machine learning interpretability: a survey on methods and metrics. Electronics **8**(8), 832 (2019)
5. Deb, K., Pratap, A., Agarwal, S., Meyarivan, T.: A fast and elitist multiobjective genetic algorithm: NSGA-II. IEEE Trans. Evol. Comput. **6**(2), 182–197 (2002)
6. Doran, D., Schulz, S., Besold, T.R.: What does explainable AI really mean? A new conceptualization of perspectives. arXiv preprint arXiv:1710.00794 (2017)
7. Doshi-Velez, F., Kim, B.: Towards a rigorous science of interpretable machine learning. arXiv preprint arXiv:1702.08608 (2017)

8. Dou, R., Zong, C., Li, M.: Application of an interactive genetic algorithm in the conceptual design of car console. Tianjin University (2014)
9. Fitzgerald, J., Ryan, C.: Exploring boundaries: optimising individual class boundaries for binary classification problem. In: Proceedings of the 14th annual conference on Genetic and evolutionary computation, pp. 743–750 (2012)
10. Gilpin, L.H., Bau, D., Yuan, B.Z., Bajwa, A., Specter, M., Kagal, L.: Explaining explanations: an overview of interpretability of machine learning. In: 2018 IEEE 5th International Conference on data science and advanced analytics (DSAA), pp. 80–89. IEEE (2018)
11. Goertzel, T.: The path to more general artificial intelligence. J. Exp. Theoret. Artif. Intell. **26**(3), 343–354 (2014)
12. Goodman, B., Flaxman, S.: European union regulations on algorithmic decision-making and a "right to explanation". AI Mag. **38**(3), 50–57 (2017)
13. Guidotti, R., Monreale, A., Ruggieri, S., Turini, F., Giannotti, F., Pedreschi, D.: A survey of methods for explaining black box models. ACM Comput. Surv. (CSUR) **51**(5), 93 (2018)
14. Huang, Z., Gedeon, T.D., Nikravesh, M.: Pattern trees induction: a new machine learning method. Trans. Fuzzy Syst. **16**(4), 958–970 (2008). https://doi.org/10.1109/TFUZZ.2008.924348
15. Huysmans, J., Dejaeger, K., Mues, C., Vanthienen, J., Baesens, B.: An empirical evaluation of the comprehensibility of decision table, tree and rule based predictive models. Decis. Support Syst. **51**(1), 141–154 (2011)
16. Ishibuchi, H., Tsukamoto, N., Nojima, Y.: Evolutionary many-objective optimization: a short review. In: 2008 IEEE Congress on Evolutionary Computation (IEEE World Congress on Computational Intelligence), pp. 2419–2426. IEEE (2008)
17. Koza, J.R., Koza, J.R.: Genetic Programming: On the Programming of Computers by Means of Natural Selection, vol. 1. MIT Press, Cambridge (1992)
18. Krakovna, V., Doshi-Velez, F.: Increasing the interpretability of recurrent neural networks using hidden Markov models. arXiv preprint arXiv:1606.05320 (2016)
19. Lipton, Z.C.: The mythos of model interpretability. arXiv preprint arXiv:1606.03490 (2016)
20. Marcus, G.: Deep learning: a critical appraisal. arXiv preprint arXiv:1801.00631 (2018)
21. Moore, A., Murdock, V., Cai, Y., Jones, K.: Transparent tree ensembles. In: The 41st International ACM SIGIR Conference on Research & #38; Development in Information Retrieval, SIGIR 2018, pp. 1241–1244. ACM, New York (2018). https://doi.org/10.1145/3209978.3210151, https://doi.org/10.1145/3209978.3210151
22. Murphy., A., Ali., M.S., Dias., D.M., Amaral., J., Naredo, E., Ryan., C.: Grammar-based fuzzy pattern trees for classification problems. In: Proceedings of the 12th International Joint Conference on Computational Intelligence - Volume 1: ECTA, pp. 71–80. INSTICC, SciTePress (2020). https://doi.org/10.5220/0010111900710080
23. Murphy, A., Ryan, C.: Improving module identification and use in grammatical evolution. In: Jin, Y. (ed.) 2020 IEEE Congress on Evolutionary Computation, CEC 2020. IEEE Computational Intelligence Society, IEEE Press (2020)
24. Nordin, P., Francone, F., Banzhaf, W.: Explicitly defined introns and destructive crossover in genetic programming. Adv. Genet. Program. **2**, 111–134 (1995)
25. O'Neill, M., Ryan, C.: Grammatical evolution. IEEE Trans. Evol. Comput. **5**(4), 349–358 (2001)

26. Patten, J.V., Ryan, C.: Attributed grammatical evolution using shared memory spaces and dynamically typed semantic function specification. In: Machado, P., et al. (eds.) EuroGP 2015. LNCS, vol. 9025, pp. 105–112. Springer, Cham (2015). https://doi.org/10.1007/978-3-319-16501-1_9

27. Ribeiro, M.T., Singh, S., Guestrin, C.: Why should I trust you?: Explaining the predictions of any classifier. In: Proceedings of the 22nd ACM SIGKDD International Conference on Knowledge Discovery and Data Mining, pp. 1135–1144. ACM (2016)

28. Ryan, C., Azad, R.M.A.: Sensible initialisation in grammatical evolution. In: GECCO, pp. 142–145. AAAI (2003)

29. Ryan, C., Collins, J.J., Neill, M.O.: Grammatical evolution: evolving programs for an arbitrary language. In: Banzhaf, W., Poli, R., Schoenauer, M., Fogarty, T.C. (eds.) EuroGP 1998. LNCS, vol. 1391, pp. 83–96. Springer, Heidelberg (1998). https://doi.org/10.1007/BFb0055930

30. Ryan, C., Collins, J.J., Neill, M.O.: Grammatical evolution: evolving programs for an arbitrary language. In: Banzhaf, W., Poli, R., Schoenauer, M., Fogarty, T.C. (eds.) EuroGP 1998. LNCS, vol. 1391, pp. 83–96. Springer, Heidelberg (1998). https://doi.org/10.1007/BFb0055930

31. Ryan, C., O'Neill, M., Collins, J.: Handbook of Grammatical Evolution, 1st edn., p. 497. Springer, Cham (2018). https://doi.org/10.1007/978-3-319-78717-6

32. dos Santos, A.R., do Amaral, J.L.M.: Synthesis of fuzzy pattern trees by cartesian genetic programming. Mathware Soft Comput. **22**(1), 52–56 (2015)

33. Schneider, J., Handali, J.: Personalized explanation in machine learning: a conceptualization. arXiv preprint arXiv:1901.00770 (2019)

34. Silver, D., et al.: A general reinforcement learning algorithm that masters chess, shogi, and Go through self-play. Science **362**(6419), 1140–1144 (2018)

35. Takagi, H.: Interactive evolutionary computation: Fusion of the capabilities of EC optimization and human evaluation. Proc. IEEE **89**(9), 1275–1296 (2001)

36. Yi, Y., Fober, T., Hüllermeier, E.: Fuzzy operator trees for modeling rating functions. Int. J. Comput. Intell. Appl. **8**, 413–428 (2009)

37. Zou, J., Schiebinger, L.: AI can be sexist and racist–it's time to make it fair (2018)

Evolutionary Neural Architecture Search Supporting Approximate Multipliers

Michal Pinos[(✉)], Vojtech Mrazek[iD], and Lukas Sekanina[iD]

Faculty of Information Technology, IT4Innovations Centre of Excellence, Brno University of Technology, Božetěchova 2, 612 66 Brno, Czech Republic
{ipinos,mrazek,sekanina}@fit.vutbr.cz

Abstract. There is a growing interest in automated neural architecture search (NAS) methods. They are employed to routinely deliver high-quality neural network architectures for various challenging data sets and reduce the designer's effort. The NAS methods utilizing multi-objective evolutionary algorithms are especially useful when the objective is not only to minimize the network error but also to minimize the number of parameters (weights) or power consumption of the inference phase. We propose a multi-objective NAS method based on Cartesian genetic programming for evolving convolutional neural networks (CNN). The method allows approximate operations to be used in CNNs to reduce power consumption of a target hardware implementation. During the NAS process, a suitable CNN architecture is evolved together with approximate multipliers to deliver the best trade-offs between the accuracy, network size and power consumption. The most suitable approximate multipliers are automatically selected from a library of approximate multipliers. Evolved CNNs are compared with common human-created CNNs of a similar complexity on the CIFAR-10 benchmark problem.

Keywords: Approximate computing · Convolutional neural network · Cartesian genetic programming · Neuroevolution · Energy efficiency

1 Introduction

Machine learning technology based on deep neural networks (DNNs) is currently penetrating into many new application domains. It is deployed in such classification, prediction, control, and other tasks in which designers can collect comprehensive data sets that are mandatory for training and validating the resulting model. In many cases (such as smart glasses or voice assistants), DNNs have to be implemented in low-power hardware operated on batteries. Particularly, the inference process of a fully trained DNN is typically accelerated in hardware to meet real-time time requirements and other constraints. Hence, drastic optimizations and approximations have to be introduced at the level of hardware [2]. On the other hand, DNN training is typically conducted on GPU servers.

© Springer Nature Switzerland AG 2021
T. Hu et al. (Eds.): EuroGP 2021, LNCS 12691, pp. 82–97, 2021.
https://doi.org/10.1007/978-3-030-72812-0_6

Existing DNN architectures have mostly been developed by human experts *manually*, which is a time-consuming and error-prone process. The current approach to hardware implementations of DNNs is based on semi-automated simplifying of a network model, which was initially developed for a GPU and trained on GPU without considering any hardware implementation aspects. There is a growing interest in automated DNN design methods known as the *neural architecture search* (NAS) [4,26]. Evolutionary NAS, introduced over three decades ago [28], is now intensively adopted, mostly because it can easily be implemented as a multi-objective design method [12,20].

This paper is focused on the NAS applied to the automated design of *convolutional neural networks* (CNNs) for image classification. Current NAS methods only partly reflect hardware-oriented requirements on resulting CNNs. In addition to the classification accuracy, some of them try to minimize the number of parameters (such as multiply and accumulate operations) for a GPU implementation, which performs all operations in the floating-point number representation [4,12]. Our research aims to propose and evaluate a NAS method for the highly automated design of CNNs that reflect hardware-oriented requirements. We hypothesize that *more energy-efficient hardware implementations of CNNs can be obtained if hardware-related requirements are specified, reflected, and exploited during the NAS*. In this paper, we specifically focus on the automated co-design of CNN's topology and approximate arithmetic operations. The objective is to automatically generate CNNs showing good trade-offs between the accuracy, the network size (the number of multiplications), and a degree of approximation in the used multipliers.

The proposed method is based on a multi-objective Cartesian genetic programming (CGP) whose task is to maximize the classification accuracy and minimize the power consumption of the most dominated arithmetic operation, i.e., multiplications conducted in convolutional layers. To avoid the time-consuming automated design of approximate multipliers, CGP selects suitable multipliers from a library of approximate multipliers [14]. While CGP delivers the network topology, the weights are obtained using a TensorFlow. The NAS supporting approximate multipliers in CNNs is obviously more computationally expensive than the NAS of common CNNs. The reason is that TensorFlow does not support the fast execution of CNNs that contain non-standard operations such as approximate multipliers. We propose eliminating this issue by employing TFApprox [25], which extends TensorFlow to support approximate multipliers in CNN training and inference. Evolved CNNs are compared with common human-created CNNs of a similar complexity on the CIFAR-10 benchmark problem.

To summarize our key contributions: We present a method capable of an automated design of CNN topology with automated selection of suitable approximate multiplier(s). The methodology uniquely integrates a multi-objective CGP and TFApprox-based training and evaluation of CNNs containing approximate circuits. We demonstrate that the proposed method provides better trade-offs than a common approach based on introducing approximate multipliers to CNNs developed without reflecting any hardware aspects.

2   Related Work

Convolutional neural networks are deep neural networks employing, in addition to other layer types, the so-called *convolutional layers*. These layers are capable of processing large input vectors (tensors). Simultaneously, the number of parameters (the weights in the convolutional kernels) they use is small compared to the common fully-connected layers. Because the state of the art CNNs consist of hundreds of layers and millions of network elements, they are demanding in terms of the execution time and energy requirements. For example, the inference phase of a trained CNN such as ResNet-50 requires performing $3.9 \cdot 10^9$ multiply-and-accumulate operations to classify one single input image. Depending on a particular CNN and a hardware platform used to implement it, arithmetic operations conducted in the inference are responsible for 10% to 40% of total energy [23].

To reduce power consumption, hardware-oriented optimization techniques developed for CNNs focus on optimizing the data representation, pruning less important connections and neurons, approximating arithmetic operations, compression of weights, and employing various smart data transfer and memory storage strategies [8,16]. For example, the Ristretto tool is specialized in determining the number of bits needed for arithmetic operations [5] because the standard 32-bit floating-point arithmetic is too expensive and unnecessarily accurate for CNNs. According to [23], an 8-bit fixed-point multiply consumes 15.5× less energy (12.4× less area) than a 32-bit fixed-point multiply, and 18.5× less energy (27.5× less area) than a 32-bit floating-point multiply. Further savings in energy are obtained not only by the bit width reduction of arithmetic operations but also by introducing approximate operations, particularly to the multiplication circuits [15,18]. Many approximate multipliers are available in public circuit libraries, for example, EvoApproxLib [14]. All these techniques are usually applied to CNN architectures initially developed with no or minimal focus on a potential hardware implementation.

NAS has been introduced to automate the neural network design process. The best-performing CNNs obtained by NAS currently show superior performance with respect to human-designed CNNs [4,26]. NAS methods can be classified according to the *search mechanism* that can be based on reinforcement learning [29], evolutionary algorithms (EA) [21], gradient optimization [11], random search [1], or sequential model-based optimization [10]. NAS methods were initially constructed as single-objective methods to minimize the classification error for a CNN running on a GPU [17,22]. Recent works have been devoted to *multi-objective* NAS approaches in which the error is optimized together with the cost, whose minimizing is crucial for the sustainable operation of GPU clusters [7,12].

As our NAS method employs genetic programming, which is a branch of evolutionary algorithms, we briefly discuss the main components of the EA-based approaches. Regarding the *problem representation*, direct [12,22] and indirect (generative) [20] encoding schemes have been investigated. The selection of *genetic operators* is tightly coupled with the chosen problem representation. While mutation is the key operator for CGP [22], the crossover is crucial for binary encoding of CNNs as it allows population members to share common building-blocks [12]. The *non-dominated sorting*, known from, e.g., the NSGA-II algorithm [3], enables to maintain diverse trade-offs between conflicting design objectives. The evolutionary search is often combined with *learning* because it is very inefficient to let the evolution find the weights. A candidate CNN, constructed using the information available in its genotype, is trained using common learning algorithms available in popular DNN frameworks such as TensorFlow. The number of epochs and the training data size are usually limited to reduce the training time, despite the fact that by doing so the fitness score can wrongly be estimated. The CNN accuracy, which is obtained using test data, is interpreted as the fitness score. The best-evolved CNNs are usually *re-trained* (fine-tuned) to further increase their accuracy.

The entire *neuro-evolution* is very time and resources demanding and, hence, only several hundreds of candidate CNNs can be generated and evaluated in one EA run. On common platforms, such as TensorFlow, all mathematical operations are highly optimized and work with standard floating-point numbers on GPUs. If one needs to replace these operations with approximate operations, these non-standard operations have to be expensively emulated. The CNN execution is then significantly slower than with the floating-point operations. This problem can partly be eliminated by using TFApprox in which all approximate operations are implemented as look-up tables and accessed through a texture memory mechanism of CUDA capable GPUs [25].

A very recent work [8] presents a method capable of jointly searching the neural architecture, hardware architecture, and compression model for FPGA-based CNN implementations. Contrasted to our work, arithmetic operations are performed on 16 bits, and no approximate operations are employed. High-quality results are presented for CIFAR-10 and ImageNet benchmark data sets.

3   Evolutionary NAS with Approximate Circuits

The proposed evolutionary NAS is inspired in paper [22] whose authors used CGP to evolve CNNs. We extend this work by (i) supporting a multi-objective search, (ii) using an efficient seeding strategy and (iii) enabling the approximate multipliers in convolutional layers. The method is evaluated on the design of CNNs for a common benchmark problem – the CIFAR-10 image classification data set [9]. The role of CGP is to provide a good CNN architecture. The weights are obtained using Adam optimization algorithm implemented in TensorFlow. Our ultimate goal is to deliver new CNN architectures that are optimized for hardware accelerators of CNNs in terms of the parameter count and usage of low-energy arithmetic operations.

In this section, we will describe the proposed CGP-based NAS which is developed for CNNs with floating-point arithmetic operations executed on GPU. In Sect. 3.5, the proposed evolutionary selection of approximate multipliers for CNNs will be presented.

3.1   CNN Representation

CGP was developed to automatically design programs and circuits that are modeled using directed acyclic graphs [13]. A candidate solution is represented using a two-dimensional array of $n_c \times n_r$ nodes, consuming n_i inputs and producing n_o outputs. In the case of evolutionary design of CNNs, each node represents either one layer (e.g., fully connected, convolutional, max pooling, average pooling) or a module (e.g., residual or inception block) of a CNN. Each node of j-th column reads a tensor coming from column $1, 2, \ldots, j-1$ and produces another tensor. In our case study, CNNs accept one 4D input tensor (of shape [batch_size, height, width, depth]) holding one batch of input images and produce one 2D output tensor (of shape [batch_size, class_probs]) which is treated as a matrix, in which each row corresponds to a vector of class probabilities.

Figure 1 shows how resulting CNN is obtained from an array of CGP nodes (called the template) and an individual, which is represented as a graph $I = (V, E)$, where V denotes a set of vertices (nodes of template) and E is a set of edges. Individual representation (in a form of the graph I) in a conjunction with the template creates a candidate solution. The nodes that are employed in the CNN are called the active nodes and form a directed acyclic graph (DAG), that connects the input node with the output node. When a particular CNN has to be built and evaluated, this DAG is extracted (from a candidate solution) and transformed to a computational graph which is processed by TensorFlow.

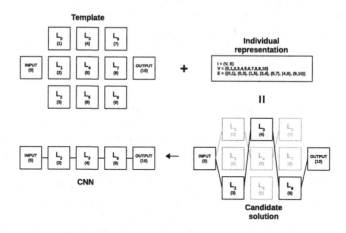

Fig. 1. A template combined with an individual representation creates a candidate solution, which is transformed into a CNN.

The following layers are supported: fully connected (FC), convolutional (CONV), summation (SUM), maximum pooling (MAX) and average pooling (AVG). Inspired in [27], CGP can also use inception (INC), residual (RES), and (residual) bottleneck (RES-B) modules [6] that are composed of several elementary layers as shown in Fig. 2. Selected layers and modules are introduced in the following paragraphs; the remaining ones are standard.

The *summation layer* accepts tensors t_1 and t_2 with $shape(t_1) = (h_1, w_1, c_1)$ and $shape(t_2) = (h_2, w_2, c_2)$, where h_x, w_x and c_x are height, width and the number of channels respectively ($x \in \{1, 2\}$). It outputs t_o, i.e. the sum of t_1 and t_2, defined as

$$t_o = t_1 + t_2 \iff t_o^{ijk} = t_1^{ijk} + t_2^{ijk} \text{ for } i = 0, ..., c - 1 \qquad (1)$$
$$j = 0, ..., h - 1$$
$$k = 0, ..., w - 1.$$

It has to be ensured that the height and width of both the tensors are identical. If it is not so, the pooling algorithm is applied to the 'bigger' tensor to unify these dimensions. The problem with unmatched number of channels is resolved by zero padding applied to the 'smaller' tensor, i.e., $shape(t_o) = (h_o, w_o, c_o)$, where $h_o = min(h_1, h_2)$, $w_o = min(w_1, w_2)$ and $c_o = max(c_1, c_2)$.

The *inception module*, showed in Fig. 2c, performs in parallel three convolutions with filters 5×5, 3×3 and 1×1 and one maximum pooling. The results are then concatenated along the channel dimension. Additionally, 1×1 convolutions are used to reduce the number of input channels. Parameters C_1, C_2 and C_3 correspond to the number of filters in 5×5, 3×3 and 1×1 convolutions, whereas R_1, R_2 and R_3 denote the number of filters in 1×1 convolutions. All convolutional layers operate with stride 1 and are followed by the ReLU activation.

The *residual module* contains a sequence of NxN and MxM convolutions that can be skipped, which is implemented by the summation layer followed by the ReLU activation. The residual module, shown in Fig. 2b, consists of two convolutional layers with the filters $N \times N$ and $M \times M$, both followed by batch normalization and ReLU activation. In parallel, one convolution with filter 1×1 is computed. Results of $M \times M$ and 1×1 convolution are added together to form a result. Convolutional layers with filters NxN and 1×1 operate with stride n.

We also support a bottleneck variant of the residual module, shown in Fig. 2a, which comprises of one convolutional layer with filter $N \times N$, which applies batch normalization and ReLU activation to its input and output. This convolutional layer is surrounded by two 1×1 convolutional layers. In parallel, another 1×1 convolutional layer is employed. The first two parallel 1×1 convolutional layers operate with stride n, whereas all other layers use stride 1. The outputs of the last two parallel 1×1 convolutional layers are then batch-normalized and added together. The final output is obtained by application of ReLU activation to the output of the addition layer.

3.2 Genetic Operators

CGP usually employs only one genetic operator – mutation. The proposed mutation operator modifies architecture of a candidate CNN; however, the functionality (layers and their parameters) implemented by the nodes are not directly

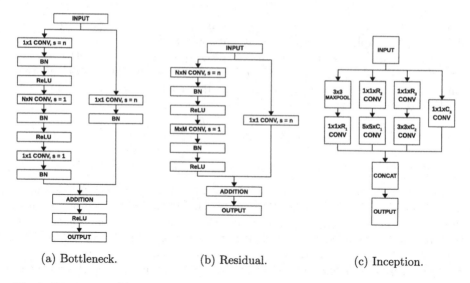

(a) Bottleneck.   (b) Residual.   (c) Inception.

Fig. 2. Diagrams of (a) bottleneck residual module, (b) residual module and (c) inception module.

changed, except some specific cases, see below. A randomly selected node is mutated in such a way that all its incoming edges are removed and a new connection is established to a randomly selected node situated in up to L previous columns, where L is a user-defined parameter. This is repeated k times, where k is the node's arity. If the mutation does not hit an active node it is repeated to avoid generating functionally identical networks. One mutation can thus modify several inactive nodes before finally modifying an active node. The weights associated with a newly added active node are randomly initialized. If the primary output undergoes a mutation, its destination is a randomly selected node of the last column containing FC layers.

3.3 Fitness Functions

The objectives are to maximize the CNN accuracy and to minimize the CNN complexity (which is expressed as the number of parameters), and power consumption of multiplication in the convolutional layers. The objective function expressing the accuracy of a candidate network x (evaluated using a data set D), is calculated using TensorFlow as $f_1(x, D) = accuracy(x, D)$. The number of parameters in the entire CNN x is captured by fitness function $f_2(x)$. Power consumption is estimated as $f_3(x) = N_{mult}(x) \cdot P_{mult}$, where N_{mult} is the number of multiplications executed during inference in all convolutional layers and P_{mult} is power consumption of used multiplier.

3.4   Search Algorithm

The search algorithm (see Algorithm 1) is constructed as a multi-objective evolutionary algorithm inspired in CGP-based NAS [22] and NSGA-II [3]. The initial population is heuristically initialized with networks created according to a template shown in Fig. 3. The template consists of typical layers of CNNs, i.e., convolutional layers in the first and middle parts and fully connected layers at the end. All connections in the template (including the link to the output tensor) and all associated weights are randomly generated. The proposed template ensures that even the networks of the initial populations are reasonable CNNs which reduces the computational requirements of the search process.

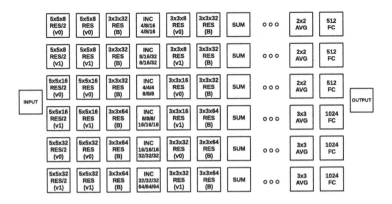

Fig. 3. The template used to initialize CGP.

Training of a CNN is always followed by testing to obtain fitness values $f_1(x)$, $f_2(x)$, and $f_3(x)$. To reduce the training time, a randomly selected subset D_{train} of the training data set can be used. The same subset is used for training all the individuals belonging to the same population. Training is conducted for E_{train} epochs. The accuracy of the candidate CNN (i.e., f_1) is determined using the entire test data set D_{test} (Algorithm 1, line 2). To overcome the overfitting during the training, data augmentation and L2 regularization were employed [19].

The offspring population (O) is created by applying the mutation operator on each individual of the parental population P. The offspring population is evaluated in the same way as the parental population (Algorithm 1, line 5). Populations P and O are joined to form an auxiliary population R (line 6). The new population is constructed by selecting non-dominated individuals from Pareto fronts (PF) established in R (lines 9–10). If any front must be split, a crowding distance is used for the selection of individuals to P (lines 12–13) [3]. The search terminates after evaluating a given number of CNNs.

As the proposed algorithm is multi-objective, the result of a single CGP run is a set of non-dominated solutions. At the end of evolution, the best-performing individuals from this set are re-trained (fine-tuned) for $E_{retrain}$ epochs on the complete training data set $D_{retrain}$ and the final accuracy is reported on the complete test data set D_{test}.

Algorithm 1. Neuroevolution

1: $P \leftarrow$ initial_population(); $g \leftarrow 0$
2: training_evaluation($P, E_{train}, D_{train}, D_{test}$)
3: **repeat**
4:     $P' \leftarrow$ replicate(P); $O \leftarrow$ mutate(P')
5:     training_evaluation($O, E_{train}, D_{train}, D_{test}$)
6:     $R \leftarrow P \cup O$; $P \leftarrow \emptyset$
7:     **while** $|P| \neq population\_size$ **do**
8:         $PF \leftarrow non\_dominated(R)$
9:         **if** $|P \cup PF| \leq population\_size$ **then**
10:             $P \leftarrow P \cup PF$
11:         **else**
12:             $n \leftarrow |PF \cup P| - population\_size$
13:             $P \leftarrow P \cup crowding\_reduce(PF, n)$
14:         $R \leftarrow R \setminus PF$
15:     $g \leftarrow g + 1$
16: **until** stop_criteria_satisfied()
17: training_evaluation($P, E_{retrain}, D_{retrain}, D_{test}$)
18: **return** (P)

3.5 NAS with Approximate Multipliers

So far we have discussed a NAS utilizing standard floating-point arithmetic operations. In order to find the most suitable approximate multiplier for a CNN architecture, we introduce the following changes to the algorithm. (i) The problem representation is extended with one integer specifying the index I_m to the list of available 8-bit approximate multipliers, i.e. to one of the 14 approximate multipliers included in EvoApproxLib-Lite[1] [14]. These approximate multipliers show different trade-offs between power consumption, error metrics and other parameters. Please note that the selection of the exact 8-bit multiplier is not excluded. (ii) The mutation operator is modified to randomly change this index with probability p_{mult}. (iii) Before a candidate CNN is sent to TensorFlow for training or testing, all standard multipliers used in convolutional layers are replaced with the 8-bit approximate multiplier specified by index I_m. TensorFlow, with the help of TFApprox, then performs all multiplications in the convolution computations in the forward pass of learning algorithm with the approximate multipliers, whereas all computations in the backward pass are done with the standard floating-point multiplications.

---

[1] http://www.fit.vutbr.cz/research/groups/ehw/approxlib/.

4   Results

Table 1 summarizes all parameters of CGP and the learning method used in our experiments. These parameters were experimentally selected based on a few trial runs. Because of limited computational resources, we could generate and evaluate only $pop\_size + G \times pop\_size = 88$ candidate CNNs in each run.

Table 1. Parameters of the experiment.

Parameter	Value	Description
n_r	6	Number of rows in the CGP grid
n_c	23	Number of columns in the CGP grid
L	5	L-back parameter
pop_size	8	Number of individuals in the population
G	10	Maximum number of generations
D_{train}	50000	Size of the data set used during the evolution
$D_{retrain}$	50000	Size of the data set for re-training
D_{test}	10000	Size of the test data set
E_{train}	20	Number of epochs (during the evolution)
$E_{retrain}$	200	Number of epochs (for re-training)
$batch\_size$	32	Batch size
$rate$	0.001	Initial learning rate for all CNNs
p_{arch}	1.0	Probability of mutation of the architecture
p_{mult}	1.0	Probability of mutation of I_m

4.1   The Role of Approximate Multipliers in NAS

We consider four scenarios to analyze the role of approximate multipliers in NAS: (S1) CNN is co-optimized with the approximate multiplier under fitness functions f_1 and f_3 (denoted 'CGP+auto-selected-mult-A/E' in the following figures); (S2) CNN is co-optimized with the approximate multiplier under fitness functions f_1, f_2 and f_3 (denoted 'CGP+auto-selected-mult-A/E/P'); (S3) A selected approximate multiplier is always used in NAS (denoted 'CGP+fixed-approx-mult-A/E'); (S4) The 8-bit exact multiplier is always used in NAS (denoted 'CGP+accurate-8-bit-mult-A/E'). Note that symbols A, E and P denote Accuracy, Parameters and Energy. Because of limited resources we executed 5, 2, 13, and 2 CGP runs for scenarios S1, S2, S3, and S4.

Figure 4 plots a typical progress of a CGP run in S1 scenario. The blue points represent the initial population – all parents and offspring are depicted in Fig. 4a. The remaining subfigures show generations 3, 6, and 9. The grey points are candidate solutions created in the previous generations and their purpose is to emphasize the CGP progress. As the best trade-offs (Accuracy vs. Energy) are moving to the top-left corner of the figures, we observe that CGP can improve candidate solutions despite only 10 populations are generated.

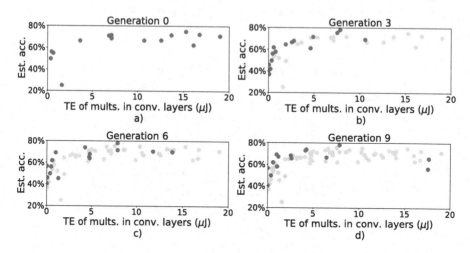

Fig. 4. A typical progress of evolution in scenario S1 (Estimated Accuracy vs. Total Energy). The blue points represent the current generation (all parents and offspring). The grey points are all previously generated solutions.

Trade-offs between the accuracy (estimated in the fitness function) and the total energy of multiplications performed in convolutional layers during inference are shown in Fig. 5. The Pareto front is mostly occupied by CNNs evolved in scenario S3, i.e. with a pre-selected approximate multiplier. CNNs utilizing the 8-bit accurate multiplier are almost always dominated by CNNs containing some of the approximate multipliers. CNNs showing the 70% and higher accuracy never use highly approximate multipliers (see the bar on the right hand side) in Fig. 5. Figure 6 shows that re-training of the best evolved CNNs conducted for $E_{retrain}$ epochs significantly improves the accuracy.

Final Pareto fronts obtained (after re-training) in our four scenarios are highlighted in Fig. 7. When an approximate multiplier is fixed before the NAS is executed (S3), CGP is almost always able to deliver a better trade-off than if a suitable multiplier is automatically selected during the evolution (in S1 or S2). However, CGP has to be repeated with each of the pre-selected multipliers to find the best trade-offs. We hypothesize that longer CGP runs are needed to benefit from S1 and S2.

Finally, Table 2 lists key parameters of selected CNNs (the final and estimated accuracy, the energy needed for all multiplications in convolutional layers, and the number of multiplications) and used approximate multipliers (the identifier and the energy per one multiplication). One of the evolved CNNs is depicted in Fig. 8.

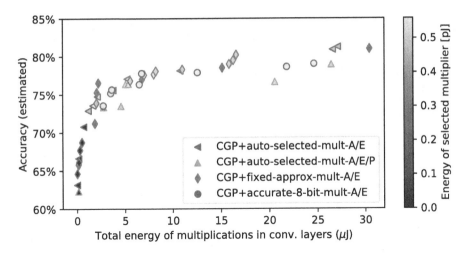

Fig. 5. Trade-offs between the accuracy and the total energy of multiplications performed in convolutional layers during one inference obtained with different design scenarios.

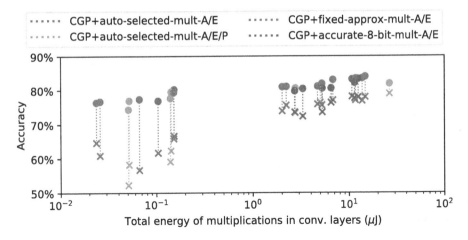

Fig. 6. The impact of re-training on the accuracy of best-evolved CNNs. Crosses/points denote the accuracy before/after re-training.

4.2 Execution Time

Experiments were performed on a machine with two 12-core CPUs Intel Skylake Gold 6126, 2.6 GHz, 192 GB, equipped with four GPU accelerators NVIDIA Tesla V100-SXM2. A single CGP run with CNNs utilizing approximate multipliers takes 48 GPU hours; the final re-training requires additional 56 GPU hours on average. When approximate multipliers are emulated by TFApprox, the average time needed for all inferences in ResNet-8 on CIFAR-10 is 1.7 s (initialization) + 1.5 s (data processing) = 3.2 s. If the same task is performed by

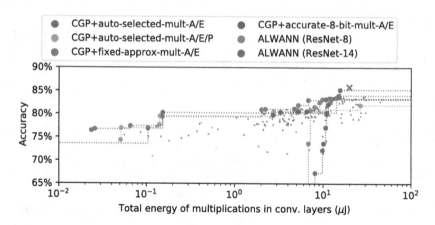

Fig. 7. Pareto fronts obtained in four scenarios compared with ResNet networks utilizing 8-bit multipliers (crosses) and the ALWANN method.

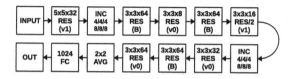

Fig. 8. Evolved CNN whose parameters are given in the first row of Table 2.

TensorFlow in the 32-bit FP arithmetic, the time is $1.8\,s + 0.2\,s = 2.0\,s$. Hence, the time overhead coming with approximate operations is 37.5%.

4.3   Comparison with Other Similar Designs

The results are compared with human-created ResNet networks of similar complexity as evolved CNNs. Parameters of ResNet-8 and ResNet-14 (utilizing the 8-bit exact multiplier) are depicted with crosses in Fig. 7. While ResNet-8 is dominated by several evolved CNNs, we were unable to evolve CNNs dominating ResNet-14. We further compared evolved CNNs with the CNNs optimized using the ALWANN method [15]. ALWANN tries to identify the best possible assignment of an approximate multiplier to each layer of ResNet (i.e., different approximate multipliers can be assigned to different layers). For a good range of target energies, the proposed method produces better trade-offs than ALWANN.

Paper [26] reports 31 CNNs generated by various NAS methods and five CNNs designed by human experts. On CIFAR-10, the error is between 2.08% and 8.69%, the number of parameters is between 1.7 and 39.8 millions and the design time is between 0.3 and 22,400 GPU days. Our results are far from all these numbers as we address much smaller networks (operating with 8-bit multipliers) that must, in principle, show higher errors. However, paper [24] reports a number of human-created CNN hardware accelerators with the classification

Table 2. Key parameters of selected CNNs and used multipliers. Symbol * denotes the 8-bit accurate multiplier.

Method	Accuracy		Energy [μJ]	Mults ×10⁶	Approx. mult. ID	Energy of 1 mult. [pJ]
	Final	Estimated				
Proposed	83.98	78.01	14.88 μJ	30.9	mul8u_JD	0.48 pJ
	83.50	76.88	13.82 μJ	30.9	mul8u_C1	0.45 pJ
	83.18	78.14	10.76 μJ	28.5	mul8u_GR	0.38 pJ
	83.01	77.02	6.79 μJ	22.9	mul8u_M1	0.30 pJ
	82.53	75.85	9.22 μJ	31.7	mul8u_85Q	0.29 pJ
	82.15	77.66	11.48 μJ	20.5	mul8u_JFF*	0.56 pJ
	81.03	75.54	2.23 μJ	7.7	mul8u_85Q	0.29 pJ
	79.55	62.32	0.14 μJ	27.2	mul8u_KX	0.01 pJ
	79.20	69.13	1.05 μJ	6.8	mul8u_2N4	0.15 pJ
	78.64	66.28	4.54 μJ	8.1	mul8u_JFF*	0.56 pJ
	77.66	59.12	0.14 μJ	26.8	mul8u_KX	0.01 pJ
	77.60	67.21	1.68 μJ	5.7	mul8u_M1	0.30 pJ
	76.73	60.88	0.03 μJ	4.9	mul8u_KX	0.01 pJ
	74.34	44.37	0.05 μJ	3.2	mul8u_8DU	0.02 pJ
ALWANN	85.81	ResNet-14	19.76 μJ	35.3	mul8u_JFF*	0.56 pJ
	82.85	ResNet-8	11.84 μJ	21.2	mul8u_JFF*	0.56 pJ

accuracy 80.77–81.53% on CIFAR-10, and with the total energy consumption $34.2 - 335.7\,\mu J$ (energy of multiplications is not reported separately). These numbers are quite comparable with our results even under the conservative assumption that multiplication requires 20% of the total energy of the accelerator.

5 Conclusions

We developed a multi-objective evolutionary design method capable of automated co-design of CNN topology and approximate multiplier(s). This is a challenging problem not addressed in the literature. On the standard CIFAR-10 classification benchmark, the CNNs co-optimized with approximate multipliers show excellent trade-offs between the classification accuracy and energy needed for multiplication in convolutional layers when compared with common ResNet CNNs utilizing 8-bit multipliers and CNNs optimized with the ALWANN method. Despite very limited computational resources, we demonstrated that it makes sense to co-optimize CNN architecture together with approximate arithmetic operations in a fully automated way.

Our future work will be devoted to extending the proposed method, employing more computational resources, and showing its effectiveness on more complex problems instances. In particular, we will extend the CGP array size whose current setting was chosen to be comparable with the ALWANN method. It also seems that we should primarily focus on optimizing the convolutional layers and leave the structure of fully connected layers frozen for the evolution.

Acknowledgements. This work was supported by the Czech science foundation project 21-13001S. The computational experiments were supported by The Ministry of Education, Youth and Sports from the Large Infrastructures for Research, Experimental Development and Innovations project "e-Infrastructure CZ – LM2018140".

References

1. Bergstra, J., Bengio, Y.: Random search for hyper-parameter optimization. J. Mach. Learn. Res. **13**(10), 281–305 (2012)
2. Capra, M., Bussolino, B., Marchisio, A., Shafique, M., Masera, G., Martina, M.: An updated survey of efficient hardware architectures for accelerating deep convolutional neural networks. Future Internet **12**(7), 113 (2020)
3. Deb, K., Pratap, A., Agarwal, S., Meyarivan, T.: A fast and elitist multiobjective genetic algorithm: NSGA-II. IEEE Trans. Evol. Comput. **6**(2), 182–197 (2002)
4. Elsken, T., Metzen, J.H., Hutter, F.: Neural architecture search: a survey. J. Mach. Learn. Res. **20**(55), 1–21 (2019)
5. Gysel, P., Pimentel, J., Motamedi, M., Ghiasi, S.: Ristretto: a framework for empirical study of resource-efficient inference in convolutional neural networks. IEEE Trans. Neural Netw. Learn. Syst. **29**(11), 5784–5789 (2018)
6. He, K., Zhang, X., Ren, S., Sun, J.: Identity mappings in deep residual networks. In: Leibe, B., Matas, J., Sebe, N., Welling, M. (eds.) ECCV 2016. LNCS, vol. 9908, pp. 630–645. Springer, Cham (2016). https://doi.org/10.1007/978-3-319-46493-0_38
7. Hsu, C., et al.: MONAS: multi-objective neural architecture search using reinforcement learning. CoRR abs/1806.10332 (2018). http://arxiv.org/abs/1806.10332
8. Jiang, W., Yang, L., Dasgupta, S., Hu, J., Shi, Y.: Standing on the shoulders of giants: hardware and neural architecture co-search with hot start (2020). https://arxiv.org/abs/2007.09087
9. Krizhevsky, A., Nair, V., Hinton, G.: CIFAR-10 (Canadian Institute for Advanced Research). http://www.cs.toronto.edu/~kriz/cifar.html
10. Liu, C., et al.: Progressive neural architecture search. In: Ferrari, V., Hebert, M., Sminchisescu, C., Weiss, Y. (eds.) ECCV 2018. LNCS, vol. 11205, pp. 19–35. Springer, Cham (2018). https://doi.org/10.1007/978-3-030-01246-5_2
11. Liu, H., Simonyan, K., Yang, Y.: DARTS: differentiable architecture search. CoRR abs/1806.09055 (2018). http://arxiv.org/abs/1806.09055
12. Lu, Z., et al.: NSGA-Net: neural architecture search using multi-objective genetic algorithm. In: Proceedings of the Genetic and Evolutionary Computation Conference, pp. 419–427. ACM (2019)
13. Miller, J.F.: Cartesian Genetic Programming. Springer, Heidelberg (2011). https://doi.org/10.1007/978-3-642-17310-3
14. Mrazek, V., Hrbacek, R., et al.: EvoApprox8b: library of approximate adders and multipliers for circuit design and benchmarking of approximation methods. In: Proceedings of DATE 2017, pp. 258–261 (2017)
15. Mrazek, V., Vasicek, Z., Sekanina, L., Hanif, A.M., Shafique, M.: ALWANN: automatic layer-wise approximation of deep neural network accelerators without retraining. In: Proceedings of the IEEE/ACM International Conference on Computer-Aided Design, pp. 1–8. IEEE (2019)

16. Panda, P., Sengupta, A., Sarwar, S.S., Srinivasan, G., Venkataramani, S., Raghunathan, A., Roy, K.: Invited - cross-layer approximations for neuromorphic computing: from devices to circuits and systems. In: 53nd Design Automation Conference, pp. 1–6. IEEE (2016). https://doi.org/10.1145/2897937.2905009
17. Real, E., et al.: Large-scale evolution of image classifiers. arXiv e-prints arXiv:1703.01041, March 2017
18. Sarwar, S.S., Venkataramani, S., Ankit, A., Raghunathan, A., Roy, K.: Energy-efficient neural computing with approximate multipliers. J. Emerg. Technol. Comput. Syst. **14**(2), 16:1–16:23 (2018)
19. Shorten, C., Khoshgoftaar, T.: A survey on image data augmentation for deep learning. J. Big Data **6**, 1–48 (2019)
20. Stanley, K.O., Clune, J., Lehman1, J., Miikkulainen, R.: Designing neural networks through neuroevolution. Nat. Mach. Intell. **1**, 24–35 (2019)
21. Stanley, K.O., Miikkulainen, R.: Evolving neural networks through augmenting topologies. Evol. Comput. **10**(2), 99–127 (2002)
22. Suganuma, M., Shirakawa, S., Nagao, T.: A genetic programming approach to designing convolutional neural network architectures. In: Proceedings of the Genetic and Evolutionary Computation Conference, GECCO 2017, pp. 497–504. ACM (2017)
23. Sze, V., Chen, Y., Yang, T., Emer, J.S.: Efficient processing of deep neural networks: a tutorial and survey. Proc. IEEE **105**(12), 2295–2329 (2017)
24. Tann, H., Hashemi, S., Reda, S.: Lightweight deep neural network accelerators using approximate SW/HW techniques. In: Reda, S., Shafique, M. (eds.) Approximate Circuits, pp. 289–305. Springer, Cham (2019). https://doi.org/10.1007/978-3-319-99322-5_14
25. Vaverka, F., Mrazek, V., Vasicek, Z., Sekanina, L.: TFApprox: towards a fast emulation of DNN approximate hardware accelerators on GPU. In: Design, Automation and Test in Europe, pp. 1–4 (2020)
26. Wistuba, M., Rawat, A., Pedapati, T.: A survey on neural architecture search. CoRR abs/1905.01392 (2019). http://arxiv.org/abs/1905.01392
27. Xie, L., Yuille, A.: Genetic CNN. In: 2017 IEEE International Conference on Computer Vision (ICCV), pp. 1388–1397. IEEE (2017)
28. Yao, X.: Evolving artificial neural networks. Proc. IEEE **87**(9), 1423–1447 (1999)
29. Zoph, B., Le, Q.V.: Neural architecture search with reinforcement learning. CoRR abs/1611.01578 (2016). http://arxiv.org/abs/1611.01578

Automatic Design of Deep Neural Networks Applied to Image Segmentation Problems

Ricardo Lima[1($\boxtimes$)], Aurora Pozo[1], Alexander Mendiburu[2],
and Roberto Santana[2]

[1] Federal University of Paraná, Curitiba, PR, Brazil
{rhrlima,aurora}@inf.ufpr.br
[2] University of the Basque Country UPV/EHU, San Sebastian, Spain
{alexander.mendiburu,roberto.santana}@ehu.eus

Abstract. A U-Net is a convolutional neural network mainly used for image segmentation domains such as medical image analysis. As other deep neural networks, the U-Net architecture influences the efficiency and accuracy of the network. We propose the use of a grammar-based evolutionary algorithm for the automatic design of deep neural networks for image segmentation tasks. The approach used is called Dynamic Structured Grammatical Evolution (DSGE), which employs a grammar to define the building blocks that are used to compose the networks, as well as the rules that help build them. We perform a set of experiments on the BSDS500 and ISBI12 datasets, designing networks tuned to image segmentation and edge detection. Subsequently, by using image similarity metrics, the results of our best performing networks are compared with the original U-Net. The results show that the proposed approach is able to design a network that is less complex in the number of trainable parameters, while also achieving slightly better results than the U-Net with a more consistent training.

Keywords: Genetic programming · Grammatical evolution · Neural architecture search · Deep learning · Edge detection

1 Introduction

Segmenting images consists of assigning a label to each pixel of an image in order to simplify the information, modifying it into a representation which is easier to analyze [32]. Pixels from a region are similar with respect to some characteristics, such as color, intensity, or texture, also, adjacent regions will be less similar regarding the same characteristics. Image Segmentation is commonly used to identify objects and boundaries (lines, curves, shapes, etc.), in images, and often applied to Medical [11,23,25,37], Security [2,8], and other modern systems, such as self-driving cars [31].

© Springer Nature Switzerland AG 2021
T. Hu et al. (Eds.): EuroGP 2021, LNCS 12691, pp. 98–113, 2021.
https://doi.org/10.1007/978-3-030-72812-0_7

Ronneberger and Fischer [28] proposed the U-Net, which was designed as a fully Convolutional Neural Network (CNN) for medical image segmentation, and it is basically composed of convolutional and pooling layers. The U-Net architecture follows, as the name suggests, a U-shaped structure, which gives the network the ability to re-use information from previous layers, through connections between both sides, in order to learn high-resolution features, and achieve higher accuracy values with limited datasets.

There are many challenges regarding the U-Net. As in any other network, the U-Net has a number of parameters that can be adjusted in order to fine tune its performance. Usually, a network is manually configured for each specific problem, and performing such a task can be very time-consuming. Some current studies [14,24,30], have been exploring and expanding the original U-Net architecture by changing parts of the network in order to achieve better results for the target problem.

Recently, Dynamic Structured Grammatical Evolution (DSGE) has been proposed for the design of CNNs [4,15,16], with the objective of offering more flexibility to the designed networks, and overcoming the issues faced by the traditional approach. DSGE is able to define the space of possible designs through a grammar that contains what we call building blocks. These building blocks can be combined in many different ways to construct an architecture which gives enough flexibility to reach a wider amount of architectures with simpler rules.

In this work, we investigate the use of DSGE towards the design of U-Nets. We use a symmetric grammar, proposed by [17], that offer an easy and flexible way to generate a variety of U-shaped networks. For our experiments, we apply the evolutionary algorithm for two image segmentation datasets, the BSDS500 and ISBI12, with the objective of searching for a network design that best performs in each dataset. Then, we compare the best designed networks with the original U-Net using 4 image similarity metrics.

In Sect. 2, we present a brief explanation about Image Segmentation and Edge detection, as well as the U-Net. Next, in Sect. 3, we present the DSGE. In Sect. 4 we present the proposed approach to design segmentation networks, including the grammar, genetic operators for the DSGE and quality metrics. In Sect. 5, the experiments are described and discussed. And finally, we present a summary of this work in Sect. 6, with some closing thoughts, and a proposal for future studies.

2 Related Work

2.1 Image Segmentation and Edge Detection

Edge detection is a fundamental tool used in most image processing applications to obtain information from the frames as a precursory step to feature extraction and object segmentation [1]. It includes a variety of methods that aim at identifying points in an image where the brightness changes sharply or, more formally, has discontinuities [36].

Edge detection techniques evolved from pioneering methods [9,26,27,34] based on low-level feature gradients, to techniques [3,10,12,22] that include manually designed features which are combined with learning based methods, and more recently, adopting deep-learning techniques [6,7,13,18,33].

Early operators, e.g., Sobel [34] and Canny [9], use the difference in intensity between the target and its surroundings to determine if the pixel is an edge or nonedge. Along with other pioneering methods, such as Roberts [27] and Prewitt [26], they are only dependent on low-level gradients. Their outputs contain many meaningless line segments, which have poor accuracy and cannot adapt to modern applications.

Later, local approaches combined manually designed features with learning-based methods, which enabled the inclusion of more information, such as color, texture and brightness. Martin [22] defined gradient operators for brightness, color, and texture, using them as input to a logistic regression classifier for predicting edge strength. Dollar [10] proposed an approach that selects a large number of features across different scales in order to train a discriminative model using the Probabilistic Boosting Tree classification algorithm.

Finally, Sun et al. [35] mention that it is hard to use low-level features to represent objects or semantic information, leading modern edge detectors to adopt deep-learning techniques.

2.2   U-Net

The U-Net was proposed by Ronneberger, Fischer and Brox [28], with the objective of overcoming the limitations of CNNs when dealing with image segmentation tasks. Classical CNNs have had limited success due to the size of available datasets and the size of the networks.

As it is mainly composed of convolutional and pooling layers, the U-Net is called a fully convolutional network (see Fig. 1). The architecture is divided into three main parts: the contracting path, the expansive path, and middle. It follows this unique U-shaped structure, in which some connections between layers are used to retrieve information from previous layers, to reconstruct the output image. The contracting path is responsible for learning basic shapes while down-sampling the image, following a typical convolutional network scheme. It does this by applying repetitions of 3×3 convolutional layers, each followed by a ReLU activation and a 2×2 max-pooling with stride 2 for down-sampling. The expansive path is then responsible for reconstructing the image, learning more complex features while also using information from previous layers. Each step consists of an up-sampling followed by a 2×2 convolution, a concatenation with the corresponding cropped image from the contracting path, and two 3×3 convolutions followed by a ReLU activation. Usually considered part of the contracting part, the middle part is composed of a few convolutional layers and dropout layers. The output of the network is given by a 1×1 convolutional layer, which performs the classification for each pixel through a Sigmoid activation function.

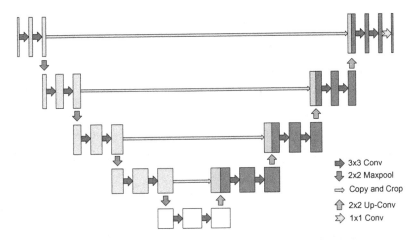

Fig. 1. Vanilla U-Net architecture.

3   Dynamic Structured Grammatical Evolution

Grammatical Evolution (GE) is considered one of the most relevant variants of Genetic Programming (GP) approaches [21]. However, it has two major issues related to locality and redundancy. The first regards the situation where small modifications to the genotype can lead to big modifications in the phenotype. The latter leads to situations where different genotypes can map to the same phenotype. Both situations affect the evolutionary process negatively, by wasting time and resources with solutions of poor quality, resembling random search.

Dynamic Structured Grammatical Evolution (DSGE) [5,19] is an improved version of GE, which is an evolutionary approach with the ability to evolve programs using an arbitrary language [29]. DSGE was proposed to address known problems with low locality and redundancy present in the original approach. Moreover, it proposes a different encoding for solutions, which affects how the grammar and mapping function work, being more efficient during the search process.

3.1   Grammar

The grammar is defined by a tuple $G = (N, T, S, P)$, where N is a non-empty set of non-terminal symbols, T is a non-empty set of terminal symbols, S is an element of N called axiom and used as the start rule, and P is a set of productions of the form $A ::= \alpha$, with $A \in N$ and $\alpha \in (N \cup T)^*$, N and T are disjoint [20].

Figure 2 shows an example of a simple grammar. The set N of non-terminals contains $\{start, expr, op, term\}$, the set of terminals T contains $\{+, -, *, /, x1, 0.5\}$, and the axiom S is given by the non-terminal $start$.

$$\langle start \rangle ::= \langle expr \rangle \langle op \rangle \langle expr \rangle \mid \langle expr \rangle$$

$$\langle expr \rangle ::= \langle term \rangle \langle op \rangle \langle term \rangle \mid (\langle term \rangle \langle op \rangle \langle term \rangle)$$

$$\langle op \rangle ::= + \mid - \mid / \mid *$$

$$\langle term \rangle ::= x1 \mid 0.5$$

Fig. 2. Example of a grammar for mathematical expressions.

3.2 DSGE Encoding

The solutions in DSGE are encoded as a list of lists, rather than a single list in classical GE, where each internal list is directly connected to one non-terminal symbol from the grammar (see Fig. 3). The length of a solution is defined by the number of non-terminals in the grammar. Moreover, the size of each internal list will depend on the number of values needed to perform a complete map, and the values will depend on the number of options for each rule. For example, the non-terminal <op> has four options $(+, -, *, /)$, so the possible values range from 0 to 3.

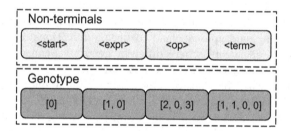

Fig. 3. DSGE encoding. Each list of integers in the genotype is related to a non-terminal.

3.3 Mapping

After the solutions have been created, by random sampling or resulting from the combinations of others solutions, the mapping is responsible for translating a solution into an executable program. What it does is, starting from the axiom, perform a grammar expansion, always replacing the leftmost non-terminal by one of its productions. The values are selected from the list related to the non-terminal being evaluated. For example, if the left-most terminal is <expr>, the values will be extracted from the list [1, 0] as in Fig. 3. Moreover, the values for each non-terminal are sampled respecting the number of options, which removes the need for using the mod operator as in classical GE.

Considering the solution present in Fig. 3, the mapping would happen as in Fig. 4. Starting from the axiom <start>, the first value from the first list is

Derivation step	Integers left
<start>	[[0], [1, 0], [2, 0, 3], [1, 1, 0, 0]]
<expr><op><expr>	[[], [1, 0], [2, 0, 3], [1, 1, 0, 0]]
(<term><op><term>)<op><expr>	[[], [0], [2, 0, 3], [1, 1, 0, 0]]
(0.5 <op><expr>)<op><expr>	[[], [0], [2, 0, 3], [1, 0, 0]]
(0.5 / <term>)<op><expr>	[[], [0], [0, 3], [1, 0, 0]]
(0.5 / 0.5)<op><expr>	[[], [0], [0, 3], [0, 0]]
(0.5 / 0.5) + <expr>	[[], [0], [3], [0, 0]]
(0.5 / 0.5) + <expr><op><term>	[[], [], [3], [0, 0]]
(0.5 / 0.5) + x1 <op><term>	[[], [], [3], [0]]
(0.5 / 0.5) + x1 * <term>	[[], [], [], [0]]
(0.5 / 0.5) + x1 * x1	[[], [], [], []]

Fig. 4. Mapping process using the DSGE encoding.

consumed, which is related to the non-terminal <start>. The value is 0, which means that the non-terminal will be replaced by the production (according to Grammar 2) <expr><op><exp>. To follow, the next non-terminal is <expr>, and the next value related to this non-terminal is 1, which will replace <expr> by the production (<term><op><term>). The mapping procedure repeats these steps until all the values are used, and there are no non-terminals left.

3.4 Search Engine

Commonly, a Genetic Algorithm (GA) is used as the search engine, where a population of randomly generated solutions is evolved with the application of genetic operators that introduces new solutions. However, in DSGE, the genetic operators are modified to work with the new encoding.

Base parameters remain the same, such as population size, number of generations, selection, and replacement. In the mutation operator, one random value is selected from the solution to be replaced by a new one, considering the possible values according to the evaluated non-terminal. For the crossover operator, the "cut" point is chosen among the non-terminals, and two new solutions are generated by combining these parts. New solutions might not have the required number of values to accomplish a complete map. In these cases, the solution is repaired by adding random values as necessary or removing unused ones.

4 Automatic Design of U-Nets

In our approach, we use a grammar that defines the building blocks and hyperparameters that can be used to compose the networks. For designing U-shape architectures, we introduce a mirror-grammar that was proposed in a previous work [17]. It allowed us to design U-Nets with broader variety regarding the overall structure and components, while also achieving a low probability of producing invalid models during generation.

4.1   U-Net Mirror Grammar

The mirror-grammar we use is presented in Fig. 5. It is able to generate architectures that respect the specific structural characteristics of the U-Nets, finding a balance between the original aspects of the network and the possibility of exploring new designs.

This grammar assumes the U-Net as a symmetric structure, thus, it is used to design only the contracting and middle parts of the network, and then build the expanding path by exploiting the symmetry. By representing in each solution only half of the network, the representation complexity is reduced and we also decrease the chances of producing invalid connections between layers, having better control of the parameters.

$\langle unet \rangle ::= \langle conv \rangle \; \langle next \rangle$

$\langle next \rangle ::= \langle conv \rangle \; \langle next \rangle \mid \langle dropout \rangle \; \langle next \rangle \mid \langle pool \rangle \; \langle nextp \rangle \mid$ bridge $\langle pool \rangle \; \langle nextp \rangle$

$\langle nextp \rangle ::= \langle conv \rangle \; \langle next \rangle \mid \langle middle \rangle$

$\langle middle \rangle ::= \langle middle \rangle \; \langle middle \rangle \mid \langle conv \rangle \mid \langle dropout \rangle$

$\langle conv \rangle ::=$ conv $\langle filters \rangle \; \langle k\_size \rangle \; \langle strides \rangle \; \langle padding \rangle \; \langle activ \rangle$

$\langle pool \rangle ::= \langle p\_type \rangle \; \langle strides \rangle \; \langle padding \rangle \; \langle padding \rangle$

$\langle dropout \rangle ::=$ dropout $\langle rate \rangle$

$\langle p\_type \rangle ::=$ maxpool $\mid$ avgpool

$\langle filters \rangle ::= 2 \mid 4 \mid 8 \mid ... \mid 64$

$\langle k\_size \rangle ::= 1 \mid 2 \mid ... \mid 6$

$\langle strides \rangle ::= 1 \mid 2$

$\langle padding \rangle ::=$ valid $\mid$ same

$\langle activ \rangle ::=$ relu $\mid$ sigmoid $\mid$ linear

$\langle rate \rangle ::= [0.0, \, 0.5]$

Fig. 5. U-Net mirror grammar

Building the expanding path takes the pre-built structure generated from the grammar expansion, and then, for each existing node, starting from the end, new layers are added to the expanding path, considering the type of node analyzed. For example, if the analyzed node is a convolutional layer, a copy of it is added to the expanding path. For pooling layers, an up-sample and a 2×2 convolutional layer are added, working as a deconvolutional layer to reconstruct the image. Moreover, the input, classification (2×2 convolutional), and output (1×1 convolutional with sigmoid activation) layers are added to the network. After this building process, a repair function is used to ensure that the connections between the nodes are correct, i.e., the input dimension to the current node matches the output dimensions of connected nodes, so the expanding path will have no problems with reconstructing the image. It checks for unmatching layer connections, changing parameters as necessary to correct it. More details on the repair function can be found in [17].

4.2   Genetic Operators

There are four basic genetic operators in an evolutionary algorithm: the selection, crossover, mutation, and replacement. In our approach, we used a different strategy for the recombination operators. Rather than applying both crossover and mutation operators with a certain possibility, we only apply either the crossover, or the mutation.

The selection operator we use is the Tournament. For the replacement, we simply replace the parents population by the offspring population maintaining a percentage, defined by the user, of elite solutions from the parents population.

The crossover operator selects a random point on the parent solution (Fig. 6), and then creates a new solution combining the first part (entire internal lists) from one parent and the second part from the other parent.

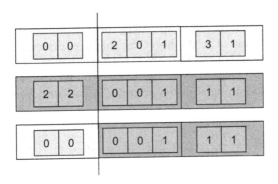

Fig. 6. DSGE crossover example.

The mutation operator we use changes one random chosen value for another valid one. The difference here is that it is only applied to portions of the solution that have non-terminal rules, those, rules that will lead to other non-terminals (Fig. 7). This way, the operator becomes much more impactful, since changes on non-terminal rules can heavily affect the whole architecture of the network.

4.3   Evaluation

First, each solution is mapped into an actual deep neural network and executed using the dataset of the problem being solved. The network is trained for a

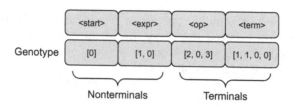

Fig. 7. This encoding is divided according to the Grammar 2 in components that are be related to nonterminals, and components related to terminals.

number of epochs using the training portion of the dataset. Then, the accuracy is calculated over the validation portion of the dataset.

For image segmentation tasks, the accuracy can be calculated using image similarity metrics. Since there is a variety of metrics, each one focuses on different characteristics of the image to calculate how similar two images are. Here, we introduce four metrics: Jaccard, Dice, Sensitivity, and Specificity. The Jaccard coefficient (Jacc, Eq. 1), also known as Intersection over Union, is a statistic used for gauging the similarity and diversity of sample sets. The Dice coefficient (DCS, Eq. 2) is similar to the Jaccard but more popular in image segmentation tasks. We also use the well-known Sensitivity and Specificity metrics. Sensitivity, or true positive rate (TPR, Eq. 3), measures the proportion of actual positives that are correctly identified as such (e.g., the percentage of foreground pixels correctly identified as foreground). Specificity, or true negative rate (TNR, Eq. 4), measures the proportion of actual negatives that are correctly identified as such (e.g., the percentage of background pixels correctly identified as background).

The fitness is then calculated as a weighted average (Eq. 5) of the presented metrics. The weights can be adjusted according to either how easy or hard is to satisfy each metric.

$$Jacc = \frac{|A \cap B|}{|A \cup B|} \quad (1) \qquad DCS = \frac{2|A \cap B|}{|A| + |B|} \quad (2)$$

$$TPR = \frac{TP}{TP + FN} \quad (3) \qquad TNR = \frac{TN}{TN + FP} \quad (4)$$

$$fitness = \frac{a * Jacc + b * DCS + c * TPR + d * TNR}{a + b + c + d} \quad (5)$$

5   Experiments

For the experiments, we focused on testing the performance of our grammar-based approach and compare the results to the original U-Net, regarding image segmentation tasks. First, our approach is executed on two problems, one of edge detection using the BSDS500 dataset, and the other is a segmentation problem, using the ISBI12 dataset. Both datasets are used to create and evolve a population of networks, and return the one design that best performed during the evolutionary process. Then, we re-execute the best performing network, one per dataset, for a higher number of epochs, aiming to reach the potential of its architecture. Finally, we compare the re-trained networks with the original U-Net, using the image similarity metrics described in Sect. 4.3.

5.1   BSDS500 Dataset

The Berkeley Segmentation Dataset and Benchmark[1] (BSDS) is a large dataset of natural images (see Fig. 8) that have been segmented by human observers. This dataset serves as ground truth for learning grouping cues as well as a benchmark for comparing different segmentation and boundary finding algorithms.

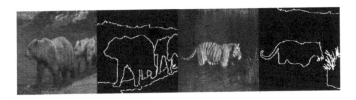

Fig. 8. Examples extracted from the BSDS500 dataset, along with their respective contour images.

The dataset is divided into the three sets usually used for learning approaches, the training, validation and test sets, with 200, 100, 200 images respectively. As the images do not share the same width and height across the dataset, we resized both the image and its corresponding contour image, to the size of 256×256 pixels. The pixels were also normalized to values between $[0, 1]$, by dividing everything by 255, to facilitate the manipulation and calculating the quality metrics.

5.2   ISBI12 Dataset

The serial section Transmission Electron Microscopy (ssTEM) dataset[2] is a set of 60 images, along with their ground truth segmentation, 512×512 pixels grayscale, divided into 30 images for training, and 30 for test. For the proposed experiments, we applied data augmentation techniques in order to enlarge the dataset. In total, we provide 300 images for training, 30 for validation, and 30 for test, all resized to 256×256 pixels.

---

[1] https://www2.eecs.berkeley.edu/Research/Projects/CS/vision/bsds/.

[2] http://brainiac2.mit.edu/isbi_challenge/.

5.3 Evolutionary Optimization

Our evolutionary approach was executed a total of 5 times per dataset, generating 5 different networks tuned specifically for segmenting images. The parameters used for the evolution are presented in Table 1. We used a population of 20 randomly generated networks, evolved through 25 generations, resulting in about 500 different networks. For the genetic operators, we apply either crossover or mutation, with 60% chance of applying the crossover, and 40% for the mutation. During the evolutionary process, the models were trained for 10 epochs, with the quality of the network being calculated using the validation set. At the end, the best performing model is delivered, and re-trained for 500 epochs, now having its performance calculated on the test data.

To compare the approaches, we used the same image similarity metrics we use to compute the quality of the networks during the evolution. As mentioned in Sect. 4.3, we used four metrics, Jaccard Index, Dice index, Sensitivity and Specificity, as well as a weighted mean of the four, giving a weight of 0.4 to Dice and Sensitivity and 0.1 to Jaccard and Specificity. The reason behind this was because the two metrics with smaller weights were too simple or too difficult to satisfy, giving less valuable feedback to the network.

Table 1. Parameters of the Evolutionary Algorithm

Parameter	Value	Parameter	Value
Population size	20	Generations	25
Crossover	60%	Mutation	40%
Tournament size	3	# of Elites	10%
Model Epochs	10/500	Model time limit	60 min

5.4 Results

Table 2 presents the image similarity metrics computed between the predictions and the ground truth, of the U-Net, the best evolved U-Net, and the mean metrics for all evolved networks, over the test set. For the BSDS500 dataset, the Specificity and Sensitivity had a greater impact on the weighted average, while the Dice and mainly the Jaccard index were more difficult to satisfy. According to the weighted average, the best evolved network is presented as slightly better than the original U-Net. Moreover, for the ISBI12 dataset, the Jaccard and Dice indexes had a bigger influence, compared to the BSDS500. Once again, the best Evolved network achieved a higher weighted average than the U-Net. For both datasets, the Dice index was the metric that differed the most, meaning that this metric was easier to satisfy on the ISBI12 dataset (segmentation problem), rather than the BSDS500 (edge detection). In general, the best evolved network is presented as a better solution than the original U-Net, although the mean among all evolved networks presented worse performance. The one design that achieved the best performance is also a smaller, less complex, and faster network to train, as it has 29,685 parameters, compared to the 31,032,837 from the U-Net.

Table 2. Similarity metrics for each dataset.

BSDS500					
Model	Jaccard	Dice	Specificity	Sensitivity	Weighted Avg
Evolved (best)	0.06	0.40	1.00	0.99	0.52
Evolved (mean)	0.06	0.26	1.00	0.99	0.47
UNET	0.06	0.38	1.00	0.99	0.51
ISBI12					
Model	Jaccard	Dice	Specificity	Sensitivity	Weighted Avg
Evolved (best)	0.54	0.87	0.69	0.99	0.85
Evolved (mean)	0.54	0.82	0.74	0.99	0.82
UNET	0.54	0.85	0.59	1.00	0.84

Figures 9 and 10 show the accuracy and loss function values over the 500 epochs of re-training of our best designed network, both best and mean runs, and the U-Net. The U-Net was able to achieve the best results in both accuracy and loss during the training, however, the same did not happen on the validation set. On the other hand, the evolved network was able to maintain consistent progress on the training and validation. Even though it did not achieve an accuracy close to the U-Net on the training, the performance on the validation was very close, along with the fact that the evolved network also produced low values on the loss function.

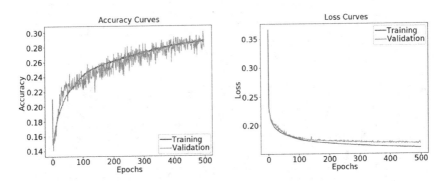

Fig. 9. Accuracy and Loss curves, for training and validation, of the best evolved architecture on the BSDS500 dataset.

Regarding the images produced by the networks, the examples in Fig. 11 show the differences between our evolved network and the U-Net. In general, the U-Net

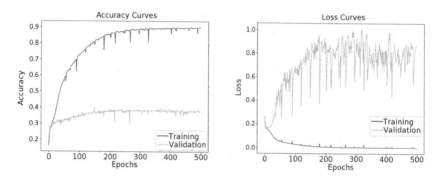

Fig. 10. Accuracy and Loss curves, for training and validation, of the U-Net architecture on the BSDS500 dataset.

Fig. 11. Examples from segmented images. The first row shows the original colored image. The second row presents the ground truth segmentation, followed by the segmentation of our evolved network in the third row and, in the last row, the segmentation of the U-Net.

was able to produce clearer lines for the contours, and capture the overall shape of the images. On the other hand, the evolved network was able to capture smaller details, being much richer in terms of information. Comparing these results to the original image and ground truth, the U-Net obtained results that are closer to the ground truth segmentation, however, the evolved network presented results that are closer to the original image, in terms of details.

6   Conclusion

The main objective of this study was to test the viability of designing deep neural networks for image segmentation tasks, and compare their results with a well-known architecture, the U-Net. To accomplish this, we used DSGE, an evolutionary grammar-based approach, along with a symmetric grammar, designed to compose a variety of networks that follows the characteristics of the U-Net. The proposed approach was tested in two real world datasets, the BSDS500 for edge detection, and the ISBI12 for image segmentation. From the experiments, we were able to obtain an architecture that performed better when compared to the U-Net in both datasets. The evolved architecture presented a smaller, and consequently faster, network in terms of number of parameters. It also presented a much more consistent performance in both training and test, regarding the accuracy and loss functions, when compared to the U-Net.

Despite the positive results, there are still many directions in which this study can be further explored, including improving the search process, decreasing the computational cost of the approach, as well as expanding the amount of networks that can be built, and testing on other domains.

Acknowledgments. This work was partially supported by Brazilian Education Ministry – CAPES and Brazilian Research Council – CNPq.

A. Mendiburu and R. Santana acknowledge support by the Spanish Ministry of Science and Innovation (projects TIN2016-78365-R and PID2019-104966GB-l00), and the Basque Government (projects KK-2020/00049 and IT1244-19, and ELKARTEK program).

References

1. Al-Amri, S.S., Kalyankar, N., Khamitkar, S.: Image segmentation by using edge detection. Int. J. Comput. Sci. Eng. **2**(3), 804–807 (2010)
2. Al-Zu'bi, S., Hawashin, B., Mughaid, A., Baker, T.: Efficient 3D medical image segmentation algorithm over a secured multimedia network. Multimedia Tools Appl. 1–19 (2020). https://doi.org/10.1007/s11042-020-09160-6
3. Arbelaez, P., Maire, M., Fowlkes, C., Malik, J.: Contour detection and hierarchical image segmentation. IEEE Trans. Pattern Anal. Mach. Intell. **33**(5), 898–916 (2010)
4. Assunçao, F., Lourenço, N., Machado, P., Ribeiro, B.: Towards the evolution of multi-layered neural networks: a dynamic structured grammatical evolution approach. In: Proceedings of the Genetic and Evolutionary Computation Conference, pp. 393–400. ACM (2017)

5. Assunçao, F., Lourenço, N., Machado, P., Ribeiro, B.: DENSER: deep evolutionary network structured representation. Genet. Program. Evolvable Mach. **20**(1), 5–35 (2019). https://doi.org/10.1007/s10710-018-9339-y
6. Bertasius, G., Shi, J., Torresani, L.: DeepEdge: a multi-scale bifurcated deep network for top-down contour detection. In: Proceedings of the 2015 IEEE Conference on Computer Vision and Pattern Recognition (CVPR 2015), pp. 4380–4389 (2015)
7. Bertasius, G., Shi, J., Torresani, L.: High-for-low and low-for-high: efficient boundary detection from deep object features and its applications to high-level vision. In: Proceedings of the 2015 IEEE International Conference on Computer Vision (CVPR 2015), pp. 504–512 (2015)
8. Bian, S., Xu, X., Jiang, W., Shi, Y., Sato, T.: BUNET: blind medical image segmentation based on secure UNET. In: Martel, A.L., et al. (eds.) MICCAI 2020. LNCS, vol. 12262, pp. 612–622. Springer, Cham (2020). https://doi.org/10.1007/978-3-030-59713-9_59
9. Canny, J.: A computational approach to edge detection. IEEE Trans. Pattern Anal. Mach. Intell. **6**, 679–698 (1986)
10. Dollár, P., Zitnick, C.L.: Structured forests for fast edge detection. In: Proceedings of the 2013 IEEE International Conference on Computer Vision (ICCV 2013), pp. 1841–1848 (2013)
11. Drozdzal, M., Vorontsov, E., Chartrand, G., Kadoury, S., Pal, C.: The importance of skip connections in biomedical image segmentation. In: Carneiro, G., et al. (eds.) LABELS/DLMIA -2016. LNCS, vol. 10008, pp. 179–187. Springer, Cham (2016). https://doi.org/10.1007/978-3-319-46976-8_19
12. Hallman, S., Fowlkes, C.C.: Oriented edge forests for boundary detection. In: Proceedings of the 2015 IEEE Conference on Computer Vision and Pattern Recognition (CVPR 2015), pp. 1732–1740 (2015)
13. Kivinen, J., Williams, C., Heess, N.: Visual boundary prediction: a deep neural prediction network and quality dissection. In: Artificial Intelligence and Statistics, pp. 512–521 (2014)
14. Kumar, A., Murthy, O.N., Ghosal, P., Mukherjee, A., Nandi, D., et al.: A dense U-Net architecture for multiple sclerosis lesion segmentation. In: Proceedings of the 2019 IEEE Region 10 Conference (TENCON 2019), pp. 662–667. IEEE (2019)
15. Lima, R.H.R., Pozo, A.T.R.: A study on auto-configuration of multi-objective particle swarm optimization algorithm. In: Proceedings of the 2017 IEEE Congress on Evolutionary Computation (CEC 2017), pp. 718–725. IEEE (2017)
16. Lima, R.H.R., Pozo, A.T.R.: Evolving convolutional neural networks through grammatical evolution. In: Proceedings of the 2019 Genetic and Evolutionary Computation Conference (GECCO 2019), pp. 179–180. ACM (2019)
17. Lima, R.H.R., Pozo, A.T.R., Mendiburu, A., Santana, R.: A Symmetric grammar approach for designing segmentation models. In: Proceedings of the 2020 IEEE Congress on Evolutionary Computation (CEC 2020), pp. 1–8. IEEE (2020)
18. Liu, Y., Cheng, M.M., Hu, X., Wang, K., Bai, X.: Richer convolutional features for edge detection. In: Proceedings of the 2017 IEEE Conference on Computer Vision and Pattern Recognition (CVPR 2017), pp. 3000–3009 (2017)
19. Lourenço, N., Assunção, F., Pereira, F.B., Costa, E., Machado, P.: Structured grammatical evolution: a dynamic approach. In: Ryan, C., O'Neill, M., Collins, J.J. (eds.) Handbook of Grammatical Evolution. LNCS, pp. 137–161. Springer, Cham (2018). https://doi.org/10.1007/978-3-319-78717-6_6
20. Lourenço, N., Pereira, F., Costa, E.: Evolving evolutionary algorithms. In: Proceedings of the 14th Annual Conference Companion on Genetic and Evolutionary Computation (GECCO 2012), pp. 51–58. ACM (2012)

21. Lourenço, N., Pereira, F.B., Costa, E.: Unveiling the properties of structured grammatical evolution. Genet. Program. Evolvable Mach. **17**(3), 251–289 (2016). https://doi.org/10.1007/s10710-015-9262-4

22. Martin, D.R., Fowlkes, C.C., Malik, J.: Learning to detect natural image boundaries using local brightness, color, and texture cues. Proc. IEEE Trans. Pattern Anal. Mach. Intell. (TPAMI) **26**(5), 530–549 (2004)

23. Milletari, F., Navab, N., Ahmadi, S.: V-Net: fully convolutional neural networks for volumetric medical image segmentation. In: 2016 Fourth International Conference on 3D Vision (3DV 2016), pp. 565–571 (2016)

24. Mirunalini, P., Aravindan, C., Nambi, A.T., Poorvaja, S., Priya, V.P.: Segmentation of coronary arteries from CTA axial slices using deep learning techniques. In: Proceedings of the 2019 IEEE Region 10 Conference (TENCON 2019), pp. 2074–2080. IEEE (2019)

25. Oktay, O., et al.: Anatomically constrained neural networks (ACNNs): application to cardiac image enhancement and segmentation. IEEE Trans. Med. Imaging **37**(2), 384–395 (2018)

26. Prewitt, J.M.: Object enhancement and extraction. Picture Process. Psychopictorics **10**(1), 15–19 (1970)

27. Roberts, L.G.: Machine perception of three-dimensional solids. Ph.D. thesis, Massachusetts Institute of Technology (1963)

28. Ronneberger, O., Fischer, P., Brox, T.: U-Net: convolutional networks for biomedical image segmentation. In: Navab, N., Hornegger, J., Wells, W.M., Frangi, A.F. (eds.) MICCAI 2015. LNCS, vol. 9351, pp. 234–241. Springer, Cham (2015). https://doi.org/10.1007/978-3-319-24574-4_28

29. Ryan, C., Collins, J.J., Neill, M.O.: Grammatical evolution: evolving programs for an arbitrary language. In: Banzhaf, W., Poli, R., Schoenauer, M., Fogarty, T.C. (eds.) EuroGP 1998. LNCS, vol. 1391, pp. 83–96. Springer, Heidelberg (1998). https://doi.org/10.1007/BFb0055930

30. Sabarinathan, D., Beham, M.P., Roomi, S., et al.: Hyper vision net: kidney tumor segmentation using coordinate convolutional layer and attention unit. arXiv preprint arXiv:1908.03339 (2019)

31. Sagar, A., Soundrapandiyan, R.: Semantic segmentation with multi scale spatial attention for self driving cars. arXiv preprint arXiv:2007.12685 (2020)

32. Shapiro, L.G., Stockman, G.C.: Computer Vision. Prentice-Hall, New Jersey (2001)

33. Shen, W., Wang, X., Wang, Y., Bai, X., Zhang, Z.: DeepContour: a deep convolutional feature learned by positive-sharing loss for contour detection. In: Proceedings of the 2015 IEEE Conference on Computer Vision and Pattern Recognition (CVPR 2015), pp. 3982–3991 (2015)

34. Sobel, I.: Camera models and machine perception. Technical report, Computer Science Department, Technion (1972)

35. Sun, W., You, S., Walker, J., Li, K., Barnes, N.: Structural edge detection: a dataset and benchmark. In: Proceedings of the 2018 Digital Image Computing: Techniques and Applications (DICTA 2018), pp. 1–8. IEEE (2018)

36. Umbaugh, S.E.: Digital Image Processing and Analysis: Human and Computer Vision Applications with CVIPtools. CRC Press, Boca Raton (2010)

37. Wang, G., et al.: Interactive medical image segmentation using deep learning with image-specific fine tuning. IEEE Trans. Med. Imaging **37**(7), 1562–1573 (2018)

On the Influence of Grammars on Crossover in Grammatical Evolution

Dirk Schweim$^{(\boxtimes)}$ (iD)

Johannes Gutenberg University, Mainz, Germany
schweim@uni-mainz.de
https://wi.bwl.uni-mainz.de/

Abstract. Standard grammatical evolution (GE) uses a one-point crossover (*"ripple crossover"*) that exchanges codons between two genotypes. The two resulting genotypes are then mapped to their respective phenotypes using a Backus-Naur form grammar. This article studies how different types of grammars affect the resulting individuals of a ripple crossover. We distinguish different grammars based on the expected number of non-terminals chosen when mapping genotype codons to phenotypes, B_{avg}. The grammars only differ in B_{avg} but can express the same phenotypes. We perform crossover operations on the genotypes and find that grammars with $B_{avg} > 1$ lead to high numbers of either very small trees or invalid individuals. Due to the re-sampling of the invalid individuals, the algorithmic runtime is higher compared to grammars with a small B_{avg}, despite being able to express the same phenotypes. In grammars with $B_{avg} \leq 1$, the bias towards small trees is reduced and instead, the frequency of valid large trees is increased. Our results give insights on favorable grammar designs and underline the central role of grammar design in GE.

Keywords: Grammatical evolution · Grammar design · Representation · Bias

1 Introduction

Grammatical evolution (GE) [22,29] is an evolutionary algorithm that uses a grammar in Backus-Naur form (BNF) to map the genotypes (variable-length binary strings) to corresponding phenotypes (e.g., computer programs or mathematical expressions). Often, crossover is applied as an operator to recombine genotypes. After crossover, the offspring genotypes are mapped to the corresponding phenotypes using the BNF grammar. Therefore, grammar design plays a central role in the success of crossover. In this article, we study the role of grammars in GE's one-point crossover (also called *ripple crossover*).

Parts of this research were conducted using the supercomputer Mogon offered by Johannes Gutenberg University Mainz (hpc.uni-mainz.de). The authors gratefully acknowledge the computing time granted on Mogon.

© Springer Nature Switzerland AG 2021
T. Hu et al. (Eds.): EuroGP 2021, LNCS 12691, pp. 114–129, 2021.
https://doi.org/10.1007/978-3-030-72812-0_8

In our experiments, we compare grammars that are able to express the same phenotypes but differ in the expected number of non-terminals chosen during mapping. First, we perform a static analysis where we compare large parent populations with the respective offspring populations, only using crossover and no selection. After that, we observe algorithm behavior over multiple generations and also take selection into account. We find that grammars with a high expected number of non-terminals (B_{avg}) lead to a strong bias towards very small trees and hardly map to large trees. Furthermore, these grammars lead to a high number of invalid individuals and, in effect, an increased algorithmic runtime due to re-sampling. In grammars with $B_{avg} \leq 1$, the bias towards small trees is reduced and instead, the frequency of valid large trees is increased.

In Sect. 2, we describe mapping, crossover, and grammar design in GE. The experiments and results are presented and discussed in Sect. 3. We end the article with concluding remarks on our findings and an overview of future work.

2 Grammatical Evolution

We discuss previous work on mapping, crossover, and grammar design in GE.

2.1 Mapping

In GE, we differentiate between the genotype representation (variable-length binary strings) and a corresponding phenotype representation (e.g., computer programs or mathematical expressions) [22,29]. To derive the phenotype representation of a particular genotype ("mapping"), a BNF grammar is used. The grammar consists of four finite sets—non-terminals N, terminals T ($N \cap T = \emptyset$), production rules P, and a start symbol S.

Independent of the genotype, deriving the phenotype from a genotype starts with the start symbol S, where S is a non-terminal ($S \in N$). Then, derivations for all non-terminals are recursively determined. Derivations can be terminals $t \in T$, non-terminals $n \in N$, or combinations of terminals and non-terminals in the form of a sequence (functions[1]). The possible derivations for every non-terminal $n \in N$ are defined by production rules $p \in P$. If more than one derivation exists for a non-terminal, the codons of the genotype are used to determine the respective derivation. A decision is made by determining the modulo of the integer codon value and the number of derivations for n. The resulting number indicates the derivation of n.

Mapping ends when the recursive process of determining the derivation for all non-terminals finishes or if no more codons are left. If the derivation can not be finished, the fitness of the respective individual is set to a high value.

The mapping can be visualized by a derivation tree (also called parse tree) where the root node represents the non-terminal start symbol S. Each node

---

[1] Unlike genetic programming [10], in GE no function set exists, but functions are defined by sequences of terminals and non-terminals.

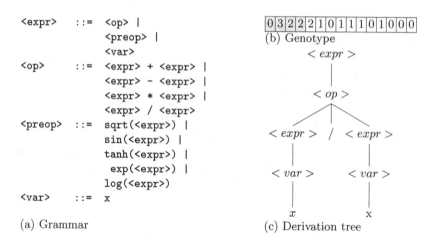

(a) Grammar

(b) Genotype

(c) Derivation tree

Fig. 1. A grammar in BNF, a genotype, and a corresponding derivation tree

that represents a non-terminal in the derivation tree has at least one child node that represents the respective derivation. All leaf nodes of the derivation tree represent terminals.

Figure 1(a) shows an example of a grammar in BNF for a symbolic regression problem with the start symbol $<expr>$. The grammar defines four production rules that map non-terminals to at least one possible derivation. For example, the production rule for the non-terminal $<var>$ maps to only one derivation, the terminal symbol x. Multiple derivations are separated by using the symbol $|$. Examples of functions can be found in the production rules for the non-terminals $<op>$ and $<preop>$, e.g., $<expr> + <expr>$ and $sin(<expr>)$. Furthermore, Fig. 1(b) shows a genotype. The genotype and the grammar are used to determine the derivation tree (Fig. 1(c)) in a depth-first, left to right order. Codons that are used during mapping are called the *effective part* of the genotype [16]—these codons are colored grey in Fig. 1(b). Codons not used when the genotype is mapped to the phenotype are called introns [23,29,35]. Since introns can only be observed at the end of the genotype [1,23,26] they form *"non-coding tails"* [16] (colored white in Fig. 1(b)).

2.2 Crossover

Similar to GAs, standard GE uses a variable length, one-point crossover operator that is applied to genotypes: first, two individuals are randomly selected in a population. Second, a crossover point in each of the genotypes is selected randomly and independently for both individuals. Then, the codons on the right side of the crossover points are exchanged between the individuals.

Unlike standard crossover in GP, crossover in GE can lead to multiple new subtrees in the offspring individuals, whereas in GP one subtree (a set of linked nodes) per individual is exchanged between the two parent individuals.

This is the reason why GE's standard crossover operator has been called *"ripple crossover"* [9,25]. Figure 2 shows an example of the "ripple" effect of crossover in GE (based on the examples presented in [9,25]). The figure shows an example grammar (Fig. 2(a)) and a genotype (Fig. 2(b)). The genotype is mapped to the derivation tree (Fig. 2(c)) in a depth-first, left to right order using the grammar. In Figs. 2(b) and (c) a possible crossover point is marked by a blue line. After cutting the codons on the right side of the crossover point, the mapping from the genotype to the phenotype can not be finished—two subtrees in the derivation tree have been deleted (Fig. 2(d)). As a consequence, some nodes in the derivation tree represent non-terminals without child nodes (*"ripple sites"* [9,25]). The derivation tree with ripple sites is called *"spine"* [9,25].

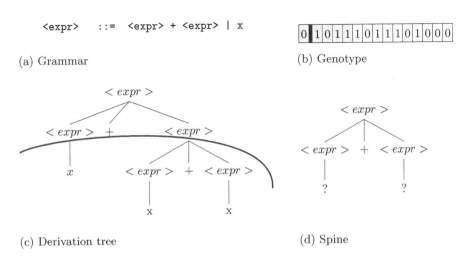

(a) Grammar

(b) Genotype

(c) Derivation tree

(d) Spine

Fig. 2. Example for the "ripple" effect of crossover in GE (based on [9,25])

Multiple studies found that a large number of introns hinder crossover (and mutation) from finding new individuals [12,19,20,22,23,27,29,35]. The reason is that codons are chosen with uniform probabilities during crossover or mutation—if there is a large number of introns compared to the number of codons in the effective part [16], introns are chosen with high probabilities as crossover or mutation points, resulting in offspring identical to their parents on the phenotype level [29]. Thus, in standard GE, variation operators often have no immediate effect on the phenotype when there is a high number of introns. Therefore, today, crossover is usually restricted to the effective part of the genotype (see modern GE implementations such as PonyGE2 [2], GEVA [18], and LibGE [17]).

Castle and Johnson [1] investigate the positional effect of ripple crossover and find that crossover applied at the beginning of the effective part of the genotype often results in large changes in the phenotype. These large changes often lead to decreasing fitness values. However, due to their exploring effect, these often destructive changes can sometimes still be useful. Crossover operations at the end of the effective part of the genotype on the other hand are less explorative and often lead to (phenoytpically) identical individuals [1].

Ripple crossover was compared to sub-tree crossover in [9,24,25]. Search using ripple crossover took more generations to find individuals of the same quality. However, evolutionary search with ripple crossover is more diverse and thus, can lead to better results when sub-tree crossover shows early convergence [9].

Thorhauer and Rothlauf [33] analyzed locality of search operators in GE and genetic programming (GP) [10]. They found that ripple crossover has a higher locality compared to subtree crossover in GP. However, the locality of ripple crossover is also low.

A number of alternative crossover operators that can be used in GE have been presented in the literature, e.g., sticky crossover [3], structure preserving crossover (LHS) [5,6], homologous crossover variants [25], syntactic geometric recombination [34], and two-point crossover variants [5,25]. In most experiments, ripple crossover led to better or comparable results compared to other crossover variants [5,6,21,25,34].

A *"headless chicken crossover"* [24,25] was used to analyze ripple crossover. One crossover operation consists of randomly choosing one individual from the population, determining a crossover point, and randomizing all codons on the right side of the crossover point. Thus, instead of exchanging codons between individuals, codons of the individuals were partially randomized. Replacing ripple crossover with the headless chicken crossover led to poor results. These findings indicate that ripple crossover is able to effectively exchange building blocks between two individuals [24,25].

2.3 Grammar Design

Many authors found that grammar design in GE has a large impact on convergence speed and solution quality (e.g., [7,8,13]). However, a recent study by Nicolau and Agapitos [15] noted that "there is surprisingly little work in the literature on the design of grammars for GE". We provide a brief overview of research on grammar design in GE. For a comprehensive discussion of grammar design please refer to [15].

O'Neill and Ryan examined the effect of genetic code degeneracy and found that certain grammars bias the search [19,26]. Genetic code degeneracy can be observed when different codon values result in the same derivation (i.e., the number of different codon values is greater than the respective number of derivations to choose from). When the number of different codon values is not a multiple of the number of derivations, some derivations are represented by more codon values than others. Thus, degeneracy can lead to a search bias [26]. To circumvent this, O'Neill et al. suggested incorporating non-functional code (introns) to the grammar [26]. Instead, this type of bias can also be reduced by setting a large maximum codon value.

Some studies [16,30] analyzed mapping termination. Both studies focus on wrapping (using the genotype multiple times during mapping) and find grammar design to be important. Ryan et al. [30] discussed different types of derivations:

producers include one or more non-terminals, whereas consumers include only terminals. Later, Harper [4] introduced the notion of GE grammars being *"balanced"* or *"explosive"*, depending on the probability to derive non-terminal rules in relation to the probability to derive terminal rules. Based on this work, [31] defined B_{avg} as the expected number of new non-terminals in one derivation step during genotype-phenotype mapping.

Assuming

- a genotype string of infinite length,
- a uniform-random distribution of codon values in the genotype, and
- a grammar with only one production rule ($|P| = 1$),

B_{avg} is calculated by

$$B_{\text{avg}} = \sum_{i \in I_p} p(i) \times B(i), \tag{1}$$

where I_p denotes the set of possible derivations for the single production rule p ($p \in P$) and $p(i)$ is the probability of choosing the derivation i. Furthermore, $B(i)$ denotes the number of non-terminals in i.

In [31], B_{avg} is used to distinguish three types of grammars: collapsing, balanced, and unbalanced grammars. Grammars with $B_{\text{avg}} < 1$ are denoted *"collapsing"* grammars since the encoded phenotype trees are finite—the probability to finish decoding is one (if the genotype is long enough). For *"balanced"* grammars, the expected number of non-terminals in each decoding step is equal to one ($B_{\text{avg}} = 1$). If $B_{\text{avg}} > 1$, a grammar is denoted *"explosive"*. For such grammars, the mapping process derives non-terminals with a higher probability than terminals [4,31]. Consequently, the probability of finishing the mapping tends to zero after a certain number of non-terminals have been derived [4,11,31]. Therefore, the expected tree size in balanced and explosive grammars is infinite.

Some studies analyze the effects of grammar design on initialization with standard random bit initialisation of genotypes [28,31,32]. The studies find that the GE encoding is strongly non-uniformly redundant and the bias depends on B_{avg} [31]. Grammars with $B_{\text{avg}} \geq 1$ result in a bias towards invalid trees that increases with higher B_{avg}. On the other hand, grammars with $B_{\text{avg}} < 1$ are biased towards small trees [31].

3   Experiments

We study the effect of different grammars on the resulting phenotypes after crossover. We first describe the grammars used throughout our analyses. Then, we present our findings of a static analysis where we consider the application of crossover operators on a large population, measuring the effects in the resulting offspring population. After that, we extend the analysis by also taking into account the effects over multiple generations and under selection pressure.

3.1   Grammars

In our analysis, we focus on single non-terminal grammars with a single production rule ($|P| = 1$). In single non-terminal grammars, codons always map to the same derivations, independent of the context given by other codons in the derivation process [30]. This simplicity is useful in the context of this work as it allows a rigorous analysis.

We compare four different grammars. All of them are able to express the same phenotypes. However, the grammars differ in the number of derivations and, as a consequence, in B_{avg}. The grammars are presented in Figs. 3, 4, 5 and 6.

```
<e> ::= <e>+<e> | <e>-<e> | <e>*<e> | pdiv(<e>,<e>) |
        psqrt(<e>) | sin(<e>)| exp(<e>)| plog(<e>) |
        x | x | x | x
```

Fig. 3. Production rules of the balanced grammar *Bal* ($B_{avg} = 1.0$)

We will use B_{avg} (see Sect. 2.3) to differentiate different types of grammars. Figure 3 presents the first grammar. For this grammar, $B_{avg} = 1.0$ and hence, the grammar is *balanced*. Therefore, it will be referred to as *Bal* in the following.

```
<e> ::= <e>+<e> | <e>-<e> | <e>*<e> | pdiv(<e>,<e>) |
        psqrt(<e>) | sin(<e>)| exp(<e>)| plog(<e>) |
        x | x | x | x | x | x
```

Fig. 4. Production rules of the collapsing grammar *Col* ($B_{avg} \approx 0.857$)

In the second grammar (Fig. 4), denoted as *Col*, two more terminal derivations (representing variables) are added compared to *Bal*. Therefore, B_{avg} is reduced ($B_{avg} \approx 0.857$) and so *Col* is a *collapsing* grammar.

```
<e> ::= <e>+<e> | <e>-<e> | <e>*<e> | pdiv(<e>,<e>) |
        psqrt(<e>) | sin(<e>)| exp(<e>)| plog(<e>) |
        x | x | x | x |
        <e>+<e> | <e>-<e>
```

Fig. 5. Production rules of the explosive grammar *Exp* ($B_{avg} \approx 1.143$)

Figure 5 presents an *explosive* grammar, *Exp*. *Exp* is a variant of *Bal* where two more derivations are added ("$< e > + < e >$" and "$< e > - < e >$"). Since both of these additional derivations contain two additional non-terminals, B_{avg} is increased ($B_{avg} \approx 1.143$).

```
<e> ::= <e>+<e> | <e>-<e> | <e>*<e> | pdiv(<e>,<e>) |
        psqrt(<e>) | sin(<e>)| exp(<e>)| plog(<e>) |
        x | x | x | x |
        <e>+<e> | <e>-<e> | <e>*<e> | pdiv(<e>,<e>)
```

Fig. 6. Production rules of the explosive grammar $Exp+$ ($B_{\mathrm{avg}} = 1.25$)

Compared to Bal, the last grammar (Fig. 6) includes four more derivations that each contain two non-terminals. This leads to a high $B_{\mathrm{avg}} = 1.25$. Since the B_{avg} of this grammar is even larger than that of Exp, we will refer to it by the name $Exp+$.

3.2 Static Analysis

In our first experiment we initialize four populations, one with each of the aforementioned grammars. Each of the four populations has a size of 100,000 individuals. Since standard random bit initialization with different grammars would lead to biased initial populations [31], we use the grow method [10]. We set the minimum depth to 3 and the maximum depth to 6. If the depth is larger than or equal to 3 and less than 6, terminals are sampled with a fixed probability of 20%. We do not allow duplicate phenotypes and ensure that the four populations initially contain *the same* phenotypes. The corresponding genotypes consist of 1,000 codons, each is a random integer between 0 and 100,000.

After initialization, we perform 200,000 onepoint crossover operations in each of the populations and observe the resulting individuals. Each crossover operation creates two children, resulting in 400,000 individuals per setting. Sampling of crossover points was restricted to the effective part of the genotypes. All of our experiments were implemented using the PonyGE2 framework [2].

The results are presented in Table 1. We first compare the number of valid individuals. With Col, crossover created only valid individuals. When using grammars with higher values of B_{avg}, crossover led to an increased number of invalid individuals.

Next, we compare diversity, measured by the number of individuals that are different from both of their parents. We observe that in crossover with Col about 275,000 of the 400,000 children were different from their parents. The diversity measure is slightly lower when using Bal and much lower with Exp and $Exp+$. Interestingly, the sum of invalid individuals and of individuals different from both parents is approximately 275,000, independent of the grammar. Thus, approximately 70% of the crossover operations resulted in genotypes where the derivations changed (i.e., the genotype did not encode the same phenotype after crossover). In effect, the mapping could not always be finished after crossover when grammars were balanced or explosive.

As expected, the size of the effective part of the genotypes before crossover ("mean number of used codons (before)") is the same for all grammars. After crossover, the average number of used codons remains similar for Col. For Bal,

Table 1. Results of 200,000 crossover operations on a population of 100,000 individuals for the grammars *Bal*, *Col*, *Exp*, and *Exp+*

	Col	*Bal*	*Exp*	*Exp+*
B_{avg}	0.857	1.000	1.143	1.250
Number of valid individuals	400,000	393,680	348,360	328,465
Number of invalid individuals	0	6,320	51,640	71,535
Num. of phenotypes different from parents	275,274	269,771	223,909	204,411
Mean number of used codons (before)	23.6	23.6	23.6	23.6
Mean number of used codons (after)	23.7	32.3	22.4	21.4
Mean number of tree nodes (before)	32.2	32.2	32.2	32.2
Mean number of tree nodes (after)	32.3	43.8	30.5	29.2

the number of used codons grows by about 36.9%, whereas less codons are used in *Exp* (−5.0%) and *Exp+* (−9.3%). The same effects can be observed with regards to the average size (number of tree nodes) of phenotype trees. With *Col*, the average tree size after crossover is similar and with *Bal*, the average tree size after crossover increases. With *Exp* and *Exp+*, on the other hand, the resulting average tree sizes are smaller.

We further investigate the bias introduced by the different grammars by analyzing the distribution of phenotype tree sizes. For the four grammars, we plot the relative frequencies of offspring individuals after crossover over the phenotype tree sizes (Fig. 7). For comparison, the dotted line shows the relative frequencies of the parent individuals. The relative frequencies are calculated using all trees (valid and invalid) but the plot only shows relative frequencies of valid phenotype trees with a size of less than or equal to 80 nodes.

We can see that all grammars are biased. Very small trees with a size of up to 10 nodes are overrepresented and for these trees, we can see no differences between the grammars. Grammars with higher values of B_{avg} lead to a lower frequency of large trees with a size of more than 10 nodes and up to 80 nodes.

The bias changes for very large trees with more than 80 nodes (not shown in Fig. 7). With *Bal*, these trees have a frequency of 6.2%, with *Col* 2.8%, with *Exp* 1.5%, and with *Exp+* 0.8%. These frequencies explain the high number of used codons and tree sizes when using *Bal* (see Table 1). The reason is that we use very long genotypes with 1,000 codons in the initial population of our experiments—with balanced grammars mapping can use many codons because, on average, the expected number of non-terminals is 1 in each derivation step. In effect, there is always a probability to create even larger trees. With explosive grammars, mapping can often not be finished and thus, the frequency of very large trees is lower for these grammars.

The results show that the genotype-phenotype mapping with *Bal*, *Exp*, and *Exp+* can not always be finished. With explosive grammars, the number of invalid individuals is high and the frequency of large trees is low. In contrast,

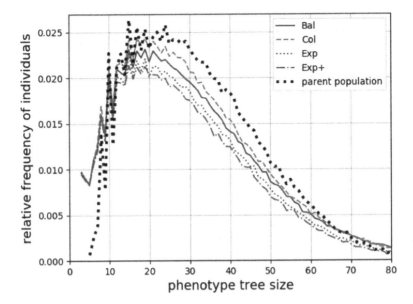

Fig. 7. Relative frequencies of individuals over the phenotype tree sizes for the grammars *Bal*, *Col*, *Exp*, and *Exp+* before and after crossover

when using *Col*, all offspring individuals were valid. With *Bal*, the frequency of very large trees with more than 80 nodes could be increased, compared to *Col*. Furthermore, the number of invalid individuals was low, compared to the explosive grammars.

3.3 Dynamic Analysis

We will extend the previous analysis by also taking into account the effects of crossover over multiple generations, using the same parameters and initialization like in Sect. 3.2. This time, we create 100,000 offspring individuals during crossover in every generation so that the number of individuals in the population remains constant. In modern GE implementations (e.g., PonyGE2 [2]), invalid individuals created during crossover are ignored. Instead, more crossover operations are performed, replacing invalid individuals with valid ones. In this experiment, we also use this approach. We perform crossover for 10 generations. The resulting distribution of phenotype tree sizes is presented in Fig. 8.

Figure 8 shows the relative frequencies of offspring individuals after 10 generations of crossover over the phenotype tree sizes for *Bal*, *Col*, *Exp*, and *Exp+*. For comparison, the dotted line shows the relative frequencies of the *initial* parent population. The plot only shows relative frequencies of phenotype trees with a size of up to 80 nodes.

We can see that the initial distribution of phenotype tree sizes has been biased towards very small trees with less than 10 nodes. For *Exp+*, 35.6% of

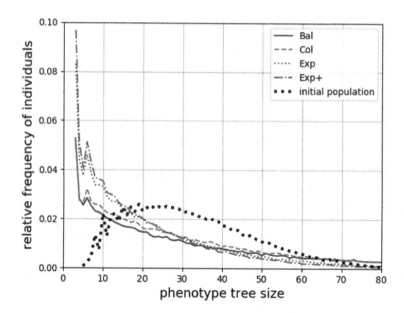

Fig. 8. Relative frequencies of individuals over the phenotype tree sizes for the grammars *Bal*, *Col*, *Exp*, and *Exp+* (initial population and after 10 generations of crossover)

individuals have a size of less than 10 nodes, while only 1.1% of the trees have at least 80 nodes. We observe a similar bias with *Exp*, where 31.7% of individuals have less than 10 nodes and 2.6% have at least 80 nodes. Crossover with *Col* leads to 21.7% of individuals having a size of less than 10 nodes and 10.3% of the trees having at least 80 nodes. For *Bal*, 20.6% of individuals have a size of less than 10 nodes and 20.2% of the trees have at least 80 nodes.

In summary, explosive grammars are not able to effectively search for large trees but are strongly biased towards very small solutions. Furthermore, collapsing and balanced grammars also bias the search towards small solutions but are also capable to find larger solutions. As a consequence, explosive grammars should be avoided.

3.4   Effects During Evolutionary Search

We study the influence of different grammars during evolutionary search under selection pressure. We use a simple test problem where the goal is to find a tree that has a given size N. The fitness (i.e., the error value) is the absolute distance between the number of nodes of an individual and N. More complex problems are not discussed due to space limitations.

The parameters used in this experiment are listed in Table 2. We do not use mutation since we focus our analysis on crossover. We use the grammars presented in Sect. 3.1 and performed 1,000 runs for each grammar. In the previous experiments, we used the grow method during initialization to get comparable initial populations. As a consequence, we were able to accurately analyze only the effects resulting from different grammars during crossover. In this experiment, we decided to use a standard GE initialization method—we use random integer initialization and allow only valid individuals and no duplicates (as recommended in [14]).

Table 2. GE parameters

Parameter	Value
Population size	1,000
Initialization	1,000 codons, each is a random integer between 0 and 100,000; we use random initialization and allow only valid individuals and no duplicates (as recommended in [14])
Elite size	5
Crossover operator	Variable onepoint crossover (sampling of crossover points is restricted to the effective part of the genotypes; invalid individuals are not selected as parents)
Crossover probability p_c	1
Mutation probability p_m	0
Duplication probability p_d	0
Wrapping	0
Selection	Tournament selection (tournament size 3)
Replacement	Generational

We analyze the fitness for *Bal*, *Col*, *Exp*, and *Exp+* over multiple generations. Figures 9(a)–(c) show the best fitness values measured for different target tree sizes N with $N \in \{50, 100, 200\}$. The presented results are averaged over 1,000 runs. We can see that the fitness values already differ in the initial generation, depending on the grammar. For all N, *Bal* leads to the best and *Exp+* to the worst initial fitnesses. *Col* and *Exp* lead to a comparable initial fitness which is better than the fitness measured with *Exp+* but worse compared to *Bal*.

During the search, the initial differences in the fitness values become smaller. For all problem instances, search with *Bal* finds better solutions earlier. The results for *Col* and *Exp* are worse but still similar to the results measured with *Bal*. *Exp+* takes more generations to converge to optimal solutions but we are able to consistently find optimal solutions with all grammars. We can see that the initially large differences between the grammars become smaller over multiple generations. Thus, for the simple problem used in this experiment, selection

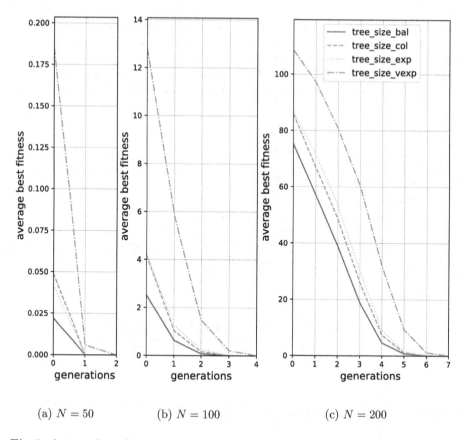

(a) $N = 50$ (b) $N = 100$ (c) $N = 200$

Fig. 9. Average best fitness over generations for the grammars *Bal*, *Col*, *Exp*, and *Exp+* and for different target tree sizes N

pressure and ignoring invalid solutions helps to counteract the problems with bias that we identified in the previous subsections.

Our preliminary results indicate that selection pressure and ignoring invalid solutions helps to reduce the bias resulting from differences in grammar design. Still, due to the lower number of invalid solutions, we recommend to use grammars where the probability for derivations representing terminals is higher than the probability to derive non-terminals.

4   Conclusions

The results of this study allow a better understanding of grammar design in GE. We analyze single non-terminal grammars that are able to express the same phenotypes but have different expected numbers of non-terminals during genotype-phenotype mapping (measured through B_{avg}). Independent of B_{avg}, all grammars are biased towards small trees. However, grammars with $B_{avg} \neq 1$

have an increased bias towards small trees and hardly map to large trees. For explosive grammars with $B_{avg} > 1$, we find a high number of invalid individuals which, in effect, leads to an increased runtime due to the re-sampling of invalid individuals.

Therefore we argue that balanced and collapsing grammars with $B_{avg} \leq 1$ are a better choice. For these grammars, we find only few or no invalid individuals. Based on our results we want to encourage GE users to carefully consider grammar design. We suggest to overrepresent derivations that lead to terminals and lower the probability to choose non-terminal derivations.

However, we note that the experiments in this paper are limited to single non-terminal grammars. In future work, we will extend our findings for grammars with multiple production rules. Furthermore, we expect differences in the performance between the grammars, depending on whether optimal solutions are small, medium, or large trees. Therefore, we plan to carefully investigate the effects of different types of grammars on solution quality.

References

1. Castle, T., Johnson, C.G.: Positional effect of crossover and mutation in grammatical evolution. In: Esparcia-Alcázar, A.I., Ekárt, A., Silva, S., Dignum, S., Uyar, A.Ş. (eds.) EuroGP 2010. LNCS, vol. 6021, pp. 26–37. Springer, Heidelberg (2010). https://doi.org/10.1007/978-3-642-12148-7_3
2. Fenton, M., McDermott, J., Fagan, D., Forstenlechner, S., Hemberg, E., O'Neill, M.: PonyGE2: grammatical Evolution in Python. In: Proceedings of the Genetic and Evolutionary Computation Conference Companion, pp. 1194–1201 (2017)
3. Francone, F.D., Conrads, M., Banzhaf, W., Nordin, P.: Homologous crossover in genetic programming. In: Proceedings of the 1st Annual Conference on Genetic and Evolutionary Computation - Volume 2, GECCO 1999, pp. 1021–1026. Morgan Kaufmann Publishers Inc., San Francisco (1999)
4. Harper, R.: GE, explosive grammars and the lasting legacy of bad initialisation. In: Proceedings of the IEEE Congress on Evolutionary Computation, CEC 2010, pp. 1–8. IEEE Press (2010)
5. Harper, R., Blair, A.: A structure preserving crossover in grammatical evolution. In: 2005 IEEE Congress on Evolutionary Computation, Edinburgh, vol. 3, pp. 2537–2544. IEEE (2005)
6. Harper, R., Blair, A.: A self-selecting crossover operator. In: 2006 IEEE International Conference on Evolutionary Computation, pp. 1420–1427. IEEE (2006)
7. Hemberg, E.: An exploration of grammars in grammatical evolution. Ph.D. thesis, University College Dublin (2010)
8. Hemberg, E., McPhee, N., O'Neill, M., Brabazon, A.: Pre-, in- and postfix grammars for symbolic regression in grammatical evolution. In: McGinnity, T.M. (ed.) IEEE Workshop and Summer School on Evolutionary Computing, pp. 18–22. IEEE (2008)
9. Keijzer, M., Ryan, C., O'Neill, M., Cattolico, M., Babovic, V.: Ripple Crossover in Genetic Programming. In: Miller, J., Tomassini, M., Lanzi, P.L., Ryan, C., Tettamanzi, A.G.B., Langdon, W.B. (eds.) EuroGP 2001. LNCS, vol. 2038, pp. 74–86. Springer, Heidelberg (2001). https://doi.org/10.1007/3-540-45355-5_7

10. Koza, J.R.: Genetic Programming: On the Programming of Computers by Means of Natural Selection. MIT Press, Cambridge (1992)
11. Luke, S.: Two fast tree-creation algorithms for genetic programming. IEEE Trans. Evol. Comput. **4**(3), 274–283 (2000)
12. Medvet, E.: A comparative analysis of dynamic locality and redundancy in grammatical evolution. In: McDermott, J., Castelli, M., Sekanina, L., Haasdijk, E., García-Sánchez, P. (eds.) EuroGP 2017. LNCS, vol. 10196, pp. 326–342. Springer, Cham (2017). https://doi.org/10.1007/978-3-319-55696-3_21
13. Nicolau, M.: Automatic grammar complexity reduction in grammatical evolution. In: The 3rd Grammatical Evolution Workshop (GECCO 2004), Seattle, Washington (2004)
14. Nicolau, M.: Understanding Grammatical Evolution: Initialisation. Genet. Program. Evolvable Mach. **18**(4), 467–507 (2017). https://doi.org/10.1007/s10710-017-9309-9
15. Nicolau, M., Agapitos, A.: Understanding grammatical evolution: grammar design. In: Ryan, C., O'Neill, M., Collins, J.J. (eds.) Handbook of Grammatical Evolution. LNCS, pp. 23–53. Springer, Cham (2018). https://doi.org/10.1007/978-3-319-78717-6_2
16. Nicolau, M., O'Neill, M., Brabazon, A.: Termination in grammatical evolution: grammar design, wrapping, and tails. In: Proceedings of the IEEE Congress on Evolutionary Computation (CEC2012), Brisbane. IEEE (2012)
17. Nicolau, M., Slattery, D.: libGE - grammatical evolution library (2006)
18. O'Neill, M., Hemberg, E., Gilligan, C., Bartley, E., McDermott, J., Brabazon, A.: GEVA: grammatical evolution in Java. SIGEVOlution **3**(2), 17–22 (2008)
19. O'Neill, M., Ryan, C.: Genetic code degeneracy: implications for grammatical evolution and beyond. In: Floreano, D., Nicoud, J.-D., Mondada, F. (eds.) ECAL 1999. LNCS (LNAI), vol. 1674, pp. 149–153. Springer, Heidelberg (1999). https://doi.org/10.1007/3-540-48304-7_21
20. O'Neill, M., Ryan, C.: Under the hood of grammatical evolution. In: Banzhaf, W., et al. (eds.) Proceedings of the 1st Annual Conference on Genetic and Evolutionary Computation, GECCO 1999. Morgan Kaufmann (1999)
21. O'Neill, M., Ryan, C.: Crossover in grammatical evolution: a smooth operator? In: Poli, R., Banzhaf, W., Langdon, W.B., Miller, J., Nordin, P., Fogarty, T.C. (eds.) EuroGP 2000. LNCS, vol. 1802, pp. 149–162. Springer, Heidelberg (2000). https://doi.org/10.1007/978-3-540-46239-2_11
22. O'Neill, M., Ryan, C.: Grammatical evolution. IEEE Trans. Evol. Comput. **5**(4), 349–358 (2001)
23. O'Neill, M., Ryan, C.: Grammatical evolution: evolutionary automatic programming in an arbitrary language. In: Genetic Programming Series. Springer, New York (2003). https://doi.org/10.1007/978-1-4615-0447-4
24. O'Neill, M., Ryan, C., Keijzer, M., Cattolico, M.: Crossover in Grammatical Evolution: The Search Continues. In: Miller, J., Tomassini, M., Lanzi, P.L., Ryan, C., Tettamanzi, A.G.B., Langdon, W.B. (eds.) EuroGP 2001. LNCS, vol. 2038, pp. 337–347. Springer, Heidelberg (2001). https://doi.org/10.1007/3-540-45355-5_27
25. O'Neill, M., Ryan, C., Keijzer, M., Cattolico, M.: Crossover in grammatical evolution. Genet. Program. Evolvable Mach. **4**(1), 67–93 (2003). https://doi.org/10.1023/A:1021877127167
26. O'Neill, M., Ryan, C., Nicolau, M.: Grammar defined introns: an investigation into grammars, introns, and bias in grammatical evolution. In: Spector, L., et al. (eds.) Proceedings of the Genetic and Evolutionary Computation Conference, GECCO 2001, pp. 97–103. Morgan Kaufmann, San Francisco (2001)

27. Rothlauf, F., Oetzel, M.: On the locality of grammatical evolution. In: Collet, P., Tomassini, M., Ebner, M., Gustafson, S., Ekárt, A. (eds.) EuroGP 2006. LNCS, vol. 3905, pp. 320–330. Springer, Heidelberg (2006). https://doi.org/10.1007/11729976_29

28. Ryan, C., Azad, R.M.A.: Sensible initialisation in grammatical evolution. In: Barry, A.M. (ed.) Proceedings of the Bird of a Feather Workshops, Genetic and Evolutionary Computation Conference, GECCO 2003, Chigaco, pp. 142–145. AAAI (2003)

29. Ryan, C., Collins, J.J., Neill, M.O.: Grammatical evolution: evolving programs for an arbitrary language. In: Banzhaf, W., Poli, R., Schoenauer, M., Fogarty, T.C. (eds.) EuroGP 1998. LNCS, vol. 1391, pp. 83–96. Springer, Heidelberg (1998). https://doi.org/10.1007/BFb0055930

30. Ryan, C., Keijzer, M., Nicolau, M.: On the avoidance of fruitless wraps in grammatical evolution. In: Cantú-Paz, E., et al. (eds.) GECCO 2003. LNCS, vol. 2724, pp. 1752–1763. Springer, Heidelberg (2003). https://doi.org/10.1007/3-540-45110-2_67

31. Schweim, D., Thorhauer, A., Rothlauf, F.: On the non-uniform redundancy of representations for grammatical evolution: the influence of grammars. In: Ryan, C., O'Neill, M., Collins, J.J. (eds.) Handbook of Grammatical Evolution, pp. 55–78. Springer, Cham (2018). https://doi.org/10.1007/978-3-319-78717-6_3

32. Thorhauer, A.: On the non-uniform redundancy in grammatical evolution. In: Handl, J., Hart, E., Lewis, P.R., López-Ibáñez, M., Ochoa, G., Paechter, B. (eds.) PPSN 2016. LNCS, vol. 9921, pp. 292–302. Springer, Cham (2016). https://doi.org/10.1007/978-3-319-45823-6_27

33. Thorhauer, A., Rothlauf, F.: On the locality of standard search operators in grammatical evolution. In: Bartz-Beielstein, T., Branke, J., Filipič, B., Smith, J. (eds.) PPSN 2014. LNCS, vol. 8672, pp. 465–475. Springer, Cham (2014). https://doi.org/10.1007/978-3-319-10762-2_46

34. Thorhauer, A., Rothlauf, F.: On the bias of syntactic geometric recombination in genetic programming and grammatical evolution. In: Silva, S. (ed.) Proceedings of the 2015 Annual Conference on Genetic and Evolutionary Computation (GECCO 2015), pp. 1103–1110. ACM Press, New York (2015)

35. Wilson, D., Kaur, D.: Search, neutral evolution, and mapping in evolutionary computing: a case study of grammatical evolution. IEEE Trans. Evol. Comput. **13**(3), 566–590 (2009)

On the Generalizability of Programs Synthesized by Grammar-Guided Genetic Programming

Dominik Sobania[✉][iD]

Johannes Gutenberg University, Mainz, Germany
dsobania@uni-mainz.de

Abstract. Grammar-guided Genetic Programming is a common approach for program synthesis where the user's intent is given by a set of input/output examples. For use in real-world software development, the generated programs must work on previously unseen test cases too. Therefore, we study in this work the generalizability of programs synthesized by grammar-guided GP with lexicase selection. As benchmark, we analyze proportionate and tournament selection too. We find that especially for program synthesis problems with a low output cardinality (e.g., a Boolean output) lexicase selection overfits the training cases and does not generalize well to unseen test cases. An analysis using common software metrics shows for such a problem that lexicase selection generates more complex programs with many code lines and a heavier use of control structures compared to the other studied selection methods. Nevertheless, the generalizability can be improved when we do not stop a GP run as usual after a first program is found that solves all training cases correctly, but give GP more time to find further solution candidates (also solving correctly all training cases) and select the smallest program (measured with different software metrics) out of these.

Keywords: Program synthesis · Genetic programming · Lexicase selection · Generalizability · Software engineering

1 Introduction

Program synthesis is an approach for the automatic generation of source code that meets the requirements of a user-defined specification. Such a specification can be given by, e.g., a natural language description, formal logic, or even a set of input/output examples [10]. A real-world example for program synthesis is the tool Flash Fill [9], which is integrated in Microsoft Excel. With Flash Fill, a user can automate string manipulation tasks by entering some input/output examples. The macro code required to solve the task is then generated automatically based on the given examples.

Genetic Programming (GP) [1,18], an evolutionary technique which automatically generates programs that solve a given problem, also uses input/output examples as training data to assess the quality of a candidate program. The

© Springer Nature Switzerland AG 2021
T. Hu et al. (Eds.): EuroGP 2021, LNCS 12691, pp. 130–145, 2021.
https://doi.org/10.1007/978-3-030-72812-0_9

programs are often generated in a domain-specific language (adjusted to the considered problem), but modern high-level programming languages (like Python) can also be used. In grammar-guided GP [7,28], a variation of the conventional GP approach, the used programming language is defined by a context-free grammar which makes it simple to support programming language features like typing constraints and control structures. In addition to the grammar, also the selection method used by GP has a great impact on the solution quality. Recent work shows that for program synthesis with grammar-guided GP, best results can be achieved with lexicase selection [4].

A challenge of program synthesis with GP is that problems are always "uncompromising problems" [15]. This means that program synthesis problems require an optimal solution, in contrast to classical machine learning tasks like regression and classification where a good approximation is often sufficient. Furthermore, the programs generated by GP must work optimally not only on the training data, but should also generalize to unseen test cases. This is relevant especially for a practical usage of GP-based program synthesis approaches in real-world software development.

In this work, we analyze the generalizability of programs synthesized by grammar-guided GP with lexicase selection. For comparison, we study proportionate and tournament selection too. As benchmark problems, we use a representative set of seven problems from the general program synthesis benchmark suite by Helmuth and Spector [13,14].

As expected, lexicase selection outperforms the other two studied selection methods on the training as well as on the test set for most benchmark problems. However, for problems with a low output cardinality, we find that lexicase selection does not generalize well to the unseen test data. E.g., for problems with a Boolean return value, less than 10% of the solutions found on the training set generalize to the unseen test set. An analysis with common software metrics shows that for such a problem lexicase selection generates, compared to proportionate and tournament selection, more complex programs using a larger number of code lines and control structures. However, if we do not stop a GP run as usual after a first program is found which is successful on the training set, GP regularly finds further solution candidates. Using the smallest out of these solution candidates (measured with the software metrics) often leads to a better generalizability.

Section 2 presents work related to GP-based program synthesis and explains briefly the used selection methods. In Sect. 3 we describe the grammar-guided GP approach, the used benchmark problems, and the software metrics. In Sect. 4 we describe our experiments and discuss the results, before concluding the paper in Sect. 5.

2   Related Work

Since the general program synthesis benchmark suite [13,14] was published in 2015, GP-based program synthesis has experienced a renaissance. This section presents the recent work on GP-based program synthesis and additionally explains briefly the selection methods used in this work.

2.1 GP-Based Program Synthesis

Program synthesis approaches generate source code in a certain programming language such that the synthesized functionality meets a given specification [10]. Grammar-guided GP approaches (e.g., grammatical evolution (GE) [22]) are suitable for representing the important properties of a programming language, like the control structures and the type system, and are therefore often used for program synthesis problems in the literature [4,5,25]. Some recent work focuses the use of domain knowledge, e.g., to reduce the search space or to guide GP approaches in promising directions. For example, Hemberg et al. [16] used the textual description of program synthesis problems to optimize a GE approach. Sobania and Rothlauf [24] used a corpus of source code mined from GitHub to guide their approaches to source code that is similar to code written by human software developers.

In addition to grammar-guided GP approaches, there exists also work using the stack-based programming language Push [12,17,23,27]. To support a correct type system, the Push programming language provides separate stacks (one for each type). Loop-like structures and conditionals can be also expressed with the Push language [27].

The generalizability of GP-based program synthesis approaches has so far only been studied in a few papers. E.g., Helmuth et al. [11] analyzed different techniques for the automatic simplification of the generated programs. For many benchmark problems, the success rates on unseen test data could be slightly improved by the use of simplification. Forstenlechner et al. [6] showed that increasing the amount of training cases often leads to a better generalization.

To our knowledge, no work so far analyzed the influence of different selection methods on the generalizability of programs synthesized by grammar-guided GP with common software metrics.

2.2 Selection Methods

In our experiments, we compare the results achieved by three different selection methods. Therefore, we briefly explain in this section the process of selecting an individual for all selection methods studied in this work.

With proportionate selection, an individual's probability of being selected as parent is proportional to its fitness. Thus, fitter individuals are selected with a higher probability [8].

Tournament selection randomly selects t individuals for a tournament and the winner (individual with the best fitness) is selected as parent [21].

Lexicase selection [23,26] differs from other selection methods, because an individual is not selected on the basis of its fitness, but rather on its performance on a set of training cases. This allows lexicase selection to incorporate

the structure given by the training cases for the selection instead of a compressed
fitness value (see evaluation bottleneck [19]). Algorithm 1 shows the process as
pseudo-code. To select an individual, lexicase selection shuffles the given training
cases (line 1) and initializes a list of candidate individuals with all individuals
from the population (line 2). After that, as long as there are remaining training cases and at least two candidate individuals (line 3), the following steps are
repeated: all individuals not achieving the exact lowest error (of all candidates)
for the currently considered training case are discarded (line 4) and the first
training case is removed from the list (line 5). Finally, one candidate individual
is returned: either the single remaining one or a random individual from the list
of remaining candidate individuals (line 7).

Algorithm 1: Lexicase selection

1   cases := shuffle(training_cases);
2   candidates := population;
3   **while** (count(cases) > 0) and (count(candidates) > 1) **do**
4 | candidates := best_individuals_for_case(candidates, cases[0]);
5 | cases := cases.remove_first();
6   **end**
7   **return** shuffle(candidates)[0];

---

3 Methodology

We describe the used software metrics which we use to analyze the functions
generated by GP, the selected benchmark problems, as well as the grammar and
the fitness function used by the GP approach.

3.1 Software Metrics

To analyze the influence of the different selection methods on the generalizability
of functions generated by GP, we use software metrics as suggested by Sobania
and Rothlauf [24,25]. Some of the metrics are computed not directly on a function's source code but on its abstract syntax tree (AST). For generating the AST
of a function, we use the Python module astdump[1]. For a given function, the
metrics are defined as follows:

- **AST Nodes:** the number of nodes in a function's AST.
- **AST Depth:** the number of edges connecting the root node with the deepest
  leaf node in a function's AST.
- **Lines of code (LOC):** the number of code lines of a function. Empty lines
  and comments are not relevant because they are not generated by the GP
  system.

---

[1] astdump module: https://pypi.org/project/astdump/.

– **McCabe metric**: the number of decision branches (usually defined by conditionals and loops) in a function incremented by one [20]. The McCabe metric is therefore suitable for measuring the use of control structures like conditionals or loops. We use the Python module `radon`[2] to compute the McCabe metric.

3.2   Benchmark Problems

For the experiments, we selected a set of seven problems from the general program synthesis benchmark suite [13,14]. To get a representative subset, we made sure that all three complexity levels, as defined by Forstenlechner et al. [6], are covered. The following problems were selected:

– **Compare String Lengths**: for the three given strings s_1, s_2, and s_3, return true if length(s_1) < length(s_2) < length(s_3), otherwise return false.
– **Count Odds**: given a list of integers, return the number of odd values in this list.
– **Grade**: for five given integer values, where the first four values define the minimum scores required for achieving the grades A to D, and the last integer value defines the achieved score, return the characters (grades) A, B, C, D, or F depending on the achieved score.
– **Median**: return the median of three given integer values.
– **Smallest**: return the smallest of four given integer values.
– **Small Or Large**: given an integer value n, return "small" if $n < 1,000$ and "large" if $n \geq 2,000$. For $1,000 \leq n < 2,000$ return an empty string.
– **Super Anagrams**: for the two given strings s_1 and s_2, return true if all characters from s_1 are also in s_2 with at least the same number of copies, otherwise return false.

In addition to complexity, the problems also differ in their output cardinality: Compare String Lengths and Super Anagrams are binary problems (Boolean output), Small Or Large is a ternary problem (returns "small", "large", or an empty string), Grade is a quinary problem (returns A, B, C, D, or F). The other problems are unlimited as they all return integer values.

For each problem, the benchmark suite defines 100 training and 1,000 test cases, except for Count Odds, Grade, and Super Anagrams where the training set consists of 200 and the test set of 2,000 cases.

3.3   Grammar-Guided GP Approach

The expressiveness of modern high-level programming languages like Python (used in this work) is high but can still be defined with context-free grammars[3]. However, with the size of a grammar, the search space grows exponentially, which makes it difficult for GP to find high quality solutions. Therefore, we use

---

[2] `radon` module: https://pypi.org/project/radon/.
[3] Python grammar: https://docs.python.org/3/reference/grammar.html.

in our experiments grammars based on the grammars provided by the PonyGE2 framework [3]. As suggested by Forstenlechner et al. [4], we support not all possible data types for each benchmark problem. To keep the grammars small but still expressive, we support in addition to some basic data types only the types specified for a benchmark problem's input parameters and return values. Table 1 shows the data types supported by the respective grammar for each studied benchmark problem. For all benchmark problems, Boolean and integer types are supported together with the elementary functions and structures like loops and conditionals. For example for the Count Odds problem, the grammar supports also integer lists (denoted as Integer[]) and the required functionality like list slicing and accessing list elements. The respective grammars for the Compare String Lengths, Grade, Small Or Large, and Super Anagrams problem support the string or char type and the required functions. For reproducibility, all grammars used in this work are available online[4].

Table 1. Data types supported by the respective grammar for each studied program synthesis benchmark problem.

Benchmark problem	Boolean	Integer	Integer[]	String	Char
Compare String Lengths	✓	✓		✓	
Count Odds	✓	✓	✓		
Grade	✓	✓			✓
Median	✓	✓			
Smallest	✓	✓			
Small Or Large	✓	✓		✓	
Super Anagrams	✓	✓		✓	

For expressive program synthesis grammars, recent work shows that the classical genotype-phenotype mapping (like in standard GE) leads to many invalid solutions [25]. Consequently, we use in our experiments a tree-based representation with position independent grow [2] as initialization method and the sub-tree variants of the variation operators. Therefore, invalid solutions do not have to be considered.

For a better inter-problem comparability, we use the same fitness function for all studied benchmark problems. The fitness function is defined for proportionate and tournament selection as

$$f(S, C, p_{\text{err}}) = \begin{cases} p_{\text{err}} \, |C| & \text{if a run-time error occurs in } S \\ \sum_{c_i \in C} d(S, c_i) & \text{else} \end{cases} \quad (1)$$

where S is a candidate solution (a Python function), C is the set of training cases, c_i is the ith case from C, and p_{err} is a penalty for solutions that produce

---

[4] Used grammars: https://gitlab.rlp.net/dsobania/progsys-grammars.

a run-time error. The function $d(S, c_i)$ returns 0 if the output of the candidate solution S is correct for the training case c_i, otherwise it returns 1. So the fitness function counts the errors of a candidate solution on the training set. In case of a run-time error, the fitness is p_{err} times the number of training cases $|C|$.

For lexicase selection, which does not use compressed fitness values, we proceed similarly, but in contrast to the other methods we consider the error separately for each training case instead of the sum of all errors.

4   Experiments and Results

To measure generalizability, Sect. 4.1 compares the achieved success rates of the different selection methods on the training and on the test sets of the studied benchmark problems. This is followed by an analysis of GP's run-time behavior using the software metrics in Sect. 4.2. Finally, in Sect. 4.3, we use the software metrics to select the smallest program found during a GP run that solves correctly all training cases to improve generalizability.

4.1   Comparison of Success Rates

To study how well programs generated by GP generalize to unseen test cases and how this is connected to the used selection method, we perform GP runs using proportionate, tournament, and lexicase selection for all studied benchmark problems and measure the success rates (percentage of successful runs) on the training and on the unseen test set. The programs generated by GP for a benchmark problem generalize well if the success rate on the test set is identical or only slightly below the success rate on the training set.

The implementation of the grammar-guided GP approach is based on the PonyGE2 framework [3]. We use a population of 3,000 individuals and initialize the population with position independent grow [2] with a maximum initial tree depth of 10. As variation operators, we use sub-tree crossover with a probability of 0.9 and sub-tree mutation with a probability of 0.05. The evaluation of a candidate solution is stopped after one second (on a system with an AMD Opteron 6272 16 × 2.10 GHz) to stop evolved endless loops. Finally, we set the error penalty $p_{err} = 2$ and stop each GP run after 100 generations.

Table 2 shows the success rates achieved on the training and on the test set for all studied benchmark problems and selection methods for 100 runs. For tournament selection, we show the results for different tournament sizes ($\forall t \in \{2, 4, 6\}$). In addition to the success rates, the table shows the average and the standard deviation (in brackets) of the generation in which the first successful solution was found on the training set. Best values are printed in **bold** font and an asterisk (*) indicates a significantly lower success rate ($p \leq 0.05$) on the unseen test set compared to the associated training set ($\Rightarrow$ poor generalization). For statistical testing, we use a chi-square test or a Fisher's exact test if one observation is lower than five.

Table 2. Success rates on the training and test set as well as the average and standard deviation (in brackets) of the generation in which a successful solution on the training set was found for all studied selection methods and program synthesis problems. Best values are printed in **bold** font. An asterisk (*) indicates a significantly lower success rate ($p \leq 0.05$) on the unseen test set compared to the associated training set.

Benchmark	Selection	Training (SR)	Test (SR)	Generation
Compare Str. Len.	Prop.	20	**6***	68.0 (22.9)
	Tour. (2)	20	2*	45.8 (14.4)
	Tour. (4)	16	4*	53.8 (26.0)
	Tour. (6)	16	4*	41.4 (**14.2**)
	Lex.	**97**	5*	**20.4** (15.5)
Count Odds	Prop.	1	1	59.0 (**0.0**)
	Tour. (2)	2	1	40.5 (20.5)
	Tour. (4)	0	0	- (-)
	Tour. (6)	3	2	51.3 (25.7)
	Lex.	3	2	**40.3** (7.4)
Grade	Prop.	0	0	- (-)
	Tour. (2)	1	1	64.0 (**0.0**)
	Tour. (4)	0	0	- (-)
	Tour. (6)	0	0	- (-)
	Lex.	**35**	**8***	**58.2** (23.0)
Median	Prop.	96	91	33.8 (16.3)
	Tour. (2)	93	91	18.1 (11.9)
	Tour. (4)	93	89	12.8 (9.4)
	Tour. (6)	94	91	11.5 (10.2)
	Lex.	**100**	**98**	**2.2** (**0.6**)
Smallest	Prop.	100	99	9.2 (3.3)
	Tour. (2)	100	98	6.1 (1.7)
	Tour. (4)	100	99	3.8 (1.1)
	Tour. (6)	100	**100**	3.2 (0.9)
	Lex.	100	98	**1.5** (**0.5**)
Small Or Large	Prop.	0	0	- (-)
	Tour. (2)	1	1	76.0 (**0.0**)
	Tour. (4)	3	3	55.7 (17.9)
	Tour. (6)	5	5	**45.0** (22.5)
	Lex.	**15**	**11**	45.7 (25.5)
Super Anagrams	Prop.	0	0	- (-)
	Tour. (2)	0	0	- (-)
	Tour. (4)	2	0	72.5 (**6.5**)
	Tour. (6)	0	0	- (-)
	Lex.	**82**	**4***	42.6 (24.8)

As expected, the grammar-guided GP approach achieves its best results with lexicase selection for most benchmark problems. On the training set, lexicase achieves best success rates for all studied benchmark problems and on the test set, only for the Compare String Lengths problem with proportionate selection and the Smallest problem with proportionate and tournament selection ($t \in \{4, 6\}$) we see slightly higher success rates.

However, for some benchmark problems, we observe a low generalizability of the programs generated by GP especially with lexicase selection. For the Compare String Lengths problem, all selection methods have a significantly lower success rate on the unseen test set compared to the training set. E.g., with lexicase selection only 5 out of 97 found programs generalize to the test set which is the lowest generalization rate compared to the other studied selection methods for this problem. We see similar results for lexicase selection also for the Grade and the Super Anagrams problem. Lexicase selection overfits the training set for the benchmark problems with a low output cardinality, e.g., for binary problems like Compare String Lengths and Super Anagrams (Boolean return value) or the quinary Grade problem which just returns the characters A, B, C, D, or F.

In addition, the results show that lexicase selection finds the successful solutions on the training set on average much faster than all other studied selection methods (except for Small Or Large). E.g., for Compare String Lengths and Super Anagrams, where we observe an extreme overfitting, GP finds solutions on average in the first half of the run. Noticeable, for Median and Smallest, lexicase finds solutions on average after 2.2 and 1.5 generations, respectively.

In summary, lexicase selection overfits the training cases for many benchmark problems. For problems with a low output cardinality (e.g., binary problems), lexicase achieves a significantly lower success rate on the test set compared to the training set.

4.2 Analysis with Software Metrics

As lexicase selection overfits the training cases for many of the considered benchmark problems, we use the software metrics as defined in Sect. 3.1 to study the development of the structure of the evolved programs over the generations of a GP run and compare the results for all studied selection methods. We present results for the Compare String Lengths problem, because all selection methods achieve a similar success rate on the test set but there are also significant differences in the generalizability of the evolved programs. Further, we present results for the Small Or Large problem where we observe no significant difference in generalizability but most selection methods find successful solutions on the test set. The other problems are not suitable for our analysis, as either the success rates are too low (for proportionate and tournament selection) or a successful solution on the training set is found on average in the first generations (e.g., with lexicase selection for the Median and Smallest problem).

Figures 1, 2, 3 and 4 plot the average AST nodes, AST depth, LOC, and McCabe metric over generations for the Compare String Lengths problem for all

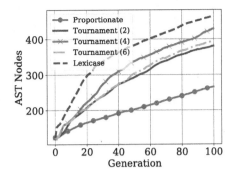

Fig. 1. AST nodes over generations for the Compare String Lengths problem for all studied selection methods.

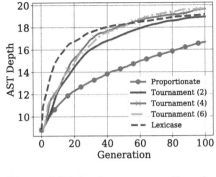

Fig. 2. AST depth over generations for the Compare String Lengths problem for all studied selection methods.

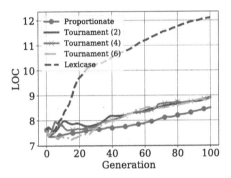

Fig. 3. LOC over generations for the Compare String Lengths problem for all studied selection methods.

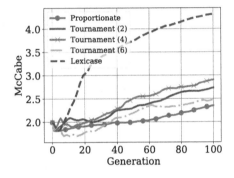

Fig. 4. McCabe metric over generations for the Compare String Lengths problem for all studied selection methods.

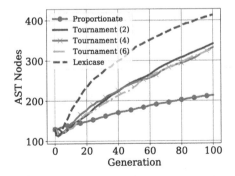

Fig. 5. AST nodes over generations for the Small Or Large problem for all studied selection methods.

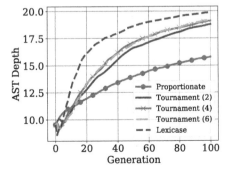

Fig. 6. AST depth over generations for the Small Or Large problem for all studied selection methods.

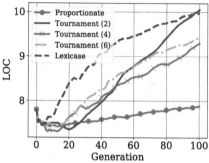
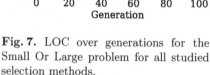
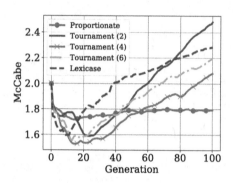

Fig. 7. LOC over generations for the Small Or Large problem for all studied selection methods.

Fig. 8. McCabe metric over generations for the Small Or Large problem for all studied selection methods.

studied selection methods. In addition to the generated code, the software metrics also consider the function's signature and the pre-defined variable initialization part. For tournament selection, all results look similar regardless of the used tournament size. In the first 40 generations, AST nodes (Fig. 1) and AST depth (Fig. 2) increase to around 300 and 18, respectively. After that, the increase slows down. LOC (Fig. 3) and McCabe metric (Fig. 4) only increase slightly over the complete run. For proportionate selection, the results are comparable with the difference that on average smaller programs are generated because AST nodes and depth are at a much lower level. However, the results for lexicase selection, which achieves the lowest generalizability on the Compare String Lengths problem, look quite different. Lexicase selection achieves the highest values for all studied software metrics except for AST depth. In addition, even though there exists a straightforward solution for the Compare String Lengths problem (a human programmer would implement) which does not require the use of conditionals or loops, lexicase achieves much higher values for LOC and McCabe metric (which increase to 12 and 4.3, respectively). As the McCabe metric is just an indicator for the use of control structures in general, we further analyzed the source code of the programs found with lexicase and find that a high number of if conditions are used. And with a high number of ifs a decision tree can be easily constructed that solves all given training cases but not generalizes well to unseen data.

Figures 5, 6, 7 and 8 plot the same analysis for the Small Or Large problem, where we observe no significant differences in the generalizability of the generated programs. Again, proportionate selection, which this time finds no successful programs (see Table 2), achieves the lowest values for all software metrics. For AST nodes (Fig. 5) and AST depth (Fig. 6) lexicase selection achieves the highest values compared to the other selection methods. For LOC (Fig. 7) and the McCabe metric (Fig. 8), lexicase selection performs similar to tournament selection (for all studied tournament sizes).

Overall, we find for the Compare String Lengths problem that lexicase selection evolves more complex programs with higher values of LOC and the McCabe metric (including ifs) than proportionate and tournament selection. For the Small Or Large problem, lexicase selection achieves results for LOC and the McCabe metric similar to the tournament selection approaches.

4.3   Software Metric-Based Program Selection

We know from the literature that smaller programs often generalize better to unseen test cases [11]. Consequently, in the next step, we do not stop a GP run as usual after a first program is found that solves all training cases correctly, but give GP more time to find further solution candidates (also solving correctly all training cases) different in structure and behavior and select the smallest program out of these. To measure the size of a program, we use the software metrics and select always the candidate solution that solves all training cases correctly and obtains the lowest value for a software metric (e.g., the program with the lowest number of AST nodes). If several different programs are found with the same value for a software metric (e.g., several programs with the identical lowest number of AST nodes), we select the program found first by GP from this group. In addition, we also determine the percentage of runs, of which at least one candidate solution generalizes to the test data in order to estimate the potential of GP. We stop each run after 100 generations.

Table 3 shows the success rates on the test set for the programs first found by GP as well as for the programs selected from all candidate solutions (working correctly on the training set) obtaining the lowest value for a software metric (AST nodes, AST depth, LOC, and McCabe metric) for all studied benchmark problems and selection methods for 100 runs. Additionally, we show the success rate that would be possible if we would know the test set (denoted as "Best"). Selection methods with a success rate of zero on the test set are omitted. The success rates for the programs first found by GP correspond to the results on the test set from Table 2.

The software metric-based selection of solution candidates achieves always identical or higher success rates compared to the programs that were first found by GP except for Small Or Large and Super Anagrams with lexicase and the Smallest problem with tournament selection ($t \in \{4, 6\}$). The results of the software metric-based selection are all very similar, regardless of the particular metric used. Only for the combination of lexicase and AST nodes-based candidate selection a notably higher value (success rate of 18%) is achieved in comparison to the other studied approaches for the Compare String Lengths problem. Again, best values are achieved with lexicase selection. In addition, by using a software metric-based selection, lexicase has now even a higher success rate than proportionate selection on the Compare String Lengths problem.

Interesting are also the success rates that are possible if we would know the test set (last column). We see that lexicase selection also has the highest potential for the generalizability of programs generated by GP. For the benchmark problems Count Odds, Median, and Smallest, this potential is even achieved

Table 3. Success rates on the test set for the programs first found by GP as well as for the programs selected from all candidate solutions (working correctly on the training set) obtaining the lowest value for a software metric (AST nodes, AST depth, LOC, and McCabe metric) for all studied benchmark problems and selection methods. Additionally, we show the success rate that would be possible if we would know the test set (denoted as "Best"). Selection methods with a success rate of zero on the test set are omitted.

Benchmark	Selection	First	Minimum of software metrics				Best
			Nodes	Depth	LOC	McCabe	
Compare Str. Len.	Prop.	6	6	6	6	6	10
	Tour. (2)	2	2	3	2	2	11
	Tour. (4)	4	6	5	6	6	11
	Tour. (6)	4	7	8	7	7	13
	Lex.	5	18	9	8	10	43
Count Odds	Prop.	1	1	1	1	1	1
	Tour. (2)	1	2	2	2	2	2
	Tour. (6)	2	2	2	2	2	2
	Lex.	2	3	3	3	3	3
Grade	Tour. (2)	1	1	1	1	1	1
	Lex.	8	10	10	11	10	16
Median	Prop.	91	96	96	93	93	96
	Tour. (2)	91	93	93	92	93	93
	Tour. (4)	89	93	91	91	91	93
	Tour. (6)	91	94	93	94	94	94
	Lex.	98	100	99	99	99	100
Smallest	Prop.	99	100	100	100	100	100
	Tour. (2)	98	100	100	100	100	100
	Tour. (4)	99	100	100	98	99	100
	Tour. (6)	100	100	98	100	100	100
	Lex.	98	100	100	99	100	100
Small Or Large	Tour. (2)	1	1	1	1	1	1
	Tour. (4)	3	3	3	3	3	3
	Tour. (6)	5	5	5	5	5	5
	Lex.	11	10	10	10	10	12
Super Anagrams	Lex	4	3	3	4	4	21

by using the software metric-based candidate selection. However, for the benchmark problems Compare String Lengths, Grade, and Super Anagrams, where we observe significantly lower success rates on the test set compared to the training set (see Table 2), the results are notably below the possible potential.

To summarize, for most studied benchmark problems a software metric-based candidate selection can improve the success rates in comparison to selecting the first solution that correctly solves all training cases found in a GP run.

5 Conclusions and Future Work

Grammar-guided GP is an approach suitable for program synthesis, as it can generate programs in a high-level programming language that meet the requirements of a user's specification defined with input/output examples. Typical features of programming languages like conditionals, loops, and typing constraints can be supported by using a context-free grammar. However, in order to use program synthesis as a support system for real-world software development, the generated programs must not only work correctly on the training cases but also on previously unseen test cases.

Consequently, we studied in this work the generalizability of programs synthesized by grammar-guided GP with lexicase selection. As benchmark, we analyzed proportionate and tournament selection too.

We found that lexicase selection achieves high success rates on the training set but for many benchmark problems the found programs do not generalize well to unseen test cases. E.g., for the Compare String Lengths and the Super Anagrams problem less than 10% of the programs solving correctly all training cases generalize to the unseen test cases.

Exemplary, we found for the Compare String Lengths problem that lexicase selection generates more complex programs with higher values for LOC and McCabe metric, which indicates an extensive use of control structures including `if` conditions, compared to the other studied selection methods.

Further, we found that if we do not stop a GP run as usual after a first program is found which successfully solves all training cases, GP regularly finds further solution candidates. Using the software metrics to select the smallest out of these candidates often improves the generalizability.

In future work, we will further analyze the structure and behavior of the programs synthesized by GP with lexicase selection and develop methods that predict if a program overfits the training cases or will generalize well to unseen test cases. Such a classifier could then be used to improve GP-based program synthesis.

References

1. Cramer, N.L.: A representation for the adaptive generation of simple sequential programs. In: Proceedings of an International Conference on Genetic Algorithms and the Applications, pp. 183–187 (1985)
2. Fagan, D., Fenton, M., O'Neill, M.: Exploring position independent initialisation in grammatical evolution. In: 2016 IEEE Congress on Evolutionary Computation, pp. 5060–5067. IEEE (2016)

3. Fenton, M., McDermott, J., Fagan, D., Forstenlechner, S., Hemberg, E., O'Neill, M.: PonyGE2: grammatical evolution in Python. In: Proceedings of the Genetic and Evolutionary Computation Conference Companion, pp. 1194–1201 (2017)
4. Forstenlechner, S., Fagan, D., Nicolau, M., O'Neill, M.: A grammar design pattern for arbitrary program synthesis problems in genetic programming. In: McDermott, J., Castelli, M., Sekanina, L., Haasdijk, E., García-Sánchez, P. (eds.) EuroGP 2017. LNCS, vol. 10196, pp. 262–277. Springer, Cham (2017). https://doi.org/10.1007/978-3-319-55696-3_17
5. Forstenlechner, S., Fagan, D., Nicolau, M., O'Neill, M.: Extending program synthesis grammars for grammar-guided genetic programming. In: Auger, A., Fonseca, C.M., Lourenço, N., Machado, P., Paquete, L., Whitley, D. (eds.) PPSN 2018. LNCS, vol. 11101, pp. 197–208. Springer, Cham (2018). https://doi.org/10.1007/978-3-319-99253-2_16
6. Forstenlechner, S., Fagan, D., Nicolau, M., O'Neill, M.: Towards understanding and refining the general program synthesis benchmark suite with genetic programming. In: Congress on Evolutionary Computation. IEEE (2018)
7. Forstenlechner, S., Nicolau, M., Fagan, D., O'Neill, M.: Grammar design for derivation tree based genetic programming systems. In: Heywood, M.I., McDermott, J., Castelli, M., Costa, E., Sim, K. (eds.) EuroGP 2016. LNCS, vol. 9594, pp. 199–214. Springer, Cham (2016). https://doi.org/10.1007/978-3-319-30668-1_13
8. Goldberg, D.E.: Genetic Algorithms in Search Optimization and Machine Learning. Addison-Wesley, Boston (1989)
9. Gulwani, S., Hernández-Orallo, J., Kitzelmann, E., Muggleton, S.H., Schmid, U., Zorn, B.: Inductive programming meets the real world. Commun. ACM **58**(11), 90–99 (2015)
10. Gulwani, S., Polozov, O., Singh, R.: Program synthesis. Found. Trends® Program. Lang. **4**(12), 1–119 (2017)
11. Helmuth, T., McPhee, N.F., Pantridge, E., Spector, L.: Improving generalization of evolved programs through automatic simplification. In: Proceedings of the Genetic and Evolutionary Computation Conference, pp. 937–944. ACM, New York (2017)
12. Helmuth, T., McPhee, N.F., Spector, L.: Program synthesis using uniform mutation by addition and deletion. In: Proceedings of the Genetic and Evolutionary Computation Conference, pp. 1127–1134. ACM, New York (2018)
13. Helmuth, T., Spector, L.: Detailed problem descriptions for general program synthesis benchmark suite. University of Massachusetts Amherst, Technical report, School of Computer Science (2015)
14. Helmuth, T., Spector, L.: General program synthesis benchmark suite. In: Proceedings of the Genetic and Evolutionary Computation Conference, pp. 1039–1046. ACM, New York (2015)
15. Helmuth, T., Spector, L., Matheson, J.: Solving uncompromising problems with lexicase selection. IEEE Trans. Evol. Comput. **19**(5), 630–643 (2014)
16. Hemberg, E., Kelly, J., O'Reilly, U.M.: On domain knowledge and novelty to improve program synthesis performance with grammatical evolution. In: Proceedings of the Genetic and Evolutionary Computation Conference, pp. 1039–1046. ACM, New York (2019)
17. Jundt, L., Helmuth, T.: Comparing and combining lexicase selection and novelty search. In: Proceedings of the Genetic and Evolutionary Computation Conference, pp. 1047–1055. ACM, New York (2019)
18. Koza, J.R., Koza, J.R.: Genetic Programming: On the Programming of Computers by Means of Natural Selection, vol. 1. MIT press, Cambridge (1992)

19. Krawiec, K.: Behavioral Program Synthesis with Genetic Programming, vol. 618. Springer, Cham (2016). https://doi.org/10.1007/978-3-319-27565-9
20. McCabe, T.J.: A complexity measure. IEEE Trans. Softw. Eng. **4**, 308–320 (1976)
21. Poli, R., Langdon, W.B., McPhee, N.F., Koza, J.R.: A Field Guide to Genetic Programming. Lulu.com, Morrisville (2008)
22. Ryan, C., Collins, J.J., Neill, M.O.: Grammatical evolution: evolving programs for an arbitrary language. In: Banzhaf, W., Poli, R., Schoenauer, M., Fogarty, T.C. (eds.) EuroGP 1998. LNCS, vol. 1391, pp. 83–96. Springer, Heidelberg (1998). https://doi.org/10.1007/BFb0055930
23. Saini, A.K., Spector, L.: Effect of parent selection methods on modularity. In: Hu, T., Lourenço, N., Medvet, E., Divina, F. (eds.) EuroGP 2020. LNCS, vol. 12101, pp. 184–194. Springer, Cham (2020). https://doi.org/10.1007/978-3-030-44094-7_12
24. Sobania, D., Rothlauf, F.: Teaching GP to program like a human software developer: using perplexity pressure to guide program synthesis approaches. In: Proceedings of the Genetic and Evolutionary Computation Conference, pp. 1065–1074. ACM, New York (2019)
25. Sobania, D., Rothlauf, F.: Challenges of program synthesis with grammatical evolution. In: Hu, T., Lourenço, N., Medvet, E., Divina, F. (eds.) EuroGP 2020. LNCS, vol. 12101, pp. 211–227. Springer, Cham (2020). https://doi.org/10.1007/978-3-030-44094-7_14
26. Spector, L.: Assessment of problem modality by differential performance of lexicase selection in genetic programming: a preliminary report. In: Proceedings of the 14th Annual Conference Companion on Genetic and Evolutionary Computation, pp. 401–408 (2012)
27. Spector, L., Robinson, A.: Genetic programming and autoconstructive evolution with the push programming language. Genet. Program Evolvable Mach. **3**(1), 7–40 (2002)
28. Whigham, P.A.: Grammatically-based genetic programming. In: Proceedings of the Workshop on Genetic Programming: From Theory to Real-world Applications, pp. 33–41 (1995)

Evolution of Complex Combinational Logic Circuits Using Grammatical Evolution with SystemVerilog

Michael Kwaku Tetteh[1]([📧]) [ID], Douglas Mota Dias[1,2] [ID], and Conor Ryan[1] [ID]

[1] Lero and CSIS, University of Limerick, Limerick, Ireland
{michael.tetteh,douglas.motadias,conor.ryan}@ul.ie
[2] UERJ, Rio de Janeiro State University, Rio de Janeiro, Brazil
douglas.dias@uerj.br
http://bds.ul.ie/

Abstract. Scalability problems have hindered the progress of Evolvable Hardware in tackling complex circuits. The two key issues are the amount of testing (for example, a 64-bit × 64-bit add-shift multiplier problem has 2^{64+64} test cases) and low level that hardware works at: a circuit to implement 64-bit × 64-bit add-shift multiplier would require approximately 33,234 gates when synthesized using the powerful Yosys Open SYnthesis Suite tool. We use Grammatical Evolution and SystemVerilog, a Hardware Description Language (HDL), to evolve fully functional **parameterized** adder, multiplier and selective parity circuits with default input bit-width sizes of 64-bit + 64-bit, 64-bit × 64-bit and 128-bit respectively.

These are substantially larger than the current state of the art for evolutionary approaches, specifically, 6.4× (adder), 10.7× (multiplier), and 6.7× (parity). We are able to scale so dramatically because our use of an HDL permits us to operate at a far higher level of abstraction than most other approaches. This has the additional benefit that no further evolutionary experiments are needed to design different input bit-width sizes of the same circuit as is the case for existing EHW approaches. Thus, one can evolve once and reuse multiple times, simply by specifying the newly desired input/output bit-width sizes during module instantiation.

For example, 32-bit × 32-bit and 256-bit × 256-bit multipliers can be instantiated from an evolved parameterized multiplier. We also adopt a method for reducing testing from Digital Circuit Design known as *corner case testing*, well-known technique heavily relied upon by circuit designers to avoid time-consuming exhaustive testing; we demonstrate a simple way to identify and use corner cases for evolutionary testing and show that it enables the generation of massively complex circuits with a huge number of inputs.

The authors are supported by Research Grant 16/IA/4605 from the Science Foundation Ireland and by Lero, the Irish Software Engineering Research Centre. The second author is partially financed by the Coordenação de Aperfeiçoamento de Pessoal de Nível Superior - Brasil (CAPES) - Finance Code 001.

T. Hu et al. (Eds.): EuroGP 2021, LNCS 12691, pp. 146–161, 2021.
https://doi.org/10.1007/978-3-030-72812-0_10

We obtain successful results (ranging from 72% to 100%) on each benchmark and all three problems were tackled without resorting to the use of any standard decomposition methods due to our ability to use high-level programming constructs and operators available in SystemVerilog.

Keywords: Grammatical Evolution · Digital circuit design · Evolvable Hardware · Hardware Description Languages (HDLs) · Verilog · SystemVerilog

1 Introduction

Evolvable Hardware (EHW) is a field that deals with the application of evolutionary algorithms to conventional circuit design and adaptive hardware. The latter refers to devices that are capable of autonomous reconfiguration and repair over their lifetime in the deployed environment. Since its inception, much innovative research have been conducted to advance the field. However, impeding the progress of EHW to tackle complex circuits are the two major scalability problems: *scalability of representation* and *scalability of fitness evaluation*. A complex circuit has at least tens of inputs and thousands of gates [20]. Despite the design of good methodologies to address the issues of scalability in EHW, circuit design benchmarks remain relatively complex. For example, a 64-bit × 64-bit add-shift multiplier would require approximately 33,234 gates when synthesized using Yosys [23].

In industry, Hardware Description Languages (HDLs) are used to design digital circuits due to the high level of abstraction at which circuit design can be done. The two dominant HDLs in industry today are Verilog/SystemVerilog (SV) and VHDL. For example, Verilog/SV supports circuit design at different levels of abstraction; starting as low as switch-level modelling, gate-level modelling, dataflow modelling and as high as behavioural modelling. Some of the benefits of HDLs such as Verilog/SystemVerilog that make them convenient for adoption in EHW are: *interpretability, modifiability, design module reuse through parameterization, support for mixed-style design in a single module, the availability of high-level constructs/operators such as* `always block`, `generate-loop` *(synthesizable* `for-loop`*)*, `reduction operators`, `binary operators`, *etc. These features reduce the complexity when dealing with high input size circuits unlike current approaches in the field. To date, the most complex circuits evolved are: 10-bit + 10-bit adder [3], 6-bit × 6-bit multiplier [17], 19-bit parity circuit [14] and 28-input frg1 circuit [20].

In this work, we address the scalability problem through the use of SV with Grammatical Evolution (GE) to design fully functional complex conventional combinational circuits; moreover, we do this without the use of decomposition methods. The main contributions of this paper are:

1. The evolution of complex accurate combinational digital circuits: 64 × 64-bit multiplier, 64 + 64-bit adder and 128-bit selective parity circuit;

2. All evolved circuits are parameterized; thus the design modules are reusable and only require the specification of input and output bit-width sizes without the need for re-run of experiments. The bit-width sizes mentioned in (1) above are the default bit-width sizes for the evolved circuits;
3. Significant reduction in simulation time through the use of appropriate operators and the use of corner cases in addition to sampled test cases in testbenches.

The outline for the rest of the paper is as follows: Sect. 2 gives a brief overview of EHW scalability problems and some steps taken to address them. Section 3 provides a summary of some existing approaches designed to address EHW scalability problems. Section 4 describes our experimental setup. In Sect. 5, we present our results with discussions. Finally, in Sect. 6, we conclude and provide the roadmap for future works.

2   Background

Scalability of representation and of evaluation are the two major scalability problems hindering the progress of Evolvable Hardware to evolve complex circuits [13]. The former refers to the scenario where long chromosomes are required to represent complex circuit solutions, resulting in difficult to search large solution spaces. The latter which is usually associated with complex combinational circuits occurs when exhaustive testing is used. Thus, an increase in input bit-width size directly increases evaluation time making it difficult to evolve complex circuits.

Existing methodologies to address EHW scalability of representation limitation in current literature have followed three major directions, namely: *problem decomposition, functional level evolution* and increasing evolvability through the *improvement of genetic operators*. In functional level evolution, larger building blocks such as multipliers, multiplexers, adders, etc. are used as functions to scale up evolution instead of the use of primitive logic gates [10].

A number of problem decomposition techniques have been devised with the aim of breaking a complex problem into sub-problems in order to reduce the search space. These decomposition approaches are usually based on the circuit's outputs or inputs. Some decomposition techniques are manual, requiring the designer to dictate the decomposition process while others are done automatically using algorithms. In other works such as [4], multi-threaded parallel implementations of evolutionary algorithms, specifically CGP, have been developed to exploit modern processor architectures to allow for more fitness evaluations. However, just a single run was performed to evolve 5-bit × 5-bit multiplier due to the associated high computational effort [4]. In [20], CGP candidate circuits are transformed into a Binary Decision Diagram (BDD) and a comparison is made with the circuit specification also in a BDD format. The resulting hamming distance from the functional similarity comparison is the fitness value of the CGP circuit candidate. In comparison to CGP's traditional fitness evaluation, BDD-based evaluation is faster. Existing scalability approaches in current literature have proved their superiority to direct evolution. However, these approaches have only been capable of evolving relatively complex circuits.

2.1 Cartesian Genetic Programming and Grammatical Evolution

Cartesian Genetic Programming (CGP) is a GP variant that represent programs using direct acyclic graphs [9]. A CGP genotype consist of function, connection and output genes. CGP is widely used in the evolutionary design of digital circuits and has made a lot of progress [13], mainly at the gate level, but also at the functional-level.

Grammatical Evolution (GE) is a grammar-based GP system that evolves programs in any arbitrary languages using a Backus-Naur Form (BNF) grammar [11]. A mapper uses a linear genome and the provided grammar to synthesize the programs. The linear genome consists of codons which are used by the *modulo rule* to dictate production rule selection. The process continues until all non-terminals are expanded into terminals. GE has been used to evolve relatively complex circuits in [12].

3 Related Work

3.1 Functional-Level Evolution

In [6], half-adder, full adder and multiplier circuits were used as functions to design adders and multipliers. In comparison to gate-level evolution, function-level evolution obtained higher success rate as well as significant reduction in the number of generations in some instances [6]. Three-bit multipliers were evolved using binary multipexers in [22]. Approximate 9-input and 25-input median circuits [21], and an image filter [16] have also been evolved at functional-level.

3.2 Problem Decomposition

Increased complexity evolution (ICE), also known as divide-and-conquer methodology, breaks a complex system into simpler systems before evolution is performed on each sub-system in a bottom-up manner [18,19]. Sub-systems can be evolved in parallel (if no dependence exist between them) or sequentially. These evolved sub-systems are used as building blocks in a more complex sub-system(s) up the chain. The challenge with ICE is the definition of the fitness functions for the sub-systems has to be manually done. However, for certain problems such as circuit design, partitioning of training vectors based on circuit outputs is one option or the training set can be partitioned [18,19].

In contrast to ICE, Bidirectional Incremental Evolution (BIE) performs automatic decomposition of a complex circuit into subsystems using either a suitable standard decomposition technique (such as Shannon's theorem) or an EHW-oriented decomposition technique or a combination of both [5]. BIE progressively decomposes complex circuits in a top-down fashion while evolving each subsystem. Subsystem(s) are further broken down if evolution is unable to obtain optimal solutions. During the second stage of BIE, the evolved subsystems are assembled and optimized in a bottom-up fashion. In comparison, BIE outperformed direct evolution on 7-inputs and 10-output circuit benchmark problem.

When tested on more complex circuits, BIE performed poorly [17]. As a result, instead of output decomposition in the case of BIE, an input decomposition technique named Generalized Disjunction Decomposition (GDD) was proposed [17]. GDD automatically decomposes a complex circuit into two subcircuits: the evolvable and multiplexer subcircuits [17]. The number of inputs for the evolvable circuit is defined by the user which must be less than the initial number of inputs of the original system. Consequently, two truth tables are derived; one for each subcircuit. The evolvable subcircuit can be evolved using any EHW methods such IEC or BIE. The output of the evolvable subsystem serve as the inputs for the multiplexer sub-system. The remaining inputs not used in the evolvable subsystem are used as select lines for the multiplexer subsystem. The output of the multiplexer subsystem is that of the original complex system. GDD required fewer number of generations, time and obtained better fitness across randomly generated circuit problems and a selection of circuit benchmark problems from Microelectronics Center of North Carolina (MCNC) benchmark suite when compared to BIE [17].

Stepwise Dimension Reduction (SDR) is a layered output decomposition approach that decomposes a circuit into two subcircuits. The first and second subcircuits are evolved to handle input combinations with an output value of 1 and 0 respectively [14]. Internal intermediate mappings are devised if subcircuits are not of evolvable complexity. SDR evolved a 19-bit circuit which GDD was unable to evolve. SDR obtained comparable results for few of the benchmark problems in less time compared to GDD, but not on more complex multiple output circuit benchmarks [14]. SDR is effective on single output circuit problems such as the parity circuit.

3.3 Increasing Evolvability Through the Improvement of Genetic Operators

Biased Single Active Mutation is a variant of Single Active Mutation (SAM) devised to improve SAM's robustness for tackling combinational circuits design [8]. SAM ensures a single active gene is mutated during a mutation operation [2], unlike standard CGP point mutation which mutates either an active or inactive gene. In the event of an inactive gene mutation, offspring has the same fitness as it's parent as there is no change to the phenotype. In biased SAM, initial evolutionary experiments on selected benchmark problems are performed, during which the transition of functional gene mutations which result in the increase of offsprings fitness are recorded.

A transition probability matrix is constructed from the transitions. Functional mutation(s) that increase the fitness of offspring(s) are recorded (transition from previous function to current function). Subsequently, during mutation roulette wheel selection is applied on the transition probability matrix to determine the function the selected functional node should be mutated to [8].

Biased SAM outperformed SAM on all circuit design benchmarks used. Subsequently, Guided Active mutation (GAM) was proposed which mutates active node(s) in a subgraph corresponding to a single output in an attempt to increase the overall score of the output when compared to the truth table of the circuit. Results obtained from experiments using GAM revealed although GAM required fewer fitness evaluations to find feasible solutions, it recorded low success rates [15].

As a result, SAM and GAM were combined in order to exploit the advantages of both mutation operators, which resulted in high success rates and best results on the benchmark problems used [15]. Semantically-oriented mutation operator (SOMO) performs mutation in the phenotype space after which the resultant phenotype is encoded to its corresponding phenotype [3]. SOMO randomly selects an active node for mutation. A mutation operation may affect a node function or a single node input connection. During the node input connection mutation, semantics is applied to determine the best connection point that increases the fitness score of the circuit [3]. SOMO evolved combinational circuits significantly faster compared to the multi-threaded parallel CGP implementation in [4].

4   Proposed Approach and Experimental Design

4.1   Problems

Three circuit benchmark problems are used: *multiplier, adder* and *parity generator*. These are representative of evolutionary circuit design benchmark problems in current literature. All three circuit problems are evolved as parameterized design modules; thus, although all three circuits are evolved with default input(s)/output(s) bit-width sizes, once evolved, instances of the same module can be instantiated simply by changing the parameter values prior to simulation or synthesis without a re-run of evolutionary experiments as is the case for existing EHW methodologies. Parameterized design modules are designed using the keyword **parameter** in SV. The usage of the *parameter* keyword is shown in the corresponding production of ⟨design-module⟩ rule in all three circuit grammars.

Parameterizable N-bit Parity Generator. A parity generator circuit evaluates and generates a single bit (either 0 or 1) based on data to be transmitted in order to obtain an even or odd number of 1s. An odd parity generator ensures an odd number of 1's; conversely, an even parity circuit ensures an even number of 1's.

We design two different parity generator circuit grammars: *Parity Grammar A* and *Parity Grammar B* shown in Fig. 1 and Fig. 2 respectively. *Parity Grammar A* uses generate loops (synthesizable ⟨for-loop⟩) and bitwise operators (⟨bitwise-op⟩) to loop through the data bits while performing bitwise operations until a parity bit is obtained. *Parity Grammar B* uses both reduction operators (⟨reduction-op⟩) and bitwise-operators (⟨bitwise-op⟩). Reduction operators apply bitwise operations on the bits of an $n-bit$ operand (a vector) recursively to produce a scalar output.

The bitwise operators are used to construct variable length equations ($\langle$expr$\rangle$) using the scalar outputs of reduction operations as operands. We speculate that evolutionary runs using *Parity Grammar B* will be faster than using *Parity Grammar A* because the use of generate loop together with bitwise operators requires a minimum of *width* evaluation events to compute the parity of the data. However, in the case of *Parity Grammar B*, the reduction operators require a single evaluation event to return a scalar output when applied to an $n - bit$ operand or a vector.

```
⟨design-module⟩ ::= ⟨begin-module⟩⟨declarations⟩⟨initialize⟩⟨code-block⟩⟨output⟩⟨end-module⟩
   ⟨code-block⟩ ::= ⟨for-loop⟩⟨newline⟩
     ⟨for-loop⟩ ::= "for(i = 0; i < width; i = i + 1)"begin⟨newline⟩⟨stmt⟩end⟨newline⟩
         ⟨stmt⟩ ::= assign intmd_parity[i+1]"="⟨expr⟩;⟨newline⟩
         ⟨expr⟩ ::= ⟨select-bit⟩ | ⟨select-bit⟩⟨bitwise-op⟩⟨expr⟩ | ~(⟨expr⟩)
   ⟨select-bit⟩ ::= intmd_parity[i] | data[i]
       ⟨output⟩ ::= assign parity "=" intmd_parity[width];⟨newline⟩
   ⟨initialize⟩ ::= assign parity "=" even_odd;⟨newline⟩
   ⟨bitwise-op⟩ ::= ^ | & | "|" | ~^
 ⟨declarations⟩ ::= "logic [width : 0] intmd_parity; \n genvar i; \n"
 ⟨begin-module⟩ ::= "module parity \#(parameter width=128)(input logic [width-1:0]
                     data, input logic even_odd, output logic parity);"⟨newline⟩
   ⟨end-module⟩ ::= endmodule
      ⟨newline⟩ ::= "\n"
```

Fig. 1. N-bit Parity Generator Grammar A (default input bit-width is 128). This uses generate loop and bitwise operators.

Parameterizable N-bit Adder. An adder circuit performs addition in digital electronic devices. The adder grammar is shown in Fig. 7. It uses the always ($\langle$always-block$\rangle$) procedural block which takes a sensitivity list as arguments and executes the statements within its code-block whenever a signal within the list changes. The operators used are binary arithmetic operator ($+$) and bitwise operators ($\&, |, \hat{}$). The default input bit-width of the addends is 128 specified using the *parameter* keyword in the $\langle$begin-module$\rangle$ rule.

Parameterizable N-bit Multiplier. A multiplier performs multiplication in digital electronic devices such as computers, calculators etc. The particular multiplier type considered here is the Add-Shift Multiplier. The Add-Shift Multiplier's operation is based on longhand multiplication. Each digit of the multiplier multiplies the multiplicand to obtain an intermediate product shifted a digit to the left of the preceding intermediate product. All intermediate products are then summed up to obtain the product of the multiplication. The *Multiplier Grammar* is shown in Fig. 4. The grammar makes use of always ($\langle$always-block$\rangle$),

```
⟨design-module⟩ ::= ⟨begin-module⟩⟨code-block⟩⟨end-module⟩
   ⟨code-block⟩ ::= ⟨always-block⟩⟨newline⟩
 ⟨always-block⟩ ::= always"@(data or even_odd)"⟨newline⟩⟨stmt⟩
         ⟨stmt⟩ ::= parity "="⟨expr⟩;
         ⟨expr⟩ ::= ⟨reduct-expr⟩ | (⟨reduct-expr⟩⟨bitwise-op⟩⟨reduct-expr⟩)
                    | (⟨reduct-expr⟩⟨bitwise-op⟩⟨expr⟩)
   ⟨reduct-expr⟩ ::= ⟨reduction-op⟩⟨input⟩ | ⟨reduction-op⟩(⟨reduct-expr⟩)
                    | (⟨reduction-op⟩{⟨multi-concat-expr⟩})
⟨multi-concat-expr⟩ ::= ⟨input⟩ | ⟨reduct-expr⟩ | ⟨multi-concat-expr⟩,⟨multi-concat-expr⟩
        ⟨input⟩ ::= data | even_odd
 ⟨reduction-op⟩ ::= & | ~& | "|" | ~"|" | ^ | ~^
   ⟨bitwise-op⟩ ::= ^ | & | "|" | ~^
 ⟨begin-module⟩ ::= "module parity \#(parameter width=128)(input logic
                    [width-1:0] data, input logic even_odd, output logic parity);\n"
   ⟨end-module⟩ ::= endmodule
      ⟨newline⟩ ::= "\n"
```

Fig. 2. N-bit Parity Generator Grammar B (default input bit-width is 128). This uses *reduction* and *bitwise* operators.

for-loop (⟨for-loop⟩) and if-else (⟨if-else⟩) programming constructs in SV. Three different operators (⟨op⟩) are used: *binary arithmetic operator (+), shift operators (<<, >>)* and *bitwise operators (&, |)*.

4.2 Evolutionary Parameters

Preliminary evolutionary runs were performed in order to determine the appropriate parameters to use. Results obtained from the preliminary evolutionary runs showed the parity generator circuit is trivial to evolve. As a result large population sizes are not necessary. A population size of 200 is used for the parity generator circuits and 1,000-population is used for both adder and multiplier circuits. All other parameters remain the same across all three circuit benchmark problems. Table 2 details the evolutionary parameters used.

4.3 Training and Testing

Given the high input bit-width of these combinational circuits to be evolved, exhaustive testing is not feasible. Therefore, we create our test cases using two strategies as shown in Table 1. First, we identify the corner test case(s) for each circuit problem, usually targeting the test vectors located at the boundaries of all the possible test vectors (truth table). Next, we generate the remaining test cases by uniform random sampling (using $urandom() function in SV) the internal test vectors within the input range of each circuit. This ensures our testbenches have good coverage over all possible test vectors. Given that our parity generator circuit can behave as an odd or even parity based on the even_odd input signal, during training we use the same test cases to test both behaviours.

```
⟨design-module⟩ ::= ⟨always -block⟩⟨begin-module⟩⟨end-module⟩
 ⟨always -block⟩ ::= always @(a, b or carry_in)begin⟨newline⟩⟨stmt⟩end⟨newline⟩
  ⟨sum-output⟩ ::= {carry_out, sum} "=" ⟨expr⟩;⟨newline⟩
          ⟨io⟩ ::= a | b | carry_in
        ⟨expr⟩ ::= ⟨io⟩ | ⟨io⟩⟨op⟩(⟨expr⟩) | ~(⟨expr⟩)
          ⟨op⟩ ::= + | & | "|" | ^
⟨begin-module⟩ ::= "module adder \#(parameter width=128)(input logic [width-1:0] a, b,
                   input logic carry_in, output logic carry_out,
                   output logic [width-1:0] sum);"⟨newline⟩
  ⟨end-module⟩ ::= endmodule
     ⟨newline⟩ ::= "\n"
```

Fig. 3. N-bit + N-bit adder grammar

```
   ⟨design-module⟩ ::= ⟨begin-module⟩⟨declarations⟩⟨always⟩⟨end-module⟩
    ⟨declarations⟩ ::= integer⟨loop-var⟩;⟨next-line⟩
         ⟨always⟩ ::= always @(multiplicand or multiplier)⟨next-line⟩begin⟨next-line⟩
       ⟨for-loop⟩ ::= for(i"="0; i < i_width; i"="i+1)
                      begin⟨next-line⟩⟨if-else⟩⟨next-line⟩end⟨next-line⟩
         ⟨if-else⟩ ::= if(⟨condition⟩)⟨next-line⟩begin⟨next-line⟩ product "=" ⟨expr⟩;
                      ⟨next-line⟩end | if(⟨condition⟩)⟨next-line⟩begin⟨next-line⟩
                      product "=" ⟨expr⟩;⟨next-line⟩end⟨next-line⟩
                      else⟨next-line⟩begin⟨next-line⟩ product "=" ⟨expr⟩;⟨next-line⟩
       ⟨condition⟩ ::= ⟨io⟩[i]"=="⟨bit⟩
           ⟨expr⟩ ::= ⟨io⟩ | ⟨io⟩⟨op⟩(⟨expr⟩)
             ⟨op⟩ ::= + | << | >> | & | "|"
             ⟨io⟩ ::= multiplier | multiplicand | product | i
            ⟨bit⟩ ::= 1'b0 | 1'b1
   ⟨begin-module⟩ ::= module mult \#(parameter i_width=64, o_width=128)(input
                      logic [i_width-1":"0] multiplier, multiplicand,
                      output logic [o_width-1":"0] product);⟨next-line⟩
    ⟨end-module⟩ ::= endmodule
      ⟨next-line⟩ ::= "\n"
```

Fig. 4. N-bit × N-bit multiplier grammar

In order to ensure the evolved optimal solutions are indeed accurate, testing is performed. In a similar approach described above for training, we test optimal candidate circuits by choosing input bit-width sizes less and greater than the specified input bit-width with which the circuits are evolved. We then generate the test cases accordingly. For example, we tested the adder using 32-bit + 32-bit and 256-bit + 256-bit test vectors as shown in Table 1. Recall all evolved circuits are parameterized.

Experiments were ran on a Dell OptiPlex-5060 Desktop with a RAM size of 32 gigabyte and an Intel Core i7-8700 CPU with 6 cores and a processor base frequency of 3.20 GHz.

Table 1. Test cases for benchmark problems. a and b refers to addends for the adder circuit. For the multiplier circuit, a and b are *multiplier* and *multplicand* respectively. $N = $ bit-width

Problem	Corner cases	Training	Testing	Test cases
N-bit Parity (default N = 128)	1. data = 0 2. data = $2^N - 1$	N = 128	N = 32 N = 1024	48 sampled test inputs 128-bit data
N-bit + N-bit adder (default N = 64)	1. a = 0, b = 0 2. a = $2^N - 1$, b = $2^N - 1$ 3. a = 0, b = N-bit number	N = 64	N = 32 N = 256	47 sampled test inputs between 0 to $(2^N - 1)$
N-bit × N-bit multiplier (default N = 64)	1. a = 0, b = 0 2. a = $2^N - 1$, b = $2^N - 1$ 3. a = 0, b = N-bit number 4. a = 1, b = N-bit number	N = 64	N = 32 N = 256	46 sampled test inputs between 0 to $(2^N - 1)$

Table 2. Experimental run parameters

Parameter type	Parameter value
Initialization	Sensible Initialization
N$^{\underline{o}}$ of generations	50
Mutation rate	0.01
Crossover rate	0.8
Replacement rate	0.5
N$^{\underline{o}}$ of runs	50
Population	200 for Parity Generator Circuit 1,000 for Adder and Multiplier Circuits
Selection	Lexicase Parent Selection

5 Results and Discussion

In order to visualize the trend of evolution taking place, we plotted the mean best and average fitnesses against generation with error bars for each of the three circuit benchmark problems. The error bars represent standard deviation. Figures 5 and 6 show the plot for the *Parity Generator Grammar A* and *Parity Generator Grammar B* respectively. Both parity grammars attained maximum mean fitness right from the initial generation. However, *Parity Generator Grammar*

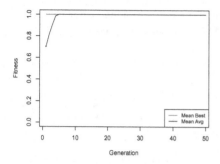

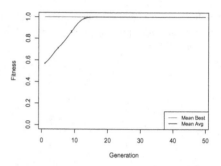

Fig. 5. Mean best and mean average with error bars for N-bit Parity Generator Grammar A

Fig. 6. Mean best and mean average with error bars for N-bit Parity Generator Grammar B

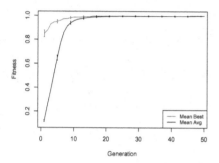

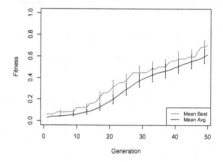

Fig. 7. Mean best and mean average with error bars for N-bit + N-bit adder

Fig. 8. Mean best and mean average with error bars for N-bit × N-bit multiplier

B recorded a slightly lower mean average fitnesses during its initial generations compared to *Parity Generator Grammar A*. We conclude that the parity generator circuits are trivial to evolve as optimal solutions are found in the initial generations as observed in Figs. 5 and 6. In Fig. 7, the plot for the adder circuit is shown; clearly, in this case, evolution is working hard. Similarly, the same observation is made for the multiplier circuit in Fig. 8. However, in the case of the adder circuit, the mean fitness increases rapidly as the evolution progresses, while in the case of the multiplier circuit, fitness increases slowly as the evolution progresses. Short to non existent error bars are observed for the parity and adder circuits in Figs. 5, 6 and 7 indicating the fitness values for candidate solutions in a specified generation are close or almost equal to the mean fitness. For the multiplier circuit, short error bars are observed in the earlier generations and widens gradually in subsequent generations signifying increasing variability in individual fitness values compared to the mean fitness value.

In Table 3, we tabulated the number of successful runs obtained for each of the three circuit benchmark problems. We recorded 100% success rate for the parity generator circuit for both grammars and the adder circuit. 36 out of 50 optimal solutions were obtained for the multiplier circuit corresponding to 72% success rate.

To gain insight into the 14 non-optimal solutions obtained for the multiplier circuit benchmark problem, we conducted post-testing on each. In our post-testing, each non-optimal circuit was tested using the same testbench used in the evolutionary experiments. We then studied the test cases (test vectors) passed and failed by each circuit. Recall, we had two set of test cases: corner cases and the sampled test cases within the circuit's input range. We observed all 14 unsuccessful runs were only able to solve the 4 corner cases shown in the Table 1. This observation is of utmost significance as it proves sampling test vectors from the circuit's input range alone is not sufficient to avoid exhaustive testing for complex combinational circuits. Corner case testing is equally important as it ensures valid inputs likely to cause circuit malfunction are explicitly tested.

Table 4 details the average evolutionary time per run for each of the three circuit benchmark problems. On average an experimental run takes 18.14 min for the N-bit + N-bit adder (N = 64) and 55.28 min for the N-bit × N-bit multiplier (N = 64). The multiplier has a higher average evolutionary run because it performs several additions to sum up the partial products computed in addition to other operations. The N-bit parity generator circuit (N = 128) using Grammar A takes 1,056.83 min while Grammar B takes 0.99 min. In order to assess the effect of input bit-width sizes on the evolutionary time, we conducted separate experiments using smaller input-width sizes, N = 32 for adder and multiplier circuits; N = 64 for the parity circuit. It took 17.99 min for $32 - bit + 32 - bit$ adder and 48.91 min for the $32 - bit \times 32 - bit$ multiplier. We observe, no significance impact in terms of input sizes on both the adder and multiplier circuits. It took 15.89 min on average per run for the $32 - bit$ parity generator. We also observe that the average duration per run for the parity generator circuit using Grammar A is far greater than Grammar B. This is because in grammar A, we used bitwise operators together with a `for-loop` as a result it requires a minimum of *width* evaluation events each time an input changes to generate the parity. Grammar B on the other hand make use of reduction operators that takes a vector and return a single bit and they do so in a single evaluation event. Thus, the use of reduction operators is more efficient in regards to simulation time for the parity generator circuit; therefore suggest the choice of operators to be incorporated in grammars to be carefully selected.

In the Appendix, we show an optimal solution for each of the benchmark problems.

Table 3. Success rate

Problem	Successful runs (out of 50)
N-bit + N-bit Adder	50
N-bit × N-bit Multiplier	36
N-bit Parity Generator Grammar A	50
N-bit Parity Generator Grammar B	50

Table 4. Average duration per run in minutes

Problem	Input size	Average duration per run (Minutes)
N-bit + N-bit Adder	32 + 32	17.99
	64 + 64	18.14
N-bit × N-bit Multiplier	32 × 32	48.91
	64 × 64	55.28
N-bit Parity (Grammar A)	64	62.57
	128	1056.83
N-bit Parity (Grammar B)	64	1.01
	.128	0.99

6   Conclusion and Future Work

In this work, we have demonstrated that, when using GE with HDLs, specifically SV, we are capable of designing complex circuits. This is because of the high level of abstraction at which circuits can be designed through the use of HDLs. We evolved fully functional parameterized N-bit parity generator circuit, N-bit + N-bit adder and N-bit × N-bit multiplier within reasonable evolutionary time.

We also proved how appropriate selection of operators can create efficient circuit designs that require significant less simulation time than others in the case of the parity generator circuit. We obtained 100% success rate for the parity and adder circuits; and 72% success rate on the multiplier circuit problem. In comparison to current literature, the circuits evolved in this work represent the most complex accurate adder, multiplier and parity circuits evolved [3,4,8,17]. In addition, the evolved circuits are parameterized. Thus, they have the additional advantage of being reusable because the same circuit can be instantiated to handle different bit-width sizes without the need for a re-run of evolutionary experiments as is the case for existing methodologies within the EHW field.

Moving forward, there is the need to investigate the limitations of evolving more complex circuits other than those used in this work. This will give as insight regarding the limitations of our approach and how to address them. Very large complex circuit will be slower to test and therefore the conventional generate and test approach of standard GP systems may not suffice. A more efficient approach that will exploit the power of modern processors will be of high priority when we begin to venture into industrial scale circuit designs. Furthermore, in a typical circuit design flow, our SV evolved circuits will have to go through the synthesis phase, where synthesis tools are used to obtain the equivalent gate-level representation. As a result, circuit optimization is dependent on the robustness of open-source or commercial synthesis tools. However, progress made in Evolutionary Optimization of Digital Circuits, a sub-field of EHW which focuses on the optimization of functional circuits, have obtained competitive results compared to conventional synthesis tools [1,7].

Exploiting the capabilities of GE and CGP for functional evolution and optimization of complex circuits respectively will be the starting point of realizing evolutionary circuit design tool chains. Finally, for very large complex circuits that naturally require decomposition, HDLs support hierarchical modelling. In hierarchical modelling low-level design modules are included in high-modules and communication is established through the inputs and output ports of the low-level design modules. Our future work will employ this approach to design other complex circuits.

Appendix

```
module parity
#(parameter width=128)
(input logic [width-1:0] data, input
logic even_odd, output logic parity);
logic [width : 0] intmd_parity;
genvar i;
assign intmd_parity[0] = even_odd;
for(i = 0; i < width; i = i + 1)
begin
assign intmd_parity[i+1] = data[i] ~^
  intmd_parity[i] | data[i] ~^
  intmd_parity[i];
end
assign parity = intmd_parity[width];
endmodule
```

Listing 1. An optimal solution obtained for N-bit Parity Generator (Grammar B) (N = 128).

```
module parity
#(parameter width=128)
(input logic [width-1:0] data, input
logic even_odd, output logic parity);
  always @(data or even_odd)
    parity = (~|((|{even_odd})) ^ ~^
       ((^{data})));
endmodule
```

Listing 2. An optimal solution obtained for N-bit Parity Generator (Grammar B) (N = 128).

```
module adder
#(parameter width=64)
(input logic [width-1 : 0] a, b,
  input   carry_in,
  output logic carry_out,
  output logic [width-1:0] sum);
always @(a, b or carry_in) begin
{carry_out, sum} = a + (b + (carry_in));
end
endmodule
```

Listing 3. An optimal solution obtained for N-bit + N-bit Adder (N = 64).

```
module mult
#(parameter i_width=64, o_width=128)
(input logic [i_width-1:0] multiplier,
  multiplicand, output logic
  [o_width-1:0] product );
integer i;
always @(multiplicand or multiplier)
begin
product = 1'b0;
for(i=0;i<i_widthi=i+1) begin
  if(multiplier[i] == 1'b1) begin
    product = product + (
    multiplicand << (i));
  end
end
end
endmodule
```

Listing 4. An optimal solution obtained for N-bit × N-bit Adder (N = 64).

References

1. Fišer, P., Schmidt, J., Vašíček, Z., Sekanina, L.: On logic synthesis of conventionally hard to synthesize circuits using genetic programming. In: 13th IEEE Symposium on Design and Diagnostics of Electronic Circuits and Systems, pp. 346–351 (2010). https://doi.org/10.1109/DDECS.2010.5491755

2. Goldman, B.W., Punch, W.F.: Reducing wasted evaluations in cartesian genetic programming. In: Krawiec, K., Moraglio, A., Hu, T., Etaner-Uyar, A.Ş., Hu, B. (eds.) EuroGP 2013. LNCS, vol. 7831, pp. 61–72. Springer, Heidelberg (2013). https://doi.org/10.1007/978-3-642-37207-0_6

3. Hodan, D., Mrazek, V., Vasicek, Z.: Semantically-oriented mutation operator in cartesian genetic programming for evolutionary circuit design. In: Proceedings of the 2020 Genetic and Evolutionary Computation Conference, GECCO 2020, pp. 940–948. Association for Computing Machinery, New York (2020). https://doi.org/10.1145/3377930.3390188

4. Hrbacek, R., Sekanina, L.: Towards highly optimized cartesian genetic programming: from sequential via SIMD and thread to massive parallel implementation. In: Proceedings of the 2014 Annual Conference on Genetic and Evolutionary Computation, GECCO 2014, pp. 1015–1022. Association for Computing Machinery, New York (2014). https://doi.org/10.1145/2576768.2598343

5. Kalganova, T.: Bidirectional incremental evolution in extrinsic evolvable hardware. In: Proceedings of the Second NASA/DoD Workshop on Evolvable Hardware, pp. 65–74 (2000). https://doi.org/10.1109/EH.2000.869343

6. Kalganova, T.: An extrinsic function-level evolvable hardware approach. In: Poli, R., Banzhaf, W., Langdon, W.B., Miller, J., Nordin, P., Fogarty, T.C. (eds.) EuroGP 2000. LNCS, vol. 1802, pp. 60–75. Springer, Heidelberg (2000). https://doi.org/10.1007/978-3-540-46239-2_5

7. Kocnova, J., Vasicek, Z.: Towards a scalable EA-based optimization of digital circuits. In: Sekanina, L., Hu, T., Lourenço, N., Richter, H., García-Sánchez, P. (eds.) EuroGP 2019. LNCS, vol. 11451, pp. 81–97. Springer, Cham (2019). https://doi.org/10.1007/978-3-030-16670-0_6

8. Manfrini, F.A.L., Bernardino, H.S., Barbosa, H.J.C.: A novel efficient mutation for evolutionary design of combinational logic circuits. In: Handl, J., Hart, E., Lewis, P.R., López-Ibáñez, M., Ochoa, G., Paechter, B. (eds.) PPSN 2016. LNCS, vol. 9921, pp. 665–674. Springer, Cham (2016). https://doi.org/10.1007/978-3-319-45823-6_62

9. Miller, J.F., Thomson, P.: Cartesian genetic programming. In: Poli, R., Banzhaf, W., Langdon, W.B., Miller, J., Nordin, P., Fogarty, T.C. (eds.) EuroGP 2000. LNCS, vol. 1802, pp. 121–132. Springer, Heidelberg (2000). https://doi.org/10.1007/978-3-540-46239-2_9

10. Murakawa, M., Yoshizawa, S., Kajitani, I., Furuya, T., Iwata, M., Higuchi, T.: Hardware evolution at function level. In: Voigt, H.-M., Ebeling, W., Rechenberg, I., Schwefel, H.-P. (eds.) PPSN 1996. LNCS, vol. 1141, pp. 62–71. Springer, Heidelberg (1996). https://doi.org/10.1007/3-540-61723-X_970

11. Ryan, C., Collins, J.J., Neill, M.O.: Grammatical evolution: evolving programs for an arbitrary language. In: Banzhaf, W., Poli, R., Schoenauer, M., Fogarty, T.C. (eds.) EuroGP 1998. LNCS, vol. 1391, pp. 83–96. Springer, Heidelberg (1998). https://doi.org/10.1007/BFb0055930

12. Ryan., C., Tetteh., M.K., Dias., D.M.: Behavioural modelling of digital circuits in system verilog using grammatical evolution. In: Proceedings of the 12th International Joint Conference on Computational Intelligence, ECTA, vol. 1, pp. 28–39. INSTICC, SciTePress (2020). https://doi.org/10.5220/0010066600280039
13. Sekanina, L., Walker, J.A., Kaufmann, P., Platzner, M.: Evolution of electronic circuits. In: Miller, J. (eds) Cartesian Genetic Programming. Natural Computing Series. Springer, Heidelberg, pp. 125–179 (2011). https://doi.org/10.1007/978-3-642-17310-3_5
14. Henriques da Silva, J.E., Soares Bernardino, H.: A 3-step cartesian genetic programming for designing combinational logic circuits with multiplexers. In: Moura Oliveira, P., Novais, P., Reis, L.P. (eds.) EPIA 2019. LNCS (LNAI), vol. 11804, pp. 762–774. Springer, Cham (2019). https://doi.org/10.1007/978-3-030-30241-2_63
15. da Silva, J.E.H., de Souza, L.A.M., Bernardino, H.S.: Cartesian genetic programming with guided and single active mutations for designing combinational logic circuits. In: Nicosia, G., Pardalos, P., Umeton, R., Giuffrida, G., Sciacca, V. (eds.) LOD 2019. LNCS, vol. 11943, pp. 396–408. Springer, Cham (2019). https://doi.org/10.1007/978-3-030-37599-7_33
16. Slaný, K., Sekanina, L.: Fitness landscape analysis and image filter evolution using functional-level CGP. In: Ebner, M., O'Neill, M., Ekárt, A., Vanneschi, L., Esparcia-Alcázar, A.I. (eds.) EuroGP 2007. LNCS, vol. 4445, pp. 311–320. Springer, Heidelberg (2007). https://doi.org/10.1007/978-3-540-71605-1_29
17. Stomeo, E., Kalganova, T., Lambert, C.: Generalized disjunction decomposition for evolvable hardware. IEEE Trans. Syst. Man Cybern. Part B (Cybernetics) **36**(5), 1024–1043 (2006)
18. Torresen, J.: A divide-and-conquer approach to evolvable hardware. In: Sipper, M., Mange, D., Pérez-Uribe, A. (eds.) ICES 1998. LNCS, vol. 1478, pp. 57–65. Springer, Heidelberg (1998). https://doi.org/10.1007/BFb0057607
19. Torresen, J.: Two-step incremental evolution of a prosthetic hand controller based on digital logic gates. In: Liu, Y., Tanaka, K., Iwata, M., Higuchi, T., Yasunaga, M. (eds.) ICES 2001. LNCS, vol. 2210, pp. 1–13. Springer, Heidelberg (2001). https://doi.org/10.1007/3-540-45443-8_1
20. Vasicek, Z., Sekanina, L.: How to evolve complex combinational circuits from scratch? In: 2014 IEEE International Conference on Evolvable Systems, pp. 133–140 (2014)
21. Vasicek, Z., Sekanina, L.: Evolutionary approach to approximate digital circuits design. IEEE Trans. Evol. Comput. **19**(3), 432–444 (2015). https://doi.org/10.1109/TEVC.2014.2336175
22. Vassilev, V.K., Miller, J.F.: Embedding landscape neutrality to build a bridge from the conventional to a more efficient three-bit multiplier circuit. In: Proceedings of the Genetic and Evolutionary Computation Conference. Morgan Kaufmann (2000)
23. Wolf, C.: Yosys open synthesis suite. http://www.clifford.at/yosys/

Evofficient: Reproducing a Cartesian Genetic Programming Method

Lorenz Wendlinger[✉], Julian Stier, and Michael Granitzer

Chair of Data Science, University of Passau, Innstraße 31, 94032 Passau, Germany
`lorenz.wendlinger@uni-passau.de`

Abstract. Designing Neural Network Architectures requires expert knowledge and extensive parameter searches. Neural Architecture Search (NAS) aims to change that by automating the design process. It is important that these approaches are reproducible so they can be used in real-life scenarios. In our work, we reproduce a genetic programming approach to designing convolutional neural networks called CGP-CNN. We show that this is difficult and requires many changes to the training scheme, reducing real-life applicability. We achieve a final accuracy of $90.6\% \pm 0.005$, substantially lower than the reported $93.7\% \pm 0.005$. This negates some of the benefits of using CGP-CNN for NAS. We establish a random search as a consensus baseline and show that it produces similar results to the evolutionary method of CGP-CNN. To assess the adaptability and generality of the presented algorithm, it is applied to CIFAR-100 and SVHN with a final accuracy of 63.1% and 95.6%, respectively. We extend the investigated NAS by two methods for predicting candidate fitnesses from partial learning curves. This improves CGP-CNN runtime efficiency by a factor of 1.69.

Keywords: Neural Architecture Search · Reproduction · Object recognition · Convolutional Neural Network

1 Introduction

Two major reasons drive the field of Neural Architecture Search (NAS), a sub-field of automated machine learning. First, the automation of repeated work. The design of neural networks involves expert knowledge and extensive work. Human experts need substantial knowledge about the interplay of various possible structural components of a network design and the effects of various hyper-parameter choices. Further work emerges from tying such a network's design then into a machine learning pipeline. Automated machine learning strives to automate design choices and integration labor. The second reason driving NAS is to gain insights on new design choices or even on relationships between design choices and performance metrics.

This work has been partially funded by the "Bavarian Ministry of Economic Affairs, Regional Development and Energy" under the grant 'CrossAI' (IUK593/002).

T. Hu et al. (Eds.): EuroGP 2021, LNCS 12691, pp. 162–178, 2021.
https://doi.org/10.1007/978-3-030-72812-0_11

One of these popular NAS methods are evolutionary searches and genetic programming in particular. CGP-CNN [26] by Suganuma et al. is such a method.

This work studies the reproducibility of results obtained by Suganuma et al. and reports various issues. These issues shed light on the difficulty of comparing research results in Neural Architecture Search and using it in practice. Furthermore, performance predictions are used as a way to improve CGP-CNN runtime and influence the exploration phase of the search method. Our **contributions** comprise:

- results on the reproducibility of CGP-CNN [26] on the CIFAR-10[1] image classification task[2] including many necessary changes,
- an analysis of the low repeatability of various CGP-CNN components,
- random search as a consensus baseline for CGP-CNN, rivaling the evolutionary search strategy in performance,
- results on the surprisingly high adaptability of CGP-CNN to SVHN[3] and CIFAR-100,
- and accelerating CGP-CNN using performance prediction yielding a $1.69\times$ speed-up.

2   Background

According to [10], a survey on NAS, three properties characterize a NAS approach: the search space, search strategy and performance estimation strategy.

The most simple architecture space is sequential stacking of hyper-parameterized layers. However, Suganuma et al. define their search space using a cartesian grid (c.f. [21]). This represents a restriction on arbitrary directed acyclic graphs and allows for more complex multi-branch networks. The CGP search space consists of high-level functional blocks such as convolutions or pooling. This is in contrast to many cell-based methods, such as [28,30], that search for repeated motifs. These cells are then stacked to create the final model.

The search strategy employed by Suganuma et al. is a variation of the greedy $(\mu + \lambda)$ evolutionary strategy (c.f. [6]). Similar strategies have been used for NAS as early as 1994 (c.f. [2,25]). However, the formulation of NAS as a Bayesian optimization problem has lead to many successful methods as well, such as [5,8, 20]. Reinforcement learning can also be used for NAS, e.g. in [3,29] or [28].

For comparing results between NAS runs, we adopt the notion of a mean testing accuracy (MTA) from [24]. It measures the test accuracy of the top percentile selected via validation accuracy and is therefore more robust than only the top testing accuracy (TTA).

---

[1] CIFAR-10 and CIFAR-100 [16] are image classification datasets of 32×32 color images.

[2] Code and experimental setup: https://zenodo.org/record/2611575.

[3] Street View House Numbers (SVHN) [22] is an image classification task, "seen as similar in flavor to MNIST", containing images of digits from house numbers.

3   Reproduction

CGP-CNN is a Neural Architecture Search (NAS) based on an evolutionary $(1 + \lambda)$ strategy. During the search, individuals are trained for 50 epochs and evaluated on a validation set to measure their fitness. After the search, the winning individual is trained for 500 epochs with a polishing-up schema and evaluated on the test set.

For real-life applicability, NAS needs to be reproducible. The main goal of the study was to fully reproduce CGP-CNN as described in Suganuma's original paper. This includes the re-implementation of CGP-CNN in a different deep-learning framework, namely `tensorflow` [1].

As the high-level description was not sufficient to achieve a level of performance comparable to the one reported, we performed several experiments to justify changes in the following areas: The *polishing-up schema* is used to fully train the final found architecture which directly influences the result reported for a NAS run. The *fitness evaluation schema* is used during the NAS and determines which architectures are selected.

A full-stack comparison finally shows how successful the reproduction was. We furthermore present a random search baseline for method-agnostic comparison between search spaces.

Like in CGP-CNN, two dataset scenarios have been considered: the full dataset scenario on CIFAR-10 and a small dataset scenario in which only 5 000 images are used for training.

3.1   Polishing-Up Schema

In [26], only two architectures are reported, so the first step in reproduction is to verify that these architectures can be trained to the reported performance level. We had to make two alterations for the polishing-up schema to work to an appropriate degree, namely the learning rate schedule and weight decay. However, evaluation using two *winning* architectures for both dataset scenarios from the original paper shows that our schema does not achieve the same results as reported in [26]. We observe a margin of 2.83% (91.37% over 3 runs vs. 94.2% reported) for the full dataset scenario and 2.81% for the small dataset scenario (c.f. Table 1).

Learning Rate Schedule. The learning rate schedule of [26] could not be used in our implementation since it resulted in gradient explosions immediately after increasing the learning rate to 0.1. While the reason for this is difficult to find, it probably being related to slightly different uses of the GPU computing API between frameworks, a heuristic for setting the maximum possible learning rate proved a viable workaround. As the numerical error manifests in the first few steps, progressively lowering the learning rates to the point at which it vanishes is quite effective. This is done in steps of 0.01 from 0.1 to 0.01. Architectures that diverge later on or require a lower learning rate than 0.01 as per this heuristic are assigned a final fitness of 0. This schedule works better than a fixed, lower learning rate, but still falls short of the results reported by Suganuma et al.

Table 1. Test accuracy for winning architectures from [26] after full training on small or full dataset using different frameworks. For `tensorflow` results over 3 trials are aggregated.

Dataset	Framework	Test accuracy
Full	chainer	**94.2%**
	tensorflow	91.37% ± 0.068
Small	chainer	**76.52%**
	tensorflow	73.71 % ± 0.79

Weight Decay. With a decay factor of 5×10^{-4} as suggested in [26] and [11], in our experiments networks consistently achieve lower accuracy than without. Applying weight decay also results in much more erratic learning curves and corresponding variation of final accuracy between runs. We believe that the negative effects of applying weight decay is a result of the change in framework and therefore not directly comparable to the results of [26].

Evaluation Result Selection. Suganuma et al. employ a *top-k* strategy to select the best network weights for an individual after training. For the k last epochs they are evaluated on a set of unseen data. The best of these results is then reported. *Top-450* is also used for polishing-up, however with the reserved cifar-10 test partition as a validation set. We investigated the effects of this methodologically problematic selection.

Tested in a small-dataset scenario on the same 100 random architectures used for Sect. 3.2, using the top-450 strategy results in a marginal improvement (66.61% vs. 66.34% on average) over evaluating after the last epoch. This concordance is a result of the consistency and timely convergence the learning curves exhibit (with no weight decay and more conservative learning rates). Consequently, we decided to reuse the *top-450* evaluation strategy, which allows us to have one fewer changing variable in reproduction.

3.2 Fitness Evaluation Schema

The candidate fitness is evaluated on the validation set after 50 training epochs and can be seen as an approximation of the final evaluation with the polishing-up schema. It is used to select the highest performing individuals during the NAS and thereby directly influences its outcome. For this reason it should also be repeatable.

We investigated the choices for optimizer and learning rate and how they influence repeatability as well as how it compares to the polishing-up schema.

Learning Rate. Similarly to the findings for polishing up, high learning rates prevent convergence for many architectures (53 out of a random sample of 100), while also considerably decreasing repeatability. *Adam* [14] could not be used with a learning rate of 0.01. We therefore tried adjusting the learning rate to achieve convergence for most randomly generated architectures. With a tenfold reduction to 0.001, all of the tested 100 architectures could be trained and evaluate to much higher accuracies with a mean of 0.667 ± 0.04 compared to a mean of 0.351 ± 0.23 with the higher learning rate. An investigation into repeatability compared to other optimizers (c.f. Sect. 3.2) suggests it is also advantageous in this regard. The learning rate schedule (now simply 50 epochs with $\eta = 0.001$) was not modified to keep results comparable.

Final Accuracy Approximation Quality. The explicit goal of using the fast candidate evaluation method is to exploit a linear relationship between validation accuracy (VA) and testing accuracy (TA) that allows the implication $VA(x) > VA(y) \Rightarrow TA(x) > TA(y)$ to be used with some uncertainty. We use 100 randomly generated architectures and compute both their TA, using the polishing-up schema described in Sect. 3.1, and VA using the different optimizers. The learning rate is set to *0.001* for all except *Adadelta*, which is used with no predefined learning rate (i.e. a learning rate of 1) as proposed in [27]. The chosen optimizers are *Adam* [14], as used in the original *CGP-CNN*, *Adagrad* [9] plus its variation *AdaDelta*, plain *GradientDescent* as well as *RMSProp* [12].

While *RMSProp* shows slightly higher correlation, it attains significantly lower R^2 score. *Adadelta* is almost on par and might also be a reasonable choice as it not requiring a predetermined learning rate removes some complexity. Plain Gradient Descent and *Adagrad* perform much worse and are not suitable for this task (Table 2).

Table 2. Final accuracy approximation quality with different optimizers; Error between approximated performance and full training, both evaluated on validation set.

Optimizer	r2	corr	mse	mean	std
RMSProp	0.289	**0.772**	0.002	0.665	0.042
Adam	**0.327**	0.77	**0.001**	**0.667**	**0.042**
Adadelta	−2.15	0.69	0.007	0.616	0.046
Adagrad	−30.225	0.579	0.066	0.438	0.051
Gradient Descent	−51.166	0.41	0.11	0.364	0.054

Repeatability. Due to the random initialization as well as the non-deterministic nature of training neural networks on GPUs, validation accuracies fluctuate between runs. We decided to investigate whether this can be improved by changing the used optimizer.

For 10 randomly generated architectures, the validation accuracy timeline is obtained via *best_of_k* with $k = 10$ and 50 epochs by computing the validation accuracy after every epoch. We do this for 20 independent runs to assess consistency. The initialization is kept identical between all optimizers and runs. The same is true for any other non-deterministic elements of training, namely dataset splitting, batch shuffling and image augmentations.

Adam and *RMSProp* are on par for most architectures. *Adadelta*, *Adagrad* and *GradientDescent* don't achieve accuracies high enough to be considered in this task (c.f. Fig. 1). However, we include them for their very interesting property of showing no or minute variation between runs (c.f. Fig. 2). It can be assumed that this is partly due to smaller gradients that reduce the effect of non-determinism in updates.

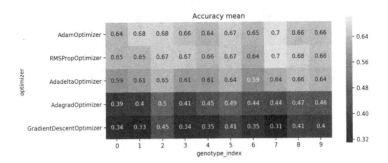

Fig. 1. Mean validation accuracy achieved after training of 10 randomly generated individuals with different optimizers across 20 runs.

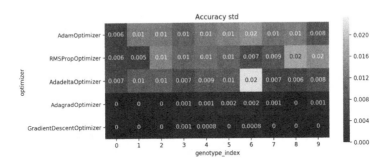

Fig. 2. Standard Deviation of validation accuracy achieved after training of 10 randomly generated individuals with different optimizers across 20 runs.

Unfortunately, all approaches that achieve adequate accuracy add noise to the selection process that can change results of the NAS between runs.

To isolate the effects of update size, the step size η can be varied while keeping the used optimizer constant. As previous experiments suggest *Adam* as the most suitable candidate, it was chosen for this ablation study. The same architectures as before were used, also using the same random configuration for each trial.

Results (c.f. Fig. 2) suggest that update size is a large factor in repeatability. It has to be noted that the runs with 0 variation for learning rates 0.01 and 0.005 all resulted in 0.1 accuracy, i.e. the network could not be trained.

The lowest tested step size, $\eta = 5e{-}05$, achieves repeatability on par with *Adagrad*, the best of considered optimizers that can be considered *repeatable*. However, Adam with $\eta = 5e{-}05$ achieves this in conjunction with significantly higher resulting accuracy. This shows that update size is a more important factor than the optimization algorithm itself.

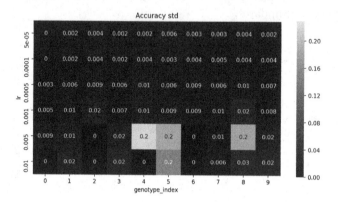

Fig. 3. Standard Deviation of accuracy achieved after partial training of 10 randomly generated individuals using *Adam* with different learning rates in 10 runs. Note how lower learning rates result in higher repeatability.

These two studies highlight the difficulty in finding a training schema that is both repeatable and shows good convergence. However, the configuration of *Adam* with $\eta = 0.001$ that was chosen based on previous experiments is a good compromise.

3.3   Full-Stack Comparison

With both the polishing-up schema and the fitness evaluation schema evaluated against and aligned with the reported values as far as possible, a test of the full NAS stack can be performed. Comparison is complicated by the performance of our polishing-up being slightly worse than what is reported in [26]. If, however, our NAS produces results on par with the values our polishing-up schema generates for winners reported by Suganuma et al., we consider the NAS similar.

Small-Dataset-Scenario. If the CGP is on par with Suganuma et al.'s implementation, a winner with a TVA of 70.4% and TTA of 73.71% should be found (c.f. Sect. 3.1). Three trials with fixed parameters but different random seeds were performed. As apparent from Table 3, results are as expected concerning TTA. However, the validation accuracy of the found winner is about 4% higher than the reference and on par with the polished-up performance.

Table 3. Results for small dataset modified $1 + \lambda$ using different frameworks. Standard deviation is given where available. Values for *CGP-CNN* taken from [26]. Aggregated over 3 trials for *evofficient*.

Framework	TTA	TVA	params (Mio)	GPU time
Evofficient	0.743 ± 0.009	0.745 ± 0.02	**1.01** ± 0.11	4d 10 h ± 18 h
CGP-CNN	**0.765**	–	3.9	–

Full-Dataset-Scenario. Since using the full dataset more computationally demanding than the small-dataset scenario and not the focus of this work, only two NAS runs were undertaken.

As before, the accuracies obtained in Sect. 3.1 serve as a reference with a VA of 88.0% and TA of 91.37%. Results are analogous to the small dataset scenarios, with equivalent test accuracy and a slightly higher VA than expected based on the investigated architectures reported in [26] (c.f. Table 4).

Table 4. Results for full dataset modified $1 + \lambda$ using different frameworks. Standard deviation is given wherever available. Values for *CGP-CNN* taken from [26]. Aggregated over 3 trials for *CGP-CNN* and over 2 runs for *evofficient*.

Framework	TTA	TVA	params (Mio)	GPU time
Evofficient	0.906 ± 0.005	0.888 ± 0.001	**1.13** ± 0.09	6d 21h ± 11 h
CGP-CNN	**0.937** ± 0.005	–	1.75 ± 0.23	15d 2 h ± 20 h

This suggests that the evolutionary strategy discovers competitive architectures, while only the difficulties in reproducing the polishing-up schema result in lower test accuracies than Suganuma et al. reported.

3.4   Random Search Baseline

Random Search (RS) is the most basic approach to hyper-parameter tuning and can be applied to most problems, making it ideal for comparison.

Each random search run is assigned the same 3 000 evaluations budget that results from 1 500 generations of the CGP-CNN default $1 + \lambda$ with $\lambda = 2$. The variation of random seeds leads to a change in genotype initialization, dataset split, batch composition, image augmentation and weight initialization between each trial. The best VA is achieved by RS outliers. Furthermore the MVA of $1 + \lambda$ is significantly higher. We can see (c.f. Table 5) that the clustering of test accuracies is much higher for $1 + \lambda$, as indicated by the higher average MTA.

Overall the comparison to random search presents mixed results that allow for two conclusions: The architecture search space is well-constructed for CIFAR-10 and random search is a sufficient strategy for sampling it.

Table 5. Results of NAS trials using different methods and random seeds in the small dataset scenario. Aggregated over three trials with random seeds $\{2016, 42, 31415\}$.

Method	MTA	TTA	MVA	TVA	params (Mio)
$1 + \lambda$	**0.742**	0.743	**0.730**	**0.745**	1.013
RS	0.722	**0.750**	0.718	0.739	0.723

4   Accelerating Neural Architecture Search Using Accuracy Prediction

The most costly step in Neural Architecture Search is evaluating the individuals' fitness. This evaluation process is called *performance estimation* and is usually done by training and measuring individuals on a potentially large dataset. However, this process also shows patterns such as similar learning curves [8,15] that can be exploited, allowing to predict performance for multiple individuals. Two performance prediction approaches can be differentiated by the type of features they require. *Genotypical prediction* needs only the genotype, an untrained network topology, for inference, whereas *phenotypical prediction* necessitates at least partial training. Genotypical features exploiting architectural characteristics such as the number of blocks, block types, tensor shapes, connection n-grams were tried but found to require extensive amounts of training data for acceptable performance, thus achieving no tangible speed-up. We will therefore focus on phenotypical prediction via learning curves and how it can be applied to CGP-CNN in the following.

Methodology and Evaluation. Data for this task can be gained from random search trials with different random seeds, yielding a training and a test set with 3 000 trained individuals each. An emphasis on performance in data sparsity can be achieved by running many (e.g. 100) folds in which models are trained on a small random subset (e.g. 100 samples, as in [4]) and evaluated on the remaining samples. The best model found in this way can then be tested on a set of unseen instances, in the same shuffle-split trials. We chose coefficient of determination R^2 (c.f. [23]) to evaluate different approaches, with Pearson correlation (c.f. [17]) reported as well.

Learning Curve Prediction. In learning curve prediction, the goal is to predict a networks' final performance after full training for T epochs based on a partial *learning curve* of length $\tau < T$. Baker et al. [4] base the predictions on the time-series of validation accuracy for each training epoch as well as first- and second-order differences of the time series. They achieve very good results using a *sequential regression model* (SRM) that consists of $\tau - 1$ base regressors, each of which is trained with one more learning curve point than the previous one.

In our work, time series for training accuracy, validation loss and training loss were extracted as well. For two or more learning curves, one SRM is trained for each feature and the predictions averaged. We found the two best performing single features to be validation loss and validation accuracy, whereas their combination does not seem to increase capability, see Fig. 4.

Among the base estimators, OLS regression, linear SVR, RBF-kernel SVR and Random Forest as in Baker et al.'s work, linear regression shows the best performance by a small margin.

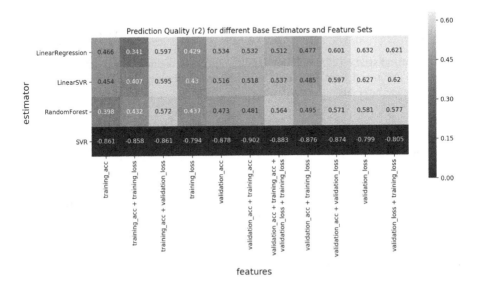

Fig. 4. R^2 on test set for different combinations of feature set and base learner (*estimator*) for the SRM.

We can also perform different ablation studies to find an efficient configuration for the SRM, meaning sufficient performance with as little data as possible. When increasing training data quantity, performance initially grows drastically, up to about 900 instances (c.f. Fig. 5a). Increasing the observed proportion of the learning curve results in a noticeable performance boost at first (c.f. Fig. 5b), but shows a negative impact beyond 50%. The model scales well with an increase in both parameters and can therefore be considered well-conditioned.

4.1 Time Series Based Accuracy Prediction Accelerated CGP-CNN

In [4], Baker et al. propose a strategy that incorporates performance prediction into NAS methods. First a training S set is created by generating n random individuals and fully training them. This is used to fit a SRM fitness estimator predicting the performance of partially trained offspring, meaning individuals need to be trained to convergence only if their predicted performance indicates high potential. A parameter Δ that serves as a probability threshold for which architectures to fully train is introduced.

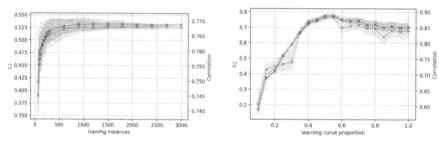

(a) Effect of training data quantity n.   (b) Effect of learning curve proportion

Fig. 5. Ablation studies on prediction quality of a SRM trained on validation accuracy time series. Averaged over 100 trials with different subsets, shaded region indicates IQR confidence intervals.

With the goal of keeping S bias free, none of the discovered architectures are added during the search. The best performing architecture in S serves as the initial parent for $1 + \lambda$.

Simulated Accelerated Random Search. Similar to experiments described in Baker et al.s' work [4], the potential speed-up and the expected effects on selection optimality can be simulated by applying the above describe procedure over multiple (e.g. 10) re-orderings of 3 000 training samples previously generated through random exploration.

The learning curve proportion τ was increased to 18 and the training set size to $n = 200$. Those two changes improve the explained variance of the SRM to $R^2 = 0.746$ with a Pearson correlation of $\rho = 0.867$.

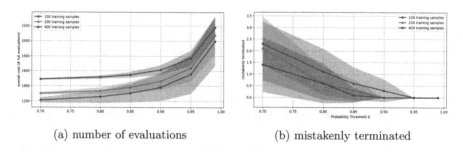

(a) number of evaluations   (b) mistakenly terminated

Fig. 6. Effect of the probability threshold Δ and initial training size set n for simulated accelerated NAS. 10 trials per configuration with $\pm 1\sigma$ confidence intervals.

Baker et al. report a Δ of 0.99 to be necessary for no erroneous termination to occur in their simulations, resulting in a 3.4× speed-up. Due to the higher used learning curve proportion, we observed fewer accidentally discarded optimal solutions (c.f. Fig. 6), allowing for a more liberal Δ of 0.9. However this also results in a longer initial training period, and consequently a speed-up of only 2.14× with $n = 200$.

Accelerated $1 + \lambda$. Whereas in random search all discoveries are independent, an evolutionary strategy makes decision based on observed points in the search space and mistakenly discarded individuals can have a large impact. Consequently, we need to actual trials for a realistic evaluation of accelerated $1 + \lambda$.

Multiple trials of accelerated $1 + \lambda$, in the same small-dataset setting as before, were performed with the SRM parameter setting derived from the previous simulation, that resulted in a simulated speed-up of 2.14×. Accordingly, we set the probability threshold to $\Delta = 0.9$, learning curve proportion to $\tau = 18$ and an initial training set size of $n = 200$.

Table 6. Results of time-series accuracy prediction accelerated $1 + \lambda$ NAS trials using different initial configurations in the small dataset scenario.

Seed	MTA	TTA	MVA	TVA	params (Mio)	Speed-up	Fully trained
2016	0.722 ± 0.006	0.716	0.751 ± 0.006	0.778	0.66	1.64×	853
31415	0.736 ± 0.005	0.731	0.725 ± 0.005	0.742	0.45	1.75×	675

The results of accelerated $1 + \lambda$ are on par with the non-modified variant (c.f. Table 6). The fitness over time (c.f. Fig. 7) shows that the initial 100 epochs of random exploration are less effective than $1 + \lambda$, however in both considered runs the NAS recovers from this.

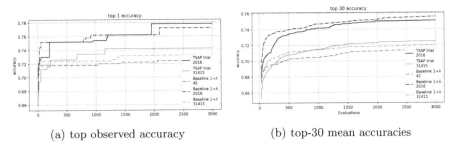

(a) top observed accuracy   (b) top-30 mean accuracies

Fig. 7. Development of top observed accuracy and top-30 mean accuracies for time-series prediction accelerated $1 + \lambda$ over 3 000 generations.

Overall, this form of acceleration is easy to implement and effects tangible speed-up while showing no negative impact on resulting fitness.

5   Adaptability

To assess how well CGP-CNN works on data-sets that it was not developed for, we can try it on different image recognition tasks, c.f. Table 7. For SVHN the image augmentation pipeline was changed to include no horizontal flips as these are not label-preserving for digits.

Table 7. Image Recognition datasets used for adaptability studies. *current SotA* gives the state of the art performance for an estimation of task difficulty.

Dataset	Training samples	Test samples	Classes	Current SotA	NiN [18] performance
CIFAR-10 [16]	50 000	10 000	10	99.0% [13]	91.2%
CIFAR-100 [16]	50 000	10 000	100	91.3% [13]	64.3%
SVHN [22]	73 257	26 032	10	98.98% [7]	97.65%

5.1   Full-Dataset-Scenario

In the full-dataset scenario, results are relatively close to the performance of Network-in-Network (c.f. [18], see Table 8a). For SVHN the 1,85% margin to Network-in-Network is significant. It suggests that the NAS has difficulties adapting to the task of recognizing digits, as these require much different filters than the real world objects of CIFAR.

Table 8. Results of NAS trials on different image recognition datasets.

dataset	MTA	TTA	MVA	TVA	params	MTA	TTA	MVA	TVA	params
CIFAR-10	0.909	0.91	0.887	0.889	1.08	.749	.755	.756	.772	0.97
CIFAR-100	0.631	0.638	0.603	0.607	1.61	.30	.298	.36	.366	1.22
SVHN	0.956	0.958	0.950	0.951	0.629	.92	.921	.912	.918	1.23

(a)full dataset scenario   (b) small dataset scenario

The architecture evolved for CIFAR-100 (c.f. Fig. 8) is considerably larger than those we have previously seen, likely due to the fact that deeper networks are more suited to the difficult task as they can extract more complex features. This implies that the evolutionary strategy is successfully traversing to a more suitable part of the search space.

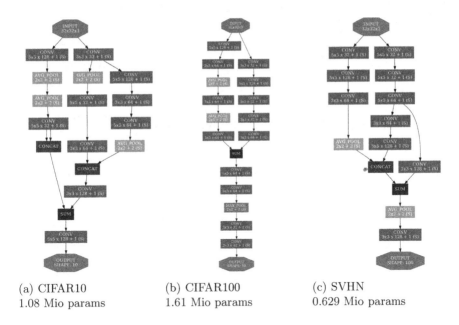

(a) CIFAR10
1.08 Mio params

(b) CIFAR100
1.61 Mio params

(c) SVHN
0.629 Mio params

Fig. 8. Winning architectures for modified $1 + \lambda$ on different datasets in full dataset scenario.

5.2   Small-Dataset-Scenario

For each dataset, one trial of $1 + \lambda$ NAS with parameters as before (1500 generations) was run using only 10% of the available training data.

Results on CIFAR-100 suffer dramatically from the data sparsity, as each of the 100 classes is only represented by 50 samples in the small-dataset setting, exacerbated to the high similarity between some classes (e.g. *maple, oak, palm, pine, willow*). Furthermore, test accuracies are consistently lower than the corresponding validation accuracies. This is an indication that the polishing-up schema is not applicable to a many-class problem such as CIFAR-100.

SVHN, on the other hand, sees only a minor decrease of 3.6% MTA in going down to 7 326 instances. This can be attributed to the slightly higher data quantity but also to the lower variability of the domain.

While the best discovered architectures for CIFAR-100 and SVHN are similar in size (both about 1.2 million parameters, c.f. Fig. 9), the architecture for SVHN is significantly deeper, while 9c is quite shallow and has almost no size reduction. This is quite different to the relatively deep topology found using the full dataset (c.f. Fig. 8b). Based on this, the assumption that extreme data sparsity makes training convolutional layers that extracting high-level features difficult seems warranted.

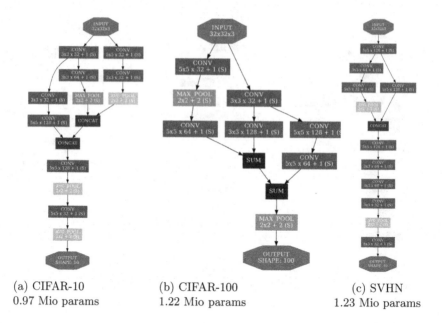

(a) CIFAR-10
0.97 Mio params

(b) CIFAR-100
1.22 Mio params

(c) SVHN
1.23 Mio params

Fig. 9. Winning architectures for modified $1 + \lambda$ on different datasets in small dataset scenario.

6 Conclusion

Our work gives insight into the reproducibility of CGP-CNN. Reproduction was achieved with a margin of 3.1% in the full-data scenario, with 2.2% in the small-data scenario. CGP-CNN and NAS in general is difficult to reproduce due to differences in frameworks, hidden hyper-parameters, large number of hyper-parameters. Therefore, provided implementation should be considered for reproduction. Consequently, this work is accompanied by source code as well as complete experimental setups and additional results, inspired by the guidelines of [19]. Still, finding the source for discrepancies is difficult, as even making training repeatable is a challenge. Overall, the conjecture can be made that tuning these hidden hyper-parameters of CGP-CNN is just as expensive as designing appropriate architectures from scratch.

CGP-CNN can easily be accelerated using time-series based accuracy prediction. Architecture-based features were tried but found to require extensive amounts of training data for acceptable performance.

However, CGP-CNN adapts well to other image recognition tasks in similar domains. It is therefore a valid approach for applications that require inductive transfer learning.

References

1. Abadi, M., et al.: Tensorflow: a system for large-scale machine learning. OSDI **16**, 265–283 (2016)
2. Angeline, P.J., Saunders, G.M., Pollack, J.B.: An evolutionary algorithm that constructs recurrent neural networks. IEEE Trans. Neural Netw. **5**(1), 54–65 (1994)
3. Baker, B., Gupta, O., Naik, N., Raskar, R.: Designing neural network architectures using reinforcement learning. arXiv preprint arXiv:1611.02167 (2016)
4. Baker, B., Gupta, O., Raskar, R., Naik, N.: Accelerating neural architecture search using performance prediction. arXiv preprint arXiv:1705.10823 (2017)
5. Bergstra, J., Yamins, D., Cox, D.D.: Making a science of model search: Hyperparameter optimization in hundreds of dimensions for vision architectures (2013)
6. Beyer, H.G., Schwefel, H.P.: Evolution strategies-a comprehensive introduction. Nat. Comput. **1**(1), 3–52 (2002)
7. Cubuk, E.D., Zoph, B., Mane, D., Vasudevan, V., Le, Q.V.: Autoaugment: learning augmentation strategies from data. In: Proceedings of the IEEE Conference on Computer Vision and Pattern Recognition, pp. 113–123 (2019)
8. Domhan, T., Springenberg, J.T., Hutter, F.: Speeding up automatic hyperparameter optimization of deep neural networks by extrapolation of learning curves. In: Twenty-Fourth International Joint Conference on Artificial Intelligence (2015)
9. Duchi, J., Hazan, E., Singer, Y.: Adaptive subgradient methods for online learning and stochastic optimization. J. Mach. Learn. Res. **12**, 2121–2159 (2011)
10. Elsken, T., Metzen, J.H., Hutter, F.: Neural architecture search: a survey. arXiv preprint arXiv:1808.05377 (2018)
11. He, K., Zhang, X., Ren, S., Sun, J.: Delving deep into rectifiers: surpassing human-level performance on ImageNet classification. In: Proceedings of the IEEE International Conference on Computer Vision, pp. 1026–1034 (2015)
12. Hinton, G., Srivastava, N., Swersky, K.: Neural networks for machine learning lecture 6a overview of mini-batch gradient descent. Cited on p. 14 (2012)
13. Huang, Y., et al.: GPipe: efficient training of giant neural networks using pipeline parallelism. In: Advances in Neural Information Processing Systems, pp. 103–112 (2019)
14. Kingma, D.P., Ba, J.: Adam: a method for stochastic optimization. arXiv preprint arXiv:1412.6980 (2014)
15. Klein, A., Falkner, S., Springenberg, J.T., Hutter, F.: Learning curve prediction with bayesian neural networks (2016)
16. Krizhevsky, A., Hinton, G.: Learning multiple layers of features from tiny images (2009)
17. Lee Rodgers, J., Nicewander, W.A.: Thirteen ways to look at the correlation coefficient. Am. Stat. **42**(1), 59–66 (1988)
18. Lin, M., Chen, Q., Yan, S.: Network in network. arXiv preprint arXiv:1312.4400 (2013)
19. Lindauer, M., Hutter, F.: Best practices for scientific research on neural architecture search. arXiv preprint arXiv:1909.02453 (2019)
20. Mendoza, H., Klein, A., Feurer, M., Springenberg, J.T., Hutter, F.: Towards automatically-tuned neural networks. In: Workshop on Automatic Machine Learning, pp. 58–65 (2016)
21. Miller, G.F., Todd, P.M., Hegde, S.U.: Designing neural networks using genetic algorithms. ICGA **89**, 379–384 (1989)

22. Netzer, Y., Wang, T., Coates, A., Bissacco, A., Wu, B., Ng, A.Y.: Reading digits in natural images with unsupervised feature learning. In: NIPS Workshop on Deep Learning and Unsupervised Feature Learning, vol. 2011, p. 5 (2011)
23. Rawlings, J.O., Pantula, S.G., Dickey, D.A.: Applied Regression Analysis: A Research Tool. Springer, New York (2001). https://doi.org/10.1007/b98890
24. Real, E., Aggarwal, A., Huang, Y., Le, Q.V.: Regularized evolution for image classifier architecture search. arXiv preprint arXiv:1802.01548 (2018)
25. Stanley, K.O., Miikkulainen, R.: Evolving neural networks through augmenting topologies. Evol. Comput. **10**(2), 99–127 (2002)
26. Suganuma, M., Shirakawa, S., Nagao, T.: A genetic programming approach to designing convolutional neural network architectures. In: Proceedings of the Genetic and Evolutionary Computation Conference, pp. 497–504. ACM (2017)
27. Zeiler, M.D.: ADADELTA: an adaptive learning rate method. arXiv preprint arXiv:1212.5701 (2012)
28. Zhong, Z., Yan, J., Wu, W., Shao, J., Liu, C.L.: Practical block-wise neural network architecture generation. In: Proceedings of the IEEE Conference on Computer Vision and Pattern Recognition, pp. 2423–2432 (2018)
29. Zoph, B., Le, Q.V.: Neural architecture search with reinforcement learning. arXiv preprint arXiv:1611.01578 (2016)
30. Zoph, B., Vasudevan, V., Shlens, J., Le, Q.V.: Learning transferable architectures for scalable image recognition. In: Proceedings of the IEEE Conference on Computer Vision and Pattern Recognition, pp. 8697–8710 (2018)

Short Talks

Software Anti-patterns Detection Under Uncertainty Using a Possibilistic Evolutionary Approach

Sofien Boutaib[1]([✉])[iD], Maha Elarbi[1]([✉])[iD], Slim Bechikh[1,2]([✉])[iD], Chih-Cheng Hung[2][iD], and Lamjed Ben Said[1][iD]

[1] SMART Lab, University of Tunis, ISG, Tunis, Tunisia
slim.bechikh@fsegn.rnu.tn, lamjed.bensaid@isg.rnu.tn
[2] Kennesaw State University, Marietta, GA, USA
chung1@kennesaw.edu

Abstract. Code smells (a.k.a. anti-patterns) are manifestations of poor design solutions that could deteriorate the software maintainability and evolution. Despite the high number of existing detection methods, the issue of class label uncertainty is usually omitted. Indeed, two human experts may have different degrees of uncertainty about the smelliness of a particular software class not only for the smell detection task but also for the smell type identification one. Thus, this uncertainty should be taken into account and then processed by detection tools. Unfortunately, these latter usually reject and/or ignore uncertain data that correspond to software classes (i.e. dataset instances) with uncertain labels. This practice could considerably degrade the detection/identification process effectiveness. Motivated by this observation and the interesting performance of the Possibilistic K-NN (PK-NN) classifier in dealing with uncertain data, we propose a new possibilistic evolutionary detection method, named ADIPOK (Anti-patterns Detection and Identification using Possibilistic Optimized K-NNs), that is able to deal with label uncertainty using some concepts stemming from the Possibility theory. ADIPOK is validated using a possibilistic base of smell examples that simulates the subjectivity of software engineers' opinions' uncertainty. The statistical analysis of the obtained results on a set of comparative experiments with respect to four state-of-the-art methods show the merits of our proposed method.

Keywords: Code smells detection · Uncertain software class labels · PK-NN evolution · Possibility theory

1 Introduction

Code smells detection is so far a very challenging research topic in the Software Engineering (SE) field. In fact, code smells (anti-patterns) [7] correspond to poor design and/or implementation that hamper the software maintenance

© Springer Nature Switzerland AG 2021
T. Hu et al. (Eds.): EuroGP 2021, LNCS 12691, pp. 181–197, 2021.
https://doi.org/10.1007/978-3-030-72812-0_12

process and may contribute to prone the occurrence of bugs over time. Many detection methods have been proposed in the literature and they can be categorized into three families: (1) rule-based methods, (2) machine learning-based methods, and (3) search-based ones. Search-based methods have shown their superior performance over the other methods thanks to their strong ability to approximate globally-optimal detectors. In fact, the detection problem corresponds to a data classification task where software classes are the data instances (records), the software metrics are the features (attributes), and the class label is just a flag indicating the existence of a code smell or not. Similarly, the identification problem is a slightly modified version of the detection one where the class label indicates the smell type (Blob, Feature Envy, Functional Decomposition, etc.). Thus, smell detection is a binary classification problem while smell identification is a multi-class one. In the data mining field, many studies were conducted to address the problem of uncertain class labels. This observation motivated us to investigate this issue in the anti-pattern detection problem. In fact, software engineers may have different and possibly conflicting opinions about whether a class in a software is smelly or not. This is mainly due to the subjective nature of human being reflection, its knowledge, and its experience. Unlikely, the existing approaches in the literature, including Search-Based Software Engineering (SBSE) methods, do not manage the uncertainty issue. They reject the uncertain data and consequently also lose an important amount of information, which in turns may significantly deteriorate their detection performances. To cope with uncertain labels in the data classification field, several tools have been proposed and the Possibility theory is one of them. For detailed about the interestingness of the use of such theory in uncertain classification, the reader could refer to [6]. Motivated by the interesting performance of the PK-NN classifier [20] in handling the inherent label uncertainty, we propose in this paper, for the first time within the SBSE field, a *possibilistic search-based method*, named ADIPOK, that evolves a set of optimized smells detectors each corresponding to a PK-NN using a GA (Genetic Algorithm). The main contributions of this work could be summarized as follows:

1. Proposing ADIPOK as a new *possibilistic SBSE* method for smells detection and identification in uncertain environments;
2. Developing a new dataset of software classes with uncertain class labels for the case of detection, where the label name could be either "smelly" or "non-smelly" and the label value is a possibility degree expressing the likelihood of smelliness;
3. Developing a supplementary dataset of smelly classes for the identification task, where the class label name corresponds to the smell type, while its value is a possibility degree expressing the belonging degree to the considered smell type;
4. Showing the outperformance and merits of ADIPOK with respect to four competitive existing methods, including the baseline PK-NN, on six object-oriented software projects.

Table 1. List of the adopted metrics

ANA - Average Number of Ancestors	DCC - Direct Class Coupling	NOF - Number of Fields
AOFD - Access Of Foreign Data	DSC - Design Size in Classes	NOH - Number of Hierarchies
CAM - Cohesion Among Methods of Class	LOC - Lines of Code	NOM - Number of Methods
CBO - Coupling Between Objects	MFA - Measure of Functional Abstraction	NOPA - Number of Public Attributes
CIS - Class Interface Size	MOA - Measure of Aggregation	NPA - Number of Private Attributes
CM - Changing Method	NOA - Number of Attributes	TCC - Tight Class Cohesion
DAM - Data Access Metric	NOAM - Number of Accessor Methods	WMC - Weighted Methods per Class
WOC - Weight Of Class		

The rest of this paper is structured as follows. Section 2 is devoted to present our ADIPOK method. Section 3 describes the experimental setup. Section 4 reports an analysis of the comparative results while Sect. 5 summarizes the related work. Finally, Sect. 6 concludes the paper and gives some promising paths for future research.

2 The Proposed Approach: ADIPOK

This section presents our proposed ADIPOK method. It starts by giving an overview on the working principle of detectors generation process. Then, it describes how the uncertain datasets are built. Furthermore, the GA operators are explained in detail including the fitness assignment, the selection mechanism, and the variation operators. Finally, the way in which a software engineer could use ADIPOK detectors (i.e., PK-NN classifiers) is described.

2.1 A Brief Overview of ADIPOK

In this study, we decided to focus on eight code smells that are: God Class (aka Blob), Data Class, Feature Envy, Long Method, Duplicate code, Long Parameter List, Spaghetti Code, and Functional Decomposition. In fact, these smells are among the most studied ones in the literature. Moreover, we considered the widely used structural (quality) metrics presented in Table 1. To build our ADIPOK approach, the first step is the development of the Possibilistic Base of Examples (PBEs), which is characterized by uncertainty inherent at the class labels. It is important to know that the main source of uncertainty is the subjectivity and uncertainty of software engineers' opinions regarding the smelliness of software class and the residing smell types. Thus, a set of probabilistic classifiers (Naïve Bayes classifier (NB) [8], Probabilistic K-NN (PrK-NN) [10], Bayesian Networks (BN) [17], Naïve Bayes Nearest Neighbor (NBNN) [1], and Probabilistic Decision Tree (PrDT) [18]) are employed to predict the probability distribution for every software class (i.e., instance in the BE). The idea of using a set of probabilistic classifiers is extended from the work of [2] in which the classifiers are used to simulate the software engineers' uncertainty in labeling the software classes, as it is easier and more flexible to express an opinion in a likelihood form. Then, the generated probability distributions are converted into possibility ones. Once the PBEs are created, the GA generates a set of optimized PK-NN classifiers by optimizing a fitness function (i.e., the Possibilistic

G-mean distance (PG-mean)), which is calculated according to the PBEs. Once a number of optimized possibilistic detectors are generated, they are utilized to detect and/or identify the existing of anti-patterns on unseen software systems. We recall that for the detection operation the BE is composed of smelly and non-smelly classes; while for the case of identification, each BE contains a single type of smells.

2.2   Construction of PBEs

The real-world environment of the SE industry is far from being perfect. Like other domains, the uncertainty issue is also present in SE. In fact, the BE could be contaminated with the uncertainty of class label. The sources of this uncertainty could be the subjectivity of opinions and/or the lack of expert knowledge. In such setting, the expert can express an opinion in the form of likelihood values each expressing the membership degree of each software class to each class label. To deal with such uncertain environment, a PBE is a good choice since each instance could be assigned a set of labels each having a possibility degree. As far as we know, we have not found a dataset in the SE literature for us to explore the uncertainty issue in this study. To do so, we have built Possibilistic datasets as follows. First, we adopted five different advisors (DECOR [15], JDeodorant [23], INFUSION[1], IPLASMA[2], and PMD [9]) to produce five crisp BEs. Second, we run autonomously five probabilistic classifiers (i.e., NB, PrK-NN, BN, NBNN, and PrDT). Then, we use the average operator twice to apply the voting fusion. For the first time, we use the voting fusion with the aim to aggregate the resulted probabilistic BE for every classifier. For the second time, it was used to get a single probabilistic BE. Finally, we employed the following conversion formula (detailed in [12]) to convert the obtained probability distributions into possibility ones:

$$\pi(\omega_i) = i \times p(\omega_i) + \sum_{j=i+1}^{n} p(\omega_j), \forall i = 1..n \tag{1}$$

where p refers to the probability distribution defined on the universe of discourse Ω and n represents the number of states of knowledge. Before starting the transformation process from p to π, the probability values should be sorted in descending order, $p(\omega_1) \geq p(\omega_2) \geq ... \geq p(\omega_n)$. It is important to know that the constraint $\sum_{j=i+1}^{n} p(\omega_j) = 1$ must be satisfied.

2.3   Chromosome Encoding

The PK-NN performance mainly depends on three parameters: (1) the FS (Feature Subset), (2) the number of nearest neighbors K, and (3) the reliability degree α. The latter parameter indicates to what extent the current detector is reliable. To optimize these parameters, the solution encoding in ADIPOK is a

---

[1] http://www.intooitus.com/products/infusion.
[2] http://loose.upt.ro/iplasma/.

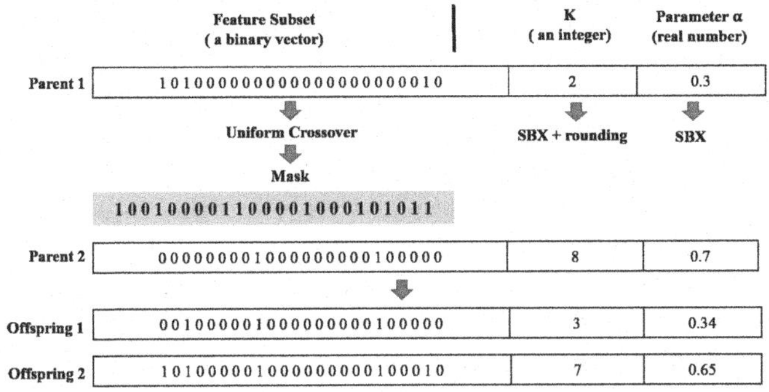

Fig. 1. Illustration of the crossover operation in ADIPOK. A recombination mask of zeros and ones is randomly generated following a uniform distribution. The offspring-1 is generated by taking the bit from parent-1 if the corresponding mask bit equals 0 or from parent-2 if the corresponding mask bit equals 1.

vector containing all these parameters as illustrated in Fig. 1. As these parameters are of different numerical types, the crossover operation will be applied on each part separately as follows:

- The FS subset is a binary vector and is varied using uniform crossover [22];
- The K value is an integer and is varied using SBX [5] followed by a rounding up to the nearest integer;
- α adopts real numbers in $[0, 1]$ and are crossed-over using SBX.

It is worth noting that the initialization of these parameters is randomly performed at the beginning of the GA while respecting the definition domain of each gene.

2.4 Fitness Function

To compute the fitness function value, an important step should be performed consisting in selecting the K nearest neighbors of the current individual based on the Euclidean distance. Then, a combination of the possibility degrees for every class label should be performed to produce a final possibility distribution for the new unseen instance using Eq. (2). Afterwards, the found information (possibility distribution) for the unseen software class is updated based on (i.e., the reliability of the detector that exists in the vector presentation) Eq. (3). We notice that ω_q represents the class of the ith instance among the K chosen nearest neighbors.

$$\forall \omega_q \in \Omega, \pi_{\sum}(\omega_q) = \frac{\sum_{i=1}^{K} \pi(\omega_q^{(i)})}{\sum_{i=1}^{K} \pi(\omega^{(i)})} \tag{2}$$

$$\pi' = \alpha * \pi + 1 - \alpha \tag{3}$$

It is worth noting that code smells detection could be matched to an imbalanced binary classification issue. In such problem, the BE is composed of two main subsets: (1) the majority class and (2) the minority one. The latter cardinality is much less than the former one, which involves an imbalance problem that should be considered by the classifier. The same issue applies for the case of smell identification, but with a more important imbalance ratio because this problem corresponds to a detection task with only one smell type. To deal with data imbalance, our fitness function is designed based on the G-mean classification metric. Our choice is justified by the fact that the G-mean corresponds to the geometric mean of Sensitivity and Specificity over the minority class [14]; this makes it insensitive to the imbalance issue. As the G-mean is not adequate for the case of uncertain class labels, we propose a possibilistic version of this metric that is named Possibilistic G-mean (PG-mean) and expressed in Eq. (4). The PG-mean considers the mean distances between the generated possibility distribution (π^{res}) and the initial possibility distribution (π^{init}) of every classified unseen software class $\overrightarrow{I_j}$. When PG-mean is close to 1, the obtained detector is accurate as well as the generated possibility distribution are characterized by high quality and faithful compared to the initial possibility distribution. However, the detector is considered as a bad detector if its fitness function (PG-mean) falls to 0. The analytical expression of the PG-mean is as follows:

$$PG - mean = \sqrt{Sensitivity\_dist \times Specificity\_dist} \tag{4}$$

$$Specificity\_dist = \frac{TN\_dist}{TN\_dist + FP\_dist} \tag{6}$$

$$Sensitivity\_dist = \frac{TP\_dist}{TP\_dist + FN\_dist} \tag{5}$$

$$TN\_dist = \sum\nolimits_{\overrightarrow{I_j} \in \text{ANSCcc}} NSD(\overrightarrow{I_j}) \tag{8}$$

$$TP\_dist = \sum\nolimits_{\overrightarrow{I_j} \in \text{ASCcc}} NSD(\overrightarrow{I_j}) \tag{7}$$

$$FN\_dist = \sum\nolimits_{\overrightarrow{I_j} \in \text{ANSCms}} NSD(\overrightarrow{I_j}) \tag{10}$$

$$FP\_dist = \sum\nolimits_{\overrightarrow{I_j} \in \text{ASCmNs}} NSD(\overrightarrow{I_j}) \tag{9}$$

$$NSD(\overrightarrow{I_j}) = 1 - \frac{Sd(\overrightarrow{I_j})}{2} \tag{12}$$

$$Sd(\overrightarrow{I_j}) = \sum\nolimits_{i=1}^{|C|} (\pi^{res}(C_i) - \pi^j(C_i)) \tag{11}$$

where ASCcc, ANSCcc, ASCmNs, and ANSCms abbreviations refer to Actual Smelly classes correctly classified, Actual Non-smelly classes correctly classified, Actual Smelly classes miss-classified as Non-smelly, and Actual Non-smelly classes miss-classified as Smelly, respectively. $Sd(\overrightarrow{I_j})$ (Similarity distance) (cf. Eq. 11) represents the distance between the generated possibility distribution (π^{res}) and the initial possibility distribution (π^{init}). Such distance is in the range of [0, 2]. To give the $Sd(\overrightarrow{I_j})$ a significance close to G-mean, we made changes on $Sd(\overrightarrow{I_j})$ to obtain the Normalized Similarity Distance $(NSD(\overrightarrow{I_j}))$ where values between 0 and 1 (cf. Eq. 12). Based on the obtained position of the most plausible classes, the $NSD(\overrightarrow{I_j})$ is added to the adequate quantity (i.e., TP_dist (cf. Eq. 7) or TN_dist (cf. Eq. 8) or FP_dist (cf. Eq. 9) or FN_dist (cf. Eq. 10)). According to these distances, the $Sensitivity\_dist$ (cf. Eq. 5) and $Specificity\_dist$ (cf. Eq. 6) are computed to obtain at the end the PG-mean. For example, if π^{init} = [1 0.4] and π^{res} = [1 0.2], then based on the calculated distance between those possibility distributions, we will add the obtained distance to the TP_dist. Conversely, if π^{res} = [0.2 1], then the obtained distance will be added to FP_dist. As in the comparative experiments below, we compare ADIPOK to some relevant state-of-the-art approaches that do not consider the uncertainty aspect such as (DECOR [15], GP [16], and BLOP [19]), their crisp results should be transformed into a set of possibility distributions. For example, if the predicted class label of GP is C_1, then its possibility distribution would be [1, 0].

2.5 Mating Selection Operator

As ADIPOK evolves a set of PK-NNs, it should encourage the selection of good parents at each generation of the GA, while allowing less effective individuals to participate in the reproduction process in order to escape local optima and converge towards the globally optimum PK-NN model. To do so, the tournament selection operator is adopted to choose parents for reproduction. Indeed, at each generation (N/2) individuals are selected as parents. This allows the acceptance of worse movements in the search space which allows escaping from locally-optimal PK-NN models.

2.6 Crossover and Mutation Operators

As noted in Sect. 2.3, the chromosome is encoded with three parts where the first part is encoded as a binary string, the second part is an integer, and the third part is a vector of two positive real numbers. As illustrated in Fig. 1, the crossover is performed on each part separately. The binary string part is varied using uniform crossover [22] which in turn uses a random binary mask. The K real value is varied using the Simulated Binary Crossover (SBX) operator with a rounding up mechanism [5]. As SBX outputs real numbers and the K value should be an integer, the obtained value from the SBX is rounded up to the nearest integer. Finally, the third part, which encodes the real-valued α reliability parameter is crossed-over using SBX.

The mutation operation is also performed on each part separately. The first part is mutated using the one-point mutation operator [21]. The polynomial-based mutation operator [5] is applied on the second part with a rounding up and then on the third part without rounding up. It is worth mentioning that once the mutation is triggered, it modifies the three chromosome parts simultaneously.

2.7   Optimized Possibilistic Detectors Application Module

Once the optimized PK-NN detectors are generated by the GA, the software engineer could use them to detect and/or identify anti-patterns and/or their types. In fact, the human expert could use the best detector(s) or all of them. We recommend the use of all detectors based on a voting procedure as presented in Fig. 2. In fact, each detector has a possibility distribution expressing the possibility degree of its membership to each class label. As the detectors' distributions could be in agreement or disagreement with respect to one or several class labels, we adopt the AFO (Adaptive Fusion Operator) (for more details please refer to [12]) to aggregate the various possibility distributions using the following equation:

$$\forall \omega \in \Omega, \ \pi_{AD}(\omega) = max(\pi_\wedge(\omega), \ min(\pi_\vee(\omega), \ 1 - h(\pi_1, \pi_2))) \qquad (13)$$

where $\pi_\wedge(\omega) = \frac{min(\pi_1(\omega), \pi_2(\omega))}{h(\pi_1, \pi_2)}$ is the conjunctive operator, $\pi_\vee(\omega) = max(\pi_1(\omega), \pi_2(\omega))$ is the disjunctive operator, and $h(\pi_1(\omega), \pi_2(\omega))$ represents the degree of agreement between two detectors [12]. The disjunctive operator is used when detectors disagree while the conjunctive one is applied for the agreement case. The AFO operator works as follows. For the case of agreement between distributions, it combines the distributions using the disjunction operator. In contrast, for the case of disagreement between distributions, the AFO aggregates the distributions using the conjunction operator. We notice that the agreement/disagreement detection is based on the amount of conflict between detectors' distributions (cf. Eq. (14)). In fact, two detectors are in disagreement if $Inc(\pi_1 \wedge \pi_2) \neq 0$.

$$Inc(\pi_1, \pi_2) = 1 - max_{\omega_i \in \Omega}\{min_{\omega_i \in \Omega}\{\pi_1(\omega), \pi_2(\omega)\}\} \qquad (14)$$

3   Experimental Validation

To evaluate the performance of ADIPOK, we set two RQs (Research Questions):

- **RQ1:** How does ADIPOK perform in code smells detection under uncertainty compared to the considered relevant peer methods?
- **RQ2:** How is the performance of ADIPOK in smell type identification under uncertainty with regard to the chosen competitor methods?

We applied our approach on commonly used Java software projects, namely: ArgoUML[3], Xerces-J[4], GranttProject[5], Ant-Apache[6], Azureus[7], and

---

[3] http://argouml.tigris.org/.
[4] http://xerces.apache.org/xerces-j/.
[5] https://sourceforge.net/projects/ganttproject/files/OldFiles/.
[6] http://ant.apache.org.
[7] http://vuze.com/.

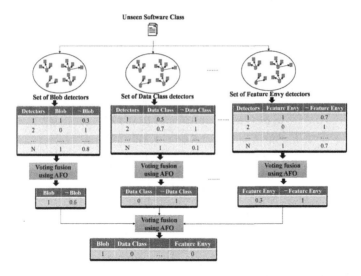

Fig. 2. Illustrating the use of ADIPOK for anti-pattern type identification on an unseen software class.

JFREECHART[8]. ArgoUML is a well-known UML modeling tool. Xerces-J is a popular system for parsing XML files. GanttProject is an open source cross-platform for project management. Ant-Apache is a building automation system for Java applications. Azureus is a client program devoted to sharing files. JFreechat is a powerful Java open-source library that displays professional graphical charts. Table 2 summarizes some descriptive statistics about the employed systems. These systems are commonly-used in the SBSE community as they contain an important number of different code smells. In our experiments, the PBE is adopted as ground truth since this base is an aggregation of the simulated subjective uncertain opinions of different experts expressed in the form of likelihood values. In this work, we assess our approach using a five-fold cross-validation procedure. Then, the generated metrics' results on the test data are averaged over the five folds.

3.1 Performance Metrics and Statistical Testing

To quantify the performance of the different considered methods, we used two classification performance metrics that are suitable for uncertain environments. The first one is the *PG-mean*, previously detailed in Sect. 2.4. The second one is the Information Affinity-based Criterion (IAC) [13], which measures the distance between two possibility distributions, the initial possibility distribution (π^{init}) and the resulting one (π^{result}). The IAC takes into account the uncertainty aspect and it is expressed as follows:

---

[8] http://www.jfree.org/jfreechart/.

Table 2. Software adopted in our experimentats

Systems	Version	NOC	KLOC
GanttProject	1.10.2	245	41
ArgoUML	0.19.8	200	300
Xerces-J	2.7.0	991	240
JFreeChart	1.0.9	521	170
Ant-Apache	1.7.0	1,839	327
Azureus	2.3.0.6	1,449	42

[a]Number of Classes.
[b]Thousands of Lines Of Code.

Table 3. Parameters settings

Parameters	ADIPOK	GP	BLOP
Crossover rate	0.9	0.9	0.8
Mutation rate	0.1	0.5	0.5
Population size	200	100	30

$$IAC = \frac{1}{n}\sum_{i=1}^{n} Aff(\pi_i^{initial}, \pi_i^{predicted}) \tag{15}$$

where Aff refers to the Information Affinity distance measure (presented in [12]). As all the compared methods have stochastic behaviors, except DECOR, the generated results could vary from one run to another on the same experiment. To deal with this stochastic nature, we used the Wilcoxon test [4] in a pairwise fashion with a significance level of 5%. To do so, each experiment was repeated 31 times and then the median metrics' values were collected and analyzed to detect the performance differences between the compared methods. To quantify the amount of performance difference, we used the Cohen's d statistic as an effect size measure [3]. The size is considered: (1) large if $d \geqslant 0.8$, (2) medium if $0.5 \leqslant d < 0.8$, (3) small if $0.2 \leqslant d < 0.5$, and (4) very small if $d < 0.2$.

3.2 Parameters Settings

An important issue that should be considered before running search algorithms is their parameter tuning. In fact, the parameter setting has an important impact on the performance of metaheuristics. To deal with this issue, we used the trial-and-error method to tune the parameters' values of ADIPOK. The other search algorithms' parameters were set based on their original papers (cf. Table 3). To ensure fairness of comparisons, the same stopping criterion was used for all the search methods. Indeed, each run is stopped after 256500 fitness evaluations.

Table 4. PG-mean (PGm) and IAC median scores of ADIPOK, DECOR, GP, BLOP, and PK-NN over 31 runs on the detection process with an uncertainty level $UL = 50\%$.

Systems	ADIPOK		DECOR		GP		BLOP		PK-NN	
	PGm	IAC	PGm	IAC	PGm	IAC	PGm	IAC	PGm	IAC
GanttProject	**0.9045**	**0.9108**	0.1519	0.1721	0.1753	0.1908	0.2252	0.2436	<u>0.5006</u>	<u>0.5215</u>
	(+ + + +)	(+ + + +)	(− + +)	(− + +)	(+ +)	(+ +)	(+)	(+)		
	(l l l l)	(l l l l)	(s l l)	(s l l)	(m l)	(m l)	(l)	(l)		
ArgoUML	**0.9162**	**0.9246**	0.128	0.1428	0.1522	0.1745	0.2249	0.2417	<u>0.4991</u>	<u>0.5068</u>
	(+ + + +)	(+ + + +)	(− + +)	(− + +)	(+ +)	(+ +)	(+)	(+)		
	(l l l l)	(l l l l)	(s l l)	(s l l)	(m l)	(m l)	(l)	(l)		
Xercess-J	**0.8954**	**0.9130**	0.0814	0.0917	0.1413	0.1609	0.2078	0.2160	<u>0.4639</u>	<u>0.4920</u>
	(+ + + +)	(+ + + +)	(+ + +)	(+ + +)	(+ +)	(+ +)	(+)	(+)		
	(l l l l)	(l l l l)	(m l l)	(m l l)	(m l)	(m l)	(l)	(l)		
JFreeChart	**0.9213**	**0.9407**	0.0807	0.0906	0.1251	0.1380	0.1805	0.1913	<u>0.4117</u>	<u>0.4253</u>
	(+ + + +)	(+ + + +)	(− + +)	(− + +)	(+ +)	(+ +)	(+)	(+)		
	(l l l l)	(l l l l)	(s l l)	(s l l)	(m l)	(m l)	(l)	(l)		
Azureus	**0.9383**	**0.9356**	0.0495	0.0653	0.1158	0.1207	0.1644	0.1682	<u>0.3680</u>	<u>0.3941</u>
	(+ + + +)	(+ + + +)	(+ + +)	(+ + +)	(+ +)	(+ +)	(+)	(+)		
	(l l l l)	(l l l l)	(m l l)	(m l l)	(m l)	(m l)	(l)	(l)		
Ant-Apache	**0.9081**	**0.9293**	0.0451	0.0624	0.0827	0.0988	0.1540	0.1637	<u>0.3582</u>	<u>0.3703</u>
	(+ + + +)	(+ + + +)	(− + +)	(− + +)	(+ +)	(+ +)	(+)	(+)		
	(l l l l)	(l l l l)	(s l l)	(s l l)	(m l)	(m l)	(l)	(l)		

The sign "−" means the opposite. Similarly, the effect sizes values (small (s), medium (m), and large (l)) using the Cohen'd statistics are given. Best PG-mean (or IAC) values are in Bold. Second-best PG-mean (or IAC) values are underlined.

[a] We used the original version of DECOR, which works only on three smell types: Blob, SC, and FD.

4 Comparative Results

4.1 Results for RQ1

Table 4 presents the metrics' results along with the effect size values for the five detection methods on the considered software systems. As we need to show that ADIPOK performs well for both cases: (1) with uncertainty and (2) without uncertainty; we used two levels of uncertainty. The first case is expressed with an uncertainty level $UL = 50\%$; while for the second case, $UL = 0\%$. Based on this table, ADIPOK outperforms all the other considered methods with a PG-mean varying between 0.9045 and 0.9383. The second-best method is PK-NN with a PG-mean lying between 0.3582 and 0.5006. The three other methods DECOR, GP, and BLOP produced poor results with maximum PG-mean values of 0.1519, 0.1753, and 0.2252, respectively. The outperformance of ADIPOK and PK-NN over GP and BLOP could be explained by the fact that these two latter methods do not consider the uncertainty factor in the solution evaluation process. Indeed, the ADIPOK fitness function is the PG-mean, which is a well-suited metric for uncertain environments. PK-NN optimizes the PCC (Percentage of Correct Classifications) over the most plausible classes. Furthermore, ADIPOK's superiority over PK-NN could be explained by two factors. On the one hand, ADIPOK employs the EA to evolve the PK-NN classifier, which allows to gain a globally-optimal PK-NN configurations. Moreover, ADIPOK performs feature

Table 5. PG-mean (PGm) and IAC median scores of ADIPOK, DECOR, GP, BLOP, and PK-NN over 31 runs on the detection process with an uncertainty level $UL = 0\%$.

Systems	ADIPOK		DECOR		GP		PK-NN		BLOP	
	PGm	IAC	PGm	IAC	PGm	IAC	PGm	IAC	PGm	IAC
GanttProject	**0.9398**	**0.9477**	0.35328	0.37815	0.4041	0.4216	0.5236	0.5329	0.5678	0.5691
	(+ + + +)	(+ + + +)	(− + +)	(− + +)	(+ +)	(+ +)	(−)	(−)		
	(l l l l)	(l l l l)	(s l l)	(s l l)	(m m)	(m m)	(s)	(s)		
ArgoUML	**0.9322**	**0.9597**	0.32848	0.33428	0.3589	0.3846	0.5107	0.5315	0.5576	0.5659
	(+ + + +)	(+ + + +)	(− + +)	(− + +)	(+ +)	(+ +)	(−)	(−)		
	(l l l l)	(l l l l)	(s l l)	(s l l)	(m m)	(m m)	(s)	(s)		
Xercess-J	**0.9203**	**0.9405**	0.19698	0.21018	0.3189	0.3375	0.4566	0.4721	0.5043	0.5211
	(+ + + +)	(+ + + +)	(+ + +)	(+ + +)	(+ +)	(+ +)	(−)	(−)		
	(l l l l)	(l l l l)	(m l l)	(m l l)	(m m)	(m m)	(s)	(s)		
JFreeChart	**0.9486**	**0.9622**	0.17068	0.20368	0.3048	0.3096	0.3833	0.4062	0.5128	0.5098
	(+ + + +)	(+ + + +)	(+ + +)	(+ + +)	(+ +)	(+ +)	(+)	(+)		
	(l l l l)	(l l l l)	(m l l)	(m l l)	(m l)	(m l)	(m)	(m)		
Azureus	**0.9312**	**0.9593**	0.12958	0.14618	0.2417	0.2728	0.3489	0.3605	0.4231	0.437
	(+ + + +)	(+ + + +)	(+ + +)	(+ + +)	(+ +)	(+ +)	(+)	(+)		
	(l l l l)	(l l l l)	(m l l)	(m l l)	(m l)	(m l)	(m)	(m)		
Ant-Apache	**0.9395**	**0.9522**	0.11188	0.12168	0.2138	0.2255	0.3359	0.3482	0.3368	0.3527
	(+ + + +)	(+ + + +)	(+ + +)	(+ + +)	(+ +)	(+ +)	(−)	(−)		
	(l l l l)	(l l l l)	(m l l)	(m l l)	(m m)	(m m)	(s)	(s)		

The sign "−" means the opposite. Similarly, the effect sizes values (small (s), medium (m), and large (l)) using the Cohen'd statistics are given. Best PG-mean (or IAC) values are in Bold. Second-best PG-mean (or IAC) values are underlined.

(metric) selection task (cf. Fig. 1). However, the probability of a greedy PK-NN (i.e., the baseline one) to find a near-optimal configuration is extremely small. Additionally, it does not consider the feature selection task. On the other hand, PK-NN does not consider the data imbalance issue since PCC is not a good choice for imbalanced classification. Additionally, the PG-mean is insensitive to data imbalance. Similar results are obtained for the IAC metric because the certain case (i.e., the ground truth) is a subcase of the uncertain one. More specifically, the possibility distribution for the certain case would be in the form of a binary vector containing a unique value of 1 and all the other values are equal to 0; where the value of 1 refers to the real (certain) class label. This makes ADIPOK suitable regardless of the uncertainty level including the absence of uncertainty. Table 5 reports the metrics' results and the effect sizes of the five detection methods for the case when there is no uncertainty (ULevel = 0%). Based on this fact, the PG-mean performance metric behaves like the G-mean. Based on the data shown in this table, it is remarkable ADIPOK outperforms the four considered methods thanks to the adopted fitness function (i.e., PG-mean), which is insensitive to data imbalance. In fact, The results obtained by DECOR, BLOP, and PK-NN are biased and mostly affected by the stochastic noise as these methods are not able to cope with the data imbalance issue. The worst results are provided by the DECOR method as the detection rules are manually fixed, which is ineffective in the case of data imbalance. Similar interpretation is valid for the IAC metric in certain environment.

Table 6. PG-mean (PGm) and IAC median scores of ADIPOK, DECOR, GP, BLOP, and PK-NN over 31 runs on smell type identification process with an uncertainty level $UL = 50\%$.

Code Smell	ADIPOK		DECOR		GP		BLOP		PK-NN	
	PGm	IAC	PGm	IAC	PGm	IAC	PGm	IAC	PGm	IAC
Blob	**0.9303**	**0.9318**	0.0853	0.0927	0.1499	0.1615	0.2086	0.2190	<u>0.3691</u>	<u>0.3841</u>
	(+ + + +)	(+ + + +)	(+ + +)	(+ + +)	(+ +)	(+ +)	(+)	(+)		
	(1 1 1 1)	(1 1 1 1)	(m m l)	(m m l)	(m l)	(m l)	(m)	(m)		
Data	**0.9067**	**0.9133**	N/A	N/A	0.1210	0.1243	0.1839	0.1906	<u>0.3510</u>	<u>0.3762</u>
Class	(+ + +)	(+ + +)			(+ +)	(+ +)	(+)	(+)		
	(1 1 1)	(1 1 1)			(m l)	(m l)	(l)	(l)		
Feature	**0.8901**	**0.8962**	N/A	N/A	0.1137	0.1195	0.1785	0.1832	<u>0.316</u>	<u>0.3288</u>
Envy	(+ + +)	(+ + +)			(+ +)	(+ +)	(+)	(+)		
	(1 1 1)	(1 1 1)			(m l)	(m l)	(l)	(l)		
Long	**0.86723**	**0.8835**	N/A	N/A	0.1079	0.1107	0.1502	0.1528	<u>0.3045</u>	<u>0.3109</u>
Method	(+ + +)	(+ + +)			(+ +)	(+ +)	(+)	(+)		
	(1 1 1)	(1 1 1)			(m l)	(m l)	(m)	(m)		
Duplicate	**0.8547**	**0.8821**	N/A	N/A	0.0834	0.0890	0.1279	0.1348	<u>0.2952</u>	<u>0.3082</u>
Code	(+ + +)	(+ + +)			(+ +)	(+ +)	(+)	(+)		
	(1 1 1)	(1 1 1)			(m l)	(m l)	(m)	(m)		
Long	**0.8622**	**0.8741**	N/A	N/A	0.0663	0.0724	0.1137	0.1201	<u>0.2831</u>	<u>0.2976</u>
Parameter	(+ + +)	(+ + +)			(+ +)	(+ +)	(+)	(+)		
List	(1 1 1)	(1 1 1)			(m l)	(m l)	(m)	(m)		
Spaghetti	**0.8728**	**0.8976**	0.0350	0.0447	0.0495	0.0625	0.0927	0.1030	<u>0.2368</u>	<u>0.2413</u>
Code	(1 1 1 1)	(1 1 1 1)	(− + +)	(− + +)	(+ +)	(+ +)	(+)	(+)		
	(+ + + +)	(+ + + +)	(s m m)	(s m m)	(m m)	(m m)	(m)	(m)		
Functional	**0.8507**	**0.8639**	0.0226	0.0335	0.0476	0.0584	0.0603	0.0716	<u>0.1980</u>	<u>0.2113</u>
Decomposition	(+ + + +)	(+ + + +)	(− + +)	(− + +)	(− +)	(− +)	(+)	(+)		
	(1 1 1 1)	(1 1 1 1)	(s m l)	(s m l)	(s m)	(s m)	(m)	(m)		

The sign "−" means the opposite. Similarly, the effect sizes values (small (s), medium (m), and large (l)) using the Cohen'd statistics are given. The N/A signifies that the given approach is Not Applicable (N/A) on the corresponding smell. Best PG-mean (or IAC) values are in Bold. Second-best PG-mean (or IAC) values are underlined.

4.2 Results for RQ2

The goal of this subsection is to study the performance of the five considered methods on the identification task for both cases: (1) uncertain class labels and (2) certain ones. It is very important to note that the identification task is characterized by a higher data imbalance ratio. We recall that identifying the smell type corresponds to detecting a smell while considering only one smell type. This fact makes the number of smelly software classes much less than the number of non-smelly ones. This issue is present in both environments: (1) the crisp environment and (2) the uncertain one. For the latter environment, the class label of each software class is characterized by a possibility distribution encoded as a vector of two real numbers. Each number refers to the possibility degree of the membership of the considered software class to each of the two possible class labels: (1) Smell-type or (2) Non-smelly. Based on Table 6 and Table 7, we observe that the same conclusions of RQ1 could be deduced, but with less PG-mean and IAC values for all compared methods on both uncertain and certain datasets. This general observation is mainly due to the increase of the imbalance ratio,

Table 7. PG-mean (PGm) and IAC median scores of ADIPOK, DECOR, GP, BLOP, and PK-NN over 31 runs on the smell type identification process with an uncertainty level $UL = 0\%$.

Code Smell	ADIPOK		DECOR		GP		PK-NN		BLOP	
	PGm	IAC	PGm	IAC	PGm	IAC	PGm	IAC	PGm	IAC
Blob	**0.9158** (+ + + +) (1111)	**0.9476** (+ + + +) (1111)	0.306 (− + +) (s m m)	0.317 (− + +) (s m m)	0.3316 (+ +) (m m)	0.3514 (+ +) (m m)	0.4026 (−) (s)	0.4125 (−) (s)	0.4322	0.4507
Data Class	**0.8911** (+ + +) (1 1 1)	**0.9154** (+ + +) (1 1 1)	N/A	N/A	0.267 (+ +) (m m)	0.2802 (+ +) (m m)	0.3088 (+) (m)	0.3207 (+) (m)	0.3713	0.3819
Feature Envy	**0.8722** (1 1 l) (+ + +)	**0.8901** (1 1 l) (+ + +)	N/A	N/A	0.2516 (− +) (s m)	0.2721 (+ +) (m m)	0.2960 (+) (m)	0.3302 (+) (m)	0.3675	0.395
Long Method	**0.864** (+ + +) (1 1 l)	**0.8820** (+ + +) (1 1 l)	N/A	N/A	0.2392 (+ +) (m m)	0.256 (+ +) (m m)	0.2811 (+) (m)	0.3177 (+) (m)	0.3418	0.3782
Duplicate Code	**0.8562** (+ + +) (1 1 l)	**0.8715** (+ + +) (1 1 l)	N/A	N/A	0.1964 (+ +) (m m)	0.2397 (+ +) (m m)	0.267 (+) (m)	0.2957 (+) (m)	0.3270	0.3374
Long Parameter List	**0.861** (+ + +) (1 1 l)	**0.8844** (+ + +) (1 1 l)	N/A	N/A	0.1412 (+ +) (m m)	0.1632 (+ +) (m m)	0.2204 (+) (m)	0.2492 (+) (m)	0.2992	0.3011
Spaghetti Code	**0.855** (1 1 1 1) (+ + + +)	**0.8672** (1 1 1 1) (+ + + +)	0.0813 (− + +) (s m l)	0.1210 (− + +) (s m l)	0.1130 (+ +) (m m)	0.1329 (+ +) (m m)	0.206 (−) (s)	0.2301 (−) (s)	0.2536	0.2644
Functional Decomposition	**0.8412** (+ + + +) (1 1 1 1)	**0.8703** (+ + + +) (1 1 1 1)	0.0635 (− + +) (s m m)	0.0923 (− + +) (s m m)	0.1022 (− +) (s m)	0.1281 (− +) (s m)	0.1436 (+) (m)	0.1589 (+) (m)	0.2074	0.2093

The sign "−" means the opposite. Similarly, the effect sizes values (small (s), medium (m), and large (l)) using the Cohen'd statistics are given. N/A means that the given approach is Not Applicable (N/A) on the corresponding smell. Best PG-mean (or IAC) values are in Bold. The Second-best PG-mean (or IAC) values are underlined.

which in turns augments the resolution difficulty. The performance degradation did not affect all the algorithms with the same magnitude degree. In fact, the quality of ADIPOK results is slightly decreased vis-à-vis its performance on the detection task. However, DECOR, GP, BLOP, and PK-NN performance indicators' values are dramatically degraded. This phenomenon could be explained as follows:

- Despite the fact that PK-NN could face uncertainty, its performance is significantly deteriorated due to the use of the PCC as a fitness function, which is unsuitable with highly imbalanced data;
- GP and BLOP results are poor due to not only the imbalance issue but also the uncertainty one; and
- DECOR results are extremely degraded because it was not conceived to take into account data uncertainty and imbalance.

5   Related Work

Code smells detection is still so far a very active and timely research topic in the SE community, including the community of SBSE. Several researchers have proposed many automatic detection methods that could help the human expert either in the detection task or in the manual design of detectors. These methods could be classified into three main categories: (1) Rule-based methods, (2) Machine learning-based methods (including deep learning), and (3) Search-based ones. In what follows, we give details in each category in the case of crisp data, since almost all existing works did not consider the data uncertainty issue; which is the main goal of this work. The first group of methods that were proposed in the literature are rule-based ones. Indeed, the software engineer designs a combination of metrics that closely capture the bad design, where each metric is subject to threshold calibration. One of the main issues in these rules is the absence of consensus on threshold calibration. In this way, the anti-pattern definition may considerably differ from one engineer to another. The lack of compromise could incur poor detection accuracy results. One of the most known and used rule-based methods is DECOR [15], which is a tool that uses predefined rule-cards to define the symptoms of each considered smell. To deal with the difficulty of manual design, researchers have proposed the use of machine learning models and algorithms. The idea is to train a classifier with datasets to make the classifier able to distinguish between defected software classes and non-smelly ones. The most used classifier models for smell detection are Decision Trees (DTs), Bayesian Networks (BN), Support Vector Machines (SVMs), and Deep Neural Networks (DNNs). These methods have shown very interesting results on many software systems based on varied classification metrics such as accuracy, PCC, the G-mean, and the Area Under Curve (AUC). The main critic of learning methods is that the classifier induction algorithm is greedy, which means that it may get stuck in the first encountered local optimum. In this way, the generated classifier model is usually not the globally optimal. The third category corresponds to the SBSE methods, which were proposed to deal with the issue of stagnation in locally-optimal classifier models. The main idea consists in optimizing a set of detectors using a particular metaheuristic. The most used one is the GA [11] thanks to its global search ability and its probabilistic acceptance of fitness deterioration. Among the most effective methods through the SBSE community, GP [16] and BLOP [19] are ranked as the top methods. GP evolves a set of detection rules each corresponding to a combination of quality metrics and thresholds with the aim to maximise the number of truly defected classes based on a BE containing only smelly classes. As the performance of GP detectors depends on the BE, the authors proposed a bi-level optimization approach, called BLOP [19], to diversify the training data. The idea is to formulate the detection problem in a bi-level fashion where: (1) the upper-level generates a set of detection rules and (2) the lower-level produces a set of artificial code smells. The upper-level optimizes the ability of the rules to detect not only smells contained in the BE but also those artificially generated by the lower-level. The lower-level optimizes the ability of the artificial anti-patterns to escape the upper-level detection rules.

6   Conclusions and Future Work

In this paper, we have developed ADIPOK as a new approach and tool, that is capable of effectively detecting and identifying code smells under both uncertain and certain environments. Our approach evolves a set of PK-NN classifiers by optimizing a possibilistic version of the G-mean (i.e., the PG-mean). ADIPOK has shown its outperformance over four relevant state-of-the-art approaches, including the baseline PK-NN. The obtained evaluation results show the merits of our proposed approach as it adopts the possibility distribution concept to model uncertainty and the AFO to merge the (possibly) conflicting distributions. Several perspectives could be extracted from this work. First, the code smell detection problem could be tackled by the semi-supervised techniques since a huge amount of data could be unlabeled. Second, we aim to merge various information types (historical as well as structural) and adopting uncertain classifiers to learn under uncertainty. Third, we intend to use ADIPOK for the identification of smell types residing on web services.

References

1. Behmo, R., Marcombes, P., Dalalyan, A., Prinet, V.: Towards optimal Naive Bayes nearest neighbor. In: Daniilidis, K., Maragos, P., Paragios, N. (eds.) ECCV 2010. LNCS, vol. 6314, pp. 171–184. Springer, Heidelberg (2010). https://doi.org/10.1007/978-3-642-15561-1_13

2. Bounhas, M., Hamed, M.G., Prade, H., Serrurier, M., Mellouli, K.: Naive possibilistic classifiers for imprecise or uncertain numerical data. Fuzzy Sets Syst. **239**, 137–156 (2014)

3. Cohen, J.: Statistical Power Analysis for the Behavioral Sciences. Erlbaum Associates, Hillsdale (1988)

4. Conover, W.J., Conover, W.J.: Practical Nonparametric Statistics. Wiley, New York (1980)

5. Deb, K., Agrawal, R.B., et al.: Simulated binary crossover for continuous search space. Complex Syst. **9**(2), 115–148 (1995)

6. Dubois, D., Prade, H.: Possibility theory: an approach to computerized processing of uncertainty. Plenum Press, New York (1988)

7. Fowler, M., Beck, K.: Refactoring: Improving the Design of Existing Code. Addison-Wesely, Boston (1999)

8. Friedman, N., Geiger, D., Goldszmidt, M.: Bayesian network classifiers. Mach. Learn. **29**(2–3), 131–163 (1997)

9. Gopalan, R.: Automatic detection of code smells in Java source code. Ph.D. thesis, University of Western Australia (2012)

10. Holmes, C., Adams, N.: A probabilistic nearest neighbour method for statistical pattern recognition. J. Roy. Stat. Soc. B (Stat. Methodol.) **64**(2), 295–306 (2002)

11. Jain, A., Jatain, A.: Search based software engineering techniques. Int. J. Comput. Appl. **975**, 8887 (2015)

12. Jenhani, I.: From Possibilistic Similarity Measures to Possibilistic Decision Trees: Decision Tree Approaches for Handling Label-uncertainty in Classification Problems. LAP LAMBERT Academic Publishing, Saarbrücken (2010)

13. Jenhani, I., Ben Amor, N., Elouedi, Z., Benferhat, S., Mellouli, K.: Information affinity: a new similarity measure for possibilistic uncertain information. In: Mellouli, K. (ed.) ECSQARU 2007. LNCS (LNAI), vol. 4724, pp. 840–852. Springer, Heidelberg (2007). https://doi.org/10.1007/978-3-540-75256-1_73

14. Li, L., Zhao, K., Sun, R., Gan, J., Yuan, G., Liu, T.: Parameter-free extreme learning machine for imbalanced classification. Neural Process. Lett. **52**(3), 1927–1944 (2020). https://doi.org/10.1007/s11063-020-10282-z

15. Moha, N., Gueheneuc, Y.G., Duchien, L., Meur, A.F.L.: DECOR: a method for the specification and detection of code and design smells. IEEE Trans. Softw. Eng. **36**(1), 20–36 (2009)

16. Ouni, A., Kessentini, M., Sahraoui, H., Boukadoum, M.: Maintainability defects detection and correction: a multi-objective approach. Autom. Softw. Eng. **20**(1), 47–79 (2013)

17. Pearl, J.: Bayesian networks: a model CF self-activated memory for evidential reasoning. In: Proceedings of the 7th Conference of the Cognitive Science Society, University of California, Irvine, CA, USA, pp. 15–17 (1985)

18. Quinlan, J.R.: Decision trees as probabilistic classifiers. In: the Proceedings of the 4th International Workshop on Machine Learning, pp. 31–37. Elsevier (1987)

19. Sahin, D., Kessentini, M., Bechikh, S., Deb, K.: Code-smell detection as a bilevel problem. ACM Trans. Softw. Eng. Methodol. **24**(1), 1–44 (2014)

20. Saied, S., Elouedi, Z.: K-nearest neighbors classifier under possibility framework. In: Proceedings of the 27th La Logique Floue est ses Applications, LFA, pp. 1–8 (2018)

21. Srinivas, M., Patnaik, L.M.: Genetic algorithms: a survey. Computer **27**(6), 17–26 (1994)

22. Talbi, E.G.: Metaheuristics: From Design to Implementation, vol. 74, pp. 214–215. Wiley, New York (2009)

23. Tsantalis, N., Chatzigeorgiou, A.: Identification of move method refactoring opportunities. IEEE Trans. Softw. Eng. **35**(3), 347–367 (2009)

Probabilistic Grammatical Evolution

Jessica Mégane[(✉)], Nuno Lourenço, and Penousal Machado

CISUC, Department of Informatics Engineering, University of Coimbra,
Polo II - Pinhal de Marrocos, 3030 Coimbra, Portugal
jessicac@student.dei.uc.pt, {naml,penousal}@dei.uc.pt

Abstract. Grammatical Evolution (GE) is one of the most popular
Genetic Programming (GP) variants, and it has been used with success
in several problem domains. Since the original proposal, many enhance-
ments have been proposed to GE in order to address some of its main
issues and improve its performance.

In this paper we propose Probabilistic Grammatical Evolution (PGE),
which introduces a new genotypic representation and new mapping mechanism for GE. Specifically, we resort to a Probabilistic Context-Free
Grammar (PCFG) where its probabilities are adapted during the evolutionary process, taking into account the productions chosen to construct
the fittest individual. The genotype is a list of real values, where each
value represents the likelihood of selecting a derivation rule. We evaluate
the performance of PGE in two regression problems and compare it with
GE and Structured Grammatical Evolution (SGE).

The results show that PGE has a better performance than GE, with
statistically significant differences, and achieved similar performance
when comparing with SGE.

Keywords: Genetic Programming · Grammatical Evolution ·
Probabilistic Context-Free Grammar · Probabilistic Grammatical
Evolution · Genotype-to-Phenotype Mapping

1 Introduction

Evolutionary Algorithms (EAs) are loosely inspired by the ideas of natural evolution, where a population of individuals evolves through the application of selection, variation (such as crossover and mutation) and reproduction operators.
The evolution of these individuals is guided by a fitness function, which measures the quality of the solutions that each individual represents to the problem
at hand. The application of these elements is repeated for several iterations and
it is expected that, over time, the quality of individuals improves.

Genetic Programming (GP) [1] is an EA that is used to evolve programs.
Over the years many variants of GP have been proposed, namely concerned
with how individuals (i.e., computer programs) are represented. Some of these
variants make use of grammars to enforce syntactic constraints on the individual
solutions. The most well known grammar-based GP approaches are Context-
free Grammar Genetic Programming (CFG-GP), introduced by Whigham in

© Springer Nature Switzerland AG 2021
T. Hu et al. (Eds.): EuroGP 2021, LNCS 12691, pp. 198–213, 2021.
https://doi.org/10.1007/978-3-030-72812-0_13

[2], and Grammatical Evolution (GE) introduced by Ryan *et al.* [3]. The main distinction between the two approaches is the representation of the individual's solution (genotype) in the search space. CFG-GP uses a derivation-tree based representation, and the mapping is made by reading the terminal symbols (tree leaves), starting from the left leaf to the right. In GE there is a distinction between the genotype, a variable length string of integers, and the phenotype of the individual. The mapping between the genotype and the phenotype is performed through a Context-Free Grammar (CFG).

GE is one of the most popular GP variants, in spite of the debate in the literature [4] concerning its relative performance when compared to other grammar-based variants. To address some of the main criticisms of GE, several improvements have been proposed in the literature related to the population initialisation [5], grammar design [6] and the representation of individuals [7–10].

In this paper we introduce a new representation to GE. In concrete, we proposed a new probabilistic mapping mechanism to GE, called Probabilistic Grammatical Evolution (PGE). In PGE the genotype is a list of probabilities and the mapping is made using a Probabilistic Context-Free Grammar (PCFG) to choose the productions of the individual's phenotype. All derivation rules in the grammar start with the same chance of being selected, but over the evolutionary process, the probabilities are updated considering the derivation rules that were selected to build the fittest individual. To evaluate the performance of PGE, we compare its performance with GE and SGE [11] in two benchmark problems. PGE showed statistically significant improvements when compared with GE and obtained similar performance when compared to SGE.

The remainder of the paper is structured as follows: Sect. 2 introduces Grammatical Evolution and related work. Section 3 describes our approach called Probabilistic Grammatical Evolution (PGE), Sect. 4 details the experimental framework used to study the performance of PGE, and Sect. 5 describes the main results. Finally, Sect. 6 gathers the main conclusions and provides some insights towards future work.

2   Grammatical Evolution

GE [3] is a Grammar-based GP approach where the individuals are presented as a variable length string of integers. To create an executable program, the genotype (i.e., the string of integers) is mapped to the phenotype (program) via the productions rules defined in a Context-Free Grammar (CFG). A grammar is a tuple $G = (NT, T, S, P)$ where NT and T represent the non-empty set of *Non-Terminal* (NT) and *Terminal* (T) symbols, S is an element of NT called the axiom and P is the set of production rules. The rules in P are in the form $A ::= \alpha$, with $A \in NT$ and $\alpha \in (NT \cup T)^*$. The NT and T sets are disjoint. Each grammar defines a language $L(G) = \{w : S \stackrel{*}{\Rightarrow} w, w \in T^*\}$, that is the set of all sequences of terminal symbols that can be derived from the axiom.

The genotype-phenotype mapping is the key issue in GE, and it is performed in several successive steps. To select which derivation rule should be selected to replace a NT, the mapping relies on the modulo operator. An example of this process is shown in Fig. 1. The genotype is composed of integers values randomly generated between [0,255]. The mapping starts with the axiom $<start>$. In this case, there is only one derivation possible, and we rewrite the axiom with $<expr>$. Then we proceed the expansion of $<expr>$. Since this NT has two possible expansion rules available, we need to select which one will be used. We start by taking the first unused value of the genotype, which is 54, and divide it by the number of possible options. The remainder of this operation indicates the option that should be used. In our example, $54mod(2) = 0$, which results in the first production being selected. This process is performed until there are no more NT symbols to expand or there are no more integers to read from the genotype.

In this last case and if we still have NT to expand, a wrapping mechanism can be used, where the genotype will be re-used, until it generates a valid individual or the predefined number of wraps is over. If after all the wraps we still have not mapped all the NT, the mapping process stops, and the individual will be considered invalid.

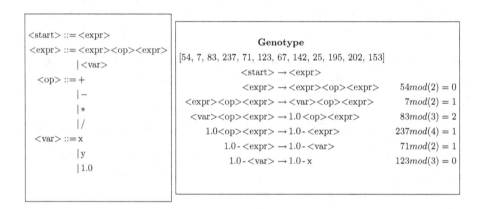

Fig. 1. Example of GE mapping

Even though GE has been applied to several problem domains, there is a debate in the literature concerned with its overall performance [4,12]. GE has been criticised for having high redundancy and low locality [13,14]. A representation has high redundancy when several different genotypes correspond to one phenotype. Locality is concerned with how changes in the genotype are reflected on the phenotype. These criticisms have triggered many researchers into looking how GE could be improved [7,11,15,16].

2.1 Representation Variants

O'Neill *et al.* [7] proposed Position Independent GE (πGE), introducing a different mapping mechanism that removes the positional dependency that exists in GE. In πGE each codon is composed of two values (nont, rule), where nont is used to select the next non-terminal to be expanded and the rule selects which production rule should be applied from the selected non-terminal. In Fagan *et al.* [17] several different mapping mechanisms where compared, and πGE showed better performance over GE, with statistical differences. Another attempt to make GE position independent is Chorus [15]. In this variant, each gene encodes a specific grammar production rule, not taking into consideration the position. This proposal did not showed significant differences when comparing with standard GE.

Structured Grammatical Evolution is a recent proposal to address the locality and redundancy problems of GE [10,11]. SGE proposes a one-to-one mapping between the genotype and the non-terminal symbols of the grammar. Each position in the genotype of SGE is a list of integers, where each element of this list is used to select the next derivation rule. This genotype structure, ensures that the modification of a codon does not affect the chosen productions of other non-terminals, reducing the overall changes that can occur at the phenotypical level, which results in an higher locality.

In [11] different grammar-based GP approaches were compared, and the authors showed that SGE achieved a good performance when compared with several grammar-based GP representations. These results were in line with Fagan *et al.* [17], which showed that different genotype-phenotype mapping can improve the performance of grammar-based GP.

Some probabilistic methods have been proposed to try to understand more about the distribution of fitter individuals and have been effective in solving complex problems [18]. Despite its potential, few attempts have been made to use probabilities in GE.

In [8], was implemented a PCFG (Fig. 2) to do the mapping process of GE, where the genotype of the individual is a vector of probabilities used to choose the productions rules. This approach also implements Estimation of Distribution Algorithms (EDA) [19], a probabilistic technique that replaces the mutation and crossover operators, by sampling the probability distribution of the best individuals, to generate the new population, each generation. The probabilities start all equal and are updated each generation, based on the frequency of the chosen rules of the individuals with higher fitness. The experiments were inclusive, since the proposed approach had a similar performance to GE.

Kim *et al.* [9] proposed Probabilistic Model Building Grammatical Evolution (PMBGE), which utilises a Conditional Dependency Tree (CDT) that represents the relationships between production rules used to calculate the new probabilities. Similar to [8], the EDA mechanism was implemented instead of the genetic operators. The results showed no statistical differences between GE and the proposed approach.

3 Probabilistic Grammatical Evolution

Probabilistic Grammatical Evolution (PGE) is a new representation for Grammatical Evolution. In PGE we rely on a Probabilistic Context-Free Grammar

(PCFG) to perform the genotype-phenotype mapping. A PCFG is a quintuple $PG = (NT, T, S, P, Probs)$ where NT and T represent the non-empty set of *Non-Terminal* (NT) and *Terminal* (T) symbols, respectively, S is an element of NT called the axiom, P is the set of production rules, and *Probs* is a set of probabilities associated with each production rule. The genotype in PGE is a vector of floats, where each element corresponds to the probability of choosing a certain derivation rule. The overall mapping procedure is shown in Algorithm 1 and Fig. 2 shows an example of the application of the PGE mapping.

The panel on the left shows a PCFG, where each derivation rule has a probability associated. The set of NT is composed of $<start>, <expr>, <op>$ and $<var>$. The right panel of Fig. 2 shows how the mapping procedure works.

<start> ::= <expr>	(1.0)
<expr> ::= <expr><op><expr>	(0.5)
| <var>	(0.5)
<op> ::= +	(0.33)
| *	(0.33)
| −	(0.33)
<var> ::= x	(0.5)
| 1.0	(0.5)

Genotype

[0.8, 0.2, 0.98, 0.45, 0.62, 0.37, 0.19]

<start> → <expr>	(0.8)
<expr> → <expr><op><expr>	(0.2)
<expr><op><expr> → <var><op><expr>	(0.98)
<var><op><expr> → x <op><expr>	(0.45)
x<op><expr> → x * <expr>	(0.62)
x * <expr> → x * <var>	(0.37)
x * <var> → x * x	(0.19)

Fig. 2. Example of mapping with PCFG

It begins with the axiom, $<start>$. We start by taking the first value of the genotype, which is 0.8, and since there is only one expansion available, the non-terminal $<expr>$ will be chosen. Next, we need to rewrite $<expr>$, which has two derivation options. We take the second value of the genotype, 0.2, and compare it to the probability associated with the first derivation option ($<expr><op><expr>$). Since $0.2 < 0.5$, we select this derivation option to rewrite $<expr>$. This process is repeated until there are no more non-terminals left to expand, or no probabilities left in the genotype. When this last situation occurs, we use a wrapping mechanism similar to the standard GE, where the genotype will be reused a certain number of times. If after the wrapping we still have not mapped the individual completely, the mapping process stops, and the individual will be considered invalid.

In PGE, the probabilities are updated each generation after evaluating the population, based on how many times each derivation rule has been selected by the best individual of the current generation or the best individual overall. When a derivation rule is used to create one of these individuals, its probability should be increased, otherwise if a derivation rule is not used, we should decrease it.

Algorithm 1. Mapping with PCFG

```
 1: procedure GENERATEINDIVIDUAL(genotype, pcfg)
 2:     start = pcfg.getStart()
 3:     phenotype = [start]
 4:     for codon in genotype do
 5:         symbol = phenotype.getNextNT()
 6:         productions = pcfg.getRulesNT(symbol)
 7:         cum_prob = 0.0                          ▷ Cumulative Sum of Probabilities
 8:         for prod in productions do
 9:             cum_prob = cum_prob + prod.getProb()
10:             if codon < cum_prob then
11:                 selected_rule = prod
12:                 break
13:             end if
14:         end for
15:         phenotype.replace(symbol, selected_rule)
16:         if phenotype.isValid() then
17:             break
18:         end if
19:     end for
20: end procedure
```

Alternating between these two bests helps us to avoid using the same individual in consecutive generations to adjust the probabilities of the PCFG, balancing global exploration with local exploration. All the adjustments are performed using a parameter λ called *learning factor* which smooths the transitions on the search space. The lambda value should be between 0% and 100%. At each generation, each individual is mapped using an updated version of grammar.

To update the probabilities in the grammar, we use Algorithm 2, where j is the number of productions of a non-terminal symbol of the grammar, i is the index of the production probability that is being updated and λ is the learning factor.

The probabilities are updated based on two different rules. The first rule increases the probability of a derivation rule, taken into account the frequency that it was selected by the best individual (Algorithm 2 line 5). The second rule decreases the probability of the derivation options that are never used to expand a non-terminal (Algorithm 2 line 7). The *min* operator ensures that when we update the probabilities they are not greater than 1.

After the update of the probabilities for each derivation rule, we make sure that the sum of the probabilities of all derivation rules, for a non-terminal, is 1. If the sum surpasses this value, the excess is proportionally subtracted from the derivation options for a non-terminal. If the sum is smaller than one, the missing amount is added equally to the production rules of the non-terminal.

We are going to use the example of grammar and individual presented Fig. 2, to show how the probabilities are updated. On the left panel of Fig. 3 we can see

Algorithm 2. Probabilistic Grammatical Evolution

1: **procedure** UPDATEPROBABILITIES(*best*)
2:     $counter = best.getCounter()$ ▷ list with times each rule was expanded
3:     **for** each production rule i of each NT **do**
4:         **if** $counter_i > 0$ **then**
5:             $prob_i = min(prob_i + \frac{\lambda*counter_i}{\sum_{k=1}^{j} counter_k}, 1.0)$
6:         **else**
7:             $prob_i = prob_i - \lambda * prob_i$
8:         **end if**
9:     **end for**
10:    **while** $\sum_{k=1}^{j} prob_i \neq 1.0$ **do**
11:       $extra = (1.0 - \sum_{k=1}^{j} prob_i)/j$
12:       **for** each production rule i **do**
13:          $prob_i = prob_i + extra$
14:       **end for**
15:    **end while**
16: **end procedure**

---

the derivation tree of the individual that was used to update the probabilities of the PCFG on the right. The learning factor used was 0.01 (1%).

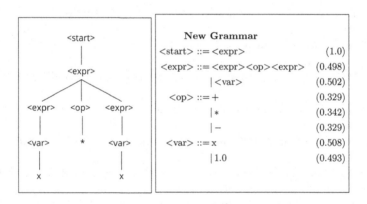

Fig. 3. Example of probability updating in PGE

Since the symbol $<start>$ has only one expansion rule, the probability of choosing $<expr>$ stays always 1. Looking at the derivation tree, we can see that the first derivation rule ($<expr><op><expr>$) of the non-terminal $<expr>$ was selected once, and the second derivation rule ($<var>$) was selected twice.

Using the Algorithm 2, the new probabilities for the first derivation option is $min(0.5 + \frac{0.01*1}{3}, 1)$ equals 0.5033(3), and for the second rule, $min(0.5 + \frac{0.01*2}{3}, 1)$ equals 0.5066(6). As the sum of the probabilities surpass 1, the excess ((1 − 0.5066 + 0.5033)/2 = 0.00495) is subtracted from both probabilities and the value is rounded to 3 decimal places. Then we distribute the excess for the derivations rules: the first rule is updated to 0.498 and the second rule is updated to 0.502. This process is applied to the other symbols. For the non-terminal $<op>$ the rule + and − were never chosen so they will update equally $((0.33 − 0.01 * 0.33)$ that equals 0.3267), and the rule * was chosen once $(min(0.33 + \frac{0.01*1}{1}, 1)$ that equals 0.34). As the sum of the three probabilities is smaller than one, 0.0022 must be added to the three probabilities, and the result rounded, staying with 0.329 for the + and − symbols, and 0.342 for the *. The non-terminal $<var>$ was expanded twice for the terminal x and never expanded for the terminal 1.0. By applying the algorithm, the first rule (x) should be updated to 0.51 $(min(0.5 + \frac{0.01*2}{2}, 1))$ and the second to 0.495 $(0.5 − 0.01 * 0.5)$, being the sum of the two probabilities different than one, the adjustment and rounding should be done and they are updated to 0.508 and 0.493, respectively.

4   Experimental Analysis

Over the years, several genotype-phenotype mapping alternatives have been proposed to increase the performance of GE. One that has obtained promising results is Structured Grammatical Evolution (SGE) [10,11]. To evaluate the performance of PGE, we considered the standard GE and SGE algorithms in two different benchmark problems. These benchmark problems were selected taking into account the comparative analysis followed by [11] and the recommendations presented in [20]. For our experimental analysis we selected the Pagie Polynomial and the Boston Housing prediction problem.

4.1   Problem Description

Pagie Polynomial. Popular benchmark problem for testing Genetic Programming algorithms, with the objective of finding the mathematical expression for the following problem:

$$\frac{1}{1 + x^{-4}} + \frac{1}{1 + y^{-4}}. \tag{1}$$

The function is sampled in the interval [-5, 5.4] with a step of 0.4, and the grammar used is:

$\langle start \rangle$ ::= $\langle expr \rangle$

$\langle expr \rangle$ ::= $\langle expr \rangle \langle op \rangle \langle expr \rangle$ | ($\langle expr \rangle \langle op \rangle \langle expr \rangle$)
              | $\langle pre\_op \rangle$ ($\langle expr \rangle$) | $\langle var \rangle$

$\langle op \rangle$ ::= + | - | * | /

$\langle pre\_op \rangle$ ::= sin | cos | exp | log | inv

$\langle var \rangle$ ::= x | y | 1.0

The division and logarithm functions are protected, i.e., $1/0 = 1$ and $log(f(x)) = 0$ $if f(x) \leq 0$.

Boston Housing. This is a famous Machine Learning problem to predict the prices of Boston Houses. The dataset comes from the StatLib Library [21] and has 506 entries, with 13 features. It was divided in 90% for training and 10% for testing. The grammar used for the Boston Housing regression problem is as follows:

⟨*start*⟩   ::= ⟨*expr*⟩

⟨*expr*⟩   ::= ⟨*expr*⟩ ⟨*op*⟩ ⟨*expr*⟩ | (⟨*expr*⟩ ⟨*op*⟩ ⟨*expr*⟩)
         | ⟨*pre_op*⟩ (⟨*expr*⟩) | ⟨*var*⟩

⟨*op*⟩   ::= + | - | * | /

⟨*pre_op*⟩ ::= sin | cos | exp | log | inv

⟨*var*⟩   ::= x[1] |...| x[13] | 1.0

4.2   Parameters

For all the experiments reported, the fitness function is computed using the Root Relative Squared Error (RRSE), where lower values indicate a better fitness. The parameters are presented in Table 1. These parameters were selected in order to make the comparisons between all the approaches fair. Additionally, and to avoid side effects, the wrapping mechanism was removed from GE and PGE. Concerning the variation operators for PGE, we used the standard one-point crossover, and float mutation which generates a new random float between [0,1]. Additionally, PGE uses a learning factor of $\lambda = 1.0\%$.

Table 1. Parameters used in the experimental analysis for GE, PGE and SGE

	Value		
Parameters	GE	PGE	SGE
Population size		1000	
Generations		50	
Elitism		10%	
Mutation probability		5%	
Crossover probability		90%	
Tournament		3	
Max number of wraps	0		-
Size of genotype	128		-
Min tree depth	-		-
Max tree depth	-		-

5   Results

The experimental results in this section will be presented in terms of the mean best fitness, which results from the execution of 100 independent runs. To compare all approaches we performed a statistical study. Since the results did not follow any distribution, and the populations were independently initialised, we employed the Kruskal-Wallis non-parametric test to check if there were meaningful differences between the different groups of approaches. When this happened we used the Mann-Whitney *post-hoc* test with Bonferroni correction. For all the statistical tests we considered a significance level $\alpha = 0.05$.

Figure 4 depicts the results for the Pagie Polynomial. It is possible to see that all the methods start from similar fitness values, but as the evolutionary process progresses, differences between the approaches emerge. The fitness of the solutions being evolved by SGE rapidly decrease in the early generations, but slows down after a certain number of generations (≈ 20). For GE, the fitness decreases slowly through the generations. This results are in line with the ones presented in [10].

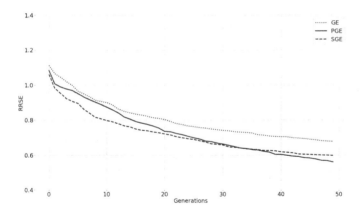

Fig. 4. Results for the Pagie Polynomial

The PGE performance is different from both SGE and GE. In the early generations PGE decreases slowly (following the same trend as GE), but then, around the 10th generation, the fitness of PGE starts to rapidly decrease. Around generation 35 it surpasses the quality of SGE. The first row of Table 2 shows the Mean Best Fitness and the Standard Deviation for each approach. We can see that for the Pagie Polynomial problem PGE obtains the lowest error.

In terms of statistical significant differences, the Kruskall-Wallis showed meaningful differences between the approaches. The *post-hoc* results are depicted in Table 3. Looking at the results it is possible to see that both PGE and SGE are better than GE with statistical significant differences. When comparing PGE and SGE we only found marginal differences (p-value = 0.04) on the Boston Housing Training.

Table 2. Mean Best Fitness and Standard Deviation for all the methods used in the comparison. Results are averages of 100 independent runs.

Problem	PGE	GE	SGE
Pagie polynomial	**0.56 ± 0.16**	0.68 ± 0.17	0.59 ± 0.13
Boston housing train	0.82 ± 0.12	0.88 ± 0.14	**0.78 ± 0.13**
Boston housing test	0.84 ± 0.13	0.90 ± 0.15	**0.79 ± 0.12**

Table 3. Results of the Mann-Whitney *post-hoc* statistical tests. Bonferroni correction is used and the significance level $\alpha = 0.05$ is considered.

	PGE - GE	PGE - SGE
Pagie polynomial	**0.00**	0.24
Boston housing training	**0.00**	0.04
Boston housing test	**0.00**	0.10

Figure 5 shows the results for the Boston Housing problem. Looking at the training results (Fig. 5 (a)), it is possible to see that the fitness of SGE individuals rapidly decrease, and continue too over the entire evolutionary process. The performance of GE is in line with what we observed previously, i.e., a slow decrease on the fitness. Even though the training results are important to understand the behaviour of the methods, the testing results are more relevant, because they allow us to evaluate the generalisation ability of the models evolved by each approach. Looking at the test results (Fig. 5(b)) we can see that SGE and PGE are building models that can generalise better to unseen data.

Once again we applied a statistical analysis to check whether there were differences between the approaches (Table 3). The results, for both training and test, show that PGE is statistically significant than GE, but there are no differences between PGE and SGE.

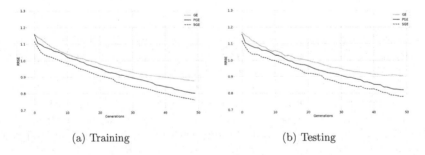

(a) Training   (b) Testing

Fig. 5. Results for the Boston Housing problem

Finally we present an analysis on how the probabilities of certain derivation rules progress over the generations. This analysis will give us insights into what are the rules that are more relevant.

For the Pagie Polynomial, Fig. 6 presents the evolution of the PCFG's probabilities for the non-terminal $<op>$ over the generations. As one would expect, the probabilities associated with the symbols that are required to solve the problem are higher, namely the ones associated with the terminal symbols $+$ and $/$.

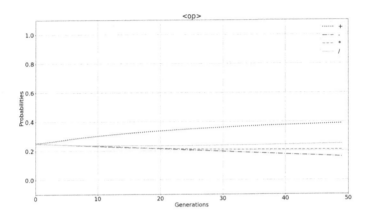

Fig. 6. Evolution of grammar probabilities of non-terminal $<op>$ with the Pagie Polynomial. Results are averages of 100 runs.

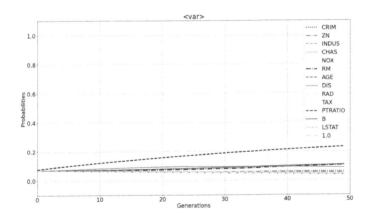

Fig. 7. Evolution of grammar probabilities of non-terminal $<var>$ with the Boston Housing problem. Results are averages of 100 runs.

Concerning the Boston Housing, the progression of the probabilities are depicted in Fig. 7 and in Table 4. Concretely, the results show the probabilities for the derivation options of the non-terminal $<var>$. This symbol was selected because it contains the features that describe the problem. Looking at the evolution of the probabilities associated with each production, we can understand which of these features are more relevant to accurately predict the price of houses. Looking at the results (Fig. 7), one can see that PTRATIO stands out in terms of the probability of being selected. PTRATIO represents the pupil-teacher ratio by town. This is in line with the results reported by [22]. Another interesting result is to see that the feature RM (the third most important feature in [22]), which is the average number of rooms per dwelling, is also on the top three of our results. These results confirm not only the relevance of these features to the Boston Housing problem, but also allow us to perform feature selection and provide an explanation to the results achieved. This means that at the end of the evolutionary process one can look at the final distribution of the probabilities in the grammar, and analyse the relative importance of each production and derivation rules, and see how they are used to create the best models.

Table 4. Probabilities of the Boston Housing Dataset's productions of the non-terminal $<var>$ at the end of the evolutionary process. Results are averages of 100 runs.

Production	Probability
PTRATIO	0.23
B	0.11
RM	0.1
DIS	0.09
LSTAT	0.07
ZN	0.06
NOX, CRIM, 1.0	0.05
RAD, TAX, RADIUS, CHAS, AGE	0.04

6   Conclusion

Grammatical Evolution (GE) has attracted the attention of many researchers and practitioners. Since its proposal in the late 1990s, it has been applied with success to many problem domains. However, it has been shown that it suffers from some issues.

In this paper we proposed a new mapping mechanism and genotypic representation called Probabilistic Grammatical Evolution (PGE). In concrete, in PGE the genotype of an individual is a variable length sequence of floats, and the genotype-phenotype mapping is performed using a Probabilistic Context-Free Grammar (PCFG). Each derivation rule has a probability associated, and they are updated with taking into account the number of times that the derivation rules were selected by the best individuals. In order to maintain a balance between global and local exploration we alternate between the best overall individual and the best individual of generation, respectively.

PGE was compared with standard GE and SGE in two different benchmarks. The results show that for both problems PGE is statistically better that GE and has a similar performance when compared to SGE. We also analyse how the probabilities associated the different productions progress over time, and it was possible to see that the production rules that are more relevant to the problem at hand have higher probabilities of being selected.

In terms of future work one needs to consider alternative mechanisms to adjust probabilities of the productions rules. Another line of work that needs to be conducted is concerned with the analysis of the locality and redundancy in PGE.

Acknowledgements. This work is partially funded by the project grant DSAIPA/DS/0022/2018 (GADgET), by national funds through the FCT - Foundation for Science and Technology, I.P., within the scope of the project CISUC - UID/CEC/00326/2020 and by European Social Fund, through the Regional Operational Program Centro 2020. We also thank the NVIDIA Corporation for the hardware granted to this research.

References

1. Koza, J.R.: Genetic Programming: On the Programming of Computers by Means of Natural Selection. MIT Press, Cambridge (1992)
2. Whigham, P.A.: Grammatically-based genetic programming. In: Proceedings of the Workshop on Genetic Programming: From Theory to Real-World Applications, vol. 16, pp. 33–41 (1995)
3. Ryan, C., Collins, J.J., Neill, M.O.: Grammatical evolution: evolving programs for an arbitrary language. In: Banzhaf, W., Poli, R., Schoenauer, M., Fogarty, T.C. (eds.) EuroGP 1998. LNCS, vol. 1391, pp. 83–96. Springer, Heidelberg (1998). https://doi.org/10.1007/BFb0055930
4. Whigham, P.A., Dick, G., Maclaurin, J., Owen, C.A.: Examining the best of both worlds of grammatical evolution. In: Proceedings of the 2015 Annual Conference on Genetic and Evolutionary Computation, pp. 1111–1118. ACM (2015). https://doi.org/10.1145/2739480.2754784
5. Nicolau, M.: Understanding grammatical evolution: initialisation. Genet. Program. Evolvable Mach. **18**(4), 467–507 (2017). https://doi.org/10.1007/s10710-017-9309-9
6. Nicolau, M., Agapitos, A.: Understanding grammatical evolution: grammar design. In: Ryan, C., O'Neill, M., Collins, J.J. (eds.) Handbook of Grammatical Evolution, pp. 23–53. Springer, Cham (2018). https://doi.org/10.1007/978-3-319-78717-6_2
7. O'Neill, M., Brabazon, A., Nicolau, M., Garraghy, S.M., Keenan, P.: πGrammatical evolution. In: Deb, K. (ed.) GECCO 2004. LNCS, vol. 3103, pp. 617–629. Springer, Heidelberg (2004). https://doi.org/10.1007/978-3-540-24855-2_70
8. Kim, H.-T., Ahn, C.W.: A new grammatical evolution based on probabilistic context-free grammar. In: Handa, H., Ishibuchi, H., Ong, Y.-S., Tan, K.-C. (eds.) Proceedings of the 18th Asia Pacific Symposium on Intelligent and Evolutionary Systems - Volume 2. PALO, vol. 2, pp. 1–12. Springer, Cham (2015). https://doi.org/10.1007/978-3-319-13356-0_1

9. Kim, H.T., Kang, H.K., Ahn, C.W.: A conditional dependency based probabilistic model building grammatical evolution. IEICE Trans. Inf. Syst. **E99.D**(7), 1937–1940 (2016). https://doi.org/10.1587/transinf.2016edl8004

10. Lourenço, N., Pereira, F.B., Costa, E.: Unveiling the properties of structured grammatical evolution. Genet. Program. Evolvable Mach. **17**(3), 251–289 (2016). https://doi.org/10.1007/s10710-015-9262-4

11. Lourenço, N., Ferrer, J., Pereira, F.B., Costa, E.: A comparative study of different grammar-based genetic programming approaches. In: McDermott, J., Castelli, M., Sekanina, L., Haasdijk, E., García-Sánchez, P. (eds.) EuroGP 2017. LNCS, vol. 10196, pp. 311–325. Springer, Cham (2017). https://doi.org/10.1007/978-3-319-55696-3_20

12. Ryan, C.: A rebuttal to Whigham, Dick, and Maclaurin by one of the inventors of grammatical evolution: commentary on on the mapping of genotype to phenotype in evolutionary algorithms by Peter A. Whigham, Grant Dick, and James Maclaurin. Genet. Program. Evolvable Mach. **18**(3), 385–389 (2017). https://doi.org/10.1007/s10710-017-9294-z

13. Keijzer, M., O'Neill, M., Ryan, C., Cattolico, M.: Grammatical evolution rules: the mod and the bucket rule. In: Foster, J.A., Lutton, E., Miller, J., Ryan, C., Tettamanzi, A. (eds.) EuroGP 2002. LNCS, vol. 2278, pp. 123–130. Springer, Heidelberg (2002). https://doi.org/10.1007/3-540-45984-7_12

14. Rothlauf, F., Oetzel, M.: On the locality of grammatical evolution. In: Collet, P., Tomassini, M., Ebner, M., Gustafson, S., Ekárt, A. (eds.) EuroGP 2006. LNCS, vol. 3905, pp. 320–330. Springer, Heidelberg (2006). https://doi.org/10.1007/11729976_29

15. Ryan, C., Azad, A., Sheahan, A., O'Neill, M.: No coercion and no prohibition, a position independent encoding scheme for evolutionary algorithms – the chorus system. In: Foster, J.A., Lutton, E., Miller, J., Ryan, C., Tettamanzi, A. (eds.) EuroGP 2002. LNCS, vol. 2278, pp. 131–141. Springer, Heidelberg (2002). https://doi.org/10.1007/3-540-45984-7_13

16. Bartoli, A., Castelli, M., Medvet, E.: Weighted hierarchical grammatical evolution. IEEE Trans. Cybern. **50**(2), 476–488 (2018). https://doi.org/10.1109/tcyb.2018.2876563

17. Fagan, D., O'Neill, M., Galván-López, E., Brabazon, A., McGarraghy, S.: An analysis of genotype-phenotype maps in grammatical evolution. In: Esparcia-Alcázar, A.I., Ekárt, A., Silva, S., Dignum, S., Uyar, A.Ş. (eds.) EuroGP 2010. LNCS, vol. 6021, pp. 62–73. Springer, Heidelberg (2010). https://doi.org/10.1007/978-3-642-12148-7_6

18. Kim, K., Shan, Y., Hoai, N.X., McKay, R.I.: Probabilistic model building in genetic programming: a critical review. Genet. Program. Evolvable Mach. **15**(2), 115–167 (2013). https://doi.org/10.1007/s10710-013-9205-x

19. Larrañaga, P., Lozano, J.A. (eds.): Estimation of Distribution Algorithms: A New Tool for Evolutionary Computation. Springer, New York (2002). https://doi.org/10.1007/978-1-4615-1539-5

20. McDermott, J., et al.: Genetic programming needs better benchmarks. In: Proceedings of the Fourteenth International Conference on Genetic and Evolutionary Computation Conference - GECCO 2012. ACM Press (2012). https://doi.org/10.1145/2330163.2330273

21. Harrison, D., Rubinfeld, D.: Boston Housing Data (1993). http://lib.stat.cmu.edu/datasets/boston. Accessed 27 Dec 2020

22. Che, J., Yang, Y., Li, L., Bai, X., Zhang, S., Deng, C.: Maximum relevance minimum common redundancy feature selection for nonlinear data. Inf. Sci. 409–410, 68–86 (2017). https://doi.org/10.1016/j.ins.2017.05.013

Evolving Allocation Rules for Beam Search Heuristics in Assembly Line Balancing

João Pedro Gonçalves Moreira and Marcus Ritt[✉]

Instituto de Informática, Universidade Federal do Rio Grande do Sul,
Av. Bento Gonçalves, 9500 Porto Alegre, Rio Grande do Sul, Brazil
{joaopedro.goncalvesmoreira,marcus.ritt}@inf.ufrgs.br

Abstract. We study the evolution of rules that define how to assign tasks to workstations in heuristic procedures for assembly line balancing. In assembly line balancing, a set of partially ordered tasks has to be assigned to workstations. The variant we consider, known as the assembly line worker assignment and balancing problem (ALWABP), has a fixed number of machines and workers, and different workers need different times to execute the tasks. A solution is an assignment of tasks and workers to workstations satisfying the partial order of the tasks, and the problem is to find a solution that maximizes the production rate of the assembly line. These problems are often solved by station-based assignment procedures, which use heuristic rules to select the tasks to be assigned to stations. There are many selection rules available in the literature. We show how efficient rules can be evolved, and demonstrate that rules evolved for simple assignment procedures are also effective in stochastic heuristic procedures using beam search, leading to improved heuristics.

Keywords: Combinatorial optimization · Genetic programming · Allocation rules · Station-based allocation procedures · Assembly line balancing

1 Introduction

Assembly lines are common in the mass production of goods. The assembly of a product is divided into a number of tasks, usually with precedence constraints, which are assigned to a series of workstations. The products pass through the assembly line in a pipelined fashion: an assembly line with m workstations holds m partially assembled products, one per station, and in one work cycle each station executes the tasks assigned to it, and all products move on to the next

Our research has been supported by CNPq (grant 420348/2016-6), Coordenação de Aperfeiçoamento de Pessoal de Nível Superior - Brasil (CAPES) - Finance Code 001, and by Google Research Latin America (grant 25111).

T. Hu et al. (Eds.): EuroGP 2021, LNCS 12691, pp. 214–228, 2021.
https://doi.org/10.1007/978-3-030-72812-0_14

station. The *cycle time* thus depends on the largest station time, since all stations work synchronously, and *balancing* a line means minimizing the cycle time, which is equivalent to maximizing the production rate.

Formally, let $(T, \preceq)$ be a set of $n = |T|$ tasks equipped with a partial order $\preceq$, and assume we are given m workstations and a set W of workers, where $|W| = m$. It is convenient to represent the partial order $\preceq$ by a directed acyclic graph $G = (T, A)$ with arcs $(i, j) \in A$ such that task i is an immediate predecessor of task j, and to write F_i and F_i^* for the set of immediate and all followers of task i, and P_i and P_i^* for the set of immediate and all predecessors of task i [18]. The execution time of task $i \in T$ by worker $w \in W$ is $t_{wi} \geq 0$. A value of $t_{wi} = \infty$ is allowed and indicates that worker w is unable to execute task i. We are interested in assignments $a : T \rightarrow [m]$ of tasks and $w : W \rightarrow [m]$ of workers to the m stations[1], where w is bijective and a respects the partial order, i.e. for $i, j \in T$, $i \preceq j$ we have $a(i) \leq a(j)$. For a pair (a, w) we have *station loads* (i.e. total execution times on stations) $T(s) = \sum_{i \in a^{-1}(s)} t_{w^{-1}(s),i}$, for each station $s \in [m]$, and the maximum station load $C = \max_{s \in [m]} T(s)$ defines the *cycle time*.

This problem is called the Assembly Line Worker Assignment and Balancing Problem (ALWABP) of type II. Type II problems minimize the cycle time for a fixed number of stations, type I problems the number of stations for a fixed cycle time. The ALWABP is NP-complete, since for worker-independent times $t_{wi} = t_i$ it reduces to the NP-complete Simple Assembly Line Balancing Problem (SALBP) of type II [16]. The ALWABP has been introduced by [10] to model workers of varying capabilities in sheltered work centers for persons with disabilities. [10] have shown that individual disabilities can be often hidden in assembly lines, and that well balanced lines can have an efficiency similar to lines where all workers have the same (standard) performance. Therefore the problem has a practical social value, since sheltered work centers often are under pressure in having to operate efficiently, with limited subsidy from the state.

Several heuristic methods for the ALWABP have been proposed [1–3,5,11, 12,14]. Many of them are based on constructive, station-based assignment procedures (SBAP) which consider each station in turn, and repeatedly assign an available task to the current station, until the station is completely loaded, and then move on to the next station. For each station, a SBAP has to choose an available worker, and a subset of the available tasks. SBAP have been studied thoroughly for the SALBP [13]. [11] propose constructive heuristics based on task and worker selection rules, and study sixteen task selection rules for the ALWABP, extending well-known task selection rules for the SALBP adapted for the specific characteristics of the ALWABP. [3] propose a probabilistic beam search for the ALWABP-2 and show that it produces robust results that outperform state-of-the-art heuristic methods for the ALWABP-2, in a set of 320 instances proposed by [4], when using some of the best known task and worker selection rules.

---

[1] We write $[n] = \{1, 2, \ldots, n\}$.

In this paper we are interested in evolving such selection rules using Genetic Programming to use them in SBAP for the ALWABP. Genetic Programming is a method to evolve programs, and has been applied successfully to a broad range of problems (see e.g. [8,15]), including many combinatorial optimization problems in areas related to assembly line balancing such as scheduling [20,21], and resource allocation [6,19].

We build on earlier work from [7] who have proposed a language for expressing task selection rules, and have shown that it is possible to apply genetic programming to evolve these rules, and that their performance in constructive SBAP is competitive with manually designed rules from the literature. In this paper we investigate evolving rules that perform well in complete heuristic procedures for the ALWABP. The main contributions of this paper are: (1) an improvement of current SBAP for the ALWABP by including a constraint propagation that improves the lookahead of a SBAP, and a better task selection strategy, (2) an experimental demonstration that rules evolved for such SBAP work well within probabilistic beam searches, and (3) a detailed experimental analysis, comparing the resulting heuristics to a state-of-the-art heuristic for the problem.

The remainder of the paper is organized as follows. In Sect. 2 we explain SBAP and heuristic searches that use them, and their application to the ALWABP. We then present in Sect. 3 briefly the language for expressing task selection rules, and the genetic algorithm (GA) introduced by [7], and then present strategies to improve the search for good selection rules. In Sect. 4 we report on computational experiments. We conclude in Sect. 5.

2   Station-Oriented Heuristics for the ALWABP

Being a type II problem, the objective of the ALWABP is to find the smallest feasible cycle time, such that valid assignments a and w of tasks and workers to workstations exist. This is usually reduced to a sequence of feasibility problems, that try to find such an assignment for a fixed cycle time C. The search strategies in the C-space include lower bound searches, that start from a lower bound on the cycle time, and increase it until a feasible solution is found, or binary searches in a range of feasible C-values. These strategies are discussed in more detail in Sect. 2.1.

For a given cycle time C, a SBAP tries to construct a feasible solution. Algorithm 1 outlines the main steps of a SBAP [11]. A problem instance is a pair $I = (G, p)$ of a directed acyclic graph G representing the task precedences, a matrix of processing times p, together with a trial cycle time C. The algorithm maintains a set U of unassigned workers, initially set to all available workers, and current partial assignments a and w of tasks and workers to workstations, initially empty. For each workstation $s \in [m]$, and for each available worker $u \in U$ it repeatedly selects a task from a set of candidate tasks $C(I, T, u)$ and assigns it to the station, until no more tasks can be assigned to the station. Candidate tasks are all tasks whose predecessors have been already assigned, and whose addition to the current station does not exceed the cycle time, namely

$C(I, T, u) = \{i \in V(G) \mid T + t_{ui} \leq C \wedge P_i^* = \emptyset\}$. The procedure stops when all stations have been processed or all tasks have been assigned, and is successful if a is a complete assignment.

Input : An instance $I = (G, p)$ and a cycle time C.
Output: Assignments a and w.
$U = [m]$
initialize a and w to empty assignments
for $s \in [m]$ **do**
    for $u \in U$ **do**
        $a_u := a; G_u := G$
        $T := 0$
        while $C(I, T, u) \neq \emptyset$ **do**
(*)   use the task selection rule to choose some $t \in V(G)$
            extend assignment a_u by $t \mapsto s$
            $G_u := G \setminus \{t\}$
    use the worker selection rule to choose the best worker $u \in U$
    $a := a_u$
    $G := G_u$
    $U := U \setminus \{u\}$
    extend assignment w by $u \mapsto k$

Algorithm 1: Station-based assignment procedure for the ALWABP.

The quality of the solutions found by priority-based heuristics for the ALWABP strongly relies on the task and worker selection rules used by the heuristics. For the SALBP, choosing a task $t \in T$ of maximum *positional weight* $\mathrm{PW}_i = \sum_{j \in F^*(i)} t_j$ is one of the most effective rules [17]. [11] have studied several task and worker allocation rules for the ALWABP and confirmed that the extension of the positional weights to the ALWABP, taking as the task time the minimum time over all workers $\underline{t}_i = \min_{w \in W} t_{wi}$ remains effective. This rule is called MaxPWMin. They further have identified that for a residual instance with graph G and unassigned workers U, choosing the worker that minimizes the lower bound on the cycle time $\sum_{i \in T} \underline{t}_i / |U|$ is the most effective worker selection rule analyzed (called MinRLB).

2.1 Iterated Probabilistic Beam Search

Given a SBAP, a heuristic has to search for the smallest cycle time that produces a feasible solution. For the SALBP several strategies have been used in the literature, which similarly apply to the ALWABP. A *lower bound search* starts from a lower bound on the cycle time, and increases it until finding a feasible solution. Similarly, an *upper bound search* starts from an upper bound on the cycle time and repeatedly decreases it. One can also apply a *binary search*. However, if the allocation procedure for a fixed cycle time is a heuristic, there can be inversions where a larger cycle time is not feasible, although a smaller cycle time is. For this reason, a binary search can mislead the search to the wrong part of the search space, and usually is used only with exact procedures. In this paper we follow previous approaches and apply an upper bound search.

The upper bound search maintains the current feasible cycle time C. Following [3] we cyclically search for a feasible solution in an interval $[l, u]$ of cycle times, where $l = \lfloor ru \rfloor$ and $u = C - 1$, with a search rate $r \in (0, 1)$. This strategy allows for a larger reduction of the cycle time when C is high, and diversifies the search on different cycle times, since a heuristic search may work better for some cycle times. If the number of cyclic searches in $[l, u]$ reaches an upper bound M (i.e. after $(l - u + 1)M$ trials), which is a parameter of the method, the search is considered to have stagnated and terminates.

An additional strategy that improves SBAP assignment is to use forward as well as backward assignment. In the forward assignment the SBAP is applied to the given precedence graph. However, it is also possible to apply a SBAP to the precedence graph where all arcs have been inverted, which is equivalent to assigning tasks from last to the first station. For some precedence graphs this strategy is more effective. For this reason we apply for each given cycle time C the SBAP always in forward manner first, and if this does not succeed, try to assign the tasks in a backward manner.

The search for a fixed cycle time itself is extended from a simple SBAP to a *probabilistic beam search*. A beam search, introduced by [9] is a constructive procedure that maintains a set of solutions B, called the *beam*, of a fixed size $|B|$ (the beam size). Repeatedly, each solution is expanded several times to produce a set of candidate solutions, and among all candidate solutions from all solutions in the current beam, the best $|B|$ solutions are selected to form the beam in the next step. The number of expansions per solution is called the *beam factor*. Since a deterministic expansion would produce always the same candidate solution, the expansion is probabilistic. In this paper we propose to use the task allocation rule to rank all candidate tasks in line (*) of the SBAP (Algorithm 1) and select a task of rank r with probability proportional to $r^{-\tau}$ for a greediness parameter τ (for $\tau \to \infty$ we obtain the normal deterministic selection of a task of highest priority, for $\tau = 0$ a uniform random selection).

For local assignment we additionally propose a new domain-dependent constraint propagator, which maintains the current task-worker assignment and a list of excluded task-worker pairs. When assigning a new task to the current worker, all free tasks that exceed the worker's idle time are removed as candidates for the current worker. Furthermore, all successors of such tasks can no longer be assigned to the current worker. If any free task has no remaining candidate, the allocation is declared infeasible; if it has only one remaining candidate, it is assigned to the only remaining worker. This may lead to other infeasible task-worker pairs that can be excluded from consideration, or that can be assigned to the last remaining worker. In particular, if a non-minimal task is assigned to the current worker, all its predecessors are also assigned. These propagation rules are applied until no more task-worker pairs are forced or can be removed.

The complete procedure is referred to as the Iterated Probabilistic Beam Search (IPBS).

Table 1. Task attributes [7].

Name	Value	Description
Time	t_{wi}	Task time of current task for the current worker
MaxTIC	$\max_{w' \in U_w} t_{w'i}$	Maximum task time of unassigned workers
MaxTEC	$\max_{w' \in U_w^-} t_{w'i}$	Maximum task time of unassigned workers, excluding the current worker
MinTIC	$\min_{w' \in U_w} t_{w'i}$	Minimum task time of unassigned workers
MinTEC	$\min_{w' \in U_w^-} t_{w'i}$	Minimum task time of unassigned workers, excluding the current worker
SumTIC	$\sum_{w' \in U_w} t_{w'i}$	Sum over unassigned worker times
SumTEC	$\sum_{w' \in U_w^-} t_{w'i}$	Sum over unassigned worker times, excluding the current worker
Rank	$\sum_{w' \in U_w} [t_{w'i} < t_{wi}]$	Number of unassigned workers of smaller task time than the current worker
IF	$|F_i|$	Number of immediate followers
F	$|F_i^*|$	Number of total followers

3   Genetic Programming Applied to Task Selection Rules

Genetic programming (GP) is a form of evolutionary computation that evolves computer programs, with the aim of solving exactly or approximately a problem of interest. GP maintains a population of computer programs, often represented by expression trees. The tree representation of individuals allow the application of several crossover and mutation strategies to search for good solutions in the program space. In our case individuals represent task selection rules. To represent them, we use the language defined in [7]. Tables 1 and 2 give a brief overview on the available task attributes and operators of the language.

3.1   Crossover and Mutation Strategies

Crossover is applied to generate new individuals that share some of the structural characteristics of selected parents. Mutation produces a random small modification to an individual's structure. In case of GP, it is necessary to define ways of combining and modifying the structure of trees representing valid programs, such that the resulting tree is also a valid program.

In our study, we defined two strategies for crossover and mutation. The first strategy follows [7]. Their crossover operation consists of generating new individuals by combining the trees of the two parents using one of the followin operators:

DIV, RND, WCMB, WCMB*, OS, OS*, MIN, MAX.

For the RND operator, we generate a new individual for each probability $p \in \{0.1, 0.3, 0.5, 0.7, 0.9\}$. We select either operator WCMB or WCMB* with uniform probability, and generate six individuals for the selected operator using randomly chosen weights from the set $\{100, 10, 5, 2, 1, 0.5, 0.2, 0.1, 0.01\}$. In the first strategy, the mutation applied to an individual with expression tree p generates two new individuals. One is obtained by rounding the expression p using the ROUND operator, generating (ROUND α p), for a random rounding factor $\alpha \in \{0.01, 0.033, 0.1, 0.33\}$ following [13]. The second mutation consists of traversing the expression tree p and replacing each subtree s with (INV s) with

Table 2. Operators [7].

Name	Value	Description
Unary operators		
INV p	$-P(p)$	Negated priority
TSUM S p	$\sum_{j \in S \cup \{i\}} P(j, p)$	Sum of priorities of current task and all tasks in S. Set S may be F_i or F_i^*
ROUND α p	$\lceil P(p)/(\alpha C) \rceil$	Aggregation by αC.
Binary operators		
ADD l r	$P(l) + P(r)$	Sum of priorities
SUB l r	$P(l) - P(r)$	Difference of priorities
MULT l r	$P(l)P(r)$	Product of priorities
DIV l r	$P(l) \div P(r)$	Division of priorities
RND p l r		With probability p, return $P(l)$, else return $P(r)$
OS l r	$o\,P(l) + (1-o)\,P(r)$	Convex combination according to order strength[a] o
OS* l r		With probability o, return $P(l)$, else return $P(r)$
CMB w l r	$wP(l) + (1-w)P(r)$	Convex combination with weight w
CMB* w l r	$w'P(l) + (1-w')P(r)$	Convex combination with random weight $w' \sim U[w/1.1, 1.1w]$
WCMB w l r	$wP(l) + P(r)$	Combination with weight w
WCMB* w l r	$w'P(l) + P(r)$	Combination with random weight $w' \sim U[0.2w, 5w]$
MIN l r	$\min\{P(l), P(r)\}$	Minimum priority
MAX l r	$\max\{P(l), P(r)\}$	Maximum priority

[a]The order strength is the fraction of possible precedence relations, namely if $\bar{G} = (V, A)$ is the transitive closure of the precedence graph, the order strength is $|A|/\binom{|V|}{2}$.

probability $1/m$, where m is the number of nodes in p, i.e. the expected value of inverted nodes is 1. If no inversion is performed, it generates a new individual (INV p).

The second strategy for crossover and mutation uses *subtree crossover* and *subtree mutation*, which are common operations in GP. Given two parent trees p_1 and p_2, the subtree crossover randomly selects one node n_1 in p_1 and another node n_2 in p_2. Nodes n_1 and n_2 are called *crossover points*. Then, it generates as offspring a new individual by first making a copy of p_2 and replacing the subtree rooted at n_2 by a copy of the subtree rooted at n_1. Similarly to the subtree crossover, the subtree mutation also selects a random node n in an expression tree p, and replaces it with a randomly generated new subtree. A random tree is generated by selecting a random node, and recursively expanding it until a leaf node is produced, or a fixed depth is reached, in which case a leaf node is forced.

3.2   Strategies to Enhance the Search for Good Programs

We apply three additional strategies to improve the GP. The strategies primarily help the algorithm to explore the program space faster and find better programs by starting from an improved initial population.

Two-Step Evaluation. To compute the fitness of an individual we perform a SBAP as described in Algorithm 1 with a lower bound search on the cycle time, using the individual as task selection rule, over the set I of 320 instances with known optimal solution proposed by [4]. We evaluate the fitness of an individual by its average relative deviation from the best known solution value over all 320 instances. Since evaluating rules in this manner can be costly, we use a surrogate fitness which is the average relative deviation over a subset $I' \subseteq I$ of all instances. We proceed to evaluate the individual on all instances I only if its surrogate fitness is at most τ above surrogate fitness of the best individual, where τ is a parameter.

Non-repetition of Individuals. In later generations we have observed a high probability of generating repeated individuals. We avoid early convergence by not accepting the same individual twice. Technically this is achieved by storing and comparing hash values of the trees.

Initial Population. We use two strategies to start the evolution on a good initial population: tournament selection and seeding with known rules. The tournament selection follows [7]. To create a single individuals in the initial population we generated P random individuals and then select the one of best surrogate fitness. This step is effective, since the rule space permits rules of inferior performance (e.g. a rule with constant value for all tasks). We fill the population in this manner, except for seven individuals which are initialized with rules that are known to perform well. These rules include the three best performing rules for the ALWABP (namely MaxPWMin, MaxPWMax and MaxPWAvg), and also four more rules that select tasks according to a single attribute (namely the rank among the workers that can perform the task, the number of total and immediate followers, and the task time). These rules are listed in Table 3 which gives their name, the representation as an expression, and their definition. In the table, U represents the set of free workers and w the worker in the current station being constructed during the SBAP. Task i is the current task whose priority value is being computed. As priorities are by default maximized in GP, individuals that represent a minimization rule have their priority negated by the INV operator.

Table 3. Seed individuals in the initial population.

Rule	Program	Value
MaxPWMin	(TSUM F (MinTEC))	$\sum_{j \in F_i^* \cup \{i\}} \min_{w' \in U \setminus \{w\}} t_{w'j}$
MaxPWMax	(TSUM F (MaxTEC))	$\sum_{j \in F_i^* \cup \{i\}} \max_{w' \in U \setminus \{w\}} t_{w'j}$
MaxPWAvg	(TSUM F (SumTEC))	$\sum_{j \in F_i^* \cup \{i\}} \sum_{w' \in U \setminus \{w\}} t_{w'j}$
MinRank	(INV Rank)	$-|\{ w' \in U \mid t_{w'i} < t_{wi} \}|$
MaxF	(F)	$|F_i^*|$
MaxIF	(IF)	$|F_i|$
MinTime	(INV Time)	$-t_{wi}$

4   Computational Experiments

In this section we present the results of three experiments. We first calibrate GP, and in particular show experimentally that the new crossover operator improves its performance. We then conduct experiments that demonstrate that the performance of rules evolved for single allocation correlates well to the performance when used in search methods such as IPBS. Our third experiment then evaluates the performance of IPBS on the best rule found by GP, and compares it to the literature.

4.1   Instances

Table 4 summarizes the instances used in the computational experiments. We use the standard set of 320 instances proposed by [4], which is used in the majority of the publications in computational tests and in the genetic algorithm to evolve allocation rules. The instances are based on four SALBP instances (namely heskia, roszieg, wee-mag, and tonge), selected to represent two experimental factors at two levels, namely a low and high number of tasks, and a low and high order strength. For the ALWABP three experimental factors at two levels have been added, with 10 replications in each of the 32 resulting groups. The factors are a low ($m = \lceil n/7 \rceil$) or high ($m = \lceil n/3 \rceil$) number of workers, a low ($t_{iw} \sim U[1, t_i]$) or high ($t_{iw} \sim U[1, 2t_i]$) task time variability where t_i is the time of task i in

Table 4. Experimental factors and levels of the instance sets used in the computational experiments.

Factor	Levels	
	L	H
Number of tasks n	25, 28	70, 75
Order strength	[.22, .23]	[.59, .72]
Number of workers w	$\lceil n/7 \rceil$	$\lceil n/4 \rceil$
Task time variability	$\sim U[1, t_i]$	$\sim U[1, 2t_i]$
Number of task-worker incompatibilities (%)	10	20

the underlying SALBP instance, and a low (10 %) or high (20 %) percentage of task-worker incompatibilities.

The experiments were done on a PC with an AMD Ryzen 9 3900X processor, 32 GB of RAM, running Ubuntu Linux. All algorithms were implemented in C++ and compiled with gcc 9.3.0 and maximum optimization.

4.2   Experiment 1: Calibration of the Genetic Algorithm

As explained in Sect. 3, a new rule is first evaluated on a subset S of all instances, and only if the fitness on these instances is at most τ from the best fitness, we evaluate it on all 320 instances. We have used $\tau = 3 \%$ in these experiments. We test subset sizes in $|S| \in \{32, 96, 160, 192, 256, 320\}$ for both crossover operators. Subset sizes are always multiples of the 32 factor combinations, and if $|S| = 32k$ we select k individuals from each factor combination for the subset S. The experiments in this section are limited to a single run, since each run takes about 120 hours. Following [7] we set the population size in this an subsequent experiments to 750, and stop after a fixed time limit.

Table 5. Comparison of combination crossover and subtree crossover, for different sizes of the set S of instances.

$|S|$	Combination			Subtree		
	Min.	Avg.	Max.	Min.	Avg.	Max.
32	14.17	14.63	14.80	13.67	14.08	14.20
96	14.43	14.97	15.16	14.18	14.60	14.74
160	14.65	15.38	15.64	13.66	13.94	14.02
192	14.60	15.66	16.03	13.95	14.43	14.56
256	14.44	15.22	15.55	14.25	14.69	14.83
320	14.69	15.38	15.66	14.24	14.79	14.97

Table 5 presents the results. Rules generated by the genetic algorithm have been evaluated by their average relative deviation of the best found cycle time from the optimal values over all 320 instances. The cycle times are obtained by a deterministic lower bound search with a forward allocation followed by a backward allocation. The table shows for the 100 best individuals found the minimum, mean, and maximum average relative deviation from the optimal values. We can see that the combination crossover obtains the best results for the smallest number of trial instances, while subtree crossover finds the best results for $|S| = 160$. We can also see that subtree crossover consistently finds better results than the combination crossover. Therefore we use subtree crossover set to 160 candidate evaluations for the remaining experiments.

4.3   Experiment 2: Performance of Evolved Rules in Beam Searches

In this experiment we analyze the performance of rules evolved for a deterministic lower bound search in more advanced heuristic searches. Since the running time of an advanced heuristic search can be one to two orders of magnitude slower than a deterministic lower bound search, evaluating rules in the genetic algorithm directly with such methods is be prohibitively slow. Therefore we are interested, if the rules evolved for deterministic lower bound searches, also perform well in a lower bound beam search, and in an IPBS. We use two rules in this experiment, the rule MaxPWMin which is the best performing rule from the literature [11], and a rule evolved by GP. Following [3] we set the parameters of the IPBS to the values shown in Table 6.

Table 6. Parameter setting for the IPBS.

Parameter	Value	Parameter	Value
Beam size	125	Beam factor	5
Search rate r	0.95	Task selection greediness τ	2.5
Allocation strategy	Forward and backward	Repetitions until stagnation	20

Table 7 shows the results when applying these two rules in a deterministic lower bound search (LBS), in a lower bound beam search (LBS/Beam), and in the full iterated probabilistic beam search (IPBS). We can see that the average solution quality improves with the complexity of the method. The largest improvement comes from using the beam search, and the IPBS can improve the relative deviation from the optimal values by another 1.5 % taking about four times longer. We can also see that the rule evolved by GP is better in a simple lower bound search, and that this advantage carries over to the more complex heuristic searches, although the difference decreases. The correlation between the values of LBS and LBS/Beam for rule MaxPWMin is 68 % between LBS/Beam and IPBS 85 %. For rule R-GP these values are 68 % and 78 %. This experiment confirms that the strategy to evaluate rules using simpler, faster procedures is effective.

Table 7. Comparison of the best rule from the literature and the rule found by genetic programming in a simple lower bound search, a lower bound beam search, and IPBS.

Rule	LBS		LBS/Beam		IPBS	
	Rel. dev. (%)	t (s)	Rel. dev. (%)	t (s)	Rel. dev. (%)	t (s)
MaxPWMin	15.90	0.02	3.37	6.61	1.89	27.04
R-GP	14.51	0.04	3.07	10.47	1.48	40.90

4.4   Experiment 3: Performance of the Best Evolved Rules

In our third experiment we investigate the robustness of the genetic algorithm, and compare the best found allocation rule to a state-of-the-art heuristic.

We have run five replications of the genetic algorithm with a time limit of 12 h. The best rules resulting from these runs had an overall average relative deviation of 1.7 % from the optimal values when used in an IPBS, with a standard deviation of 0.2 %. Thus the GP approach can consistently produce effective rules.

We have selected the best rule from these five runs as the overall best rule found by GP. The detailed results for this rule in comparison to the best rule MaxPWMin from the literature, both applied in an IPBS, can be seen in Table 8. The table shows the overall average relative deviation from the optimal values over 20 replications of the IPBS ("Gap") and the relative deviation of the best solution found in all 20 replications ("Gap_b") as well as the average total running time in seconds ("t (s)") for rule MaxPWMin and rule R-GP found by Genetic Programming. The experimental setup, as well as the results for the MaxPWMin rule, follow [3]. Instance groups 1–4 have a low, groups 4–8 a high number of workers, groups 1, 2, 5, 6 a low, groups 3, 4, 7, 8 a high task variability, and odd groups a low and even groups a high number of task-worker incompatibilities as defined in Table 4. We can see that the evolved rule performs better than the best rule from the literature, with an overall improvement of 0.4 %. The performance is in particular significantly better for instances "wee-mag" with a low order strength. The best values over all replications show a similar behaviour. Computation times of both rules are comparable. Although the computational environment of [3] is about a factor two slower, the rule produced by GP is not optimized and could be improved, and all computation times are small enough for practical applications. In terms of the experimental factors, the order strength has the strongest influence on performance, followed by the number of task-worker incompatibilities, with instances of a low order strength and a high number of incompatibilities being harder to solve.

Table 8. Detailed comparison of the best rule from the literature and the best rule found by genetic programming in an IPBS.

Inst.	Grp.	MaxPWMin			R-GP		
		Gap	Gap$_b$	t (s)	Gap	Gap$_b$	t (s)
Heskia	1	0.0	0.0	6.0	0.0	0.0	1.1
Heskia	2	0.0	0.0	6.0	0.1	0.0	0.8
Heskia	3	0.0	0.0	6.0	0.0	0.0	2.0
Heskia	4	0.0	0.0	6.0	0.0	0.0	1.5
Heskia	5	0.0	0.0	5.4	0.0	0.0	1.0
Heskia	6	0.5	0.3	4.3	0.0	0.0	0.9
Heskia	7	0.0	0.0	2.5	0.0	0.0	1.4
Heskia	8	0.0	0.0	3.7	0.0	0.0	1.4
Roszieg	1	0.0	0.0	6.0	0.0	0.0	0.3
Roszieg	2	0.0	0.0	5.4	0.0	0.0	0.2
Roszieg	3	0.0	0.0	6.0	0.0	0.0	0.4
Roszieg	4	0.0	0.0	6.0	0.0	0.0	0.4
Roszieg	5	0.0	0.0	6.0	0.0	0.0	1.0
Roszieg	6	0.0	0.0	6.0	0.0	0.0	0.9
Roszieg	7	0.0	0.0	6.0	0.0	0.0	1.4
Roszieg	8	0.0	0.0	6.0	0.0	0.0	1.4
Tonge	1	1.9	0.9	56.2	1.6	0.8	53.2
Tonge	2	2.3	1.0	58.9	2.8	1.7	56.4
Tonge	3	1.4	0.9	89.2	2.9	1.8	88.7
Tonge	4	2.2	1.2	91.0	2.2	1.4	88.1
Tonge	5	2.8	1.9	61.2	4.2	2.6	58.5
Tonge	6	6.9	5.6	60.5	6.9	5.6	58.0
Tonge	7	3.0	2.3	96.7	2.7	2.5	97.0
Tonge	8	4.5	3.2	107.7	4.6	3.9	104.7
Wee-Mag	1	5.8	3.8	25.1	2.4	1.1	33.0
Wee-Mag	2	4.6	2.9	25.1	1.9	1.0	31.5
Wee-Mag	3	5.6	3.7	37.1	3.1	1.7	49.6
Wee-Mag	4	4.5	2.6	36.1	1.9	1.2	46.2
Wee-Mag	5	4.6	3.2	39.9	3.6	2.1	41.4
Wee-Mag	6	3.6	1.8	39.0	1.1	0.9	40.1
Wee-Mag	7	4.6	3.7	38.3	2.9	1.7	39.2
Wee-Mag	8	3.2	2.9	41.6	1.9	0.7	44.9
Avgs.		1.9	1.3	31.0	1.5	1.0	29.6

5 Conclusions

We have studied the evolution of task priority rules in station-based allocation procedures for a line balancing problem with workers of different capabilities. We have proposed an improved GP approach to evolve such rules, and an improved SBAP to apply them. We find that the performance of rules which have been evolved for deterministic lower bound searches generalizes to simple and probabilistic beam searches. The results show that the rules in these search procedures can improve over the best known rules from the literature. The resulting heuristics have a better performance than state-of-the-art heuristics using station-based allocation.

References

1. Blum, C., Miralles, C.I.: On solving the assembly line worker assignment and balancing problem via beam search. Comput. Oper. Res. **38**(2), 328–339 (2011)
2. Borba, L.M., Ritt, M.: A task-oriented branch-and-bound method for the assembly line worker assignment and balancing problem. In: XLIV Simpósio Brasileiro de Pesquisa Operacional, pp. 3192–3291 (2012)
3. Borba, L.M., Ritt, M.: A heuristic and a branch-and-bound algorithm for the assembly line worker assignment and balancing problem. Comput. Oper. Res. **45**, 87–96 (2014). https://doi.org/10.1016/j.cor.2013.12.002. Online supplement: http://www.inf.ufrgs.br/algopt/alwabp2
4. Chaves, A.A., Lorena, L.A.N., Miralles, C.I.: Clustering search approach for the assembly line worker assignment and balancing problem. In: International Conference on Computers and Industrial Engineering, Alexandria, Egypt, pp. 1469–1478, October 2007
5. Chaves, A.A., Lorena, L.A.N., Miralles, C.I.: Hybrid metaheuristic for the assembly line worker assignment and balancing problem. In: 6th International Workshop on Hybrid Metaheuristics, pp. 1–12 (2009)
6. Estrada, T., Wyatt, M., Taufer, M.: A genetic programming approach to design resource allocation policies for heterogeneous workflows in the cloud. In: 21st IEEE International Conference on Parallel and Distributed Systems (ICPADS), pp. 372–379 (2015). https://doi.org/10.1109/ICPADS.2015.54
7. Gonçalves, J.P., Ritt, M.: Evolving task priority rules for heterogeneous assembly line balancing. In: Proceedings of IEEE Congress on Evolutionary Computation, Wellington, pp. 1423–1430 (2019). https://doi.org/10.1109/CEC.2019.8790332
8. Langdon, W.B.: Genetic programming and evolvable machines at 20. Genet. Program. Evol. Mach. **21**(1–2), 205–217 (2020). https://doi.org/10.1007/s10710-019-09344-6
9. Lowerre, B.: The Harpy speech recognition system. Ph.D. thesis, CMU (1976)
10. Miralles, C.I., Garcia-Sabater, J.P., Andrés, C., Cardos, M.: Advantages of assembly lines in Sheltered Work Centres for Disabled. A case study. Int. J. Prod. Res. **110**(2), 187–197 (2007)
11. Moreira, M.C.O., Ritt, M., Costa, A.M., Chaves, A.A.: Simple heuristics for the assembly line worker assignment and balancing problem. J. Heuristics **18**(3), 505–524 (2012). https://doi.org/10.1007/s10732-012-9195-5

12. Mutlu, O., Polat, O., Ayca, A.: An iterative genetic algorithm for the assembly line worker assignment and balancing problem of type-II. Comput. Oper. Res. **40**(1), 418–426 (2013). https://doi.org/10.1016/j.cor.2012.07.010
13. Otto, A., Otto, C.: How to design effective priority rules: example of simple assembly line balancing. Comput. Ind. Eng. **69**, 43–52 (2014)
14. Polat, O., Kalayci, C.B., Özcan Mutlu, Gupta, S.M.: A two-phase variable neighbourhood search algorithm for assembly line worker assignment and balancing problem type-II: an industrial case study. Int. J. Prod. Res. **54**(3), 722–741 (2016). https://doi.org/10.1080/00207543.2015.1055344
15. Poli, R., Langdon, W.B., McPhee, N.F.: A Field Guide to Genetic Programming. Lulu (2008)
16. Salveson, M.E.: The assembly line balancing problem. J. Ind. Eng. **6**(3), 18–25 (1955)
17. Scholl, A.: Data of assembly line balancing problems. Technical Report 16/1993, TH Darmstadt (1993). Schriften zur Quantitativen Betriebswirtschaftslehre
18. Scholl, A., Becker, C.: State-of-the-art exact and heuristic solution procedures for simple assembly line balancing. Eur. J. Oper. Res. **168**(3), 666–693 (2006)
19. Tan, B., Ma, H., Mei, Y.: A hybrid genetic programming hyper-heuristic approach for online two-level resource allocation in container-based clouds. In: Coello, C.A.C. (ed.) Proceedings of the IEEE Congress on Evolutionary Computation, Wellington, New Zealand, pp. 2681–2688 (2019). https://doi.org/10.1109/CEC.2019.8790220
20. Yska, D., Mei, Y., Zhang, M.: Genetic programming hyper-heuristic with cooperative coevolution for dynamic flexible job shop scheduling. In: Castelli, M., Sekanina, L., Zhang, M., Cagnoni, S., García-Sánchez, P. (eds.) Genetic Programming - 21st European Conference, Parma, Italy, pp. 306–321 (2018)
21. Paquete, L., Zarges, C. (eds.): EvoCOP 2020. LNCS, vol. 12102. Springer, Cham (2020). https://doi.org/10.1007/978-3-030-43680-3

Incremental Evaluation in Genetic Programming

William B. Langdon$^{(\boxtimes)}$

CREST, Department of Computer Science, UCL,
Gower Street, London WC1E 6BT, UK
W.Langdon@cs.ucl.ac.uk
http://www.cs.ucl.ac.uk/staff/W.Langdon, http://crest.cs.ucl.ac.uk

Abstract. Often GP evolves side effect free trees. These pure functional expressions can be evaluated in any order. In particular they can be interpreted from the genetic modification point outwards. Incremental evaluation exploits the fact that: in highly evolved children the semantic difference between child and parent falls with distance from the syntactic disruption (e.g. crossover point) and can reach zero before the whole child has been interpreted. If so, its fitness is identical to its parent (mum).

Considerable savings in bloated binary tree GP runs are given by exploiting population convergence with existing GPquick data structures, leading to near linear O(gens) runtime. With multi-threading and SIMD AVX parallel computing a 16 core desktop can deliver the equivalent of 571 billion GP operations per second, 571 giga GPop/s.

GP convergence is viewed via information theory as evolving a smooth landscape and software plasticity. Which gives rise to functional resilience to source code changes. On average a mixture of $100 +, -, \times$ and (protected) $\div$ tree nodes remove test case effectiveness at exposing changes and so fail to propagate crossover infected errors.

Keywords: Parallel computing · Mutational robustness · Antifragile correctness attraction · PIE · SBSE · Software resilience · Entropy loss · Theory

1 Background: Genetic Programming Evolving Functions

Most GP problems, such as symbolic regression or classification, require the evolution of a pure function. I.e., a function without side effects. Exceptions include: problems with state, such as the truck-backer-upper problem [1] or Santa Fe Trail problem [1,2], which involve an agent moving in an environment with memory, where state is embedded in the program itself [3,4] or where genetic programming is applied to existing programs (as in genetic improvement [5–10]). Typically evolution decides the number and nature of the evolved function's inputs as well as the contents of the function itself. Essentially the idea is we do not know what we want but we can recognise a good function when GP finds one.

© Springer Nature Switzerland AG 2021
T. Hu et al. (Eds.): EuroGP 2021, LNCS 12691, pp. 229–246, 2021.
https://doi.org/10.1007/978-3-030-72812-0_15

We give evolution some way of recognising better functions from poorer ones by automatically allocating each function a fitness score. (Although fitness can be assigned manually [11].) Typically, in both regression and classification, the fitness function uses multiple examples where all the inputs and the example's expected output are known. (Backer describes dealing with missing input values [12].) An evolved function's fitness value is given by calling it with each example's inputs and comparing its return value with the expected value. Typically the differences between the function's return value and the expected answer for several test cases are combined into a single scalar fitness value. (Although multiple objective approaches are increasingly popular [13, Ch. 9]). For classification problems, we may use the area under the ROC curve [14], whilst for the continuous domain regression problems, the mean absolute error remains popular. Notice, unlike Gathercole's DSS [15] and Lexicase selection [16] or other dynamic choice of test data, e.g. [6,17], typically GP systems use all of a fixed training set of examples throughout evolution. Often a holdout set is needed to estimate the degree of overfitting [13, p140]. In most cases almost all GP's computational cost comes from running the fitness function [1]. As the evolved functions become deeper, information in their leafs is combined, eventually all of it being channeled through the limited capacity of the root node. On the way to the root information is progressively lost. Thus deep functions are resilient to changes near their leafs this, together with high selection pressure, leads to converged GP populations. We show that this can be exploited to considerably reduce fitness evaluation times and hence GP run time.

We follow common tree GP practice by representing each evolved individual as a separate tree composed of nested binary functions (ADD, SUB, MUL and DIV[1]). Each generation a new population of trees is created by recombining two parent trees from the previous generation to create a new population of trees. Koza et al. [19,20, pages 1044–1045] showed it is not necessary to store all of both populations simultaneously.

We retain GPquick's [21,22] linear prefix trees [23], although Simon Handley [24] demonstrated it is possible to store the complete evolving GP in a single directed acyclic graph (DAG). (See also Nic McPhee's Sutherland [25]). For pure functions, at the expense of memory, caches of partial results can be embedded in the DAG [26]. When a new individual is created it can be evaluated using the partial results of the subtrees from which its parents are composed. In the case of sub-tree mutation, the new random subtree (typically small) must be evaluated. But then and for subtree crossover, the rest of the individual can be evaluated, using partial results stored in the DAG, requiring only evaluation from the mutation or crossover point all the way to the root node. Ignoring the costs of accessing and maintaining the DAG memory structure, the cost of fitness evaluation of the new individual, is the product of the number of fitness cases (assumed fixed) and the height of the tree. The height of large GP trees is typically $\approx \sqrt{2\pi|\text{size}|}$ [27, page 256], [28,29] (see Fig. 7). i.e. considerably less than typical implementations,

---

[1] (DIV X Y) is protected division which returns 1.0 if Y = 0 and X/Y otherwise. Ni et al. [18] propose the analytic quotient instead of DIV.

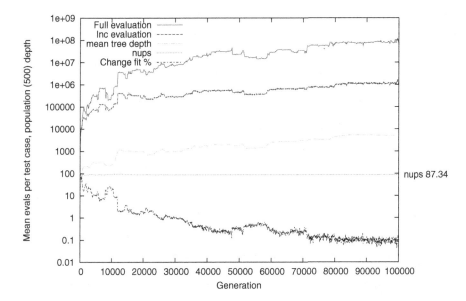

Fig. 1. Convergence of sextic polynomial. Black % parent's $\neq$ child's fitness. After gen 800 most children have identical fitness to mum, and on average (nups, dotted line) incremental evaluation evaluates subtrees of depth ≈ 100. Max saving in eval ops on traditional (top red v. dashed blue) is 100 fold. Note log scale.

which evaluate the whole tree and so scale $O(\text{size})$ rather than $O(\text{size}^{0.5})$. However the complexity of implementation, the difficulty of efficient operation on multi-core CPUs, and limited memory cache, mean DAGs are not common in GP. In principle, exploiting GP convergence allows fitness evaluation to scale independently of tree size $O(1)$, although it appears this is only approached for humongously large trees, Fig. 1.

Retaining GPquick's separate linear prefix trees suggests our approach of incremental evaluation could be used with linear postfix trees common in parallel GPs running on graphics hardware accelerators, e.g. GPUs [30,31].

2   Incremental Evaluation: How Does It Work

Since there are no side effects, the functional expressions can be evaluated in any order. In GP it is common to evaluate them recursively from the root down (see Fig. 2 left) for the first test case, then the second test case and so on until all the test cases have been run. However it is possible to start from the leafs and work to the root (see Fig. 2 right). Particularly when using parallel hardware [22,32,33], it is possible to evaluate each node in the tree on all the test cases, generating a vector of sub-results and propagate these vectors (rather than single

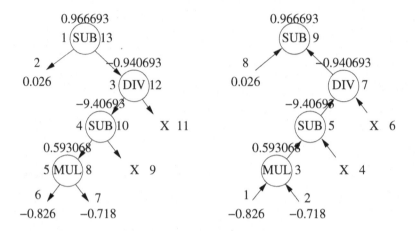

Fig. 2. Left: Conventional top-down recursive evaluation of (SUB 0.026 (DIV (SUB (MUL −0.826 −0.718) X) X)). X = 10. Blue integers indicate evaluation order, red floats are node return values. Right: an alternative ordering, starting with leaf −0.826 and working to root node. Both return exactly the same answer.

Table 1. Percentage of functions in evolved trees in ten runs where it gives the same value (0.0, 1.0 or another constant) on all 48 test cases. Data from generation 1000 in Fig. 3.

Constant	1	2	3	4	5	6	7	8	9	10	mean
0.0	0.73	1.32	0.23	0.12	0.16	0.10	4.36	2.70	1.18	1.07	1.20%
1.0	0.15	1.47	0.01	0.00	0.00	1.81	1.87	1.36	1.83	1.90	1.04%
other	9.13	1.11	17.20	9.33	5.21	16.10	6.89	10.58	12.37	4.91	9.28%

scalars) through the tree. Indeed combinations between these extremes are also valid [34]. The results are identical.

When running evolution for a long time with small populations, evolution tends to converge [35]. In GPs this can manifest itself with many different large (and hence expensive to evaluate) individuals producing children with identical fitness [29,33]. Initially it was assumed, at least in the continuous domain, that this was due to large amounts of introns [36–38], such as multiplication by zero, which would mean MUL's other subtree had no effect. However, although (SUB X X) can readily produce zero and although the fraction of zeros varies between runs (see Fig. 3 and Table 1), on average only about one percent of tree nodes evaluate to zero for all fitness cases[2].

Since the location of GP genetic operations are typically chosen at random from all the possible locations in the tree, they tend to be far from the tree's

---

[2] Trapping special cases, such as multiplication by zero, and multiplication or division by one, only sped up GP by a few percent.

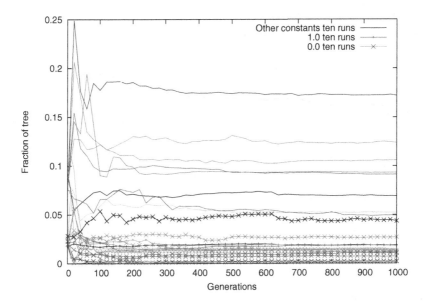

Fig. 3. Evolution of the fraction of functions in GP trees which give the same value (0.0, 1.0 or another constant) on all 48 test cases. Average across population. Tick marks every 20 generations. See also Table 1.

root. Although, Koza in [1] defined a small bias away from choosing leafs as crossover points (which we do not use in these experiments), it makes only a small difference. Effectively moving the average crossover point from near the leafs to near the outer most functions. i.e. only one level closer to the root. That is, we can view each child as being the same as the parent (for simplicity called mum) from which it inherits its root node, plus a small disruptive subtree inherited from the other parent (dad). Obviously if the dad subtree is identical to the subtree it replaces from mum, the whole offspring tree is identical to the mum tree and has identical fitness.

For near converged populations of trees of any size, a first optimisation could be to compare the child with its mum. If they are identical, the child's fitness is identical to its mum's fitness and the child does not have to be evaluated. Notice we do not even have to compare the whole of the child and mum trees. If the subtree replaced by the subtree donated by the dad are identical, then the whole of both trees are identical. In these Sextic polynomial [1] runs, by generation 1000 on average 6% of crossovers swap identical trees.

A second possibility is: what if the crossover subtrees are not genetically identical but yield the same value for all of the fitness cases. For example, we would expect evaluating (ADD X 0.837) and (ADD 0.837 X) to produce identical values. Thus a child created by replacing (ADD X 0.837) with (ADD 0.837 X) or even (SUB (ADD 0.837 X) (SUB X X)) should have the same fitness as its mum. Thus if we evaluate the child's subtree and re-evaluate the subtree which has

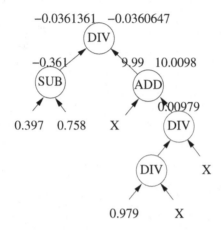

Fig. 4. Incremental evaluation of fragment of child produced by crossover. Inserted subtree (DIV (DIV 0.979 X) X) in blue. Nodes common to both mum and child in black. Red floats (left) are mum node return values. Blue floats (right) are node return values in the child. (In both X = 10.0). Notice (SUB 0.397 0.758) is not affected by the crossover and has the same value in parent and child and so is evaluated only once per test case.

just been replaced (from its mum) and for all fitness cases, the mum and child subtrees return the same value, again the child's fitness must be identical to that of the mother. So again, if the evaluation of subtree replaced and the evaluation of the subtree donated by the dad are identical, then the fitness of the whole both child and mum trees are identical. Naturally evaluating two small subtrees is typically much cheaper than evaluating the whole of the child. However crossovers that replace a subtree with a different one which gives the same evaluation are rare (about 0.2% by generation 1000).

What if the evaluation on the test cases of the old and new subtrees are not identical but are similar? We can propagate both vectors of evaluations up the tree towards the root node to the function which calls the modified code. (Fig. 4 shows a single test case.) Notice the function itself and its other argument are identical in both mum and child. To minimise cache memory load we can work with just one, typically the child. (Notice as far as this crossover is concerned we can now discard both parent trees [20].) We evaluate the calling function's other argument once (it must yield the same answers in both mum and child trees). We then evaluate the calling function twice: once for the child and once for the mum. Notice that if for any fitness test case the old and new subtrees gave identical values, then for (at least) those test cases, the evaluation of the calling function must yield the same values. Finally, if the evaluation of the calling function is identical for all test cases, then the evaluation of the whole of the child and mum trees must be identical, hence their fitness values must be the same. So we can stop the evaluation of the child and simply set its fitness to be the same as its mum.

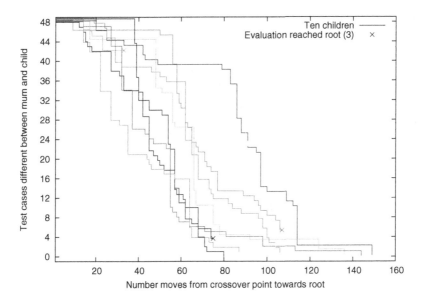

Fig. 5. Incremental evaluation of first ten members of generation 1000. Number of test cases where evaluation in the root donating parent (mum) and its offspring are identical never falls. In three cases (×) evaluation is halted by reaching the root node. Small vertical offset added to separate plots.

If the mum and child evaluation at the calling function are different for at least one test case, we can repeat the process by proceeding up the tree towards the root node and repeat the evaluation for that calling function. Again we have to evaluate (once per test case) its other argument and the function itself for both child and mum vector of evaluations (created by evaluating the lower function).

In terms of efficiency, the first thing to notice is, if we stop well before the root node, we have not evaluated the vast majority of the child tree. We have evaluated the other sub tree. But we would have had to do that anyway. And we have evaluated the calling function twice per test case. Still a large win, if the evaluation of the child and mum are identical at this point. A possible future work would be to consider if the evaluations for some test cases are different, are the difference important? Is it possible given differences in partial evaluation at this point within the tree to predict if they will have a beneficial or negative impact on fitness. Indeed will the impact on fitness (particularly where approximate answers are good enough [39]) be sufficient to cause a change in breeding pattern for the next, i.e. the grand-child's, generation?

In converged populations there are many cases where trees begat other trees with identical fitness and hence there is hope for this approach to short cut repeated evaluation of what is substantially the same code in the next generation. For example, in Fig. 1 on average only 2.6% of trees have fitness different from their mum. Indeed, there are 24 784 generations where everyone in the population has the same fitness as their mum. (After generation 100, Fig. 1 smooths the

Table 2. Mean tree size ("Full") and mean opcodes incrementally ("Inc") evaluated (per test case). "ratio" gives incremental evaluation saving. Ten runs at generation 1000.

	1	2	3	4	5	6	7	8	9	10	mean
Full	70268	14873	34546	220163	138145	36619	35890	26943	19522	35723	63269
Inc	33051	12016	22476	103503	103487	17224	7364	14880	8047	15563	33761
ratio	2.13	1.24	1.54	2.13	1.33	2.13	4.87	1.81	2.43	2.30	2.19

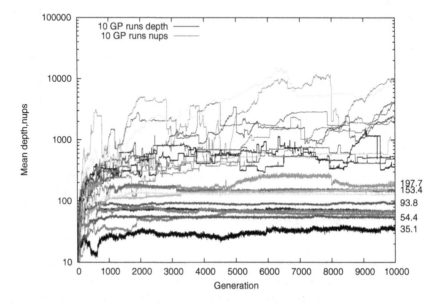

Fig. 6. Evolution of mean depth of trees and number of upward steps (nups) required by incremental evaluation. Notice nups (lower lines) tends to be more stable than tree depth. Ten runs. Last generation summarised in Table 3. Note log vertical scale.

plots by showing the means of 50 generations, so the fraction of changed fitness, lowest dashed black line, is not shown at zero).

There is a ratchet effect, whereby: if at any point the evaluation of a test case for both mum and child is identical, it will remain identical all the way up to the root node (see Fig. 5).

If at no point are all the test cases identical, we will reach the root node. But notice, even in this worst case, the overhead is modest. We will have evaluated the whole of the child, which we would have had to do anyway, plus re-evaluating the (usually small) subtree from the mum, plus evaluating all the functions from the crossover point to the root node. i.e. in the worst case the overhead is less than O (child's height), $\leq O(\text{size}^{\frac{1}{2}})$ (Sect. 1). Table 2 shows variation between runs, but even at the start of long runs, saving in terms of opcodes not evaluated can already result in evaluating on average less than half of each tree. As the

Table 3. Mean tree sizes, mean depths and mean number of upward steps, in ten GP runs at generation 10 000. $\pm$ indicates population standard deviation. The last column gives means of the ten runs. Data from Fig. 6.

run:	1	2	3	4	5	
size/1000	349 ± 4	8655 ± 5813	276 ± 4	5066 ± 1095	997 ± 4	
depth	486 ± 2	8801 ± 2230	534 ± 8	3985 ± 839	964 ± 3	
nups	94 ± 42	172 ± 127	68 ± 32	153 ± 98	198 ± 126	
run:	6	7	8	9	10	mean
size/1000	9171 ± 1345	98 ± 2	4653 ± 1075	5232 ± 1548	1567 ± 173	3606
depth	7844 ± 666	359 ± 2	4133 ± 782	1826 ± 178	2228 ± 512	3116
nups	130 ± 51	35 ± 34	69 ± 40	60 ± 33	54 ± 29	103

population converges, the saving can grow. For example, in the first run by generation 100 000 on average only $1/70^{\text{th}}$ of each tree is evaluated, Fig. 1.

3   Implementing Incremental Evaluation

From a practical point of view it is not hard to implement incremental evaluation. Firstly we need a clean implementation of EVAL, which can be directed to evaluate a subtree, rather than one dedicated to evaluating the whole of a tree. For simplicity, and as we use Intel's Advanced Vector Extensions SIMD instructions (AVX), we run EVAL on all 48 test cases and it returns a vector of 48 floats. (It would be possible to exploit the ratchet effect, Sect. 2, by keeping track of which fitness cases mum and child evaluations are different and ensuring EVAL does not executes those that are the same).

For IncFit we need the child tree, the old crossover fragment removed from the mum, and the location of the crossover point in the child. We also need an efficient way to navigate up the tree to the function calling a given subtree and to find its other subtree.

We start by calling EVAL for both the crossover fragment in the child tree and for the crossover fragment in the mum tree. Each call to EVAL returns an array of 48 floats which we bitwise compare with memcmp. If they are identical, we stop and set the child's fitness to that of the mum tree. If not, we go up one level in the child tree. (For the rest of the new tree's evaluation, it is effectively identical to its mum tree.) We locate the upper function's other argument and call EVAL for it. (I.e., we EVAL the other subtree.) We now have three vectors each of 48 floats.

The next thing to do is to evaluate the function (ADD, SUB, MUL or DIV), giving it two vectors of floats (*in order*). Remember that the other subtree may be either the function's first or second argument. For this you perhaps want a specialised version of EVAL. evalop, rather than having to recursively evaluate its two arguments, it has them passed to it directly. Our evalop takes two 48 float vectors and returns a 48 float vector of results. We call it twice, once with the other subtree's vector and that from the mum and a second time again with the other subtree's vector and this time with the child's evaluation vector.

Table 4. Evolution of Sextic polynomial symbolic regression binary trees

Terminal set:	X, 250 constants between -0.995 and 0.997
Function set:	MUL ADD DIV SUB
Fitness cases:	48 fixed input -0.97789 to 0.979541 (randomly selected from -1.0 to $+1.0$)
	Target $y = xx(x-1)(x-1)(x+1)(x+1)$
Selection:	Tournament size 7 with fitness $= \frac{1}{48}\sum_{i=1}^{48}|GP(x_i) - y_i|$
Population:	500. Panmictic, non-elitist, generational
Parameters:	Initial population ramped half and half [1] depth between 2 and 6. 100% unbiased subtree crossover. At least 1000 generations

DIV is protected division (y! = 0)? x/y: 1.0f

We compare evalop's two output vectors (again using memcmp). If they are the same we stop and use the mum's fitness, otherwise we proceed up the tree one more level and repeat. If we reach the root node, we use the child's vector of 48 floats to calculate the fitness of the child.

The GP parameters are given in Table 4. We run up to ten experiments with different pseudo random number seeds.

4   Discussion: Population Convergence

4.1   Why Does Incremental Evaluation Work?

We have a chicken and egg situation. For this (exact) version of incremental evaluation to work, we need the GP population to show significant convergence, with many children resembling their parents (i.e. have identical fitness). For convergence, we may need long runs, which implies the need for fast fitness evaluation, which incremental evaluation may provide. With many children with unchanged fitness, there is hope that chasing up the tree from the crossover point (i.e. the source of disruption) towards the root node, the difference between child and parent will dissipate.

This relies on the function set and test set being dissipative, i.e. losing information. But if the functions are perfect, i.e. never lose any information (and so are reversible), then convergence and indeed evolution is impossible [40]. However, traditional GP systems do evolve, their function sets are not reversible, they do lose information. Small GP populations, if allowed time and space, can show elements of convergence, in which case this form of incremental evaluation may flourish. Indeed by applying information theory to GP function sets, we may be able to design more evolvable GP systems.

By generation 1000 the populations have bloated and on average incremental evaluation has to process about 100 nested function calls, Table 3. Figure 8 and

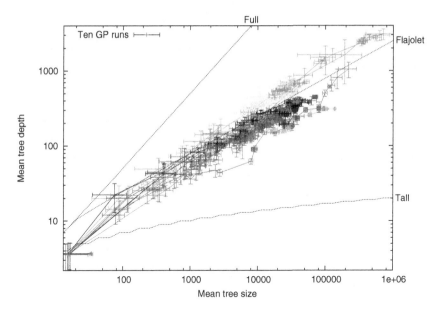

Fig. 7. Evolution of mean program size and depth in ten runs of Sextic polynomial up to generation 1000. Cross hairs show population standard deviations every 20 generations. Dotted lines show tree limits. Flajolet line is height of random trees $\sqrt{2\pi(\text{size})}$ [27]. Note log scales.

Table 5 show that the change in the difference between mum and her offspring as we evaluate each opcode during incremental fitness evaluation. The data are grouped by run and by function. There is a clear distinction between the linear functions, ADD and SUB, and the non-linear functions, MUL and DIV.

Most linear functions do not noticeably change the difference between the parent evaluation and that of the child. This is expected. e.g. if on each of the 48 test cases, the difference between the re-evaluation of the root donating parent (the mum) and that of its offspring is 1.0, we would expect after ADD, the difference would remain 1.0 no matter what ADD's other argument. However ADD is a floating point operator and so is potentially subject rounding errors. Suppose on one test case, ADD's other argument is 10^{23}, it may be that ADD's output, for both mum and child is 10^{23} and therefore on that test case their difference is now zero. Notice that ratchet effect does not apply to differences, only to the special case of values being identical (Sect. 2), and while differences tend to decrease, monotonic decrease is not guaranteed.

With non-linear operations we expect them to change the difference between mum and offspring evaluations. e.g. if MUL's other argument was 2.0 for all test cases, we would expect the difference between mum eval and child eval to double for every test cases. Table 5 largely confirms this and shows that only about 1% of MUL or DIV operations do not change the difference. Indeed MUL and, in particular, DIV can magnify the difference enormously (dotted purple

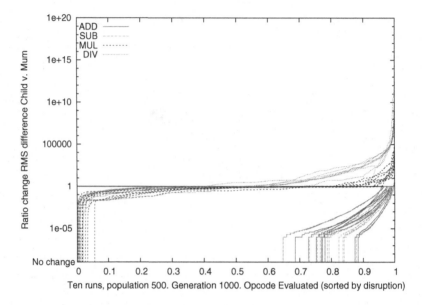

Fig. 8. Ratio of difference between mum and child before and after each function at generation 1000. Most linear functions (i.e. ADD and SUB) do not change difference. On average 86% MUL and 56% DIV decrease difference. X-axis normalised to allow easy comparison between ten runs. Note log scale.

line in Fig. 8). However there are more operations which reduce the difference than increase it. Rounding error is still active and causing information loss and although differences may rise or fall, once they reach zero on a particular test case, the difference on that test case must remain zero (Sect. 2). Typically over about one hundred evolved function calls the difference on all 48 test cases is zero and incremental fitness evaluation can stop.

There are of course considerable differences between individual crossovers but averaging at generation 1000 over the whole population and ten runs, shows on average each ADD reduces the number of test cases which are different by 13%, and the other functions by similar amounts: SUB 12%, MUL 10% and DIV 19%. If we grossly simplify by assuming the test cases are independent and there is a fixed chance of an operation clearing the difference for a given test case. The chance of test case difference being non-zero will fall geometrically (p^{nups}), with number of moves up the tree, nups. The chance of all test cases having non-zero difference is $(p^{\text{nups}})^{48}$, which is also geometric. Using the mean of the geometric distribution (here $1/p^{48}$) and the observed mean number of steps required (103.433800), and taking logs of both sides gives $-\log(p^{48}) = \log(103.433800)$ rearranging $\log(p) = -\log(103.433800)/48 = -0.0966444$. This suggests each upward move has about a 9% chance of synchronising the evaluation of a test case. i.e. each function destroys about three bits of information per test case.

Table 5. Percentages of functions in GP trees which leave unchanged, reduce or increase difference between mum and offspring in ten GP runs at generation 1000. Last column gives means of the ten runs. Data from Fig. 8.

	run	1	2	3	4	5	6	7	8	9	10	mean
No change	ADD	75.21	88.31	75.25	77.19	77.96	72.76	68.52	87.34	76.88	64.72	76.41%
	SUB	82.32	87.84	83.94	76.48	73.07	78.69	75.62	83.60	79.20	64.71	78.55%
	MUL	0.52	1.68	0.18	3.33	1.54	0.65	5.52	0.19	0.93	2.59	1.71%
	DIV	0.63	1.77	0.14	na	na	0.33	0.84	0.29	0.58	1.40	0.75%
Reduce	ADD	24.34	11.60	24.52	22.62	21.77	26.81	31.39	12.47	22.62	34.60	23.27%
	SUB	17.50	12.03	15.80	23.33	26.84	21.08	23.96	16.21	20.54	34.76	21.21%
	MUL	94.84	83.80	91.22	73.40	78.25	92.30	85.16	94.21	82.13	87.84	86.32%
	DIV	39.43	69.33	47.49	na	na	58.96	50.99	54.94	70.05	58.03	56.15%
Increase	ADD	0.45	0.09	0.23	0.19	0.26	0.43	0.09	0.19	0.50	0.67	0.31%
	SUB	0.18	0.13	0.26	0.19	0.09	0.23	0.42	0.19	0.26	0.53	0.25%
	MUL	4.64	14.52	8.60	23.27	20.20	7.05	9.31	5.59	16.94	9.57	11.97%
	DIV	59.94	28.90	52.37	na	na	40.72	48.18	44.77	29.37	40.57	43.10%

Rather more than the minimum 0.5 bits expected of well behaved floating point rounding, but similar to the last row (nups) of Table 3.

As Fig. 9 shows incremental fitness evaluation does better as the population converges and trees become larger.

4.2   Implications for Software Engineering

By software engineering standards our pure functions, even though large by GP standards, are simple. Nevertheless it is interesting that even such a pure functional program loses information and our analysis allows us to track dissipation of disruption from its cause (in the case of GP, the crossover point). Like human written software the disruption may or may not lead to a visible external affect. (In the case of GP, to be visible, the disruption must reach the root node.)

Although information loss is a general effect, in Software Engineering it is known mostly by its specific effects. In mutation testing, inserted bugs that cause no visible impact are known as equivalent mutants [41–43]. One off run time bit flips which fail to impact the program's output are known as correctness attraction [44], indeed Danglot et al. say programs are Antifragile. Coincidental correctness is another term used to describe when a program produces a correct answer despite an error in its source code, even though the error has been executed [45]. Bugs which have no visible impact (so far) are known as latent bugs [46]. The PIE (propagation, infection, and execution) view [47] considers the impact of bugs and if it propagates to the program's outputs. Failed error propagation [48] acknowledges the PIE frameworks and shows that the impact of bugs can be hidden by entropy loss and explained in terms of information theory. These can be summarised as the robustness of software [49].

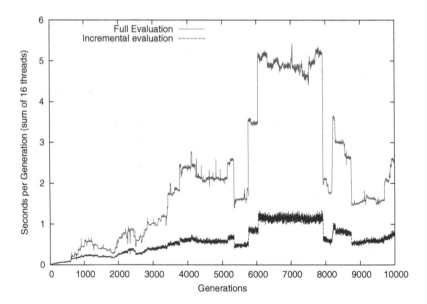

Fig. 9. Time per generation for top down recursive and bottom up incremental evaluation. 16 core 3.80 GHz i7-9800X, g++ 9.3.1. Performance equivalent of 53.1 billion GP operation per second (full, top down) and 179 10^9 GPop/s (incremental, bottom up).

5   Conclusion: Information Loss is Essential to Converge

Incremental fitness evaluation can be easily implemented and in even the worst case imposes little overhead. With very large trees, it can speed up GP by an order of magnitude. Using 48 cores of a 3.0 GHz server gave the *equivalent* of 749 billion GPop/s, exceeding the best direct interpreters [50], Table 3, [34,51].

We had assumed that the considerable bloat seen here was due to simple introns, such as multiplication or division by zero, and so runtime could be reduced by exploiting obvious fitness evaluation short cuts. However this produced only a 1% saving. Instead something much more interesting is happening.

Information flows from the leafs of GP trees via arithmetic functions to the root node. These functions are not reversible and inevitably loose information. This information loss gives rise to semantic convergence. That is, if we regard GP children as being the same as their parent plus a syntactic change (or error) made by crossover or mutation and trace fitness evaluation from the error to the root node, we see the values flowing in the parent and in the child to be increasingly similar. If the trees are large these information flows can becomes identical. If the information flow leaving the child and parent are identical then their fitness is also identical. Note GP has evolved a smooth fitness landscape.

Many GP systems do not have side effects and so their trees can be evaluated in any order. Our incremental approach evaluates trees by following the information flow. It can stop early when the data flow in the child is the same as that in its parent.

It is possible to measure the disruption to the information flow caused by the injected code. From that it may be possible to predict in advance, e.g. given the size and nature of the parent tree and the location of the injected error, how much disruption will reach the child's root node and so estimate if the injected code will change its fitness and if so by how much. Turning this about: from such an information based model, it may be possible to choose where to place new code in highly fit trees to avoid simply reproducing exactly the same fitness and perhaps even avoiding changes which will cause fitness to fall enormously.

Acknowledgements. Funded by EPSRC grant EP/P005888/1.

For GPinc C++ code see my home pages.

References

1. Koza, J.R.: Genetic Programming: On the Programming of Computers by Natural Selection (1992). http://mitpress.mit.edu/books/genetic-programming
2. Langdon, W.B., Poli, R.: Why ants are hard. In: Koza, J.R., et al. (eds.) GP, pp. 193–201 (1998). http://www.cs.ucl.ac.uk/staff/W.Langdon/ftp/papers/WBL.antspace_gp98.pdf
3. Teller, A.: The internal reinforcement of evolving algorithms. In: Spector, L., et al. (eds.) AiGP 3, pp. 325–354 (1999). http://www.cs.ucl.ac.uk/staff/W.Langdon/aigp3/ch14.pdf
4. Langdon, W.B.: Genetic Programming and Data Structures, Springer, Boston (1998). https://doi.org/10.1007/978-1-4615-5731-9
5. White, D.R., et al.: Evolutionary improvement of programs. IEEE TEVC **15**(4), 515–538 (2011). https://doi.org/10.1109/TEVC.2010.2083669
6. Langdon, W.B., Harman, M.: Optimising existing software with genetic programming. IEEE TEVC **19**(1), 118–135 (2015). https://doi.org/10.1109/TEVC.2013.2281544
7. Petke, J., Harman, M., Langdon, W.B., Weimer, W.: Using genetic improvement and code transplants to specialise a C++ program to a problem class. In: Nicolau, M., et al. (eds.) EuroGP 2014. LNCS, vol. 8599, pp. 137–149. Springer, Heidelberg (2014). https://doi.org/10.1007/978-3-662-44303-3_12
8. Petke, J.: Constraints: the future of combinatorial interaction testing. In: SBST, pp. 17–18 (2015). https://doi.org/10.1109/SBST.2015.11
9. Petke, J., et al.: Specialising software for different downstream applications using genetic improvement and code transplantation. TSE **44**(6), 574–594 (2018). https://doi.org/10.1109/TSE.2017.2702606
10. Petke, J., et al.: Genetic improvement of software: a comprehensive survey. IEEE TEVC **22**(3), 415–432 (2018). https://doi.org/10.1109/TEVC.2017.2693219
11. Takagi, H.: Interactive evolutionary computation: fusion of the capabilities of EC optimization and human evaluation. Proc. IEEE **89**(9), 1275–1296 (2001). https://doi.org/10.1109/5.949485
12. Backer, G.: Learning with missing data using genetic programming. In: The 1st Online Workshop on Soft Computing (WSC1). Nagoya University, Japan (1996). http://www.pa.info.mie-u.ac.jp/bioele/wsc1/papers/files/backer.ps.gz

13. Poli, R., et al.: A field guide to genetic programming (2008). http://lulu.com, http://www.gp-field-guide.org.uk
14. Langdon, W.B., Buxton, B.F.: Evolving receiver operating characteristics for data fusion. In: Miller, J., Tomassini, M., Lanzi, P.L., Ryan, C., Tettamanzi, A.G.B., Langdon, W.B. (eds.) EuroGP 2001. LNCS, vol. 2038, pp. 87–96. Springer, Heidelberg (2001). https://doi.org/10.1007/3-540-45355-5_8
15. Gathercole, C., Ross, P.: Dynamic training subset selection for supervised learning in genetic programming. In: Davidor, Y., Schwefel, H.-P., Männer, R. (eds.) PPSN 1994. LNCS, vol. 866, pp. 312–321. Springer, Heidelberg (1994). https://doi.org/10.1007/3-540-58484-6_275
16. Spector, L.: Assessment of problem modality by differential performance of lexicase selection in genetic programming: a preliminary report. In: McClymont, K., Keedwell, E. (eds.) GECCO Computing, pp. 401–408 (2012). https://doi.org/10.1145/2330784.2330846
17. Teller, A., Andre, D.: Automatically choosing the number of fitness cases: the rational allocation of trials. In: Koza, J.R., et al. (eds.) GP, pp. 321–328 (1997). http://www.cs.cmu.edu/afs/cs/usr/astro/public/papers/GR.ps
18. Ni, J., et al.: The use of an analytic quotient operator in genetic programming. IEEE TEVC 17(1), 146–152 (2013). https://doi.org/10.1109/TEVC.2012.2195319
19. Koza, J.R., et al.: Genetic Programming III: Darwinian Invention and Problem Solving (1999). http://www.genetic-programming.org/gpbook3toc.html
20. Langdon, W.B.: Multi-threaded memory efficient crossover in C++ for generational genetic programming. SIGEVOlution 13(3), 2–4 (2020). https://doi.org/10.1145/3430913.3430914
21. Singleton, A.: Genetic programming with C++. In: BYTE, pp. 171–176 (1994). http://www.assembla.com/wiki/show/andysgp/GPQuick_Article
22. Langdon, W.B.: Parallel GPQUICK. In: Doerr, C. (ed.) GECCO Computing, pp. 63–64 (2019). https://doi.org/10.1145/3319619.3326770
23. Keith, M.J., Martin, M.C.: Genetic programming in C++: implementation issues. In: Kinnear, Jr., K.E. (ed.) AiGP, pp. 285–310 (1994). http://cognet.mit.edu/sites/default/files/books/9780262277181/pdfs/9780262277181_chap13.pdf
24. Handley, S.: On the use of a directed acyclic graph to represent a population of computer programs. In: WCCI, pp. 154–159 (1994). https://doi.org/10.1109/ICEC.1994.350024
25. McPhee, N.F., et al.: Sutherland: An extensible object-oriented software framework for evolutionary computation. In: Koza, J.R., et al. (eds.) GP, p. 241 (1998). http://facultypages.morris.umn.edu/~mcphee/Research/Sutherland/sutherland_gp98_announcement.ps.gz
26. Ehrenburg, H.: Improved directed acyclic graph evaluation and the combine operator in genetic programming. In: Koza, J.R., et al. (eds.) GP, pp. 285–291 (1996). http://cognet.mit.edu/sites/default/files/books/9780262315876/pdfs/9780262315876_chap36.pdf
27. Sedgewick, R., Flajolet, P.: An Introduction to the Analysis of Algorithms (1996)
28. Langdon, W.B.: Fast generation of big random binary trees. Technical Report RN/20/01, Computer Science, University College, London (2020). https://arxiv.org/abs/2001.04505
29. Langdon, W.B., Banzhaf, W.: Continuous long-term evolution of genetic programming. In: Fuechslin, R. (ed.) ALIFE, pp. 388–395 (2019). https://doi.org/10.1162/isal_a_00191

30. Langdon, W.B., Banzhaf, W.: A SIMD interpreter for genetic programming on GPU graphics cards. In: O'Neill, M., et al. (eds.) EuroGP 2008. LNCS, vol. 4971, pp. 73–85. Springer, Heidelberg (2008). https://doi.org/10.1007/978-3-540-78671-9_7

31. Langdon, W.B., Harrison, A.P.: GP on SPMD parallel graphics hardware for mega bioinformatics data mining. Soft Comput. **12**(12), 1169–1183 (2008). https://doi.org/10.1007/s00500-008-0296-x

32. Poli, R., Langdon, W.B.: Sub-machine-code genetic programming. In: Spector, L., et al. (eds.) AiGP 3, pp. 301–323 (1999). http://www.cs.ucl.ac.uk/staff/W.Langdon/aigp3/ch13.pdf

33. Langdon, W.B.: Long-term evolution of genetic programming populations. In: GECCO, pp. 235–236 (2017). https://doi.org/10.1145/3067695.3075965

34. Langdon, W.B.: Genetic improvement of genetic programming. In: Brownlee, A.S., et al. (eds.) GI @ CEC 2020 Special Session (2020). https://doi.org/10.1109/CEC48606.2020.9185771

35. Langdon, W.B., et al.: The evolution of size and shape. In: Spector, L., et al. (eds.) AiGP 3, pp. 163–190 (1999). http://www.cs.ucl.ac.uk/staff/W.Langdon/aigp3/ch08.pdf

36. Altenberg, L.: The evolution of evolvability in genetic programming. In: Kinnear, Jr., K.E. (ed.) AiGP (1994)

37. Tackett, W.A.: Recombination, Selection, and the Genetic Construction of Computer Programs. Ph.D. thesis (1994)

38. Langdon, W.B., Poli, R.: Fitness causes bloat. In: Chawdhry, P.K., et al. (eds.) Soft Computing in Engineering Design and Manufacturing, pp. 13–22. Springer, London (1998). https://doi.org/10.1007/978-1-4471-0427-8_2

39. Mrazek, V., et al.: Evolutionary approximation of software for embedded systems: median function. In: Langdon, W.B., et al. (eds.) GI, pp. 795–801 (2015). https://doi.org/10.1145/2739482.2768416

40. Langdon, W.B.: The distribution of reversible functions is Normal. In: Riolo, R.L., Worzel, B. (eds.) GPTP, vol 6, pp. 173–187. Springer, Boston (2003). https://doi.org/10.1007/978-1-4419-8983-3_11

41. Yao, X., et al.: A study of equivalent and stubborn mutation operators using human analysis of equivalence. In: Briand, L., et al. (eds.) ICSE, pp. 919–930 (2014). https://doi.org/10.1145/2568225.2568265

42. Jia, Y., et al.: Learning combinatorial interaction test generation strategies using hyperheuristic search. In: Bertolino, A., et al. (eds.) ICSE, pp. 540–550 (2015). https://doi.org/10.1109/ICSE.2015.71

43. Langdon, W.B., et al.: Efficient multi-objective higher order mutation testing with genetic programming. J. Syst. Softw. **83**(12), 2416–2430 (2010). https://doi.org/10.1016/j.jss.2010.07.027

44. Danglot, B., Preux, P., Baudry, B., Monperrus, M.: Correctness attraction: a study of stability of software behavior under runtime perturbation. Empr. Soft. Eng. **23**(4), 2086–2119 (2018). https://doi.org/10.1007/s10664-017-9571-8

45. Abou Assi, R., et al.: Coincidental correctness in the Defects4J benchmark. Soft. TVR **29**(3), e1696 (2019). https://doi.org/10.1002/stvr.1696

46. Timperley, C.S., et al.: Crashing simulated planes is cheap: can simulation detect robotics bugs early? In: ICST, pp. 331–342 (2018). https://doi.org/10.1109/ICST.2018.00040

47. Voas, J.M., Miller, K.W.: Software testability: the new verification. IEEE Softw. **12**(3), 17–28 (1995)

48. Clark, D., et al.: Normalised squeeziness and failed error propagation. Info. Proc. Lets **149**, 6–9 (2019). https://doi.org/10.1016/j.ipl.2019.04.001

49. Langdon, W.B., Petke, J.: Software is not fragile. In: Parrend, P., Bourgine, P., Collet, P. (eds.) First Complex Systems Digital Campus World E-Conference 2015. SPC, pp. 203–211. Springer, Cham (2017). https://doi.org/10.1007/978-3-319-45901-1_24

50. Langdon, W.B.: Large-scale bioinformatics data mining with parallel genetic programming on graphics processing units. In: Tsutsui, S., Collet, P. (eds.) Massively Parallel Evolutionary Computation on GPGPUs. NCS, pp. 311–347. Springer, Heidelberg (2013). https://doi.org/10.1007/978-3-642-37959-8_15

51. de Melo, V.V., Fazenda, Á.L., Sotto, L.F.D.P., Iacca, G.: A MIMD interpreter for genetic programming. In: Castillo, P.A., Jiménez Laredo, J.L., Fernández de Vega, F. (eds.) EvoApplications 2020. LNCS, vol. 12104, pp. 645–658. Springer, Cham (2020). https://doi.org/10.1007/978-3-030-43722-0_41

Mining Feature Relationships in Data

Andrew Lensen$^{(\boxtimes)}$ (iD)

School of Engineering and Computer Science, Victoria University of Wellington,
PO Box 600, Wellington 6140, New Zealand
andrew.lensen@ecs.vuw.ac.nz

Abstract. When faced with a new dataset, most practitioners begin
by performing exploratory data analysis to discover interesting patterns and characteristics within data. Techniques such as association
rule mining are commonly applied to uncover relationships between features (attributes) of the data. However, association rules are primarily
designed for use on binary or categorical data, due to their use of rule-
based machine learning. A large proportion of real-world data is continuous in nature, and discretisation of such data leads to inaccurate and
less informative association rules. In this paper, we propose an alternative
approach called feature relationship mining (FRM), which uses a genetic
programming approach to automatically discover symbolic relationships
between continuous or categorical features in data. To the best of our
knowledge, our proposed approach is the first such symbolic approach
with the goal of explicitly discovering relationships between features.
Empirical testing on a variety of real-world datasets shows the proposed
method is able to find high-quality, simple feature relationships which
can be easily interpreted and which provide clear and non-trivial insight
into data.

Keywords: Association rule mining · Feature relationships · Feature
construction · Feature analysis · Unsupervised learning

1 Introduction

Exploratory data analysis (EDA) is a fundamental task in the data mining process, in which data scientists analyse the properties and characteristics of different features (or instances) in a dataset, and the relationships between them [1].
Simple linear feature relationships can be discovered through the use of statistical techniques such as Pearson's or Spearman's correlations.

Non-linear relationships are generally found by performing association rule
mining (ARM) [2], a rule-based machine learning method that produces rules
that represent relationships between discrete features in a dataset. In the case
of continuous data, discretisation techniques are commonly applied before performing ARM, limiting the quality and increasing the complexity of rules.

Genetic programming (GP) is, perhaps, most known for its success in symbolic regression tasks: the canonical tree-based GP is intrinsically suited to representing non-linear regression models. The use of GP for *interpretable* symbolic

© Springer Nature Switzerland AG 2021
T. Hu et al. (Eds.): EuroGP 2021, LNCS 12691, pp. 247–262, 2021.
https://doi.org/10.1007/978-3-030-72812-0_16

regression—where a user can understand the operation of the evolved function—has also been very successful [3].

The above properties make GP a natural choice for discovering interpretable relationships between continuous variables in data. However, no such approach has yet been proposed; all existing uses of GP for ARM use either a rule-based grammar, or discretise the input space.

This paper aims to propose the first approach to mining feature relationships (FRs), which are *symbolic* representations of intrinsic relationships between features in a dataset. A new GP method will be developed which uses a fitness function that considers both the quality of the discovered FR, as well as the potential interpretability of the FR. A speciation-based approach will also be proposed to allow for multiple distinct and complementary FRs to be automatically found as part of a single evolutionary search.

2 Background

GP has seen significant success in recent years in feature analysis applications. Tree-based GP [4], in particular, has been widely used due to its functional structure, which is well-suited to mapping a set of input features to a new *constructed feature* [5–7].

The use of GP for feature construction for regression and unsupervised learning tasks are perhaps the most closely related areas to this work: evolving feature relationships can be seen as a form of "unsupervised regression". Several works have suggested the use of methods to limit model complexity in symbolic regression, either to improve interpretability or generalisability. These include parsimony pressure and other bloat control strategies [3] as well as complexity measures such as Rademacher complexity [8]. The discovery and combination of "subexpressions" in GP (i.e. feature construction) was also shown to improve performance on symbolic regression tasks [9]. GP has been used for unsupervised tasks such as clustering [10] and nonlinear dimensionality reduction [11,12], often with a focus on interpretability [13].

2.1 Related Work

A number of evolutionary computation approaches to ARM have been proposed [14], with most using a vector-based representation such as a genetic algorithm (GA) [15] or particle swarm optimisation (PSO) [16]. The small number of papers using GP for ARM can be categorised into two paradigms: those using Genetic Network Programming (GNP) [17,18], and those using a grammar-based G3P approach [19,20]. Of these, only a handful address the task of mining ARMs from continuous data [14] (known as quantitative association rule (QAR) mining). These QAR methods, however, are all still constrained by the use of a grammar or network programming structure, and so they are unable to represent the relationships between continuous features in a more intuitive and precise symbolic manner.

3   Proposed Method: GP-FRM

The proposed method, Genetic Programming for Feature Relationship Mining (GP-FRM), aims to evolve compact rules (trees) that reconstruct a feature of the dataset from other features. In this way, the learnt rule represents a relationship between a given ("target") feature and a set of other features. A simple example is the tree $f_2 = f_1 \times f_0$, which is a non-linear relationship that would not be discovered by association rule mining algorithms. Such relationships are common: for example, the Body Mass Index (BMI) is a well-known "target" feature in the medical domain which is based on a person's mass (m) and height (h): $BMI = \frac{m}{h^2}$. As GP-FRM is an unsupervised learning method, it is also crucial that it can discover the best target features automatically without *a priori* knowledge.

3.1   Overall Algorithm

The overall GP-FRM algorithm is shown in Algorithm 1. A core component to the algorithm is the use of *speciation*: the population is split into a number of *species*, each of which share a common target feature. This niching approach serves two main purposes: it encourages multiple diverse FRs to be produced in a single GP run (rather than only a single best individual), while also restricting crossover and mutation to occurring only between individuals that share the same target feature, improving learning efficacy. The target feature of a given GP individual is automatically determined based at each generation, based on the feature which gives the best fitness, i.e. the first feature according to Eq. (1). This allows GP individuals to change more readily over time, moving between species or discovering an entirely new species niche.

$$ClosestFeatures(x|F) = \underset{f \in F}{\text{argsort}} \, |r_{x,f}| \qquad (\textit{Decreasing sort}) \qquad (1)$$

The core of Algorithm 1 is similar to a standard evolutionary search, with the main difference being the use of speciation for breeding and elitism (Lines 8–14). The speciation algorithm is shown in Algorithm 2. The number of species (N_S) is a parameter of the algorithm, and is used to constrain the number of niches in the search space: having too many species would give many poorer-quality FRs and prohibit niche-level exploitation by a group of individuals. The population is sorted by fitness (best to worst) into a Closest Features (CF) list and then each individual is considered in turn:

1. if the individual's closest feature (CF_0) has already been selected as a species, it is added to that species;
2. otherwise, if the number of species (N_S) has not been reached, a new species is created with the individual's closest feature (CF_0) as the *seed*;
3. otherwise, the individual's list of closest features ($P_j CF$) is searched to find the first seed (feature) which is in the species list, and then the individual is added to that species.

Algorithm 1. Overall GP-FRM Algorithm

Input: Dataset: X, maximum generations: G, num species N_S
Output: Set of S Feature Relationships
1: $F \leftarrow X^T$
2: Randomly initialise population P
3: **for** $i = 1$ to G **do**
4:     **for** $j = 1$ to $|P|$ **do**
5:         $P_j CF \leftarrow ClosestFeatures(P_j, F)$ using Eq. (1)
6:         P_jFitness $\leftarrow Fitness(P_j, P_j CF_0)$ using Eq. (4)
7:     **end for**
8:     $Species \leftarrow Speciate(P, N_S)$ using Algorithm 2
9:     $P_{new} \leftarrow \{\}$
10:     **for** $SP \in Species$ **do**
11:         $Offspring \leftarrow Breed(SP)$
12:         $Offspring.append(SP.seed)$
13:         $P_{new}.append(Offspring)$
14:     **end for**
15: **end for**
16: **for** $j = 1$ to $|P|$ **do**
17:     $P_j CF \leftarrow ClosestFeatures(P_j, F)$ using Eq. (1)
18:     P_jFitness $\leftarrow Fitness(P_j, P_j CF_0)$ using Eq. (4)
19: **end for**
20: $Species \leftarrow Speciate(P, N_S)$ using Algorithm 2
21: $S \leftarrow \{\}$
22: **for** $SP \in Species$ **do**
23:     $S.append(SP.seed)$
24: **end for**
25: **return** S

In this way, the species are always selected from the fittest individuals, and the species seed represents the best individual in that species. A species' seed is always transferred to the next generation unmodified during the breeding process, as a form of elitism. When breeding a species, the number of offspring produced is $\frac{|P|}{N_S}$ to ensure each species has equal weighting.

3.2   Fitness Function

A simple approach to assess the quality of a tree would be to measure the error between its output and its target feature, for example, the mean absolute error (MAE):

$$MAE(x, f) = \frac{\sum_{i=1}^{|x|} |x_i - f_i|}{|x|} \quad (2)$$

where x is the n-dimensional output of a given tree, f is the n-dimensional target feature, and n is the number of instances.

The MAE is sensitive to scale: if x was exactly 10 times the scale of f, it would give an error of 9. This presents two problems: firstly, it means that the

Algorithm 2. Speciation Algorithm

Input: Population: P, num species N_S
Output: Set of *Species*
1:   $PSorted \leftarrow Sort(P)$
2:   $Species \leftarrow []$
3:   **for** $j = 1$ to $|PSorted|$ **do**
4:      $S_{Index} \leftarrow PSorted_j CF_0$
5:      **if** $S_{Index} \in Species$ **then**
6:         $Species[S_{Index}].append(PSorted_j)$
7:      **else if** $|Species| < N_S$ **then**
8:         $Species[S_{Index}].seed \leftarrow PSorted_j$
9:         $Species[S_{Index}].append(PSorted_j)$
10:     **else**
11:       $k \leftarrow 1$
12:       **while** $S_{Index} \notin Species$ **do**
13:         $k \leftarrow k + 1$
14:         $S_{Index} \leftarrow PSorted_j CF_k$
15:       **end while**
16:       $Species[S_{Index}].append(PSorted_j)$
17:     **end if**
18: **end for**
19: **return** *Species*

GP algorithm must learn constant factors within a FR, which traditional GP algorithms struggle with due to their use of random mutation[1]. Secondly, the scale of the learnt FRs is not actually important in many cases: a relationship between weight and height, for example, is meaningful whether weight is measured in grams, kilograms, or pounds. With these issues in mind, we instead employ Pearson's correlation, $r_{x,f}$, as our cost measure, given its scale invariance:

$$\text{Cost} = r_{x,f} = \frac{\sum_{i=1}^{n}(x_i - \overline{x})(f_i - \overline{f})}{\sqrt{\sum_{i=1}^{n}(x_i - \overline{x})^2}\sqrt{\sum_{i=1}^{n}(f_i - \overline{f})^2}} \tag{3}$$

Pearson's correlation has a value between $+1$ and -1, where a value of $+1$ represents a completely positive linear relationship from x to f, 0 represents no correlation as all, and -1 represents a completely negative linear relationship. The magnitude of the correlation measures the degree of linearity in the relationship; the sign provides the directionality. We do not consider the directionality to be important in this work, as a negative feature relationship is equally as informative as a positive one. Therefore, we consider the absolute value of $r_{x,f}$ which is in the range $[0, 1]$, where 1 is optimal. Pearson's correlation has seen previous use in GP to encourage diversity and approximate fitness [21, 22].

---

[1] For example, mutating the 0.71 node of $x = f_1 \times (f_0 + 0.71)$ using a traditional mutation would give a new value in $U[0, 1]$. While local-search approaches can be used to optimise constants more cautiously, it is best if they can be avoided completely.

If an evolved FR is to be realistically useful in understanding data, it must be sufficiently small and simple for a human to easily interpret. To achieve this, we introduce a penalty term into the fitness function, with an α parameter that controls the trade-off between high correlation (high cost) and small tree size. In practice, α is generally small, so this can be seen as a relaxed version of lexicographic parsimony pressure [23]. The proposed fitness function—which should be *minimised*—is shown in Eq. (4), for an individual x with target feature f.

$$Fitness(x|f) = \begin{cases} 1 + |r_{x,f}| + \alpha \times size(x_{\text{Tree}}), & \text{if } f \in x_{\text{Tree}} \\ 1 - |r_{x,f}| + \alpha \times size(x_{\text{Tree}}), & \text{otherwise} \end{cases} \quad (4)$$

Equation (4) consists of two cases: one where the target feature f is used in the tree x_{Tree} and one where it is not. This is to penalise the evolution of naïve or self-referential trees such as $f_1 = f_1$ or $f_2 = f_1 \times \frac{f_2}{f_1}$. In the case where a target feature **is** used in x_{Tree}, the fitness is penalised by the size of the linear correlation (i.e. in the range $[1, 2]$, disregarding α). When it is not, the fitness will be in the range $[0, 1]$. In this way, the fitness of an individual not using the target feature will always be better (lower) than another that does.

3.3 Preventing the Discovery of Naïve Relationships

Often in many real-world datasets, features will be highly linearly correlated with each other: either due to redundancy in the feature set, or due to other natural linearity. For example, weight measured as a feature in kg will be perfectly correlated with weight measured in lb. While it is not incorrect for GP to discover such relationships, they are not very useful, as they can be found in $O(n^2)$ time for n features, by calculating the pairwise Pearon's correlation matrix.

We prevent GP from evolving such relationships by pre-computing a list of "matching features" for each feature. This list contains all the other features that are linearly correlated with the feature[2]. This list is used in place of f in the calculation of fitness (Eq. (4)), such that the fitness will be penalised if *any* matching features to the target feature appear in the GP tree. Note that this does not prevent any features from being used as a species seed.

4 Experiment Design

To evaluate the potential of GP-FRM, we tested it on a range of real-world classification datasets (from different domains), which were selected due to having clearly human-meaningful features. These are summarised in Table 1, ordered according to the number of features. Some minor data cleaning was done, including the removal of missing values by removing whole features or instances as appropriate.

---

[2] Two features are defined to be linearly correlated if they have an absolute Pearson's correlation greater than 0.95.

Table 1. Classification datasets used for experiments.

Dataset	Features	Instances	Classes	Source
Wine	13	178	3	[24]
WDBC	30	569	2	[24]
Dermatology	34	358	6	[24]
Steel Plates Fault	33	1941	2	[24]
PC3	37	1563	2	[25]
Spambase	57	4601	2	[24]
Arrhythmia	278	420	12	[24]
MFEAT ·	649	2000	10	[24]

Table 2. GP Parameter Settings.

Parameter	Setting	Parameter	Setting
Generations	1000	Population Size	1000
Mutation	20%	Crossover	80%
Selection	Tournament	Max. Tree Depth	6
Elitism	1-per-species	Pop. Initialisation	Half-and-half

GP-FRM was tested at three α values $(0.01, 0.001, 0.0001)$ to evaluate the trade-off between correlation and tree size. On each dataset, 30 runs of GP-FRM were performed for each value of α. The parameter settings used for GP-FRM are shown in Table 2. A reasonably high population size and number of generations was used due to the cheap computational cost of the fitness function. In practice, GP-FRM tended to convergence by about $400 - 500$ generations. A small maximum tree depth of six was used to encourage interpretable trees, which also further reduced the computational cost. The number of species, N_S, was set to 10 for all experiments based on initial tests. In future, we hope to allow the number of species to be dynamically determined during the evolutionary process.

5   Results

The mean fitness, cost, and number of nodes over 30 runs for each dataset and value of α are shown in Table 3[3].

As α is increased, there is a clear increase in mean cost and decrease in the mean number of nodes on most of the datasets in Table 3. In many cases, the proportional decrease in the number of nodes is much higher than the increases in cost: for example, on the Wine dataset, the number of nodes at $\alpha = 0.001$ is less than half that of at $\alpha = 0.0001$, but the cost only increases from 0.149 to 0.172.

---

[3] Note that Fitness = Cost + α × Nodes, but we also list the fitness separately for completeness.

Table 3. Mean results of GP-FRM across the datasets

Dataset	Alpha	Fitness	Cost	Nodes
Wine	0.0001	0.153	0.149	48.5
	0.0010	0.195	0.172	22.7
	0.0100	0.298	0.226	7.15
WDBC	0.0001	0.0203	0.018	23.4
	0.0010	0.0322	0.023	9.17
	0.0100	0.0827	0.0403	4.24
Dermatology	0.0001	0.0362	0.0334	27.9
	0.0010	0.0541	0.043	11.1
	0.0100	0.111	0.0631	4.76
Steel Plates Fault	0.0001	0.00712	0.00552	16
	0.0010	0.0166	0.00906	7.55
	0.0100	0.0573	0.0225	3.48
PC3	0.0001	0.000565	0.000162	4.04
	0.0010	0.00395	0.000334	3.62
	0.0100	0.0339	0.00379	3.01
Spambase	0.0001	0.14	0.136	35.5
	0.0010	0.16	0.144	16.1
	0.0100	0.237	0.165	7.23
Arrhythmia	0.0001	0.000298	1.63×10^{-7}	2.98
	0.0010	0.00299	1×10^{-8}	2.99
	0.0100	0.0298	4.07×10^{-7}	2.98
MFEAT	0.0001	0.00955	0.00807	14.8
	0.0010	0.0166	0.011	5.54
	0.0100	0.043	0.013	3

Similar patterns are seen for WDBC, Dermatology, Spambase, and MFEAT. When α is increased from 0.001 to 0.01, however, the increase in cost is often proportionally much higher, especially on WDBC and PC3. The Arrhythmia dataset appears to exhibit strange behaviour, as a result of it having a high number of features which are simple multiplicative combinations of other features. Such relationships could be "filtered out" as a pre-processing step, using a similar approach to that of removing highly correlated features.

Generally, as the number of features in the dataset increases, the mean cost decreases. This is not surprising: the more features available, the more likely it is to find a stronger relationship between them. From a similar perspective, higher-dimensional datasets often require the use of fewer nodes, as there are a greater number of simple FRs to be found. A multiobjective GP approach [26]

Table 4. Relative Standard Deviation of GP-FRM across the datasets

Dataset	Alpha	Fitness (%)	Cost (%)	Nodes (%)
Wine	0.0001	41.7	42.8	24.1
	0.0010	37	40	31.3
	0.0100	28.9	31.4	42.1
WDBC	0.0001	42.9	47.9	33.7
	0.0010	33.4	41.2	32.7
	0.0100	22.4	39.1	29.9
Dermatology	0.0001	40.3	43.3	37.6
	0.0010	33	36.8	42.5
	0.0100	28.5	38.9	30.7
Steel Plates Fault	0.0001	94.9	113	55.2
	0.0010	58	87.2	48.2
	0.0100	35.4	75.6	24.6
PC3	0.0001	52	161	34.6
	0.0010	24.2	182	25.6
	0.0100	18.2	159	5.41
Spambase	0.0001	61.1	62.2	43.4
	0.0010	56.9	60.8	48.4
	0.0100	43.8	59	33.1
Arrhythmia	0.0001	6.76	1.73×10^3	6.69
	0.0010	5.46	1.73×10^3	5.46
	0.0100	6.69	1.17×10^3	6.69
MFEAT	0.0001	41.7	46.8	54.4
	0.0010	28	37.2	42.9
	0.0100	13	43.1	0

would likely help to find a balance between tree and/or node count and number of FRs.

To find more complex and interesting FRs, a greater number of species should be used on high-dimensional datasets. The α parameter should be set based on initial tests of cost: on datasets such as PC3, Steel Plates Fault, and MFEAT, a high α encourages small FRs while still achieving a very good cost. On other datasets such as Wine and Spambase, a low α is needed to ensure that the FRs found are of sufficient quality.

The relative standard deviation (RSD: $100\% \times \frac{SD}{mean}$) of these results is presented in Table 4 to show the variation across the 30 runs. In general, the RSD is around 20–50%, aside from a few cases where it is much higher due to the measured values being very small. This level of variance is not unusual for GP, but

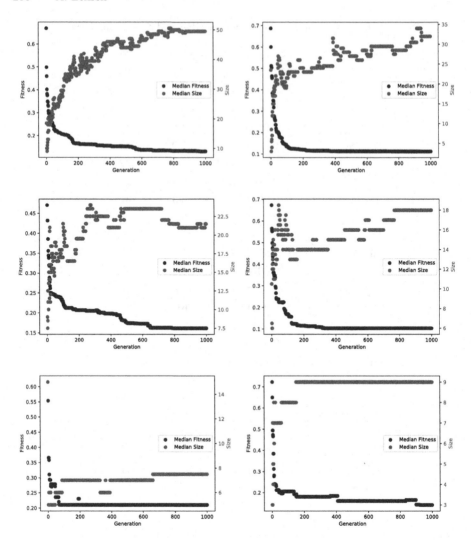

Fig. 1. Convergence Analysis for the Wine (left) and Spambase (right) datasets. Top row is $\alpha = 0.0001$, middle is $\alpha = 0.001$, and bottom is $\alpha = 0.01$. Median values of fitness and size are plotted to represent the expected average performance of a single GP run.

could be reduced further in future work through the use of a more constrained search space, or the introduction of domain knowledge to give a higher-fitness initial population.

5.1 Convergence Curves

The convergence curve for GP-FRM for each value of α is shown for two representative datasets (Wine and Spambase) in Fig. 1. Clearly, when α has a high value (0.01), convergence occurs much more quickly—the high pressure to use few nodes in a tree greatly restricts the size of trees, reducing the number of good individuals in the search space. The convergence curve is also much less granular, due to the restrictions on tree size. At a lower α, the size of individuals starts quite low, but then increases over the evolutionary process, before levelling off. This again reflects the difficulty of finding larger individuals which have sufficiently lower costs to out-perform simpler, but higher-cost individuals. Early in the evolutionary process, it is much "easier" to find small individuals that have a relatively good fitness than larger ones. In the future, it may be interesting to investigate dynamically adapting α throughout evolution, to better guide the search based on whether the cost or size of individuals is sufficiently low.

6   Further Analysis

To better understand the potential of GP-FRM for mining feature relationships which are useful for providing insight in data, we further analyse a selection of the evolved FRs in this section.

6.1   Analysis of Selected Features

Of the eight tested datasets, the four which showed the biggest decrease in tree size from $\alpha = 0.0001$ to $\alpha = 0.01$ were Wine, WDBC, Dermatology, and Spambase. A decrease in tree size will generally give a decrease in the number of feature terminals, and hence decrease the occurrence of each feature in an evolved FR. This pattern can be seen in Fig. 2, which plots the histogram of the features used to produce FRs for the five most common[4] target features in each of the datasets. As α is increased (from left to right), the number of features (the area under the histogram) decreases significantly. On three of the datasets, there are features which are never selected to be in a GP tree when $\alpha = 0.01$. This shows that the parsimony pressure is not only encouraging GP to evolve smaller trees, but also simpler trees which use fewer distinct features.

Across the four datasets, the five target features utilise clearly distinct groups of features. For example, at $\alpha = 0.0001$ on Spambase, the purple target feature mostly uses features with indices between 25 and 30. There is also a clear spike on Spambase with features above index 50 being particularly popular for the blue and orange target features. On all datasets, we can see an increase in this niching-style behaviour as α is increased. For example, on the Wine dataset, at $\alpha = 0.0001$, most features are commonly used across all the target features; at $\alpha = 0.01$, only a few different features are commonly used for each target feature. This pattern reinforces the benefit of a speciation approach (particularly at a high α) in encouraging multiple distinct FRs to be learned simultaneously. Using a more complex parsimony pressure that considers the number of unique features in a tree is likely to further improve the performance of speciation.

---

[4] Only the top five FRs are considered to make the plots easier to analyse.

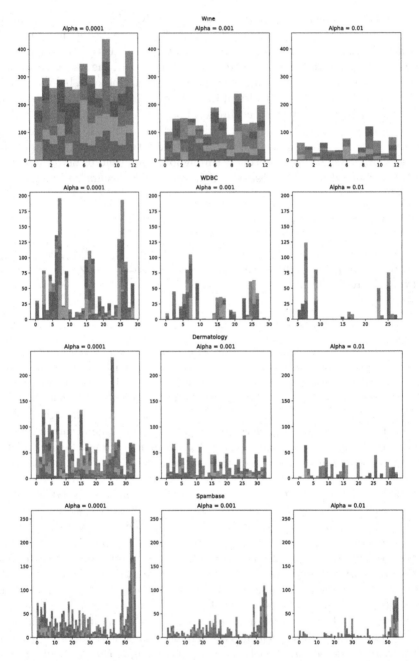

Fig. 2. Histogram of the features used to produce feature relationships (FRs) for the five most common target features on four datasets. Each colour represents one target feature. α varies from left-to-right, increasing the penalty for using more nodes in a tree. The x-axis represents each feature indexed in the order it appeared in the dataset.

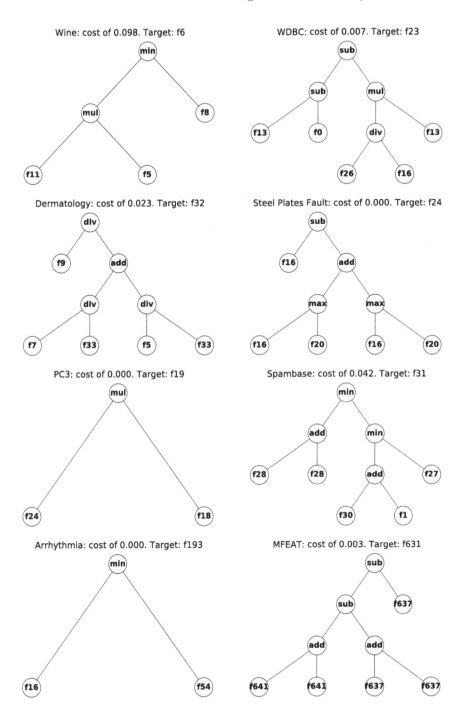

Fig. 3. Best evolved trees on each dataset that use fewer than five unique features and ten nodes in total.

6.2 Analysis of Evolved Relationships

To further understand the usefulness of the evolved FRs, we selected the tree with the lowest cost on each dataset that used fewer than five unique features and no more than ten nodes overall. While other trees had slightly lower cost, their greater complexity makes them less useful for simple analysis. The eight trees for the eight datasets are shown in Fig. 3. We analyse a sample of these trees further to evaluate their meaning in the context of the features of the dataset.

The tree shown for the Wine dataset has the highest cost across the datasets, but a cost of 0.098 still gives a Pearson's correlation of greater than 0.9, indicating a very strong correlation [27]. $f5$, $f8$, and $f11$ correspond to "total phenols", "proanthocyanins" and "hue" respectively, with the target feature being flavanoids. This FR therefore shows that flavanoids have a high linear correlation with the greater of the amount of proanthocyanins and the product of total phenols and hue. This information could be useful to a food chemist in understanding how to control the amount of flavanoids in wine.

The target feature for WDBC is "worst area": the largest cell nucleus area in the breast tissue sample. The GP tree is equivalent to the formula: worst area $=$ se area $-$ mean radius $- \left(\frac{\text{worst concavity}}{\text{se concavity}} \right) \times$ se area, where se is the standard error.

The tree evolved on the Dermatology dataset uncovers a relationship between the presence of a band-like pattern on the skin, and other skin attributes, including a clear relationship with the age of the patient: band-like infiltrate $=$ scalp involvement $\div \left(\frac{\text{oral mucosal involvement}}{\text{age}} + \frac{\text{polygonal papules}}{\text{age}} \right)$. This could be very useful to dermatologists in understanding how the likelihood of different symptoms varies as a patient gets older.

On both the PC3 and Arrhythmia datasets, GP-FRM found very simple trees. For PC3, the discovered rule is Halstead Effort $=$ Halstead Volume $\times$ Halstead Difficulty. The PC3 dataset measures various aspects of code quality of NASA software for orbiting satellites. The Halstead effort measures the "mental effort required to develop or maintain a program", and indeed is defined in the original paper in this formulation [28]. The fact that GP-FRM discovered this (already known) relationship highlights its ability to find rules that ARM algorithms would not.

Finally, on the Spambase dataset, a high correlation is found between the number of times that the token "857" occurs in an email and a number of other tokens such as "650", "telnet", "lab", and "address". A security researcher analysing this dataset may be able to use this information to better understand common patterns in spam, in order to block it more accurately.

7 Conclusion

This paper proposed the first approach to automatically discovering feature relationships (FRs): symbolic functions which uncover underlying non-linear relationships between features of a large dataset. Our proposed GP-FRM method used a variation on Pearson's correlation with a speciation-based genetic programming algorithm to automatically produce a set of distinct and meaningful feature relationships. Empirical testing across a range of real-world datasets demonstrated the ability of GP-FRM to find very strong relationships which used a small number of features, aided by the use of parsimony pressure as a secondary objective. Further analysis reinforced these findings and demonstrated how the learned relationships could be used in practice.

Future work will primarily focus on improving GP-FRM further through the use of more sophisticated parsimony pressure methods; development of approaches to minimise the number of distinct features used in a given species; and further refinements to the fitness function to better measure the interpretability and meaningfulness of feature relationships. Employing measures such as the Shapley value [29] or the Vapnik–Chervonenkis dimension [30] could give better measures of tree complexity than a simple count of nodes.

References

1. Tukey, J.W.: Exploratory data analysis, vol. 2. Reading, MA (1977)
2. Agrawal, R., Imielinski, T., Swami, A.N.: Mining association rules between sets of items in large databases. In: Proceedings of the 1993 ACM SIGMOD International Conference on Management of Data, Washington, DC, USA, pp. 207–216, May 26–28, 1993. ACM Press (1993)
3. Dick, G.: Bloat and generalisation in symbolic regression. In: Dick, G., et al. (eds.) SEAL 2014. LNCS, vol. 8886, pp. 491–502. Springer, Cham (2014). https://doi.org/10.1007/978-3-319-13563-2_42
4. Poli, R., Langdon, W.B., McPhee, N.F.: A Field Guide to Genetic Programming (2008). https://lulu.com. Accessed 27 Sept 2019
5. Neshatian, K., Zhang, M., Andreae, P.: A filter approach to multiple feature construction for symbolic learning classifiers using genetic programming. IEEE Trans. Evol. Comput. **16**(5), 645–661 (2012)
6. Tran, B., Xue, B., Zhang, M.: Genetic programming for feature construction and selection in classification on high-dimensional data. Memetic Comput. **8**(1), 3–15 (2015). https://doi.org/10.1007/s12293-015-0173-y
7. Hart, E., Sim, K., Gardiner, B., Kamimura, K.: A hybrid method for feature construction and selection to improve wind-damage prediction in the forestry sector. In: Proceedings of the Genetic and Evolutionary Computation Conference, pp. 1121–1128 (2017)
8. Chen, Q., Xue, B., Zhang, M.: Rademacher complexity for enhancing the generalization of genetic programming for symbolic regression. IEEE Trans. Cybern. 1–14 (2020)
9. Arnaldo, I., Krawiec, K., O'Reilly, U.: Multiple regression genetic programming. In: Proceedings of the Genetic and Evolutionary Computation Conference, GECCO, pp. 879–886. ACM (2014)
10. Handl, J., Knowles, J.D.: An evolutionary approach to multiobjective clustering. IEEE Trans. Evol. Comput. **11**(1), 56–76 (2007)
11. McDermott, J.: Why is auto-encoding difficult for genetic programming? In: Sekanina, L., Hu, T., Lourenço, N., Richter, H., García-Sánchez, P. (eds.) EuroGP 2019. LNCS, vol. 11451, pp. 131–145. Springer, Cham (2019). https://doi.org/10.1007/978-3-030-16670-0_9

12. Lensen, A., Zhang, M., Xue, B.: Multi-objective genetic programming for manifold learning: balancing quality and dimensionality. Genetic Program. Evolvable Mach. **21**, 399–431 (2020)
13. Lensen, A., Xue, B., Zhang, M.: Genetic programming for evolving a front of interpretable models for data visualisation. IEEE Trans. Cybern. 1–15 (2020)
14. Telikani, A., Gandomi, A.H., Shahbahrami, A.: A survey of evolutionary computation for association rule mining. Inf. Sci. **524**, 318–352 (2020)
15. Rodríguez, D.M., Rosete, A., Alcalá-Fdez, J., Herrera, F.: A new multiobjective evolutionary algorithm for mining a reduced set of interesting positive and negative quantitative association rules. IEEE Trans. Evol. Comput. **18**(1), 54–69 (2014)
16. Kuo, R.J., Chao, C.M., Chiu, Y.T.: Application of particle swarm optimization to association rule mining. Appl. Soft Comput. **11**(1), 326–336 (2011)
17. Taboada, K., Shimada, K., Mabu, S., Hirasawa, K., Hu, J.: Association rule mining for continuous attributes using genetic network programming. In: Lipson, H. (ed.) Genetic and Evolutionary Computation Conference, GECCO 2007, Proceedings, London, England, UK, p. 1758, July 7–11, 2007. ACM (2007)
18. Mabu, S., Chen, C., Lu, N., Shimada, K., Hirasawa, K.: An intrusion-detection model based on fuzzy class-association-rule mining using genetic network programming. IEEE Trans. Syst. Man Cybern. Part C **41**(1), 130–139 (2011)
19. Luna, J.M., Romero, J.R., Ventura, S.: Design and behavior study of a grammar-guided genetic programming algorithm for mining association rules. Knowl. Inf. Syst. **32**(1), 53–76 (2012)
20. Luna, J.M., Pechenizkiy, M., del Jesus, M.J., Ventura, S.: Mining context-aware association rules using grammar-based genetic programming. IEEE Trans. Cybern. **48**(11), 3030–3044 (2018)
21. Tomassini, M., Vanneschi, L., Collard, P., Clergue, M.: A study of fitness distance correlation as a difficulty measure in genetic programming. Evol. Comput. **13**(2), 213–239 (2005)
22. Haeri, M.A., Ebadzadeh, M.M., Folino, G.: Statistical genetic programming for symbolic regression. Appl. Soft Comput. **60**, 447–469 (2017)
23. Luke, S., Panait, L.: Lexicographic parsimony pressure. In: Proceedings of the Genetic and Evolutionary Computation Conference (GECCO), pp. 829–836 (2002)
24. Dheeru, D., Karra Taniskidou, E.: UCI machine learning repository (2017). http://archive.ics.uci.edu/ml
25. Sayyad Shirabad, J., Menzies, T.: The PROMISE Repository of Software Engineering Databases. School of Information Technology and Engineering, University of Ottawa, Canada (2005). http://promise.site.uottawa.ca/SERepository
26. Badran, K.M.S., Rockett, P.I.: The influence of mutation on population dynamics in multiobjective genetic programming. Genet. Program. Evolvable Mach. **11**(1), 5–33 (2010)
27. Cohen, J.: Statistical Power Analysis for the Behavioral Sciences. Academic press, Cambridge (2013)
28. Halstead, M.H., et al.: Elements of Software Science, vol. 7. Elsevier, New York (1977)
29. Roth, A.E. (ed.): The Shapley Value: Essays in Honor of Lloyd S. Cambridge University Press, Shapley, Cambridge (1988)
30. Vapnik, V.N., Chervonenkis, A.Y.: On the uniform convergence of relative frequencies of events to their probabilities. In: Vovk, V., Papadopoulos, H., Gammerman, A. (eds.) Measures of Complexity, pp. 11–30. Springer, Cham (2015). https://doi.org/10.1007/978-3-319-21852-6_3

Getting a Head Start on Program Synthesis with Genetic Programming

Jordan Wick, Erik Hemberg$^{(\boxtimes)}$, and Una-May O'Reilly

MIT, Cambridge, USA
wickj@alumn.mit.edu, {hembergerik,unamay}@csail.mit.edu

Abstract. We explore how to give Genetic Programming (GP) a head start to synthesize a programming problem. Our method uses a related problem and introduces a schedule that directs GP to solve the related problem first either fully or to some extent first, or at the same time. In addition, if the related problem's solutions are written by students or evolved by GP, we explore the extent to which initializing the GP population with some of these solutions provides a head start. We find that having a population solve one programming problem before working to solve a related programming problem helps to a greater extent as the targeted problems and the intermediate problems themselves are selected to be more challenging.

Keywords: Genetic Programming · Grammar · Program synthesis · Multi task

1 Introduction

It is possible to learn programming on one's own but following in a course with a teacher can make the learning easier. That is, teachers often give their students a head start on new problems and, prior to a problem set, they introduce examples of problems related to it. They may also provide a solution that a student only needs to extend or re-factor, with modest effort, to solve the problem, all of which provides support for learning. This notion of moving from one problem to a related one is conceptually similar to what, in Machine Learning(ML), is called multi-task learning [30]. A teacher often introduces small, modular solutions that can be easily combined in different ways with others. This head start allows them to show how to compose them in different combinations to solve larger problems(tasks) that share some subsolutions in common. This is similar to *curriculum learning* [4] in ML which starts with a small task and then introduces of a multi-stage curriculum.

We are interested in giving *Genetic Programming Used for Program Synthesis* (GP) a head start. Our desire is to improve the capacity of GP to apply existing problem solving knowledge to solve a set of similar problems. Specifically, we study how GP can, "within a run", solve multiple similar problems,

© Springer Nature Switzerland AG 2021
T. Hu et al. (Eds.): EuroGP 2021, LNCS 12691, pp. 263–279, 2021.
https://doi.org/10.1007/978-3-030-72812-0_17

whether in sequence or concurrently. This would involve only changing input-output requirements and priming the population with some solutions similar to the target problem. It would reduce reliance on manual intervention, external libraries or restarts as required by executing multiple runs. While the benefits of a head start seem obvious, it is not immediately clear how to best provide it to GP. We can draw options from a number of observations. First, instructor programs ready for modification could seed the GP's initial population. These could be starting points for GP closer to a solution to the problem or more suited to easily reach a solution. Second, we could provide elements of a human curriculum for programming. We could take two consecutive problems A and B from a programming course, and try and learn one then the other (B after A and A after B), learn them simultaneously (A and B at same time because they share common subproblems and can share subsolutions) or a new problem that is a combination of problems A and B. This set of problems would extend the current GP program synthesis benchmark suite. Currently its problems have been selected for different criteria such as solely having input/output examples, multiple solutions, no synthesis method bias and that are representative of student programming problems [10] (see Sect. 2 for related work).

To proceed with these options, we selected two similar Python programming problems from an actual programming course, specifically *MITx 6.00.1x Introduction to computer science and programming in Python (6.00.1x)*, a MOOC offered on the EdX platform. We modify a grammatical GP system [15], to allow GP to solve multiple programming problems in one run (see Sect. 3). The modifications are: **a)** a schedule to change one programming problem to another (by changing the input-output examples), **b)** initialization of the population with existing solutions to a programming problem. We seed the population with random (normal GP initialization) programs, human coded solutions, and programs generated from previous runs of GP. Our intent is to forgo inventing specialized operators or fitness measures.

We pose the following research questions (see Sect. 4 and 5) for GP: **1)** How does the quality of a solution or time to identifying a solution improve when GP switches to the problem "mid-stream", i.e. in the process of solving a similar problem? By how much does the timing of the switch impact performance? **2)** How does the quality of a solution or time to identifying a solution improve when GP's population is initialized with solutions to similar problems? What proportion of similar problem solutions helps? In the context of head starts, we will use human judgment to select problems that are similar in terms of requiring the same program conceptual knowledge.

The key contributions (see Section Sect. 6) of this paper are: **1)** Introduction of a new program synthesis problem presented as a pair that is similar according to a programming curriculum. **2)** Development of schedule for multi programming problem synthesis. **3)** Analysis of head start concept based on multiple similar programming problems, programming problem schedules and initialization.

2   Related Work

A head start for GP is intrinsically related to other attempts in GP that re-purpose solutions. In GP the seeding of initial population as a means of headstart has been studied for e.g. software improvement, controllers, symbolic regression and AI planning [2, 20, 28, 32] Another thread of work is multi-task learning. It aims to solve multiple programming problems (tasks) simultaneously to improve on the performance of solving each programming problem independently. The assumption is that there exists some subsolutions (information) in common for solving related tasks [34]. This introduces a relation between modularity and multi-task learning, since the reuse of sub-tasks is promoted by modularity. In GP there have been multiple studies regarding modularity, as reported in this survey [8], though without explicit focus on multiple tasks.

While not all this work is on program synthesis, connections exist, e.g. trans-fer learning of genetic programming instruction sets and libraries [9, 24]. Some recent work on program synthesis with GP also considers multiple functions, string library functions and vector problems [5, 25, 27]. Previous multi-task work in GP has focused on other domains for example, multi task visual learning, robot controllers, symbolic regression and Boolean problems [13, 14, 16, 18, 19, 21, 26]. Furthermore, a head start for GP is also related to non-stationary problems, due to the repurposing of the population. In non-stationary problems GP is pre-sented with a continuum of different requirements [6] whereas when looking for a head start GP pivots explicitly between explicitly different problems.

GP program synthesis has used various techniques, see [17], and also consid-ered specific programming approaches, such as recursion, lambda abstractions and reflection [1, 22, 31, 33]. An important milestone for GP is the program syn-thesis benchmark suite of 29 problems, selected from sources teaching introduc-tory computer science programming [11]. We propose a new paired problem setup that could be introduced to the suite. We differentiate from others by investigat-ing similar-problem solution initialization of the population, the switching from solving one problem to another, and a combination of the problem pair.

3   Method

In this section we first present a formalization of program synthesis and synthe-sis of multiple problems. Then we show how we proceed in a minimalist fashion by introducing two simple modifications that give GP a head start. We out-line a variety of design options this allows. We end by reviewing Grammatical Evolution [23] which our GP framework uses.

3.1   Formalization

A formulation of program synthesis is as an optimization problem: find a pro-gram (solution) q from a domain Q that minimizes combined error on a set of input-output cases $d = \{(x_0, y_0), \ldots, (x_n, y_n)\}, x \in X, y \in Y$, with $q : X \to Y$.

Algorithm 1. $GP(\mathbf{D}, S, D_K, \Theta)$ *Multi-task GP with domain knowledge*
Parameters: $\mathbf{D}$ test cases, S programming problem schedule, D_K existing solutions as knowledge base, Θ hyper parameters
Return: Population

1: $P \leftarrow \emptyset$ ▷ Population
2: $P \leftarrow P \cup$ initialize(Θ, D_K) ▷ Initialize population
3: $P \leftarrow$ evaluate(P, Θ, F) ▷ Evaluate pop fitness
4: **for** $t \in [1, \ldots, \Theta_T]$ **do**   ▷ Iterate over generations
5:      $P' \leftarrow$ selection(P, Θ) ▷ Select new population
6:      $P' \leftarrow$ variation(P', Θ) ▷ Subtree mutation and crossover
7:      $F \leftarrow$ getProgrammingProblem$(S, t, \mathbf{D})$ ▷ Get the fitness function
8:      $P' \leftarrow$ evaluate(P', Θ, F) ▷ Evaluate population on programming problem
9:      $P \leftarrow$ replacement(P', Θ) ▷ Update population
10: **return** P ▷ Return final population

Typically, an indicator function measures error on a single case: $\mathbb{1}: q(x) \neq y$. The program q can be represented by some language L. There exists a set of programs $\mathbf{q}^* = \{q_0^*, \ldots, q_n^*\}$ that can solve all input-output cases. We can formulate the program synthesis problem as

$$\underset{q \in Q}{\arg\min}(q(x) - y)$$

Here we define learning of multiple programs as

$$\underset{q \in Q}{\arg\min} \sum_{x,y \in \mathbf{D}} (q(x) - y)$$

The data set $\mathbf{D}$ is $\{d_0, \ldots, d_n\}$, where d_i has an optimal solutions $\mathbf{q}_i^*$. Domain knowledge is expressed as similar solutions or sub-solutions, $D = \{q_i, \ldots, q_j\}$. For example, initial population head start in this paper is a population of solutions $P = [q_0, \ldots, q_n]$.

3.2 GP

We use a standard GP progtram synthesis algorithm for initializing with a head start, evaluating, selecting, varying and replacing multi-programming problem program synthesis, Algorithm 1. The modifications for a head start are: **1)** Injection of previous program synthesis solutions for initialization, see Algorithm 1 line 2. **2)** A schedule to change the programming problem that is evaluated.

Scheduling Multiple Programming Problems. We design for both serial and parallel scheduling of multiple program synthesis (Algorithm 1 line 7). With a serial schedule one programming problem is first evaluated and then another. With a parallel schedule multiple programming problems are evaluated at the same time, this is done in Algorithm 1 line 7. More formally:

Serial. One programming problem, $q^t = q_0$ is evaluated at generation t (intermediate), then another programming problem, $q^{t+1} = q_1$ is evaluated at generation $t+1$. Fitness score is based on the current programming problem that is being evaluated, $F(q^t)$.

Parallel. Multiple programming problems are evaluated at the same time, $\mathbf{q} = [q_0, \ldots, q_n]$. Fitness score is the sum of each programming problem fitness score, $\sum_{q \in \mathbf{q}} F(q)$.

Serial and Parallel. Programming problems can be evaluated both in serial and parallel, $\mathbf{q}^t = [q_0]$ and $\mathbf{q}^{t+1} = [q_0, \ldots, q_n]$. Fitness score is based on the current programs that are being evaluated, $\sum_{q \in \mathbf{q}^t} F(q)$.

Existing solution initialization. Different solutions to programming problems are seeded into the initial population **a)** Existing source code(solutions) for other human student problems, D^H **b)** Existing evolved solutions in the GP representation for other program synthesis programming problem, D^S **c)** Randomly generated programs using the standard GP initialization procedures, R.

Seeding the GP search with existing similar programs (options **a** and **b**) is one way of providing domain knowledge for the program synthesis. Note, this seeding can be seen as a variant of serial multi programming problem switching, i.e. the first programming problems have been synthesized to completion and provides a starting point for the next programming problem.

To initialize with existing programs, we need to parse the codes into the representation that we use for search. We do this using a grammar. First, we preprocesses the code and refactors variables and function names to a consistent naming scheme. Then, we recursively parse a tree representation of the code depth-first left-to-right and returns a list of integers indicating production choices (GE genome). The first matching production will be returned. Note, future work will investigate if there is any search bias in GE from the code parsing.

3.3 Grammatical Evolution

Grammatical Evolution (GE) is a genetic programming algorithm where a Backus Naur Form (BNF) context free grammar is used in the genotype to phenotype mapping process [23]. A production rule is defined as a non-terminal left-hand side, a separator and a list of productions on the right hand side, each production contains terminals and/or non-terminals. In GE the probability of selecting a production from a rule is depends on the number of productions. The grammar is the starting point for a two step sequence to decode a genotype to a program(phenotype): **1) Genotype to derivation tree**: The genotype, an integer sequence, rewrites non-terminals to terminal via the production rules. This rule production sequence can be represented as a derivation tree. At each step in the rewriting the integer "gene" determines which production to expand the current production rule. The production at the (gene `modulo` number of productions in the rule) position is selected. **2) Derivation tree to phenotype/program**:

The leaves (terminals) of the derivation tree constitute the sentence (executable code) that GE can evaluate.

Synthesized candidate programs in GE are evaluated in the same way as in GP, we provide a grammar as input to Algorithm 1, and when initializing the existing solutions are parsed to a genotype representation. GE's genotype-phenotype mapping step raises locality issues [29]. One way to address the lack locality is to use variation operators that manipulate subtrees. We chose GE since it can incorporate domain information and be used with Python.

4   Experiments

First, we present the program synthesis problems and data used for the initialization experiments. Then we present the experimental setup. Finally, we show the results and discuss them.

4.1   Solutions of Similar Problems

We identify programming problems that are similar according to human experts, composable into a combined program, and for which we have a corpus of correct and incorrect human coded solutions. We draw upon *MITx Introduction to computer science and programming in Python (6.00.1x)*, a MOOC offered on the EdX platform [3]. Because they are also from an introductory programming course, they be similar in complexity to the problems in the GP program synthesis benchmark suite.

The learning design for *6.00.1x* assigns problems of progressiv complexity, e.g. Boolean operations, iterators and then combinations of iterators and Boolean operations. Because their similarity we focus on the first two problems *P1* (count_vowels) and *P2* (count_bob), which check the students' understanding of control flow. The two problems are similar, they initialize a count variable, iterate through a string, and add to a total count if some condition was met. We scraped solution history data from 2016 Term 2 and 2017 Term 1. Here we consider the correct solutions from the 3,485 who earned a certificate. We compared each solution to a gold standard solution on the basis of keyword frequencies using Pearson correlation. Most of the correct ones were correlated to the gold standard [3]. Note that privacy prevents a public release of this data set. We create a combination of *P1* and *P2* called *Combo*, all problems are in Fig. 1.

We used the grammar in Fig. 2 to both parse and generate solutions. We expect only a few distinct solutions, since we standardize them for parsing, filter for correctness, the course provides instructions for solving the problems, and solutions are available online. There are ≈2,000 solutions for *P1* but 2 distinct solutions after parsing. For *P2* there are ≈1,000 solutions and after parsing a single distinct solution. There are no existing student solutions for *Combo*, since we create it for GP. Note, GP copies the solutions in the initial population.

```
def count_vowels(s: str) -> int:
    """Assume `s` is a string of lower case characters. Write a program that counts up
the number of vowels contained in the string `s`. Valid vowels are: `'a', 'e', 'i', 'o'`,
and `'u'`. For example, if `s = 'azcbobobegghakl'`, your program should print:
`Number of vowels: 5`
    """
    ctr = 0
    for i in s:
        if i == "a" or i == "i" or i == "o" or i =="e" or i == "u":
            ctr = ctr + 1
    print("Number of vowels:", ctr)
    return ctr

def count_bob(s: str) -> int:
    """Assume `s` is a string of lower case characters. Write a program that prints the
number of times the string `'bob'` occurs in `s`. For example, if `s = 'azcbobobegghakl'`,
then your program should print
`Number of times bob occurs is: 2`
    """
    ctr = 0
    for i in range(len(s) - 2):
        if s[i] == "b" and s[i + 1] == "o" and s[i + 2] == "b":
            ctr = ctr + 1
    print("Number of times bob occurs is:", ctr)
    return ctr

def combo(s: str) -> Tuple[int, int]:
    """Assume `s` is a string of lower case characters. Write a program that prints the
number of vowels and number of times the string `'bob'` occurs in `s`. For example, if `s
= 'azcbobobegghakl'`, then your program should print
    ```
    Number of vowels: 5
    Number of times bob occurs is: 2
    ```
    """
    ctr_1 = 0
    ctr_2 = 0
    for i in range(len(s)):
        if i < (len(s) - 2) and s[i] == "b" and s[i + 1] == "o" and s[i + 2] == "b":
            ctr_2 = ctr_2 + 1
        if s[i] == "a" or s[i] == "i" or s[i] == "o" or s[i] == "e" or s[i] == "u":
            ctr_1 = ctr_1 + 1
    print("Number of vowels:", ctr_1)
    print("Number of times bob occurs is:", ctr_2)
    return ctr_1, ctr_2
```

Fig. 1. Problems *P1* (count_vowels), *P2* (count_bob) and *Combo* (combo) used for GP. In Python execution of Boolean operators is short-circuited.

4.2   Experimental Setup

We report program synthesis performance in the same way as [11], in terms of how many runs out of 100 resulted in one or more programs that solved all the out-of-sample (test) cases. All other reported values are averages over 100 runs. We ran all experiments on a cloud (OpenStack) VM with 24 cores, 24 GB of RAM using Intel(R) Xeon(R) CPU E5-2450 v2 @ 2.50 GHz. Our GP implementation is based on the PonyGE2 [7,12].

```
start : initial_assign | "i0 = int(); i1 = int(); s0 = str();
 res0 = int(); res1 = int()\n" initial_assign
initial_assign : (int_var equals num "\n" initial_assign)
               | (int_var equals num "\n" code)
               | (string_var equals "str()\n" initial_assign)
equals : " =" | "=" | " = " | " = "
plusequals : " +=" | " += " | "+=" | "+= "
code : (code statement "\n") | (statement "\n")
statement : assign | compound_stmt
compound_stmt : for | if
assign : int_assign | inc
inc : int_var plusequals int
for : for_iter_string
bool : bool_string | (bool_string bool_op bool)
bool_op : " and "|" or "
bool_string : string_cmp | in_string
in_string : "s0 in " str_tuple
str_tuple : "(" s_or_comma ")"
s_or_comma : string_alpha_low | (string_alpha_low ", " s_or_comma)
if : ("if " bool ":{:\n" code ":}") | ("if (" bool "):{:\n" code ":}")
num : "0"|"1"|"2"
int_var : "i0"|"i1"|"res0"|"res1"
int_assign : int_var "=" int
int : int_var | ("int(" num ".0)") | num
string_var : "in0[i1+" num "]" | "s0" | "in0[i1]"
string_cmp : string_var string_equals string_alpha_low
string_equals : "=="| " == " | "== " | " =="
for_iter_string : ("for s0 in in0:{:\n"if"\n:}")
                | ("for i1 in range(len(in0)-"num"):{:\n"if"\n:}")
string_alpha_low : "'b'"|"'a'"|"'e'"|"'i'"|"'o'"|"'u'"
```

Fig. 2. EBNF grammar for problems *P1*, *P2* and *Combo*

The set of parameters we use throughout all our experiments is listed in Table 1. We use subtree crossover on the GE derivation trees [7]. We use novelty selection since it was shown to be useful in program synthesis with GE [12]. Fitness is the number of correct test cases solved during training [11].

4.3   Experimental Design

For each approach, multiple variants were tested across a range of parameters. We specify both the programming problem schedule (programming problems to be solved, and in what order) and the percent of generations to spend on each programming problem. For initialization schemes, we specify which set of solutions we initialize the population with, along with the percentage of the population that is initialized from those solutions. The variants used in the experiments are described in Table 2. The names in the figures are concatenations of these. Baseline is solving only one programming problem. All variants use the same number of fitness evaluations (16,000), regardless if they solve one or multiple programming problems with GP head start during the run.

Table 1. Experimental settings for GP

Parameter	Value
Generations	200
Population Size (P)	800
Elite size	8
Replacement	Generational
Initialization	PI grow
Initial genome length	200
Max genome length	500
Max initial tree depth	15
Max tree depth	17
Crossover probability	0.8
Mutate duplicates	True
Novelty selection [15]	
Novelty archive sample size (C)	100
Novelty tournament size (ω)	6
Novelty function	Exponential
Novelty λ	Generations/10

Table 2. Experimental variants, columns show the name and a description.

Variant name	Description
Multi programming problem learning	
EarlySingleSwitch	Change programming problem after 25% of generations have passed
MedSingleSwitch	Change programming problem after 50% of generations have passed
LateSingleSwitch	Change programming problem after 75% of generations have passed
OneThenTwo	Initially optimize for *P1* and switch to *P2*
OneThenBoth	Initially optimize for *P1* and switch to *Combo*
TwoThenOne	Initially optimize for *P2* and switch to *P1*
TwoThenBoth	Initially optimize for *P2* and switch to *Combo*
Initialization Schemes	
HalfFromDir	Initialize 50% of the population from the given directory of solutions, generate the rest randomly
AllFromDir	Initialize 100% of the population from the given directory of solutions
UserSolutions	Infuse population with student-submitted solutions
NonDiverseRandom	Infuse population with multiple copies of a single program that doesn't solve either programming problem

5   Results

In summary we observe that GP variants that solve multiple programming problems can improve the quality of the solutions for the more difficult problems. However, for the simple problem the GP head start gives no benefit. Table 3 outlines the experiments and results. Although the three problems are similar in structure, they have varying difficulties given our grammar. Figure 3 shows this difference, the *Combo* alone is the most difficult, and *P1* is more easily solvable than *P2* because there are no requirements on the loop variable.

Table 3. Experimental results. Variants and problem are explained in Table 2. Percent of 100 runs solving all test cases is in the **Solved%** column for each variant.

Variant name	Problem	Solved%
Baseline		
Baseline	*P1*	(Best for *P1*) **97**
Baseline	*P2*	48
Baseline	*Combo*	3
Switching		
EarlySingleSwitch	TwoThenOne	87
MedSingleSwitch	TwoThenOne	83
LateSingleSwitch	TwoThenOne	48
EarlySingleSwitch	OneThenTwo	(Best for *P2*) **49**
MedSingleSwitch	OneThenTwo	16
LateSingleSwitch	OneThenTwo	4
EarlySingleSwitch	OneThenBoth	3
EarlySingleSwitch	TwoThenBoth	11
MedSingleSwitch	OneThenBoth	1
MedSingleSwitch	TwoThenBoth	10
LateSingleSwitch	OneThenBoth	2
LateSingleSwitch	TwoThenBoth	(Best for *Combo*) **15**
Initialization schemes		
UserSolutions, AllFromDir	*P1,*	84
UserSolutions, HalfFromDir	*P1*	(Best init. *P1*) **94**
NonDiverseRandom, AllFromDir	*P1*	93
NonDiverseRandom, HalfFromDir	*P1*	93
UserSolution AllFromDir	*P2*	37
UserSolution HalfFromDir	*P2*	42
NonDiverseRandom, AllFromDir	*P2*	(Best init. *P2*) **51**
NonDiverseRandom, HalfFromDir	*P2*	45

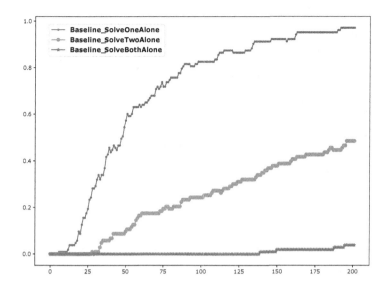

Fig. 3. Y-axis is the fraction of runs which contained a program that solved all of the test cases and x-axis is generation. Lines are a single problem (*P1*-Baseline_SolveOneAlone, *P2*-Baseline_SolveTwoAlone, or *Combo*-Baseline_SolveOneAlone)

Sequential programming problem schedules When solving a complex problem, it can be helpful to search for a problem solution to an intermediate programming problem (a sequential schedule) before solving the complete programming problem. For solving *Combo*, useful intermediate programming problems are to solve each of the *P1* and *P2* problems individually before moving to solve the combined problem. With this in mind, we solved multiple programming problem learning by starting to solve from either *P1* or *P2* and changing the programming problem to solve *Combo* at some point throughout the evolution. The percentage of runs in which at least a single program solved all given test cases is given in Fig. 4. In this plot, each of the runs was given 200 generations to run. However, they are displayed as being shifted in order to line up the point at which they started working on the final problem; for example, if a population started by spending 50 generations on *P1* and then switched to spending 150 generations on *P2*, then it would be shifted back 50 generations relative to the other lines, to get a common start point for the second problem.

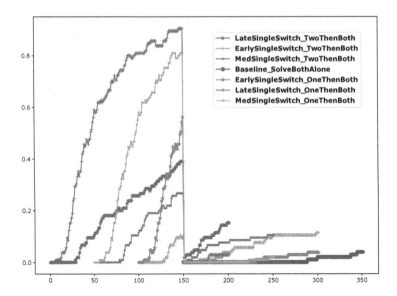

Fig. 4. Y-axis is the fraction of runs which contained a program that solved all of the test cases and x-axis is generation. The start of the lines is shifted in order to line up the point at which they started working on the final problem. The lines are the multi programming problem learning experiment, when switching from solving `OneThenBoth`, `TwoThenBoth` and not switching `Baseline_SolveBothAlone`

Populations that spent more time searching for the intermediate problem (`LateSingleSwitch`) generally had a higher upward trajectory than those that spent less time searching for it (`EarlySingleSwitch`). This effect can be seen in Fig. 5, which shows the number of test cases solved by the best individual in a run, averaged across all runs for the same problem. A longer time spent searching for the intermediate programming problem allows a population to solve a higher number of test cases from *Combo* earlier, in comparison to those that spent less time searching on the intermediate programming problem.

Additionally, this experiment revealed that harder problems can sometimes be a better intermediate signal than easier ones. *P1* is an easier problem to solve for the population than *P2*, and Fig. 4 shows better performance when searching for *P2* before *Combo*, as opposed to searching for *P1* before *Combo*.

Transferring Information from One Programming Problem to Another. The two problems are similar, in that they initialize a count variable, iterate through a string, and add to a total count if some condition was met. A population that had previously been optimized for solving *P1* could be better equipped to solve *P2* than a population solely focused on *P2* from the beginning.

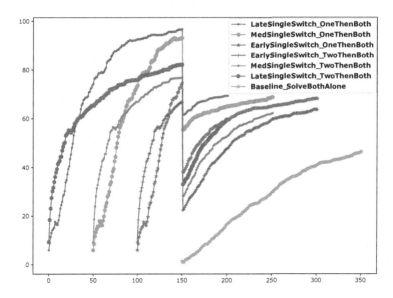

Fig. 5. Y-axis is the average number of test cases solved by the best individual and x-axis is the generation. The start of the lines is shifted in order to line up the point at which they started working on the final problem. Lines are for when switching from solving `OneThenBoth`, `TwoThenBoth` and not switching `Baseline_SolveBothAlone`

We can see that the effect of searching for a previous programming problem was different in each case. When going from *P2* to *P1* in Fig. 6, this intermediate programming problem seemed to produce positive results, as the population performed better than what it originally would have on the baseline in one case. Looking at Fig. 6, we can see that while too many generations on a related problem can be harmful, the right amount can be beneficial. E.g. the `MedSwitch` and `LateSingleSwitch` schemes perform worse than the baseline, the `EarlySingleSwitch` performed better than the baseline, even though 25% of the time was spent searching for a different problem.

Initializing with Preexisting Knowledge. Because of the similarity in the solutions to each of the given problems, our hypothesis was that initializing populations with individuals that solved *P1* would be better equipped at solving *P2*, and vice versa, by capturing common statements. None of the runs initialized with solutions to one problem did any better than the runs in which random initialization methods were used. Surprisingly, when a single program which solved neither problem was chosen as a starting point, *P2*, `NonDiverseRandom`, `AllFromDir`, performance was not hindered. In fact, it even solved the problem in a higher number of runs than the baseline.

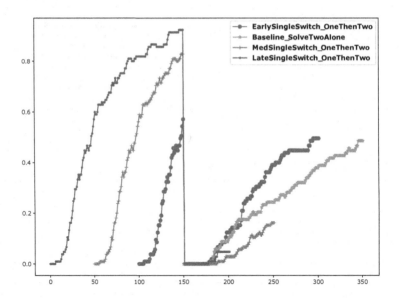

Fig. 6. Y-axis is the fraction of runs which contained a program that solved all of the test cases and x-axis is generations. The start of the lines is shifted in order to line up the point at which they started working on the final problem. Lines are for when the programming problem was switching from solving `OneThenTwo` and not switching `Baseline_SolveTwoAlone`

5.1 Discussion

This study attempts to clarify one simple approach to improve GP performance and investigate the experimental design options for solving multiple programming problems for GP. This leads to a number of limitations in our proof-of-concept study. First, the human solution data is limited and biased by amount and diversity of human solutions that are available for programming problems. Second, we have only investigated a few programming problems, and can thus not draw any strong conclusions. Another limit is that we use only informal human judgment of similarity. There exists a body of work in education and software engineering regarding programming problem similarity that may offer some help. Finally, another limit is that there is no consensus on curriculum learning design for humans, so GP learning designers might struggle to specify a curriculum as well.

It is our aim is to expand the boundaries of expectations regarding what is provided to GP. Others have questioned why GP starts "from scratch" when helpful knowledge is available. For example [12] investigated providing domain knowledge to the programming synthesis task that GP tried to solve. On the basis of our experiments, it is arguable that giving GP a head start could improve GP performance on the more difficult problems in the GP program synthesis benchmark suite assuming that similar problems could offer a head start.

6 Conclusions and Future Work

We explored transferring information within a single population by solving separate but related programming problems, the first two problems of the first MITx 6.00.1x course problem set. Specifically, we explored **1)** solution quality from a transfer between programming problem using a schedule for GP program synthesis to solve a similar programming problem, **2)** solution quality when providing information from similar programming problems during initialization. When solving the more difficult *Combo* programming problem with GP, using the P2 problem as an intermediate goal as opposed to the simpler P1 was found to be beneficial. Additionally, more time spent searching for the intermediate goal proved to be beneficial. The effects of initializing a population with solutions to a related problem were unclear.

There are multiple directions for future work. An evaluation of the difficulty of finding additional problem pairs that set up the head start could be conducted. This could also reveal whether the initial observations around ordering and problem difficulty hold more generally. Head start also could be expanded to integrate existing and new work on modularity and reuse in GP. Other metrics for comparing code similarity will also be investigated.

References

1. Agapitos, A., Lucas, S.M.: Learning recursive functions with object oriented genetic programming. In: Collet, P., Tomassini, M., Ebner, M., Gustafson, S., Ekárt, A. (eds.) EuroGP 2006. LNCS, vol. 3905, pp. 166–177. Springer, Heidelberg (2006). https://doi.org/10.1007/11729976_15
2. Arcuri, A., White, D.R., Clark, J., Yao, X.: Multi-objective improvement of software using co-evolution and smart seeding. In: Li, X., et al. (eds.) SEAL 2008. LNCS, vol. 5361, pp. 61–70. Springer, Heidelberg (2008). https://doi.org/10.1007/978-3-540-89694-4_7
3. Bajwa, A., Bell, A., Hemberg, E., O'Reilly, U.M.: Analyzing student code trajectories in an introductory programming MOOC. In: 2019 IEEE Learning With MOOCS (LWMOOCS), pp. 53–58. IEEE (2019)
4. Bengio, Y., Louradour, J., Collobert, R., Weston, J.: Curriculum learning. In: Proceedings of the 26th Annual International Conference on Machine Learning, pp. 41–48 (2009)
5. Bladek, I., Krawiec, K.: Simultaneous synthesis of multiple functions using genetic programming with scaffolding. In: Proceedings of the 2016 on Genetic and Evolutionary Computation Conference Companion, pp. 97–98 (2016)
6. Dempsey, I., O'Neill, M., Brabazon, A.: Foundations in Grammatical Evolution for Dynamic Environments, vol. 194. Springer, Heidelberg (2009). https://doi.org/10.1007/978-3-642-00314-1
7. Fenton, M., McDermott, J., Fagan, D., Forstenlechner, S., Hemberg, E., O'Neill, M.: PonyGE2: grammatical evolution in Python. In: Proceedings of the Genetic and Evolutionary Computation Conference Companion, pp. 1194–1201 (2017)
8. Gerules, G., Janikow, C.: A survey of modularity in genetic programming. In: 2016 IEEE Congress on Evolutionary Computation (CEC), pp. 5034–5043. IEEE (2016)

9. Helmuth, T., Pantridge, E., Woolson, G., Spector, L.: Transfer learning of genetic programming instruction sets. In: Proceedings of the 2020 Genetic and Evolutionary Computation Conference Companion, pp. 241–242 (2020)

10. Helmuth, T., Spector, L.: Detailed problem descriptions for general program synthesis benchmark suite. School of Computer Science, University of Massachusetts Amherst, Technical report (2015)

11. Helmuth, T., Spector, L.: General program synthesis benchmark suite. In: Proceedings of the 2015 Annual Conference on Genetic and Evolutionary Computation, pp. 1039–1046. ACM (2015)

12. Hemberg, E., Kelly, J., O'Reilly, U.M.: On domain knowledge and novelty to improve program synthesis performance with grammatical evolution. In: Proceedings of the Genetic and Evolutionary Computation Conference, pp. 1039–1046 (2019)

13. Hoang, T.H., Essam, D., McKay, R.I.B., Hoai, N.X.: Developmental evaluation in genetic programming: the TAG-based frame work. Int. J. Knowl.-Based Intell. Eng. Syst. **12**(1), 69–82 (2008). https://doi.org/10.3233/KES-2008-12106. http://content.iospress.com/articles/international-journal-of-knowledge-based-and-intelligent-engineering-systems/kes00142

14. Jaśkowski, W., Krawiec, K., Wieloch, B.: Multitask visual learning using genetic programming. Evol. Comput. **16**(4), 439–459 (2008)

15. Kelly, J., Hemberg, E., O'Reilly, U.-M.: Improving genetic programming with novel exploration - exploitation control. In: Sekanina, L., Hu, T., Lourenço, N., Richter, H., García-Sánchez, P. (eds.) EuroGP 2019. LNCS, vol. 11451, pp. 64–80. Springer, Cham (2019). https://doi.org/10.1007/978-3-030-16670-0_5

16. Koza, J.R.: Evolution of subsumption using genetic programming. In: Proceedings of the First European Conference on Artificial Life, pp. 110–119 (1992)

17. Krawiec, K.: Behavioral Program Synthesis with Genetic Programming, vol. 618. Springer, Cham (2016). https://doi.org/10.1007/978-3-319-27565-9

18. Krawiec, K., Wieloch, B.: Functional modularity for genetic programming. In: Proceedings of the 11th Annual Conference on Genetic and Evolutionary Computation, pp. 995–1002 (2009)

19. Krawiec, K., Wieloch, B.: Automatic generation and exploitation of related problems in genetic programming. In: IEEE Congress on Evolutionary Computation, pp. 1–8. IEEE (2010)

20. Langdon, W.B., Nordin, J.P.: Seeding genetic programming populations. In: Poli, R., Banzhaf, W., Langdon, W.B., Miller, J., Nordin, P., Fogarty, T.C. (eds.) EuroGP 2000. LNCS, vol. 1802, pp. 304–315. Springer, Heidelberg (2000). https://doi.org/10.1007/978-3-540-46239-2_23

21. Lopez, U., Trujillo, L., Silva, S., Vanneschi, L., Legrand, P.: Unlabeled multi-target regression with genetic programming. In: Proceedings of the 2020 Genetic and Evolutionary Computation Conference, pp. 976–984 (2020)

22. Lucas, S.M.: Exploiting reflection in object oriented genetic programming. In: Keijzer, M., O'Reilly, U.-M., Lucas, S., Costa, E., Soule, T. (eds.) EuroGP 2004. LNCS, vol. 3003, pp. 369–378. Springer, Heidelberg (2004). https://doi.org/10.1007/978-3-540-24650-3_35

23. Ryan, C., Collins, J.J., Neill, M.O.: Grammatical evolution: evolving programs for an arbitrary language. In: Banzhaf, W., Poli, R., Schoenauer, M., Fogarty, T.C. (eds.) EuroGP 1998. LNCS, vol. 1391, pp. 83–96. Springer, Heidelberg (1998). https://doi.org/10.1007/BFb0055930

24. Ryan, C., Keijzer, M., Cattolico, M.: Favourable biasing of function sets using run transferable libraries. In: O'Reilly, U.M., Yu, T., Riolo, R., Worzel, B. (eds.) Genetic Programming Theory and Practice II. Genetic Programming, pp. 103–120. Springer, Boston (2005). https://doi.org/10.1007/0-387-23254-0_7
25. Sasanka, R., Krommydas, K.: An evolutionary framework for automatic and guided discovery of algorithms. arXiv preprint arXiv:1904.02830 (2019)
26. Scott, E.O., De Jong, K.A.: Automating knowledge transfer with multi-task optimization. In: 2019 IEEE Congress on Evolutionary Computation (CEC), pp. 2252–2259. IEEE (2019)
27. Soderlund, J., Vickers, D., Blair, A.: Parallel hierarchical evolution of string library functions. In: Handl, J., Hart, E., Lewis, P.R., López-Ibáñez, M., Ochoa, G., Paechter, B. (eds.) PPSN 2016. LNCS, vol. 9921, pp. 281–291. Springer, Cham (2016). https://doi.org/10.1007/978-3-319-45823-6_26
28. Tanev, I., Kuyucu, T., Shimohara, K.: GP-induced and explicit bloating of the seeds in incremental GP improves evolutionary success. Genet. Program. Evolvable Mach. **15**(1), 37–60 (2014). https://doi.org/10.1007/s10710-013-9192-y
29. Thorhauer, A., Rothlauf, F.: On the locality of standard search operators in grammatical evolution. In: Bartz-Beielstein, T., Branke, J., Filipič, B., Smith, J. (eds.) PPSN 2014. LNCS, vol. 8672, pp. 465–475. Springer, Cham (2014). https://doi.org/10.1007/978-3-319-10762-2_46
30. Thrun, S.: Explanation-Based Neural Network Learning. Springer, Boston (1996). https://doi.org/10.1007/978-1-4613-1381-6
31. Wan, M., Weise, T., Tang, K.: Novel loop structures and the evolution of mathematical algorithms. In: Silva, S., Foster, J.A., Nicolau, M., Machado, P., Giacobini, M. (eds.) EuroGP 2011. LNCS, vol. 6621, pp. 49–60. Springer, Heidelberg (2011). https://doi.org/10.1007/978-3-642-20407-4_5
32. Henrik Westerberg, C., Levine, J.: Investigation of different seeding strategies in a genetic planner. In: Boers, E.J.W. (ed.) EvoWorkshops 2001. LNCS, vol. 2037, pp. 505–514. Springer, Heidelberg (2001). https://doi.org/10.1007/3-540-45365-2_52
33. Yu, T., Clack, C.: Recursion, lambda-abstractions and genetic programming. In: Poli, R., Langdon, W.B., Schoenauer, M., Fogarty, T., Banzhaf, W. (eds.) Late Breaking Papers at EuroGP 1998: the First European Workshop on Genetic Programming, pp. 26–30. CSRP-98-10, The University of Birmingham, UK, Paris, France, 14–15 April 1998
34. Zheng, X., Qin, A., Gong, M., Zhou, D.: Self-regulated evolutionary multi-task optimization. IEEE Trans. Evol. Comput. **24**, 16–28 (2019)

Author Index

Printed in the United States
by Baker & Taylor Publisher Services